CW01212327

Spitfire Elizabeth and the Roaring Boys

The true wartime story of one aircraft's legendary pilots

NICK ORAM

Grosvenor House
Publishing Limited

All rights reserved
Copyright © Nick Oram, 2019

The right of Nick Oram to be identified as the author of this
work has been asserted in accordance with Section 78
of the Copyright, Designs and Patents Act 1988

The author and publishers have made all reasonable efforts to contact
the copy-right holders for permission and apologise for any errors and
omissions or errors in the form of credits given. Corrections may be
made to future printings.

The book cover is copyright to Nick Oram

This book is published by
Grosvenor House Publishing Ltd
Link House
140 The Broadway, Tolworth, Surrey, KT6 7HT.
www.grosvenorhousepublishing.co.uk

This book is sold subject to the conditions that it shall not, by way of
trade or otherwise, be lent, resold, hired out or otherwise circulated
without the author's or publisher's prior consent in any form of binding or
cover other than that in which it is published and
without a similar condition including this condition being imposed
on the subsequent purchaser.

A CIP record for this book
is available from the British Library

ISBN 978-1-78623-528-2

For my wife Dawn and
our daughters Rebecca and Sophie

CONTENTS

Acknowledgements		ix
Introduction		xiii
ONE	411 Squadron	1
TWO	Bruce Whiteford	41
THREE	Charlie Trainor	93
FOUR	Ross Linquist	124
FIVE	Tommy Wheler	205
SIX	Dave Evans	259
SEVEN	Gibby Gibson	274
EIGHT	Len Harrison	301
NINE	Bob Hyndman	326
TEN	Jimmy Jeffrey	355
ELEVEN	A Phoenix Rises	382
	Appendix	392
	Glossary	397
	References and Notes	402
	Bibliography	407
	Picture Credits	410

This book is dedicated to the nine pilots of The Royal Canadian Air Force's 411 Squadron who flew spitfire NH341 Elizabeth in combat during World War II:

A B "BRUCE" WHITEFORD

H C "CHARLIE" TRAINOR

S R "ROSS" LINQUIST

T R "TOMMY" WHELER

D H "DAVE" EVANS

W R "GIBBY" GIBSON

N L "LEN" HARRISON

R S "BOB" HYNDMAN

J S "JIMMY" JEFFREY

ACKNOWLEDGEMENTS

Throughout the research and writing of this book, I have received fantastic support and encouragement from so many people. I'd like to begin with a big thank you to Aero Legends owners Keith and Suzanne Perkins, who also happen to be long-standing and great friends, and their sons Ben and Harry. Ben is now the Company Managing Director. When Aero Legends first started in 2014, Harry and I spent many days together learning the ropes as ground crew and welcoming the first customers to those wonderful Spitfires and other warbirds. They were memorable days, with hopefully plenty to come in the future.

Any true story is enriched by the personal memories, photos, and artefacts of those who were there during the war, in particular, the nine Canadian Spitfire pilots you will read about. It was very special to be able to meet and talk with one of the nine, Tommy Wheler, to read his personal logbook and hear firsthand his account of being a Spitfire pilot. Sadly, he passed away in October 2018. Tommy was brilliant, and the definition of an 'aero legend'. He was someone I'll never forget. His daughter Gail, sons Doug, Jim, and the extended Wheler family have all been wonderfully supportive and generous in sharing details of Tommy's life.

In equal measure, I would also like to offer a personal thank you to the following families of the nine for their unwavering support and encouragement:

Bruce Whiteford's son Norm, who gave me complete access to his father's logbook, records, and photos in addition to providing important details about his father and mother's lives and family history.

Robert Hyndman's daughters Brydie and Margot, who provided photos, logbooks and copies of some of their father's fantastic paintings and sketches from their private collection.

Ross Linquist's daughters Jan and Jill, who helped me uncover their father's story and provided his logbooks and entrusted me with a large collection of their father's original war time photos.

Jimmy Jeffrey's son Lawrie and his granddaughter Denise, who have given me photos, logbooks, and reached out to their connections in France. They have passed on to me several wartime stories relayed to them by Jimmy.

I have also been fortunate over the years to speak with several World War II veterans who have provided personal recollections about being in combat, on the ground, and in the air. I hope that in the book I can convey something of the courage and sacrifice they all made in the face of mortal danger. These are stories of ordinary men who each did extraordinary things yet remained modest and unassuming. All have now passed on, but their stories still live on.

My grandfather, Reg Vidler who told me at length about his combat experience from a soldier's perspective, in particular as someone who was attacked from the air several times. He served in David Stirling's 1st Special Air Service (SAS), an elite fighting force of commandos. Amongst countless hair-raising experiences, he was bombed and strafed by the Luftwaffe, including by the infamous Stuka dive bomber, whilst on a flat salt lake in the desert. He and his comrades had blown up parts of the Germans airfield the night before!

The Roaring Boys often escorted bombers on their missions and I was fortunate that Chris Yates from Headcorn aerodrome introduced me to 101 Squadron Lancaster bomber pilot George Harris DFC at an event he organised at the aerodrome. George gave me a great insight into operations from a bomber boys perspective and to flying Lancasters with the special operations 101 Squadron, who carried an extra German-speaking crewman onboard. His job was to transmit false information and to confuse enemy defences and fighters. Of course, the transmissions were intended to be picked up by Germans, hence 101 acquired the reputation of a 'chop' squadron with some of the highest losses in the RAF.

Flying a Spitfire, one of the greatest fighter aircraft of its time in air combat is a key part of this story. The aircraft's role in the lead up to D Day and beyond was much wider than the interceptor fighter role it performed during the Battle of Britain in 1940, and which propelled it to international fame. There is an extensive range of books and many firsthand accounts including the wonderful "First Light" by Squadron Leader Geoffrey Wellum DFC. Two aviation friends, Ady Shaw and

Johnny Cracknell invited me along to a couple of meetings with Geoffrey Wellum, and it was very special to speak first hand with a surviving Spitfire pilot from 1940.

Through my connections with Aero Legends, I have been fortunate to meet some leading figures within the warbird community who have offered their help and provided technical advice. I would like to give my thanks to Martin "Mo" Overall of Historic Flying Ltd, who led the project team which rebuilt Spitfire NH341 Elizabeth, and who regularly flies her today. Mo talked me through the project process and helped answer many questions about the rebuild, as well as about Spitfires in general.

Aero Legends also has on its roster some outstanding Spitfire pilots. Firstly, Antony "Parky" Parkinson MBE who has contributed to the book and answered many questions - a big thanks for your patience Parky! During the writing of this book, Squadron Leader Andrew "Milli" Millikin and F/L Charlie Brown have been kind enough to provide a great insight into all things, Spitfire, so many thanks, Milli and Charlie.

I have many friends at Headcorn Aerodrome who have helped in so many ways so thanks in particular to; Jamie Freeman, owner of Headcorn Aerodrome for providing details of the airfield's history, photographers Richard Foord and Ady Shaw for the superb photos (some of which feature in the book), and Trevor Matthews of Lashenden Air Warfare Museum for giving me access to their artefacts. A special mention also to Julie Baker who gave me complete access to her late father Vic's 126 Wing Commemorative Society records, letters, and photos. Donald Nijboer for giving me permission to quote from his book on 126 Wing. Mike Rutledge for use of his father's wartime 411 squadron photos. John Tapper, Bill Bishop and Gerry Alexander of the 411 Association who have helped track down some of the veteran's families. I was also able to meet with the current landowner of RAF Staplehurst, Simon Evans, and the former owners, Roger and Linda Munn who provided background information and photographs, so thanks to all of them.

The following people have also provided help, support, information and guidance along the way which I greatly appreciate; Steve Brocklehurst, Stephen Fulchuk, Chris Giles, Wayne Marsh, Bob Levens, Joe at fighting for your life.com, Mike Roberts, Neville Bowers, Patrick Mason, Bruce McNair, Paul Stevens, Roger Strutt, Fred Vogels. Last, and by no means least thanks to the proofreaders and editors; my wife Dawn, and daughters Rebecca and Sophie.

INTRODUCTION

My earliest memories of the Spitfire go back to the late 1960s. In a family photo, I am holding a metal Dinky Toy Mark II Spitfire in which you could insert a battery to make the propeller spin. The aircraft had a working undercarriage too, and the Spitfire fought many battles in our back garden, in Battle of Britain country near Maidstone, Kent. The toy's packaging featured the Battle of Britain film, which my twin brother, and I were taken to see. Something took hold back then. I wasn't necessarily conscious of a fascination with the Spitfire but any mention of that aircraft always caught my immediate interest and attention. And, it still does to this day. With age came a deeper understanding and appreciation of the Spitfire's legacy, along with that of the RAF's less famous but equally important fighter the Hawker Hurricane. For many people, especially, but not exclusively in Britain the Spitfire is a symbol of national resistance against an enemy intent on our destruction and that of the "free world." Britain's wartime Prime Minister Winston Churchill called the Battle of Britain "Our finest hour." The Spitfire is in the nation's heart.

In 2011, one of my oldest friends, Keith Perkins invited me to Biggin Hill airfield to meet Spitfire pilot and Heritage Hangar owner Peter Monk. Keith told me he was considering a project for Peter and his team to build a flying Spitfire. I didn't need a second invitation to go along! On 7 December 2013, Spitfire TD314 was pushed out of the hangar and the great work by Peter and his team was complete when Peter took the controls for her maiden flight. What a moment that was. The journey that led to this book was then well and truly underway.

With Spitfire TD314, now named "St George" airborne, Keith's plans started to take shape and he asked me to think about a name for his new company that would offer warbird flight experiences. One immediately leapt out of the page, Aero Legends. A short time passed and Aero Legends became firmly established as a provider of premium warbird flight experiences. Keith then commissioned a new project to rebuild a Mark IX Spitfire from the wreckage of an aircraft that was assigned to

The Royal Canadian Air Force's (RCAF) 411 Squadron. The serial number of the Spitfire was NH341 and the plan was to make the aircraft a two-seat version for customer flight experiences. Over the months and years that followed, I began work on piecing together the history of this Spitfire. There was no particular plan for a book, but as the names of the Spitfire NH341's pilots and their service history were unearthed, it was clear we were on to something quite special. The discovery that of the nine Canadian pilots who flew NH341, one, Tommy Wheler was living in Toronto was beyond anyone's expectations.

Having learned so much about Spitfire NH341 Elizabeth, her Canadian pilots, and 411 Squadron, it made me reflect on the considerable contribution made by the Canadians in World War II. More than 100 Canadian pilots took part in the Battle of Britain, with Spitfire Elizabeth's pilots joining the war much later on. I wanted to make sure each of their stories would never be forgotten. Having met and spoken with the surviving pilot, Tommy Wheler, he was very much in mind when contemplating this book. When I reflected on the contribution of the Canadians and considered that 2019 marked the 75th anniversary of D Day, and Spitfire Elizabeth's combat service commencing the book became the simplest of decisions.

I want to tell the story of these nine Canadians, who were drawn together in the RCAF's 411 Squadron, forging a special bond of comradeship and trust in the unique arena of air combat. You will find each pilot's progress from their initial flight training to joining 411 Squadron, along with a wide selection of the missions they flew during their tours of duty. As each fighter squadron comprised 12 Spitfires, the nine featured pilots flew together virtually every day and on each combat mission, they are identified when doing so. They shared several Spitfires and each had a "favourite" aircraft. These pilots had no knowledge of the extra connection that would bind them together over 70 years later, their association with one Spitfire, NH341 Elizabeth which they all flew. The nine pilots featured in this book are listed in the order they flew Spitfire NH341;

A B "Bruce" Whiteford
H C "Charlie" Trainor
S R "Ross" Linquist
T R "Tommy" Wheler

D H "Dave" Evans
W R "Gibby" Gibson
N L "Len" Harrison
R S "Bob" Hyndman
J S "Jimmy" Jeffrey

The majority of missions took place over enemy occupied Europe, rather than in the skies above Britain. Their missions included air combat, but also dive bombing and strafing ground targets. The story is a mix of first-hand accounts, official records, and extensive research. It gives an insight into the daily life of a fighter pilot, and the missions they flew in one of the most legendary fighters of the Second World War. I have interwoven a fact-based, fictional element to the story to help the understanding of their experiences. I am aware of the fact that post-publication my research work will continue as I strive to find the family and friends of four of Spitfire Elizabeth's nine pilots, who I have been unable to find. My hope is that this book will bring more of the history to light.

It is fitting to turn to another veteran, a Spitfire pilot from the Battle of Britain and Malta campaigns, Geoffrey Wellum DFC to encapsulate what I am trying to achieve with this book. When asked about the future legacy of what is often called the "greatest generation" he said:

"It's not about medals. It's not about who shot down what. It's not about thank yous, but it is nice to be remembered because being remembered covers everybody who served, flew and fought in the war."

CHAPTER ONE

411 "CITY OF NORTH YORK" SQUADRON – THE GRIZZLY BEARS

The 411 "City of North York" Squadron, also known as "The Grizzly Bears" and the "Roaring Squadron" of The Royal Canadian Airforce (RCAF) was formed on 16 June 1941 at RAF Digby, Lincolnshire. It was an Article XV Squadron comprising pilots from British Commonwealth countries, and it was to 411 Squadron that Spitfire NH341 Elizabeth would be assigned on 12 June 1944. These Canadian, Australian and New Zealand Article XV squadrons were formed from graduates of The British Commonwealth Air Training Plan (BCATP), also known as The Empire Air Training Plan. The BCATP was set up in 1939 and was under the control of The Royal Air Force (RAF).

I was interested to find out the background to 411 Squadron being known as the Roaring Squadron, and their pilots as the Roaring Boys. I had read about this association with 411 Squadron in The Canadian Department of Defence book: "The RCAF Overseas 1939-1945" which frequently refers to them by this name. Where did that name come from, and why did those boys go roaring around?

According to the official squadron history one of the ground crew, Leading Aircraftman Oliver (Ubangi) Pierce came from South Africa, and whilst at University in the USA volunteered for the RCAF. His parents sent him a parcel containing a "taste of home" which allegedly included some cured lion meat. It is not unreasonable to suspect that Pierce was simply winding up his colleagues with tall tales of wrestling lions in Africa! Many of the squadron were persuaded to try the delicacy, and shortly after they set off on a trip to the local cinema, a popular pastime of the period. Upon seeing the MGM Lion, which appeared in the title credits for the company's films, 411 Squadron let out a voluminous, collective roar which was so loud the soundtrack of the MGM lion was rendered inaudible! Thereafter, the "roar" from the 411 boys took hold and they roared on throughout the war, wherever they went, to the airfield dispersal, the mess or generally anywhere it felt right to do so!

The 411 Squadron crest contains the Latin words "INIMICUS INIMICO" which means "Hostile to an Enemy," an apt description for the brave Canadians, or Canucks as they were known (a name that refers to Jonny Canuck, a cartoon character from the 1860s who was reinvented in 1942 as a war hero) and the manner in which they conducted their war. The crest contains the drawing of a bear, harking back to their Canadian roots.

From its beginning, the squadron was equipped with the Supermarine Spitfire and it began operations in August 1941. It was allocated the squadron code "DB," which was painted on each aircraft's fuselage and which can be seen on Spitfire Elizabeth today. Throughout the war, the squadron flew various marks of the Spitfire, and by the end of the conflict, the squadron had indeed lived up to its motto.

During the war, both sides of the conflict were engaged in an arms race, particularly in the air. The Spitfire first flew on 5 March 1936. Throughout its service, it was continuously upgraded in terms of performance and firepower from the first Mark I and IIs that had fought in the Battle of Britain. Meanwhile, the Luftwaffe was undertaking similar programmes with the Messerschmitt Me 109, and the Focke Wulf FW 190 which outclassed the opposing Spitfire Mark V when it was introduced. The balance was redressed when the RAF introduced the Spitfire Mark IX, of which NH341 Elizabeth was one. Both Spitfire Marks V and IX were flown by the Roaring Boys.

During its wartime history, several of 126 Wing and 411 Squadron's pilots distinguished themselves both during combat and in escape and evasion from the enemy after being shot down. These men are worthy of inclusion in this story as they give a sense of the calibre of the Canadian pilots who served at the time. Amongst the legendary 411 Squadron pilots are H W "Wally" McLeod DSO DFC and Bar who was credited with shooting down 21.5 Luftwaffe aircraft, victories which were referred to as "kills." McLeod himself was shot down and killed on 21 September 1944. Another legendary figure was R W "Buck" McNair DSO DFC and two Bars, a Malta air campaign veteran who was credited with 16.5 kills and 5 probable and who later became a Group Captain and leader of 126 Wing.

The exploits of 411 Roaring Boy P/O William "Tex" Ash would later receive worldwide attention. His exploits were used as the basis of actor Steve McQueen's character, Virgil Hilts, "the cooler king" in the 1963 blockbuster film, *The Great Escape*. Born in Texas, Ash enlisted in the RCAF as the United States was still neutral at the time. He joined 411 Squadron in 1941, flying Spitfires on missions over France. He also flew as part of the fighter escort for bombers attacking the German battleship, Scharnhorst, as she sailed up the English Channel. Universally known, for obvious reasons by the Roaring Boys as "Tex," he was involved in several notable incidents. The 411 Squadron Operational Record Book (ORB) entry for 28 February 1942 read: "Our Ace from Texas, P/O Ash decided to prang his kite by overshooting the aerodrome at Manston. He ended by entwining his aircraft in the barbed wire at the end of the field. Why he picked the largest aerodrome in England to overshoot is not understood but fortunately, the damage was light and the pilot uninjured. So, ended a hectic day and another month."

Ash was also involved in another incident with fellow Roaring Boy, and original founding pilot of 411 Squadron, Buck McNair. Whilst performing unplanned aerobatics together in an open cockpit Tiger Moth. McNair, as passenger suddenly and dramatically made an unplanned exit from the aircraft and was fortunate to be saved by the fact that he was wearing a parachute! The subsequent investigation found that McNair had accidentally loosened the pin in his harness.

For Ash, his combat career ended on 24 March 1942. He was flying escort for Circus 116A, a daytime bomber attack with fighter escorts against short-range targets, to occupy enemy fighters and keep them in the area concerned. The squadron was attacked by around 50 FW 190s. With his guns jammed and, as Ash later recalled, only able to shout "bang" at the enemy he turned towards his attackers to minimise his profile. As they took turns to fire at him he was eventually shot down by Hauptmann Seifert. He crash landed near Vielle Eglise in France, and after initially escaping with the help of the French Resistance he made his way to Paris. He continued to move rather brazenly around the city, visiting art galleries etc. Eventually, he was arrested and subjected to beatings and interrogation by the Gestapo. Rescued from the clutches of the Gestapo by a Luftwaffe officer which wanted to deal with downed enemy airmen themselves, he was sent to Stalag Luft III, a prisoner of war camp for airmen situated near Sagan, Germany. Here, along with

Battle of Britain veteran Paddy Barthropp, he made several escape attempts, winning the admiration of his fellow prisoners. After recapture, he spent long periods in solitary confinement, the "cooler," as McQueen's character Hilts did in *The Great Escape* film. Ash was actually interned in the "cooler" when the escape of 76 prisoners, made famous by the film took place. Later, 50 of the escapees would be shot on Hitler's orders. Ash managed to escape at the end of the war and was awarded the MBE along with British citizenship. After a period at Oxford, he joined the BBC and became lifelong friends with Labour politician Tony Benn, eventually founding the Communist Party of Great Britain in the 1960s.

Another distinguished 411 Spitfire pilot was R J "Dick" Audet DFC and Bar. On one occasion he shot down 5 enemy aircraft in several minutes, qualifying him as an ace after which he became known as the "ace in a day." He went on to destroy a total of 10.5 enemy aircraft until on 3 March 1945 whilst attacking a train near Munster, his Spitfire crashed after being hit by ground fire, and he was killed. Amongst the roster of other notable pilots were Honorary Lieutenant Colonel T R "Tommy" Wheler MBE DFC CD Légion d'Honneur and H C "Charlie" Trainor DSO DFC and Bar whose stories are told in this book.

In August 1941, 411 Squadron's initial operations were patrols and bomber escorts over the French coast. Many of these patrols were routine, but the squadron did find opportunities to tangle with the Luftwaffe in air combat where victories were scored over them, but not without losses to the squadron. Later that year, the squadron was moved south to Hornchurch, and then on to Southend, Essex in March 1942 where it continued operations in support of bombers on missions over France, before returning to Digby at the end of this month.

On occasion, 411 Squadron was moved south by RAF Fighter Command to deal with the hit and run raids on south coast towns by FW 190s and Me 109s carrying single bombs, and which also strafed targets of opportunity, i.e. any useful military or civilian target that could damage Britain's ability to wage war. It was soon concluded that patrolling to prevent these so-called "tip and run" raiders was a pointless use of resources. The alternative strategy saw squadrons encouraged by Fighter Command to undertake so-called "Rhubarb" operations where small numbers of fighters would try to destroy enemy aircraft in the air, or if none were found, then preselected ground targets would be attacked.

Reading the official orders, the language used in these instructions is somewhat surprising. In RAF Fighter Command Tactical Memorandum No 21, issued on 21 March 1942 under the heading "Rhubarbs," squadron leaders were told that for target selection: "staff cars can provide lots of amusement if you find them" and with regard to flying in winter conditions: "a very serious view is taken of the dimwits who go careering round France in unsuitable weather." The memo concluded that every time fighters entered French airspace the Luftwaffe would have to scramble to meet them: "The Hun gets very fed up if he sees nothing, he binds like blazes to his controllers just as we do at times."

In one of the notable operations of 1942, on 18 August, 411 Squadron took off as fighter cover for Operation Jubilee, the Allied combined operation to capture the port of Dieppe, which was spearheaded by the Canadians. The squadron's sweeps turned into one of its busiest days with Luftwaffe aircraft shot down, however, the raid resulted in heavy casualties, and over half of the 6,000 troops landed were killed, wounded or captured. Vital lessons were learned that would prove invaluable during the invasion of Europe in June 1944, which was forever after known as D Day.

In March 1943 Exercise Spartan tested the coordination of land and air forces during a huge armoured thrust across southern England, all vital lessons that would shape the organisation of Allied forces going forward. The Roaring Boys would play their part in the air too. In April 1943, command of 411 Squadron passed to Squadron Leader Blair Dalzell (Dal) Russel DFC, a Canadian Battle of Britain veteran who had achieved ace status during that campaign. A few months later he was promoted to Wing Commander. The squadron was deployed to RAF Redhill in May. They continued operations of various types including flying as escort to bombers on short-range bombing attacks to destroy ground targets, known as Ramrods, as well as Circus missions across the channel to France. Due to the different flying range of the fighters and bombers, relays of fighters were organised to ensure the bombers always had protection to and from the target.

In July 1943, the RAF reorganised its squadron structure and operations in recognition of the vital, and the increasingly important role played by fighter bombers in support of offensives by ground forces. As a result, 411 "Grizzly Bears," Squadron joined 401 "City of Westminster,"

"The Rams," and 412 "Falcon" Squadrons, to form No 126 mobile fighter-bomber wing, which became part of the Tactical Air Force (TAF). A final change was made in May 1944 when the three squadrons became known as 126 Wing. The rationale was that the TAF would provide air combat and ground attack support to the British and Canadian armies once the Allied landings on the continent were underway. The TAF would be expected to have the capability to move swiftly in support of ground forces, operating close to the front lines. The plan was to construct temporary airfields called Advanced Landing Grounds (ALGs), which would be virtually self-sufficient in terms of operational combat and maintenance requirements. Undoubtedly, communication lines with higher command, as well as reliable supply lines were central to their success.

During the war, 411 Squadron was in combat action in the skies over Britain, France, Belgium, The Netherlands, and Germany before it was disbanded on 21 March 1946. From D Day, on 6 June 1944 to the end of the hostilities in 1945, 126 Wing was the most successful fighter wing in the 2nd TAF (renamed 2nd TAF on 15 November 1943) having shot down and destroyed 336 German aircraft. For its part, 411 destroyed 84 Luftwaffe aircraft, with 44 damaged, and 3 probably destroyed in air combat. On the ground, 5 Heinkel 177s and one Me 262 had been strafed and destroyed. The toll on German ground forces was also substantial with 367 vehicles destroyed and 353 damaged, 23 locomotives destroyed and 65 disabled. Unlike the Battle of Britain where the Spitfire was employed as an interceptor fighter, during its service with the mobile fighter wings it was also fitted with bomb racks and used extensively in dive bombing and ground attack missions.

The Spitfire itself had to perform a dual role, one in which it was a world beater, air combat, and the other dive bombing and strafing ground targets. The payload for a Spitfire was 2 x 250 lb bombs under each wing, and a single 500 lb bomb under the belly, which from an aesthetic appearance ruined the beauty and symmetry of the aircraft. It also adversely affected the aircraft's legendary nimble controls and handling. The bomb-carrying Typhoon, known as a "Bombphoon" could carry 2 x 1,000 lb bombs. The Spitfire had a weakness in the ground attack role in respect of the small tank of glycol located beneath the propeller, which was used to cool its famous Rolls Royce Merlin engine. The positioning of the tank meant that it was susceptible to damage by ground fire, something that will feature extensively in the missions flown by the Roaring Boys. Even a strike from single small calibre bullet was enough to puncture the tank, causing the engine to seize, or catch fire soon after. As the top scoring ace in the Allied air force with 34 kills, British 127 Wing Commander Air Vice Marshal James Edgar "Johnnie" Johnson, CB, CBE, DSO & Two Bars, DFC and Bar, once remarked about the Spitfire's weakness: "the prospect of being shot down by a few rounds fired by a half-baked Kraut gunner did not appeal to me in the least." For the actual dive bombing operations, the Spitfire would be put in a steep dive, rapidly increasing speed to around 300+ mph. In order to pull out of such a dive, and to avoid the pilot blacking out, the bombs were released at approximately 4,000 feet which compromised accuracy. The pilot also had to be sure to pull up just before the bomb under the belly was released to avoid it hitting the propeller. The Spitfire was not built for such stresses, and if the bombs under the wings failed to release, known as a "hang up," then it could straighten the aircraft's elliptical wing shape, necessitating a major overhaul with new wings and supporting spars. When the complications of wind direction, strength, and the distraction of incoming enemy flak were factored in it was no wonder that Johnnie Johnson described dive bombing as, "a hit and miss affair."

On 6 August 1943, 126 Wing, including 411 Squadron was posted from RAF Biggin Hill to an ALG which was located on Chickenden Lane farm near the village of Staplehurst, Kent. A few days before this move the Roaring Boys made a "liberty run" to what the Operational Record Book (ORB) described as, "the dim lights of London." Well, there was a war on and a blackout in force! The mobile nature of their forthcoming operations on the continent post-D Day meant that the aerodrome was a grass strip, hastily constructed and covered with metal Sommerfeld tracking to avoid it developing into a quagmire during wet weather. The wing's personnel had to adjust to living permanently in large tents. The plan was that these airfields could quickly be abandoned, and the wing transferred to a new airfield close to the front and just behind the advancing armies. Today, visitors can see a memorial located at the site of the RAF Staplehurst ALG which was opened in 2010 thanks to the efforts of a local man called Ted Sergison. Standing and looking out across the empty and peaceful fields it's possible to imagine the scene as squadrons of Spitfires and their mighty Merlin engines took off on bomber escort and armed fighter sweeps missions over occupied France. With the departure of 126 Airfield from RAF Staplehurst in October 1943, the ALG was later occupied from April to 4 July 1944 by the 9th United States Army Air Force's (USAAF) 363rd Fighter Group, comprising 380th, 381st and 382nd Fighter Squadrons flying P-51B Mustang fighters. It was fitting that Colonel John R Ulricson who flew his P-51 "Lolita" from Staplehurst during the war, and Lieutenant Colonel William E Bullard who also flew P51s from there, were in attendance during the ceremony to open the memorial. Some aviation friends from Headcorn Aerodrome flew over the event as a tribute. Rob Davies MBE FRAeS flew his P-51 Mustang "Big Beautiful Doll," later taking Bill Bullard up for a flight. Chris Jesson and the Tiger Club also flew their Tiger Moths and Stampe et Vertongens biplanes.

Several of Spitfire Elizabeth's pilots, Bruce Whiteford, Tommy Wheler, Bob Hyndman, Len Harrison, Charlie Trainor, Ross Linquist, and Dave Evans were based at Staplehurst during 1943. As young pilots eager to find local entertainment, the Roaring Boys soon became familiar with many of the local pubs. The Hare & Hounds, now called The Hawkenbury Inn was one such establishment, along with The Royal Star Hotel, Maidstone. On 5 October 1943, after a day of non-operational flying, which included Spitfire gun camera training, the Roaring Boys were released at 16.00 pm, and as the 411 ORB noted went on a "liberty run" to Maidstone. This involved a meal, trip to the cinema and dancing at the aforementioned Royal Star Hotel. On another occasion the squadron diarist wrote about: "the boys turning out wholeheartedly to Maidstone baths, the "flicks" and the general field of entertainment – pub crawling and the Star dance pavilion." The boozy evening pub crawls appeared to have had one unfortunate side effect of loosening tongues, resulting in sensitive classified information being released. An RCAF intelligence observer was horrified to overhear a civilian driving instructor in Maidstone, who had earlier been teaching some of 126 Airfield to drive, ask in a very loud voice: "Are you taking all three of your squadrons with you when you move to Biggin Hill?" He reported the incident which was duly investigated.

To relieve the frequent bouts of boredom there seemed to have been a fair amount of mischief and larks carried out by the young pilots and crews, who were suffering the fear and stress of combat every day and needed to let off steam. I have read a couple of reports of RCAF ground crews dealing with infestations of rats at Staplehurst ALG by pumping aviation fuel down the rat runs, followed by long blasts from an oxygen tank. The cocktail was then ignited with a lighted cloth to much hilarity from the assembled audience. The resulting explosion of flame was not only spectacular, and vaporised the pesky vermin but necessitated the rapid dispatch of a fire engine to attend to a blaze that was started in the surrounding grassland and hedgerows. The prank had literally backfired!

In trying to piece together the events of that summer of 1943, I was helped by Julie Baker whose late father, Vic was a local, part-time historian. As a young boy, he watched 126 Wing's Spitfires landing and taking off a sight which inspired in him a life-long passion, and a career in the RAF. In the 1990s he started a 126 Wing commemorative society in honour of the pilots, and in recognition was given the honorary title of Wing Leader by The Royal Canadian Air Force. Vic corresponded with several of the wartime pilots who provided memories and photos from Staplehurst, and elsewhere. By an amazing coincidence, two of the letters he received were from Spitfire Elizabeth pilot Bob Hyndman. I also later discovered two photos that Bob sent of himself, which he referred to in his letter, writing, "ghastly are they not?!" These photos are held separately in the RAF Staplehurst memorial collection.

Another of the Roaring Boys Vic Baker corresponded with, F/L Douglas R Matheson was shot down in December 1943 over France. His story is interesting as he was another fine example of the calibre of individual who joined 411 Squadron and became a Roaring Boy. After being shot down, Matheson helped the French Resistance until he was arrested in April 1944 and interrogated by the Gestapo. They were determined to break the resistance networks and identify their members. To understand how terrifying this experience would have been for Matheson I recalled the first-hand account of the German's interrogation techniques realyed to me by my grandfather. He and several other SAS troopers were captured after a fierce gun battle with German Fallschirmjäger (paratroopers) in Termoli, Italy in October 1943. They were taking part in a large scale "behind the lines" SAS raid as part of Operation Devon. My grandfather was imprisoned in squalid conditions in a cattle pen, and over the period of a few weeks, the Germans used a standard "good cop, bad cop" routine on him, including messing with his Circadian rhythm. He told me with a wry smile: "I could not reveal my actual regiment to the Germans as I knew I would be instantly shot" (as specified in Adolf Hitler's "Commando Order" for any captured Allied special forces soldiers). As a postscript to this story, my grandfather survived the war, but only after escaping from a prisoner of war camp and a subsequent encounter with a Russian army officer riding a white horse who wanted him shot as a deserter!

Douglas Matheson was interred in Stalag Luft III, along with fellow Roaring Boy, Tex Ash. Matheson helped dig some of the tunnels used for the mass escape attempt that was later immortalised in *The Great Escape* film. At the end of the war, Matheson was shot on a forced march and spent time in a British Army hospital. The Honourable Justice Douglas R Matheson of the Court of Queen's Bench of Alberta, as he became after the war, like Bob Hyndman, offered his support to Vic Baker's 126 Wing commemorations. In his letter of 27 June 1988, he said: "it's heartening to hear that someone still cares about 126 Wing. It was so long ago but to us who served, it is still a fresh memory. That summer of 1943 was a summer of anticipation – the heavy and medium bombers raids we were escorting were becoming huge." In his later years, Douglas Matheson still retained his love of flying. He tragically lost his life in a light aircraft crash on 15 June 2009, aged 88.

In September of every year, Vic Baker would organise a "Fall of Eagles" to commemorate the Canadians of 126 Wing, including a flypast by a Spitfire and Hurricane from the RAF's Battle of Britain Memorial Flight. The flypast would be followed by a service at St Georges Chapel, Staplehurst. One of Vic Baker's speeches at these events provides a useful insight into life at RAF Staplehurst. He recalled that: "at Staplehurst, the Canadians found out what life in hell is all about. They lived in a tent city, where dust clouds appeared with the departure and arrival of every Spitfire. The tents were plagued with bugs and there was a goat called 'Henniker' who would wander the tent city at night, regularly headbutting tent poles and unsuccessfully trying to leap over them. The net result was often calamitous, with the canvas and Henniker crashing down on the hapless airmen asleep inside." As if daytime tangling with the Luftwaffe and an errant night raiding goat wasn't enough, the Canadians were exposed to an equally potent danger, Kentish scrumpy cider. The Munns, a local farming family would supply the tent city with copious amounts of this lethal brew, which to their cost, the Canadians initially mistook for fruit juice! One of the farm buildings used by the Canadians had a sign carved above the entrance which said: "the fastest men in the world walk under these beams." Roger Munn's grandfather would bet the Canadians, and later the Americans that they couldn't down a pint of his farm brewed scrumpy cider, and half an hour later successfully ride a bicycle along a set distance. Apparently, no Canadians or Americans ever won that bet, and the majority of the fastest men in the world ended up going head first into the nearest hedgerow! The resulting carnage led Canadian 126 Wing Commander B D "Dal" Russel DFC to remark that the combination of cider, and Henniker the goat was doing more damage to his pilots than the Luftwaffe! And, he suspected that the Munns were in cahoots with the Germans.

During the autumn of 1943, 411 Squadron and the other squadrons of 126 and 127 Wings participated in several escape and evasion exercises, called "Ringo" operations. These were designed to prepare the pilots for the invasion of Europe, and potentially being shot down behind enemy lines. The pilots were taken by a truck several miles from their bases in civilian clothes and equipped with two pence, a small compass, and RAF identification papers and discs. Apparently, quite a few wagers were placed on the outcome of the exercise at 2/1 odds. Each squadron pilot who successfully evaded capture and returned was awarded 15 points. The pilots based at Staplehurst tried to infiltrate Headcorn to "borrow" any form of transport in which to return to their home airfield, whilst those at Headcorn did the same at Staplehurst. A cordon of Home Guard, military personnel and police were stationed in the surrounding area to catch the airmen. No violence was allowed, and the touch of a hand was enough to put the escaper "in the bag." In one exercise, S/L Ian Ormston DFC and Doug Matheson were dropped from a truck several miles from Headcorn Aerodrome. They pinched a bicycle and made their way to Headcorn, whereupon they sneaked through the barbed wire into the airfield. Both men crept into the tent of Group Captain William McBrien, 17 Wing Commander, known by the pilots as "Tin Willy." Having relieved the commander of some of his clothes they went on to steal his staff car. They did, however, draw the line at stealing his personal Spitfire as it was too closely guarded. Ormston and Matheson got into their newly acquired vehicle and brazenly drove out through the main gates, saluted on their way by the guards, following which they returned in triumph to

RAF Staplehurst. The 411 Squadron ORB enthused over the performance of the pilots in these exercises and suggested that: "when we get Spitfire Mark IXs these keen boys should pile up an imposing squadron victory score. This is the haven of their desires."

Tommy Wheler recalled the exercise with some amusement as amongst the "stolen" equipment used by the pilots to return to their bases were a few aircraft including; a Tiger Moth, a Spitfire Mark IX, and a top-secret Spitfire Mark XII which had just entered service. This action caused a huge stir amongst the top brass unsurprisingly! The Mark XII was the first Spitfire fitted with the Griffon engine, which was more powerful than the Rolls Royce Merlin turning the Mark XII into the fastest fighter of its time. Towards the end of the war, the Mark XII found a use for its incredible speed by shooting down V1 flying bombs, the "doodle bugs," or "buzz bombs." The V1 was a pilotless flying bomb and an early example of the modern cruise missile which wreaked havoc on London and the southeast of England in 1944. They were so called because of the sinister sound the engine made.

Operation Starkey took place on 9 September 1943. The Roaring Boys played their part in the operation, a deception exercise to fool the Germans into thinking that the Allies were about to launch a huge amphibious landing in the Pas de Calais. It was also intended as a dress rehearsal for D Day. Massive troop concentrations were gathered along the south coast, and bombing missions made to soften up the German coastal defences. It was anticipated that the Luftwaffe would be drawn into combat, as it had been during the Dieppe raid in 1942 and as a result, they could be destroyed in the air, and at their bases in large numbers. The end results were extremely disappointing. Only a dozen German aircraft were destroyed, despite the huge air power flying over their territory. It was suspected that the Germans didn't view the threat as serious and weren't going to risk a massive loss of aircraft to such a numerically superior force.

On 13 October 1943, after several days of abandoned flying due to dense fog, 411 Squadron transferred from the fields of Kent to their winter quarters at Biggin Hill. They were also in receipt of the new Spitfire Mark IXs which replaced their Mark Vs, a move that was eagerly anticipated and relished by all the pilots. During the winter months, a campaign of daylight bombing raids called Ramrod operations was undertaken in which the Roaring boys provided fighter escort to the bombers to and from targets in France. The mission objective was to soften up the enemy's defences ahead of D Day.

A selection of films was shown to keep the pilots amused throughout the war, and in particular on days when poor weather prevented any flying. On 19 October, *Keep 'Em Flying*, starring Bud Abbott and Lou Costello was shown to the general amusement of everyone. There were few smiles on show the next day however when WO Myers taxied his Spitfire into the tail of F/O G W Johnson. The timing of the accident caused much consternation amongst the commanders as it was only a few days after the delivery of the new Spitfire IXbs.

411 Squadron Spitfire DB-M at RAF Biggin Hill 1943

The Allied air forces began their six-month campaign against the German long-range weapons programme in early November. A significant number of 411's missions were flown against what became known as 'V Weapon' sites. Their true purpose was hidden, and aircrews were only told they were attacking construction sites. The code name, Operation Crossbow was given to the campaign to neutralise the Germans programme and the threat presented by V1 'doodle bugs,' V2 rockets, and the V3 cannon, the 'Hochdruckpumpe.' The V3 was effectively a long-range cannon, called a high-pressure pump, and it was located at Mimoyecques, Calais. The V3 was designed to send a projectile a distance of around 100 miles to explode in the London area. The plan was to build around 25 of these weapons.

The month of November also led to structural changes in the Allied air forces. Air Chief Marshall Sir Trafford Leigh-Mallory was appointed Commander in Chief of the Allied Expeditionary Air Force. There were three components; the first was the US Ninth Air Force, a tactical arm similar to the RAF's Tactical Air Force, of which 411 Squadron was part, and which, as the second component formally became 2nd Tactical Air Force (2nd TAF). And lastly, following the dissolution of Fighter Command, the Air Defence of Great Britain (ADGB) was the third component.

The 2nd TAF was commanded by Air Marshal Sir Arthur Coningham. It had three Groups, 83 Group was commanded by Air Vice Marshall (AVM) Harry Broadhurst and included amongst others, 126 Airfield (made up of 411, 401 and 412 Squadrons), 84 Group led by AVM L O Brown, and 2 Group of Bomber Command, led by AVM Basil Embry. He had been awarded 4 DSOs and made 19 operational sorties as an AVM. In an interesting coincidence, Aero Legends operate a de Havilland Devon which is used for customer flights alongside Spitfires Elizabeth and TD314 St George. This aircraft was used by Embry as his personal transport after the war.

In the months leading up to D Day, the squadron and wing were visited by a number of high-profile visitors. One such distinguished guest visited 411 on 11 December, South African Spitfire pilot, and fighter ace Group Captain Adolph G "Sailor" Malan DSO and Bar DFC and Bar, who led 74 Squadron during the Battle of Britain. He developed the 10 rules of air fighting, which by this stage of the war was pinned up on the noticeboards of most front-line squadrons.

TEN OF MY RULES FOR AIR FIGHTING – Sailor Malan

1. Wait until you see the whites of his eyes. Fire short bursts of one to two seconds only when your sights are definitely "ON".
2. Whilst shooting think of nothing else, brace the whole of your body: have both hands on the stick: concentrate on your ring sight.
3. Always keep a sharp lookout. "Keep your finger out".
4. Height gives you the initiative.
5. Always turn and face the attack.

6. Make your decisions promptly. It is better to act quickly even though your tactics are not the best.
7. Never fly straight and level for more than 30 seconds in the combat area.
8. When diving to attack always leave a proportion of your formation above to act as a top guard.
9. *INITIATIVE, AGGRESSION, AIR DISCIPLINE,* and *TEAMWORK* are words that MEAN something in Air Fighting.
10. Go in quickly – Punch hard – Get out!

With all of the operations against German military and civilian transportation targets in occupied France, there was fevered speculation about the timing for the "big show," the invasion of occupied Europe. From the German side, there was a slow, and a steady erosion in morale as the daily Ramrods, huge in terms of aircraft numbers and firepower, endlessly pounded their military, transport and communications infrastructure. In 1944, the momentous events of the Allied invasion of mainland Europe would see the 411 Squadron and their Spitfires tested to their limits.

Throughout 1943 it was becoming clear that the Allies were getting the upper hand in terms of air superiority. As the missions for each of Spitfire Elizabeth's pilots' show, most of the Ramrods and fighter sweeps were undertaken with infrequent attacks from the Luftwaffe, who were intent on saving themselves for defensive purposes after the invasion of Europe took place. With the arrival of the Spitfire Mark IXb to replace the ageing Mark V, the fighter pilots felt they had an aircraft that could really match the FW 190 and Me 109 in combat. The Roaring Boys routinely flew as escort to the USAAF's bombers. With the development of fuel drop tanks, the USAAF's P38 Lightning and P47 Thunderbolt fighters could stay in support of the heavy bombers throughout their long-range missions into the heart of Germany. As a result, 2nd TAF was given an escort role to medium range bombers on their missions, along with the responsibility to provide withdrawal support for the return leg by the "heavies" after hitting targets deep inside Germany. The Americans had also recognised the potential of the P51 Mustang as a fighter. The 354th "Pioneer Mustang" Group had undertaken escort duties for the Ninth Air Force and its capabilities made it stand out. The P51 had an enormous fuel capacity, impressive armament, and with the addition of the Rolls Merlin engine used in the Spitfire, it became a potent weapon. The aircraft could accompany bombers all the way to Berlin and gain air superiority over the Luftwaffe in air combat. The "Mighty" Eighth Air Force soon re-equipped with the P51. The sheer industrial might of America, combined with that of Allies like Britain and its Commonwealth countries including; Canada, Australia, and New Zealand allowed vast numbers of men and machines to be put into the air to support these bombing missions. On one occasion, described later, 411 Squadron was one of 20 airborne Spitfire squadrons supporting a single mission, a total of 240 aircraft. Under this pressure, it was unsurprising that the Luftwaffe withdrew from the coastal areas of France in 1943.

On 27 January 1944, the Eighth Air Force and the RAF had commenced a bombing offensive against Germany, the first time in the war that the Americans had bombed mainland Germany. The Roaring Boys would do their bit in support of this offensive. The campaign was agreed between the Allied leaders, President Franklin D Roosevelt of the United States, Prime Minister Winston Churchill for Great Britain and Charles de Gaulle leader of the Free French at The Casablanca Conference which ran from 14 to 24 January. The bombing directive read as follows;

1. Your Primary object will be the progressive destruction and dislocation of the German military, industrial, and economic system, and the undermining of the morale of the German people to a point where their capacity for armed resistance is fatally weakened.

1944 to 1945 – 411 Squadron and Spitfire NH341 Elizabeth

Following the military collapse of the Allies in 1940, and their expulsion from France and Europe in the face of the German *Blitzkrieg,* or "lightning war," on 6 June 1944 they were finally ready to return in one of the biggest military operations the world had ever seen – D Day.

This was also to be the year that a factory in Castle Bromwich, England would assemble a Mark IXb Spitfire with the serial number NH341. Following the aircraft's delivery to 411 Squadron, the name "Elizabeth," the wife of Roaring Boys pilot Bruce Whiteford was soon painted on the cowling by him. During her operational life, this aircraft would pass through the hands of 9 pilots, and daily be in the thick of the front-line fighting.

In the lead up to D Day, the Roaring Boys were engaged in numerous Ramrod missions and fighter sweeps against German military targets to disrupt aerodrome operations and denigrate the French transport and communications network. It was vital to slow any movement of reinforcements by the Germans to the front-line once the amphibious landings were underway. As described later, a significant number of the Ramrods were No Ball bombing operations as part of Operation Crossbow, a campaign which ran from 1943 until the end of the war. The campaign was the Allies attempt to disrupt all parts of the German V weapons programme, from research and production facilities to the launch sites themselves. A reconnaissance version of the Spitfire from the RAF's Photographic Reconnaissance Unit (PRU) was used to photograph targets of interest. These aircraft flew on their own at 30,000 feet and were painted a light blue/grey colour as camouflage against the sky. They took an astonishing 36 million aerial photographs during the war. There were 5 cameras on the Spitfire, including two under the wings. Jimmy Taylor, who flew them said: "the Spitfire was superb. It had no guns sticking out spoiling the outline. You could say it was like a butterfly." The aircraft could reach Berlin, and cruise at 363 miles per hour. They had to fly straight and level over their target and not alter course, all whilst avoiding flak, their giveaway contrails making them easy to pick out. And, of course, there was the additional threat of fighters.

A team of experts called Photo Interpreters "PIs" at RAF Medmenham, Danesfield House, Buckinghamshire analysed these photos. What the Germans never knew was that the photos were configured to be in 3 dimensions using a stereoscope, much like 3D glasses you would use to watch a 3D movie. Battlefield Europe was reproduced on the viewing tables at Medmenham. Its finest hour would come with Operation Crossbow when it discovered and hunted down Hitler's new V weapons, the rockets and pilotless drones. These were the first weapons of mass destruction, which Hitler and his High Command had hoped would turn the war in their favour.

It's thought that at this time around 80% of British intelligence came from photo reconnaissance and although the mathematical and geological skills of the brightest minds from the Universities of Oxford and Cambridge were required there was also a creative element to the interpretation work. In an inspired move Medmenham recruited from the Hollywood studios. Walt Disney legend Xavier Atencio, who later wrote the blockbuster film Pirates of the Caribbean was recruited as part of a large American contingent along with Hollywood actor Humphrey Bogart who worked in the army section as a PI.

As described earlier, RAF Medmenham's greatest victory was during Operation Crossbow. The chance discovery of the rocket research base on the German island of Peenemunde led to the start of the Allied campaign to destroy this programme, in which 411 Squadron and 2nd TAF took an active part. In 1942, the V1 and V2 weapons flew for the first time. Following the repeated bombing of the heavy construction and research sites, the Germans moved these facilities underground, and out of range of the reconnaissance Spitfires. The Germans then began to build the launch sites in northern France. The initial tip-off to the British came from the French Resistance, about a new clandestine building programme which they believed was for nefarious purposes. These sites included ramps, which looked like a ski on its side. The ramps were the launch sites for the V1s, so the PIs aptly called them "ski sites." Initially, no one knew what they were for as the V1 weapon was unknown to the Allies until later in 1943, when one grainy image of a blurred cross, a V1 pilotless drone, was photographed at Peenemunde. Later, over 96 sites were identified in northern France with ski ramps built to point at London, Portsmouth, and Southampton. The Germans planned to launch over 2,000 of these bombs, and V2 rockets every day. Operation Crossbow started two days before Christmas, 1943. Its success could have a major impact on the outcome of the war, and hitting these targets became a top priority. The first V1s landed on London a week after the Allies landed on D Day, 6 June. The launch sites for the V1 included on the ski jump ramp a separate rocket which was used to accelerate and launch the pilotless flying bomb into the air, whereafter the rocket motor then provided the propulsion. The V1 could be shot down by aircraft and flak, but there was no defence against the V2 rocket when they began to hit London. The rocket travelled at supersonic speed and the first one fell on Chiswick on 8 September 1944.

One launch site targeted was La forêt d'Eperlecques. In early 1943, RAF reconnaissance flights identified substantial early construction work, and although their purpose was not fully known the fact that the Germans were putting considerable manpower and resources into the site's construction, and defence meant it was worth bombing. In fact, the Blockhaus d'Eperlecques was a major complex designed to launch up to 30 V2 ballistic missiles at England each day. A liquid oxygen plant was to be included in the fortified buildings and bunkers. It was never completed due to the repeated bombing by the British and Americans. The Roaring Boys flew in support of these bombing missions, which also targeted ammunition dumps close to the launch sites. They also flew their Spitfires on dive bombing missions against various sites in northern France.

After trying to establish the reason for calling these No Ball operations, the explanations suggest that it was derived from either the sports of baseball, or cricket. With no national bias whatsoever, cricket seems to offer the most plausible explanation, as it embodies the English sense of "fair play" where a ball bowled at the opposition, which they cannot easily hit is called a "no ball." In fact, any non-cricket related matter in which the protagonist exhibits poor, even unchivalrous behaviour is seen as "just not cricket!" I recall in my meeting with Geoffrey Wellum DFC that he used this same phrase to describe the Luftwaffe's attacks in 1940. It's therefore relatively easy to see how Hitler's self-proclaimed "vengeance weapons" were simply viewed as being, "just not cricket." They were randomly targeting the civilian population, causing terror as well as widespread outrage in the British Government. Due to the censorship imposed by the government, the wider British population were initially unaware of the potential threat. The Germans were pioneers and world leaders of this type of warfare and technology. At the time, London and the South East of England were experiencing an increasing number of these attacks. Postwar, notable German rocket scientists like Wernher von Braun would move to the United States where their technical know-how was used to help the United States Army, and later the NASA's space programmes.

Many of the flight operations in the winter of 1943-44 were affected by the appalling weather. The ORBs often refer to the fighter sweeps to France turning back at the English coast. In February 1944, 411 Squadron began dive bombing and strafing missions in earnest to soften up the German defences ahead of the invasion. Adolf Hitler, *Der Fuhrer* recognised that the invasion would be a pivotal moment of the war and had tasked one of his most famous military commanders, Field Marshall Irwin Rommel, to oversee the construction of "Fortress Europe." The plan was to build an impregnable set of coastal defences running for nearly 1,670 miles from Norway, through Belgium and France, to the Spanish border. One of the other noticeable facts about 411 Squadron's winter operations were the number of times the ORBs describes the Roaring Boys as seeing the enemy, "huns," or being given their location by the fighter controllers. The Luftwaffe was not particularly keen to engage with Allied fighters. As mentioned previously, conserving pilots and equipment ahead of the expected Allied invasion of Europe was a priority, but the potential tactical disadvantages of the Me 109 and FW 190 fighters was a factor too. In addition, engaging in combat against overwhelming numbers of aircraft like the Spitfire, whose pilots were generally more experienced and highly trained, was viewed by the Luftwaffe senior command as pointless use of their valuable aircraft and pilots.

A typical example of a mission leading up to D Day took place on 5 February 1944. Six of Spitfire Elizabeth's 9 pilots; Wheler, Whiteford, Trainor, Harrison, Hyndman, and Gibson all flew together from Biggin Hill on Ramrod 514. They provided support for B17 Flying Fortresses and B24 Liberators bombing targets south west of Paris. The Roaring Boys received notification of unidentified aircraft at 12 o'clock from their position and flying at 25,000 feet. They climbed rapidly towards this threat, dropping their auxiliary fuel tanks in preparation for what the ORB described as, "a scrap with the enemy." The sighting proved to be a false alarm and was no doubt met with disappointment. As soon as visual contact was established, the "enemy" was in fact found to be P47 Thunderbolts from the USAAF. These "bounces," or attacks by friendly fighters on each other were a regular occurrence, but mercifully few engagements resulted in guns being fired in anger. Tommy Wheler also gave a clue to the other challenge of flying Spitfires at the time, the risk of mechanical failure. During this mission, he wrote in his logbook, "Jet tank trouble, no R/T." The auxiliary fuel or Jet tanks regularly caused engine failures when the pilot switched over to the aircraft's main fuel tank. On occasion, these failures resulted in the loss of life. Along with this the R/T, or radio telephone the pilots used to communicate, frequently failed.

During the close support missions, fighters like the Spitfire were positioned on both sides of the bomber formation. A single squadron on each side would contain two flights, A and B, each with two sections of three aircraft flying line abreast. A separate section of aircraft would weave around a few hundred feet above the bombers to replace any section of fighters that moved away to engage enemy fighters. With the upswing in operations and the big challenges to come, on 19 February 411 Squadron and 126 Airfield were given a talk by W/C Buck McNair. The ORB reported: "He told all the pilots to smarten up and get ready for the coming flight. He really laid into all the pilots and I'm sure his talk will have a lasting effect on all of them."

Between 20-25 February, the US and British air forces combined to launch Operation Argument, which became known as the "Big Week." The campaign was an around the clock bombing offensive against German aircraft production and airfields in France and Holland. The objective of the operation was to seriously degrade the Luftwaffe's ability to fight and 126 Wing's fighters would be deployed daily in support of the bomber formations. Despite difficult operating conditions caused by the weather the operation was a success and provided a further dent to Luftwaffe morale and defensive capabilities.

At the end of February, A and B Flights of 411 Squadron were sent on a week-long air firing course in Peterhead, Scotland. The course was designed to sharpen their skills in air to air, and air to ground firing, all vital preparation for the combat action that was to come once the weather improved, and D Day arrived. One group flew the squadron's Spitfires to Peterhead whilst the rest followed by train. It's clear that the practice was needed as the squadron's performance was only assessed as being "satisfactory," with the ORB reporting that: "air to ground firing performance was better than air to air." The night time entertainment left a lot to be desired: "some of the lads went into Peterhead to the cinema. It's only a small place and that's all there is to do!"

On their days off when the winter weather prevented flying, the Roaring Boys undertook various activities, their commanders aware of the need to keep these lively young fighter pilots busy and amused. On 26 February, as a snow blizzard closed in over Biggin Hill the Roaring Boys who weren't in Peterhead made for a dance in the mess hall which according to the ORB: "didn't break up until 1 or 2 o'clock in the morning. Good show, actually!" The next day with the weather preventing any flying, catching up on sleep was the order of the day as: "most of the boys were glad of the opportunity as they missed a lot last night at the dance." In the afternoon, and no doubt still nursing a few sore heads, the boys attended a lecture on the Spitfire's 20 mm Hispano cannon which was described in the squadron diary as, "very boring." In mid-March, 411 travelled to the White City Stadium in London to watch a rugby match between Canada and the United States. In an interesting twist, the event was staged playing Canadian rugby rules for the first half, and American rules for the second, a recipe for confusion if ever there was one! Either way, the 411 Squadron diarist wrote with good humour that the Americans, "beat the pants off us with a score of 18 – 9."

The effect on the squadron of receipt of mail and parcels from Canada cannot be overestimated. I have read entries in the squadron ORB describing when the mail was delayed, and the negative effect this could have on the men's morale. We shouldn't forget that the Canadians were a long way from home, in an era before modern communications. They were also about to take part in one of the biggest military operations in history so the chance to catch up with news and treats from home was a real tonic.

Whilst based at Biggin Hill, the Roaring Boys did get a taste of the Blitz that London had suffered in 1940, when on 22 March they were awoken, and then watched a raid on London by the Luftwaffe. It was part of the German campaign, Operation Steinbock, known as the "Baby Blitz." Steinbock ran from January to May 1944 and was the last strategic air offensive by the Germans. The ORB noted: "There was a terrific amount of A/A fire and flares and a few near hits that made the buildings shake. The boys all agree that Jerry should come over here in the day time just to give us a chance." A few days later on 26 March, the Roaring Boys returned to their old haunt at RAF Staplehurst, which they used to make a series of practice bombing runs.

On 15 April 1944, 411 Squadron moved to RAF Tangmere, living under canvas, and undertook an Army liaison exercise, vital training for a mobile fighter-bomber unit that would be operating in support of ground forces. To prepare for their ground attack role, the squadron was posted to Wales for dive bombing training.

Films were frequently shown to the squadron in the blister hangar at Tangmere in an effort to relieve some of the boredom, and the stress of daily combat operations. One of the movies recorded in the squadron diary was *A Yank at Eton*, starring Mickey Rooney. Having watched a few clips, there was more than a possibility that at the beginning of the film the appearance of the MGM lion was drowned out by the traditional riposte of roars from the squadron! The film was reported as being received, "with mixed expressions of pleasure," perhaps reflecting the fact that the story is about an American at an elite English public school.

On 28 April at the Supermarine factory in Castle Bromwich, a shiny new Mark IX Spitfire rolled off the production line, one of a batch of 43. It had the serial number NH341. Those assembly workers must occasionally have stood back, looked at their handiwork and thought "good hunting and safe returns." In a few months, Spitfire NH341 would be assigned to 411 Squadron, and 9 Roaring Boys would then fly her in combat. The aircraft was configured as a low altitude fighter fitted with a Rolls Royce Merlin Type 66 engine. The distinctive sound of that engine, the "Merlin Magic" still makes the hairs on my neck stand on end no matter how many times I hear it.

Since the Battle of Britain, the RAF had been engaged in a never-ending arms race with the German Luftwaffe to develop the capabilities of their fighter aircraft. As a front-line fighter, the Spitfire was at the forefront of this research, with over 24 different marks developed. The Type 300, which first flew on 5 March 1936 was the first, with the Mark 24 appearing in 1948. The Spitfire Mk LF IXe, of which NH341 was one, was a stop-gap solution, and a response to the appearance of the Luftwaffe's FW 190. In the pilot's logbooks and the ORBs, the aircraft is referred to as a Spitfire IXb rather than IXe, to enable the RAF to distinguish this variant from earlier versions. As a Mark IX, NH341's armament was certainly beefed up from the early Spitfires which were solely fitted with .303-inch calibre machine guns. Spitfire NH341 was fitted with 2 x 20mm Hispano cannons, along with 2 x 0.5-inch machine guns. In addition, to fulfill her role as a close support fighter-bomber she was able to carry 1,000 lb of bombs. The pilots would learn all too quickly in the months that followed the extra risk they faced by carrying these bombs. Any impact from flak or an attacking fighter could cause a sudden detonation of the ordnance, followed by almost certain death. The low altitude nature of ground attack missions was very different from the medium high-altitude air war of the Battle of Britain fought over southern England. Over English air space there was less need to concentrate on navigation, especially in Kent. Even at around 3,000 feet the south of England is laid out before you, and establishing your position can be done relatively quickly. On low altitude ground attack missions over occupied Europe, navigation became more of a consideration, and in the process of focusing on the ground, perhaps whilst establishing his position, a pilot who had a momentary lapse of concentration could suddenly find an enemy fighter appearing behind on his "6 o'clock," with deadly consequences. As Battle of Britain Spitfire pilot Jimmy Corbin DFC once remarked: "it was dangerous, and if you weren't fully aware and had someone up your arse that was good night nurse!"

As D Day drew closer, the administration and central control of RAF squadrons were lessened, as it was appreciated that once "on the ground" they would need to be virtually self-sufficient within their own temporary ALG. No 411 squadron went through endless practice drills, assembling and packing up the tents and equipment as it would be required to do when it was operational as a mobile fighting force. The Roaring Boys combat missions to soften up the enemy and destroy lines of communication continued unabated with a series of fighter sweeps, and bomber escort Ramrod operations. In addition, on 23 April 1944, 411 undertook its first bombing operations, raids on German V1 and V2 rocket research, production and launch facilities, the No Ball targets. During the spring months, 411 Squadron also kept up its impressive tally of downing enemy aircraft with 13 ½ destroyed, 2 probable and 16 damaged.

On May 15, 126 Wing renamed from 126 Airfield a few days before became a fully-fledged part of 17 (RCAF) sector, part of 83 (Composite) Group of the 2nd TAF. These changes would mark the final organisational changes ahead of D Day. In their missions, the squadron reported less contact with the Luftwaffe and operated almost with impunity, aside from the ever-present flak and ground fire which was still effective, and which downed Spitfires at regular intervals. At this stage of the conflict, the German war machine was beginning to suffer from a decline in its experienced pilots, the basic machinery and materials needed to train, and sustain them. Many units were withdrawn east into Germany, and the main threat to the Roaring Boys in the air would come from Jagdgeschwader 2 (JG 2) and Jagdgeschwader 26 (JG 26). The latter was known to the British and Americans as, "The Abbeville Boys," stationed as they were in the area of Abbeville. At one point they were commanded by legendary German Ace Adolf Galland, and JG 26 commanded almost universal respect because of their skill and fighting ability. In May, with the combined fighter numbers the of 2nd TAF, Air Defence of Great Britain, the American Eighth and Ninth Army Air Forces, the Allies could flood the skies over England and occupied Europe with around 3,000 aircraft. Meanwhile, the role of the bomber and fighter bomber was to degrade French railway and transportation networks and reduce the effectiveness of radar air defences. The 411 pilots' missions describe in detail the role they played in this campaign. Throughout occupied northern Europe, and deep into Germany, industrial centres and factories producing military equipment were a target for strategic bombing with the Roaring Boys being on hand to sweep an area for enemy fighters ahead of the bombers, whilst picking up their formations on the return legs to their bases in East Anglia, which was known as "bomber country".

Whilst the squadron was prepping itself for D Day, in late May a series of high profile "top brass" visited to brief the wing. Amongst those visitors were 2nd TAF's commanding officer Air Marshal Sir Arthur Coningham, and Air Marshal Trafford Leigh Mallory, commander in chief of the Allied Expeditionary Air Force, who led 12 Group during the Battle of Britain in 1940. Mallory stressed the importance of teamwork in the forthcoming operations, and the 411 Squadron ORB reported that: "invasion thoughts are constantly in the minds of all personnel. They will be glad when it gets underway." On 3 June, 411 Squadron's Spitfires were painted with black and white invasion stripes on their wings and fuselage. I was pleased to discover during the writing of this book that Mike Rutledge's father Don was one of the 411 crews captured in an iconic photo, paintbrush in hand, applying stripes to one of the Roaring Boys Spitfires. These stripes would help identify them as Allied aircraft preventing a friendly fire incident, often known as a "blue on blue." The squadron ORB commented, "Big things appear to be in store." In the coming days, the Roaring Boys attended the Divine Service, where prayers were said for safe passage through the forthcoming campaign. On the day before D Day, the pilots were moved from their tents to the relative luxury of Nissen huts at Crocker Hill, just a short distance along the A27 from RAF Tangmere. The South of England was filled to bursting with men and equipment waiting to set forth for Normandy. It must have been an extraordinary sight, but for many of those embarking onto ships and aircraft to take part in Operation Overlord, D Day, this would be a one-way trip. They would make the ultimate sacrifice with their lives.

Allied Supreme Commander Dwight D Eisenhower, who was in overall command of Allied forces on D Day called Operation Overlord "the Great Crusade," and in his message to the soldiers, sailors and airman said, "the eyes of the world are upon you." When D Day arrived on 6 June 1944 after a weather delay, the 411 Squadron ORB noted, "D Day is with us at last." On D Day itself, 411 was active patrolling above the Gold, Juno and Sword beachheads in Normandy providing air cover for the vast armada of ships below which were busily disgorging waves of troops and equipment onto the beaches. Despite the sky being filled with fighters, bombers and transport aircraft, Luftwaffe fighters only managed to shoot down around 20 aircraft on D Day. The main risk for pilots didn't turn out to be from the Luftwaffe, but from the potential for a mid-air collision with their own side. As the Roaring Boys patrolled above the beaches, the poor weather compressed thousands of aircraft into a relatively small amount of air space. Every pilot and bomber crew were mindful of the deadly anti-aircraft gun emplacements, known as flak batteries which the enemy had located just onshore. Flying turned into a hazardous business, necessitating the taking of evasive action to avoid the flak barrages. The rationale for the Luftwaffe's non-appearance may well have been down to Hitler's desire to reinforce the defence of the *Fatherland,* as well as the titanic struggle which was underway on the *ost* front against Russia.

411 Squadron Spitfire at RAF Tangmere with D Day invasion stripes

Spitfire NH341 Elizabeth

When D Day and after combat operations got underway 411 Squadron would fly into the Normandy battle zone from RAF Tangmere in the mornings, refuelling and rearming between missions at ALG B3 St Croix-sur-Mer, before returning to base in the evenings.

By D Day + 4, on 10 June, No 126 Wing, including 411 Squadron was operating from Normandy. They were flying missions from the newly constructed airstrips, the ALGs that were the same in construction to those they had operated, and practiced on the year before in Staplehurst. Advanced elements of the squadron had already landed in Normandy on 7 June to begin preparations for the move to ALG B4 Bény-sur-Mer. The Intelligence Officer for No 126 Wing, Monty Berger was the first RCAF ground officer to step onto French soil. A British Pathé News unit filmed the British Royal Engineers Airfield Construction Group building one of the ALGs that 411 would operate from, B3, located at St Croix-sur-Mer. They can be seen using the large-scale plant to plough an airstrip into a field of crops before rolling it flat. A short while later a squadron of Spitfires is filmed landing to refuel and rearm. There is also one section of the film which features a French farmer on a horse-drawn scythe hurriedly harvesting his remaining crops and fixing the camera with a prolonged stare. It's difficult to discern his feelings, but an easy conclusion would be that on the one hand, the loathsome Germans occupiers were in retreat, but this positive development was tempered by the fact that "Les Rosbifs" were now ploughing up his carefully nurtured crops.

Having been delivered to 411 Squadron on 12 June, two days later Spitfire NH341 Elizabeth undertook her first operation from RAF Tangmere in the hands of F/O AB "Bruce" Whiteford. I have held some of Elizabeth's original fuselage panels, and the details of several of the aircraft's missions immediately rushed into my mind. It was a quite amazing moment to hold that piece of the fuselage, taken from the engine cowling, knowing where it had been and what had happened during the aircraft's missions.

Shown in the appendix is a summary of each mission undertaken by Spitfire Elizabeth, the flight times, mission objectives and post sortie comments, along with the name of each of the nine pilots and the date they flew her. This information is drawn directly from the 411 ORBs, which frequently contain inconsistencies and spelling mistakes. I have left these errors unchanged throughout to keep the accounts from the time as authentic as possible.

Having undertaken day time operations from B3 St Croix-sur-Mer and RAF Tangmere, on 18 June 411 Squadron moved to ALG B4 at Bény-sur-Mer. The airfield was located a few miles from Juno Beach, where the Canadian divisions landed on D Day. The ground crew, non-flight crew and of course the Roaring Boys dog, and mascot Joskins Firkin of Scopwick flew over to B4 in several Dakota aircraft. Joskins was officially banned of course, but according to 411 Squadron Leading Aircraftsman, Herb Strutt, he had been trained to sit quietly in a duffle bag with his head poking out of the top, so he went too! Of the fleet of Dakota transport aircraft that left Tangmere, 4 landed at the wrong ALG and were forced to takeoff again. The ORB gave details of the event: "Today was a momentous day in the history of the squadron. Shortly after eleven in the morning notice was received to be packed within half an hour to move to France. As it usually turns out take off was about four hours later. The 'Air Lift Party' of the Wing took off in ten Dakotas. On arrival, the first and probably the impression which will last longest was the great clouds of dust which arose on the runway. After dinner thirteen pilots brought Spits over leaving five to follow later from Tangmere. Everybody busied themselves in getting settled in their tents. Our field is known as B4 and is located in the little village of Bény-sur-Mer. Two patrols were carried out from Tangmere during the day."

Herb Strutt also highlighted one of the problems experienced by the Canadians, that of the Spitfires and other aircraft generating huge clouds of dust when taking off and landing at B4. After a while, the RCAF's blue air force service uniforms began to turn to a dull grey colour, resembling that of German infantry. "After a couple of guys got shot we thought we better put on Army uniforms," Strutt later remarked. It appeared that the RCAF blue uniform was no guarantee of the squadron's safety near the American sector. The Intelligence section's situation map, used to brief pilots as to the current position of the front, in June proclaimed that near Cherbourg the, "Yanks now only 5 ½ miles away!" The next sentence again warned of the reception unwary RCAF personnel might expect to receive when straying too close: "Warning! Do not go near the American Lines in your blue uniform!"

On the following day, the rain turned the dust into sticky mud which: "brought to mind stories of the last war. The boys spent the day in digging trenches in their tents to save themselves the trouble of getting up if Jerry pays us a nocturnal visit."

In amongst the warnings the situation map contained elements of humour too. The squadron was reminded that they were, "Making the world S.H.A.E.F. for democracy" (Supreme Headquarters Allied Expeditionary Force). At this time the general movement of the squadron's equipment around the aerodrome was helped by the ever-resourceful Canadians locating and commandeering a horse. It was looked after by F/L Hayward and was named "Myrtle." The thinking was that petrol supplies might slow at some point, and it was vital to have Myrtle on board to move supplies around the vast airfield. B4 resembled a huge ammunition dump, but also had a massive engineering area for aircraft maintenance and repair, along with all the equipment and supplies needed to keep the air fighting units fully operational.

As part of the settling in process for 126 Wing and to boost morale, their commander Keith Hodson decided that a beer run was in order, and arranged for three pilots from the Roaring Boys sister squadron, 412 to transport beer in steamed out auxiliary fuel tanks, and deliver it to the expectant wing pilots and crews at Bény-sur-Mer. The three pilots selected for the mission landed back from England loaded with beer, no doubt expecting a jubilant welcome from the assembled squadrons. Instead, they were greeted by a complete absence of activity, or personnel as if the airfield had been abandoned. Eventually, a figure popped his head out from a hedge and told them in no uncertain terms that the church steeple located close to the aerodrome was loaded with German snipers. The advice offered, and immediately accepted by the pilots was to drop their precious cargo and, "bugger off!" The church steeple was eventually cleared of snipers. I was able to view the results of this attack in Herb Strutt's photo album. The steeple was no longer in place, and the area where the bells and snipers were located was bisected by an artillery round, which had left a gaping hole in the masonry. The local vicar probably just gave a Gallic shrug, "cest la Guerre" (it's the War) and attended to more pressing matters amongst his flock. Lawrie Jeffrey recalled his father Jimmy telling him of return trips being made from France in the early days after D Day with several pilots stashing bottles of champagne in their Spitfires. Much of this booze was thrust into the willing hands of the Allies by local French people jubilant at their liberation from 4 years of the German occupation. Jimmy Jeffrey said one returning pilot climbed rapidly to a high altitude in his Spitfire in order to chill the champagne ready for his triumphant return to RAF Tangmere. The unfortunate consequence was that some of the bottles and their corks exploded, whereupon he took immediate evasive action thinking he was being shot up by the enemy! The champagne-soaked pilot arrived back with a story to tell, but with a less than enthusiastic welcome from his squadron friends.

With the Squadron permanently based at B4 Bény-sur-Mer from 18 June, their role was a mix of ground attack, as well as an increasing amount of air combat as the Germans poured reinforcements into Northern France to stem the Allies advance. The Spitfire's ability as a dive bomber was open to question and is covered in some detail in other works. Certainly, it was prone to strikes from the highly accurate and effective German flak. Another hazard was the potential for a ricochet from one of the Spitfire's 20 mm Hispano cannons, which resulted in several pilots effectively shooting themselves down.

At this stage of the war many of the Luftwaffe's so-called *experten*, the elite fighter pilots, were either lost in combat or prisoners of war. There were still some highly skilled pilots in theatre, although the Luftwaffe was focusing its main strength on attacking the American sector of Normandy, to the west of the British and Canadians. For J E "Johnnie" Johnson these pilots were a pale shadow of the airmen who faced the RAF in 1940. He described them as, "a poor, ill-trained lot." The average German soldier in this area would probably have justifiably asked the question, "wo ist die Luftwaffe?" The tables had turned since the dark days of 1940 when British Tommies on the Dunkirk beaches awaiting rescue, rather unfairly asked: "where is the RAF?" To illustrate the point, on 25 June whilst the Roaring Boys were seeing little of the Luftwaffe, on the same day the USAAF had shot down 49 enemy fighters. Amongst the *experten* making an appearance in the Roaring Boys sector was a veteran of the Battle of Britain and Eastern Front. Major Walter Matoni was known to 126 Wing and their fellow pilots in 127 Wing. He was a highly skilled fighter pilot who finished the war convalescing in a hospital after a crash landing. He had 31 victories to his name, including seven Spitfires. He was reported as operating in the Normandy area and could be identified by his long-nosed FW 190, in which he led a gaggle of

ME 109s. Matoni was an elusive, and skillful opponent who, like aces on both sides of the conflict, was not easily drawn into reckless combat situations. The Canadians decided to try and lure this enemy into the fight by making rude comments about him over their radios, knowing that the Germans would probably be monitoring their transmissions. The search for this elusive quarry eventually came to the attention of the British Press who interviewed Johnnie Johnson. The story was somewhat embellished by the journalists who indicated that Johnnie Johnson had issued an old-fashioned "duel to the death" challenge to Walter Matoni, in their respective fighters. Johnson was ribbed mercilessly by his comrades as a result. The story was eventually picked up by the German Press who passed the details on to Matoni. In January 1945, Matoni was laying in hospital and was unable to take up the challenge. He later wrote to Johnson to express his regret at being unable to accept the challenge. Johnson wrote back and offered to buy him dinner, which was not taken up. In a postscript to the story, they did eventually get to meet during the filming of the British television programme, "This is your Life" in 1985 which was telling Johnnie Johnson's life story. Matoni came on as a surprise guest. To laughter from the audience, Matoni said: "I'm so happy to be here. It's better to meet here than to shoot one another from the sky!"

The Spitfire pilots of 411 were increasingly aware that post D Day German flak defences were being reinforced, and that their Spitfires were particularly vulnerable during these ground attack missions. The 411 ORBs record Spitfire Elizabeth taking part in dive bombing missions as well as strafing attacks on vehicles, tanks, and mechanised transports. Bombing during the war was generally an imprecise activity. The Spitfires were no different in this regard with their tactic of diving from around 8,000-10,000 feet and releasing their bombs at around 3,000-5,000 feet.

On 26 June, the British offensive named, Operation Epsom, was launched to the west of the strategically important city of Caen as the Allies sought to break out from their coastal bridgeheads and push inland. This offensive drew the Luftwaffe into the area in large numbers as the ORBs detailed, albeit the bad weather limited the support that Allied aircraft could offer in the offensive's first few days. On 28 June, the USAAF made very few claims, whilst 2nd TAF claimed 26 air victories, a complete reversal of the position earlier in the month. During the month of June, the Roaring Boys destroyed a total of 12 ½ Luftwaffe aircraft with another 6 damaged. In total, 411 Squadron flew 1,029 hours on combat operations for the month of June.

The month of July saw more air combat for the Roaring Boys, including for Spitfire Elizabeth in support of more ground offensives. Large groups of Luftwaffe Me 109s and FW 190s were present in support of their land forces, which were bolstered by increasing numbers of flak units, as many of the Roaring Boys were to find to their cost. The month of July was very successful for 126 Wing, with 56 Luftwaffe aircraft destroyed. There was also a slight relaxation of the restrictions on free time and movements. This enabled the Roaring Boys, and 411 personnel to sample the local delights of Normandy, including the city of Bayeux, which no doubt involved wine, cheese, calvados as well as other physical activities! The locals were also quick to exploit the opportunity of having the well paid and supplied Canadians liberators on their doorstep. After the deprivations which 4 years of war had brought them, this was too good an opportunity to miss. And, for 411 there was a chance to augment their rations with local produce.

During this time the ORBs provide details of the multiple daily missions carried out by 411, all with a level of intent and aggression to get to grips with the enemy wherever possible. It is this determination that comes through strongly in the research, and from conversations with pilots like Tommy Wheler. On 7 July, the newly promoted Dal Russel DFC would take over from Wing Commander George Keefer for his second spell as 126 Wing's commanding officer. He had previously stepped down in rank to squadron leader to lead 442 squadron. With a stalemate in the ground offensive, the RAF staged a massive raid on Caen, with over 700 Lancaster bombers rendering much of the city to rubble. It was a concerted attempt to smash the German defences around the city and open up the pathway to Paris. The sight, sounds, and tremors of the raid from the ground were all too vivid and observed keenly by 411 Squadron from their base close by at B4.

The modus operandi for armed reconnaissance missions was changed on 10 July by communiqué No 17 (F) from sector HQ, RCAF. It ordered that such missions, where a formation of Spitfires would fly over enemy territory should not be conducted at heights between 20,000 to 25,000 feet, but if weather conditions allowed, at heights 3,000 to 5,000 feet. The rationale was that maximum ground movement could be better observed closer to the ground. The communiqué also suggested that a number of aircraft in a patrol should carry bombs to increase the destructive force of an attack. If no targets were identified during the mission, then the Army Liaison Officer would brief the patrol leader of a target of last resort that could be attacked before the patrol returned to base.

On 14 July, 126 Wing was expanded with the addition of No 442 Caribou squadron. It also heralded a change at the top as Keith Hodson was replaced by Group Captain G E McGregor, a pilot who became an ace during the Battle of Britain, earning him a DFC, one of the first issued to a Canadian pilot in World War II. The land battle around Caen continued in earnest, with the attempted encirclement of the city in Operation Goodwood by British and Canadian forces, which was launched on 18 July. The summer heat also led to an infestation of flies and insects, followed almost inevitably for the weary pilots by an outbreak of dysentery, which probably curtailed any "roaring" about, other than to the latrines. The situation wasn't helped by B4 Bény-sur-Mer being adjacent to a cemetery, where on a daily basis the dead from the battle for Caen were being brought in large numbers. Members of the squadron would go over and help dig graves in the evening. Aside from dysentery, the squadron's medical team was also kept busy treating several other afflictions, including; boils, scabies, and a variety of sexually transmitted diseases! The use of chalk and opium to control the pilots dysentery and diarrhoea was well recorded and was a rather surprising medicinal combination.

The distant sound of battle was a daily accompaniment to life at B4. On 24 July, the aerodrome was rocked by a series of explosions from the armament park as a collapsing roof set off an initial blast from a belt feed of ammunition. The enormous roar provoked a domino effect around the airfield as personnel hit the ground. Fortunately, no personnel or aircraft were damaged, and an even bigger calamity with the detonation of the wing's bomb store was avoided. It was a timely reminder to all of the dangers of handling and storing ordnance.

There was no letup in the intense flying during the month of August, which would see the Germans finally removed from French soil. On the ground, the Battle of Falaise was underway with the Allies attempting to entrap and encircle General Gunther Von Kluge's Seventh German Army.

The pilots of 126 Wing, along with those from the other allied air forces, were eager to be let off the leash in a target rich environment of military vehicles streaming eastwards. The approach taken was to attack the front and rear of a column of vehicles, disabling them by bombing and strafing. This gave the remaining Spitfires and Typhoons the opportunity to fire their cannons and rockets at the trapped transports, thus exacting a heavy toll. Effectively, the retreating Germans were being funnelled by the Allies into a small "pocket" between the towns of Falaise, Trun, and Chambois which was gradually being closed, leaving them surrounded. The destruction around Chambois was such that it became known as, "The corridor of death." The Germans suffered the destruction of around eight infantry divisions and two Armoured *Panzer* Divisions. Some pilots and crews went to view the damage, as did Supreme Allied Commander Dwight D Eisenhower. None who witnessed it apparently would ever forget the scene of death and destruction that lay across the countryside. The Allies ability to breakdown and deploy at new airfields were matched by the efficient ground crews. They could refuel, rearm and where necessary repair the aircraft to allow small numbers to be almost constantly in the air harassing any Luftwaffe aircraft that should stray into their sector, as well as strafing the ground transports. The pilots often flew in pairs and could be airborne from dawn for around six to eight hours a day. The ORB reported: "Both A and B flights now have a shift system working which seems to satisfy everybody. Now a pilot flies morning and night one day and in the afternoon on the following day."

On 8 August, 411 Squadron moved forward with the advancing ground forces to ALG B.18 Cristot. The well-drilled rehearsal at ALGs like Staplehurst was put into good practice as the camp was broken down with flight operations back up and running again the next day.

The month of August would prove momentous as the Allies made significant progress, pushing the Germans back, and finally breaking free of the coastal areas. Despite the daily fighting, members of 411 were released on leave and were able to enjoy the Normandy area. Indeed, on 25 August the ORB diarist wrote: "The Wing was released at 13.00 hours for the day. At night a dance was held at the officers mess. Over a hundred nurses from hospitals in the Bayeux area attended and needless to say the 411 Squadron "Wolves" turned out en masse."

The squadron then moved onto a further 10 airfields in northern France, Belgium, and Holland in the remainder of 1944. On 1 September,

411 Squadron and 126 Wing commenced what would become a series of base "hops" as they moved from airfield to airfield to keep up with the advancing armies. In some cases, they moved in a short time after the Germans had left. The fluid nature of the battlefield and advance saw the mobile fighter wing test its metal, and name to the fullest. It was imperative that close support to the armies on the front line could be maintained around the clock. The first move of the month was from B18 to B24 St André-de-L'Eure. The following day, the Roaring Boys moved to B26 Illiers L'Eveque where they joined up with No 127 Wing, who were already based there. This rather unsatisfactory situation was soon over. A further order was received, and on 3 September 126 Wing moved to B44 Poix which is located around 15 miles to the south west of Amiens. In September 1944, from its base at B56 Evere, Belgium, 411 Squadron took part in providing local air support for Operation Market Garden, the biggest Allied airborne operation of the War to capture the strategically important bridges at Nijmegen and Arnhem. The base was too far west to allow support on the front line, and the 2nd TAF was not directly used in the operation as the fighter support for transport aircraft and gliders was provided directly from the UK. When 126 Wing moved to B68 Le Culot on 20 September, they were finally able to send patrols over Arnhem and Nijmegen.

The base at B56 Evere, near Brussels, was vacated quickly by the Luftwaffe so an improved level of comfort was experienced for the first time, and much to 411's relief there was no need to put up tents. The aerodrome was close enough to Brussels to allow the Roaring Boys the opportunity to enjoy some free time in the city. Having viewed Herb Strutt's photo album, he included several shots of Brussels showing the unbridled joy with which the Allies were received in the city after its liberation. The squadron ORB recorded that the citizens: "continue to overdo themselves in welcoming us to their country" and the squadron was inundated with invitations to dinner and parties. The welcome: "showed the justness of the cause for which we are fighting."

Having transferred to one of the Allies forward most air bases a succession of high-profile visitors duly appeared including; Generals Eisenhower and Montgomery, Prince Bernhard of the Netherlands, the Roaring Boys fellow countryman General Crerar of 1st Canadian Army, and American Generals Patton and Bradley. Amid much saluting, briefings and general interruptions caused by the dignitaries were operational log jams caused by the fact that B56 Evere was not an ALG, but was a major resupply hub. The sky was filled with Dakotas as well as "heavies" suffering from battle damage, or mechanical trouble who were looking to make an emergency landing. At any time, there could up to 40 aircraft in the circuit waiting to land, and from experience I can safely say that more than half a dozen in a circuit pattern flying at different speeds does concentrate the mind somewhat. The 126 Wing flight control staff inevitably called a halt to operations in early September as it was deemed too dangerous for the squadrons to operate safely and effectively as a mobile fighter force. In one single day, the 27th September, the Roaring Boys and their fellow pilots of 412 Squadron claimed an extraordinary 22 enemy aircraft destroyed and ten damaged. Despite their efforts, Operation Market Garden, the airborne operation was a failure for the Allies who suffered between 15,000 and 17,000 casualties. From an air support perspective, the planners had focused air support on protecting the landing grounds, thus allowing the Germans to move reinforcements into the area without being attacked from the air. The operation was later brought wider public attention in the 1977 blockbuster film "A Bridge Too Far."

411 Squadron ground crew with a captured Stuka dive bomber

From their new base at B80 Volkel, Holland in October 1944 the Roaring Boys continued to fly their Spitfires, mainly on ground attack missions utilising both bombs and cannons to attack trains, communications infrastructure, tugs, barges, bridges, oil dumps, and ground transports. Eventually, in December, the squadron moved to B88 Heesch, Holland and much to everyone's relief building accommodation was available rather than tents.

On 16 December 1944 the Germans began their last major offensive, Operation "Watch on the Rhine" through the supposedly impenetrable, and therefore lightly defended Ardennes forest. Adolf Hitler's objective was to reach the strategic port of Antwerp and cut off the Allies supply routes. After early initial gains, the offensive stalled, and Hitler's "last throw of the dice" failed to make the strategic gains he and his high command had hoped for. As a result of the offensive, there was still plenty of hunting for 411 in the air, particularly as German industry had been busily manufacturing aircraft to replace those lost after D Day and the battle of France. In the last week of December, 3 Messerschmitt Me 262 jets, an advanced fighter-bomber that signaled the beginning of the end for propeller-driven fighters, were shot down. Although German aircraft production was replacing lost aircraft, the vital components, the pilots, were not available in sufficient numbers to match the highly experienced Allied pilots, including those of 126 Wing and the Roaring Boys. Pilot training courses were shortened due to the desperate shortage of fuel meaning those entering combat for the first time were woefully short of flying experience.

The Roaring Boys provided air support in another famous action on Christmas day 1944, the Battle of the Bulge. The following day, they scored an impressive tally of air victories when they shot down 9 German fighters. Although Spitfire Elizabeth's pilots had long since departed 411 Squadron, some of the new intakes were making a name for themselves including, F/L R J "Dick" Audet who shot down 5 of the 9 aircraft on that day. He went on to shoot down 10 ½ enemy aircraft before being shot down and killed by flak whilst attacking a train on 3 March 1945.

On 1 January 1945, the Luftwaffe launched a significant air offensive with 968 fighters, against Allied airfields which was code-named Operation Baseplate. 411 Squadron, amongst others, was already airborne on routine patrols and the battle was joined. The Germans had targeted the destruction of around 400-500 allied aircraft, hangars, and equipment in the operation which would then allow their ground forces to move forward with less vulnerability to attack from the air. For the reasons outlined above, poor pilot training, skills, and experience, this target was not achieved. Many of the 290 Allied aircraft destroyed were non-operational. For the Luftwaffe, the loss of 143 pilots killed or missing, with 70 captured and 20 wounded signalled their largest defeat in a single day and another devastating blow to their offensive capabilities. The rest of the month was mixed weather wise which limited flying operations, but overall 126 Wing managed to destroy 46 aircraft and damage 17 more.

411 Squadron Spitfires with Short Stirling bombers

During the month of February, the Roaring Boys were once again assigned to dive bombing duties with the railway network being the main target. The ever-present enemy flak batteries took their toll of pilots and remained one of the greatest threats. In March 1945, the weather hampered flying operations, but on 24 March 1945, Operation Plunder saw the British and Americans cross into Germany. The Roaring Boys and 126 Wing provided bridgehead cover for the transport aircraft and won praise for the determined way in which they pressed home their attacks, a feature of their modus operandi from the beginning. Operation Varsity was part of this campaign, a highly successful airborne operation involving 16,000 paratroopers and several thousand aircraft. The Roaring Boys continued to attack ground targets, disrupting the enemy's troop movements by both road and rail. In the air, the Luftwaffe did not appear in any great numbers.

On 15 April 1945, 411 Squadron along with 126 Wing moved on to a former Luftwaffe aerodrome at B116 Wunstorf. The squadrons were delighted to find great quantities of wine and champagne had been left behind due to the rapid nature of the Allied advance. With the Luftwaffe decreasingly able to provide a significant threat in the air, the Roaring Boys were still able to harass retreating enemy troops, targeting rail links and mechanised enemy transports, although the swift pace of the Allies advance had stretched supply lines, and at times there was a shortage of ammunition and serviceable aircraft.

A momentous event happened on 30 April 1945, when the Allies on the Western front joined with the Russians advancing from the East, effectively depriving the Luftwaffe of territory in which to operate. During the month 126 Wing achieved its highest score of the war by destroying 58 enemy aircraft, with 1 probable and 31 damaged. This reflected their aggressive approach and desire to press home their attacks against an enemy who lacked the will to fight and whose airfields were well within fighter range.

On 5 May 1945, the Roaring Boys received the news they had been waiting for as it was announced that all hostilities would end at 08.00 am. The War in Europe was over.

As part of 126 Wing, 411 Squadron, the Grizzly Bears were part of one of the most successful fighting wings in the 2nd TAF. The wing destroyed an incredible 333 Luftwaffe aircraft between D Day and the declaration of Victory in Europe, VE Day. Overall, from D Day to VE Day, 411 Squadron destroyed 75 Luftwaffe aircraft. The number of trucks and mechanised transports destroyed reached over 4,400, along with nearly 500 locomotives and 1,500 rail trucks. Within 411 Squadron, were the 9 pilots who flew Spitfire NH341 Elizabeth and whose amazing stories are told in the following chapters.

In the months following the end of hostilities, the Roaring Boys were engaged in training exercises, following a suitable period of rest and relaxation. Clearly, plans had been carefully laid for some continuing celebrations at 17 Armament Practice, Camp Warmwell where 411 was posted in May. One pilot who returned from leave after the squadron had departed for England was told to follow in a Spitfire which was left behind for him. He was somewhat mystified to see a placard banning the use of fuel in the 45-gallon auxiliary tank. All was revealed when he arrived at Warmwell, and a swarm of excitable ground crew revealed the tank contents, 45 gallons of French brandy!

Upon returning to Germany as part of the Allied Occupation Forces, 411 Squadron maintained routine flight training, including being re-equipped with Spitfire Mark XVIs. In November 1945, the squadron transferred to a base on the island of Sylt, on the Danish border to practice air gunnery. Previous occupants advised them to bring playing cards as there was nothing to do. As the months rolled on it was clear that commanders were beginning the process of winding up units and demobilisation was underway. And so, on 21 March 1946, 126 Wing was stood down. The Roaring Boys had roared their last, and the Squadron's Adjutant F/L J R Hughes wrote in the Squadron's ORB: "so 411 goes down into history with a record with which we feel justly proud."

CHAPTER TWO

BRUCE WHITEFORD

Bruce Whiteford at RAF Biggin Hill

Almond Bruce Whiteford, known as Bruce, was born in Saskatoon, Saskatchewan, Canada on 3 February 1918 to John Almond Whiteford and Annie Whiteford (nee Cameron) who had emigrated from England. John enlisted shortly after the outbreak of World War 1, signing his attestation papers on 21 December 1914. Bruce married Elizabeth Willans and their son Norm Whiteford tells his remarkable family's story:

"As a Sergeant in the 42nd Battalion Royal Highlanders of Canada, Canadian Expeditionary Force my grandfather was twice wounded, badly at the Ypres salient in July 1916 with severe shrapnel wounds to his chest and was subsequently invalided out and returned to Saskatoon. His service and wartime experience most likely influenced Bruce. As a boy growing up in Saskatoon Bruce had two aims in life; to fly and to be a cowboy (in that order). The young Bruce would go to the train yards and climb up on the roofs of the small service buildings adjacent to the tracks and wait for an oncoming train. At the appropriate time, he would spread his arms ("wings") and launch himself into the onrushing air created by the vortices of the speeding locomotive and enjoy a short flight to the ground. His mother strongly disapproved of this activity. He attended the Saskatoon Technical Collegiate Institute and following a four-year course received a Certificate in Motor Mechanics. My mother frequently commented on the rapport Bruce told her he enjoyed with his ground crews; no doubt aided by his mechanical background.

"At the outbreak of World War II, Bruce enlisted in the RCAF and began his flight training at the Regina Flying Club, Regina, Saskatchewan on 27 May 1940. His early flying experience was undertaken in a De Havilland DH 60M Gypsy Moth with the serial number CF-CFQ, an aircraft type that continued to introduce a succession of trainee military pilots into flying from 1939, until it was decommissioned on 9 September 1944. Bruce flew solo in the same aircraft on 09 June after 10 hours and 20 minutes dual instruction. After a further 16 hours and 20 minutes flying time, he reported to Course No 1 BCATP, Camp Borden, Ontario which ran from 22 July to 17 September 1940. On 30 September that year, he received his "wings" in the first class of the BCATP, a ceremony for which was attended by Canadian Minister of National Defence, Hon. J. L. Ralston. Ralston addressed the 45 graduates offering them some sober advice: "The pining of these wings means more than we realise at the moment to the history of Canada, the British Commonwealth, and the world." He added that being presented with their wings: "does not make you experienced pilots. You must resist the urge to show off." On top of these warnings and perhaps driven by the audience in front of him bursting with all the vigour of youth, Ralston went on to warn of the dangers of low flying, mixing alcohol with flying and showing off to girlfriends, or anyone else! He rounded off his speech with the message that any form of ill-considered or illegal behaviour would result in drastic action, even imprisonment and dismissal from the service. He said: "It would be a loss to the people of Canada who have paid for the training." Ralston added, before giving his final sage advice to Bruce and the other 44 graduates: "Save your extra steam for Fritz when you go as a representative of this country with a personal message for Hitler – that is not against England he is making war but the British Commonwealth of Nations."

Following his completion of Course No 1, Bruce moved onto an Advanced Training Squadron (ATS) at Camp Borden on 12 November 1940 where he began flight training in the Harvard and Northrop A-17A. On 3 January 1941, he began his Instructors Course at Canadian Forces

Base Trenton flying the Fleet Canuck, Harvard, Lockheed 10, and Lockheed 12. He was then posted as a flight sergeant instructor to No 3 Service Flying Training School (SFTS) based in Calgary. It was during his time here that he met his future wife, Elizabeth Daphne Willans whose name would later be proudly painted onto the fuselage of Spitfire NH341. Norm takes up his parents story:

"Elizabeth began riding a horse virtually as soon as she began walking, and like all the members of her family was an accomplished horsewoman. Her sister-in-law, Eve Willans, ran a riding academy. After the outbreak of the war, she hosted RCAF personnel at her academy to learn to ride and provide them with a break from the monotony of service life and being away from friends and family. It was through this mechanism that Bruce met Elizabeth. She resisted his overtures initially as apparently, the "fly-boys" had already established a bit of a reputation for themselves in 1941! Bruce took to horses as a natural rider and began hanging around and making a nuisance of himself. He got along famously with Elizabeth's father and the rest of the family.

Eventually, Bruce's persistence paid off and Elizabeth relented. She started going out with him, and they were married in 1942, in a church built in 1896 by Elizabeth's father Norman Willans with logs from his own ranch." (Author's note. Norm was also married in the same church in 1979).

"The best man at Bruce and Elizabeth's wedding was his good friend Gerald (Gerry) H Cheetham who was able to join the RAF rather than the RCAF as both his parents were English. He had tried to convince Bruce to go with him overseas to fly bombers, but Bruce declined as he said he would be "going over" to fly fighters. Gerry Cheetham became a pilot flying Halifax bombers with 76 squadron. In a cruel twist of fate, all too common at the time, as Bruce commenced his initial bomber escort missions in his Spitfire with 411 Squadron in June 1943, at the same time on 25 June, one of Gerry's early missions was bombing industrial targets in the German city of Wuppertal. His Halifax was hit by flak and Gerry was killed. Along with Gerry, two others in the crew sadly lost their lives but four of the remaining survived.

"The newly married Bruce and Elizabeth spent many enjoyable hours riding together in the Foothill country west of Calgary. At the same time, he enjoyed his role as a flying instructor. Bruce had a reputation as a tough instructor, he demanded a level of performance he thought was necessary considering what he thought his pupils would potentially face in the times to come. His services as an instructor in Calgary were required for almost two years, as a result of which when he was posted overseas to a fighter squadron, he ran into several of his former students, many of whom now outranked him. Elizabeth said he told her that most of them thanked him for being an SOB (son of a bitch) as their instructor, as it had ultimately served them well (she didn't tell me what the other ones said, but as his son, I can well imagine!). My mother did tell me one story about the time they went out to a restaurant in Calgary on a busy weekend and that they had to wait up front a bit for a table. My dad was in mufti and one of his current students had eaten and was leaving. As he passed them, he held out his hand to shake and pressed a sugar cube into Bruce's hand. This was rather cheeky, and my dad took it in good humour, although I would like to know what the next instructional session was like!

"One of Bruce's students was an American who came to Canada because he wanted to fight fascism, but his government didn't at the time. After he got his wings, he was posted overseas to join a Canadian squadron but he transferred to an American one once they entered the war. He told my dad that normally he would have given his first set of (American) wings to his mother, but he gave them instead to Bruce because he said if he hadn't been his instructor, he'd be dead. I have those wings.

"In December 1942 Bruce left Calgary having been promoted twice in the March of that year initially to warrant officer and then to pilot officer. He was posted to England to No 7 (Pilot) Advanced Flying Unit (AFU) at RAF Peterborough. When he left, my mother told me one of the last things she said to him was, "Don't come home a hero, just come home."

Bruce began his training at No 7 AFU on 28 December 1942 flying the Miles Master Mark II serial number 973 and he finished the course on 26 February 1943. He then began a course at 57 Officer Training Unit at RAF Eshott, Northumberland on 05 March 1943 initially flying the Miles Master Mark I code L. On 09 March, Bruce climbed onto the wing of one of the most famous fighters in the world, a Spitfire Mark I identified with the 57 OTU training unit code "PW-G" and strapped himself in. It is not known what his initial thoughts and feelings were but the reaction of those pilots who came before and after is well documented. The power, speed, and handling were like no other aircraft they had ever flown. Upon completion of his training at 57 OTU on 23 April, the "Summary of Flying and Assessments" indicated that Bruce was "above the average" as a fighter pilot and in air gunnery. His first posting as a fighter pilot would be on 11 May 1943 to the Roaring Boys of 411 Squadron at RAF Redhill, Surrey.

Norm continues his father's story: "Unbeknownst to Bruce when he left Elizabeth in Calgary she was pregnant with their first child. Less than two months after Bruce was posted to 411 Squadron their daughter Anne was born on 26 June 1943 in the Holy Cross Hospital in Calgary. Anne was born profoundly disabled and not expected to last the day. She had spina bifida and associated hydrocephalus. With modern medicine and treatment, this would have been handled as a serious but also an eminently treatable condition in a neurological unit. In 1943, it was a death sentence. The hospital staff suggested Elizabeth go home and leave the baby with them to "deal with." Norm recalled his mother's reaction:

"They told mom that the baby would die soon regardless, Elizabeth told them: 'She's mine, and she's coming home with me.' And go home with her she did. Against all odds the baby, Anne Elizabeth Whiteford lived to the age of eight and was a source of joy to family and friends. I include this story in order that those who have worked so long and hard on the NH341 project know that this is just one way in which the woman whose name graces the cowling of this Spitfire is worthy of that honour in every respect.

"Bruce was understandably anxious about seeing his daughter before she died, but under the circumstances, he was not granted leave to go home to see her. After completing 125 combat missions Bruce went back to Canada to instruct rather than stay with his squadron in Europe. Unfortunately, the circumstances coloured Bruce's ensuing relationship with the RCAF and the government. At the war's end, he was told he was going to Staff College. Instead, he resigned his commission. Since his daughter had lived until he got home, he was going to make the most of the time she had left."

After arriving at RAF Redhill on 11 May 1943, Bruce quickly settled down to life with his new squadron and new country. The ORB announced his arrival at the same time as several other pilots including Charlie Trainor and Tommy Wheler. On 11 May Bruce was airborne for a sector reconnaissance with Art Tooley. His first operational flight took place in a Spitfire Vb with the 411 code, DB – C on 15 May, when he undertook a two-hour convoy patrol over the English Channel with one other pilot, F/O Johnny Howarth, which was recorded as uneventful. Bruce did write in his logbook that they had observed, "29 ships."

On 25 May at 10.15 am, Bruce took part in his first "big show" as the Roaring Boys lifted off in squadron strength for Circus 304, escorting six Mitchell bombers (instead of the twelve scheduled) to the aerodrome at Abbeville. They crossed the French coast at Pointe de St Quentin, which is north-west of Abbeville, at 15,000 feet. "A little heavy inaccurate flak" was detailed in the squadron ORB but Bruce and the squadron all returned safely. He had his first real taste of combat and that unnerving feeling of someone trying to take his life, an experience to which only service personnel in wartime can relate. Those seemingly innocuous black puffs of smoke which appeared all around Bruce's Spitfire were the exploding flak shells. The aerodrome defence batteries had got the range of the small formation. The ORB later recorded the fate of the beehive of 6 bombers: "One bomber was seen to dive towards cloud base, only two others were seen coming out and were escorted home. In his logbook, Bruce wrote: "2 Mitchells pranged. No E/A. 2 Spitfires pranged. One direct hit by A.A (anti-aircraft fire)."

During the month of May Bruce logged 2 hours 30 minutes of combat flying towards his tour completion target of around 200 hours. He had now spent a total of 59 hours and 55 minutes flying Spitfires, including during flight training.

Just because Bruce had qualified as a fighter pilot did not mean that his training and development journey had come to an end. On 9 June he and the squadron were sent to RAF Martlesham Heath for air to air gunnery, slow flying, and cine gun camera training, where the latest techniques were learned and practiced. This training, along with various formation flying exercises continued throughout June and all served to improve the skills and techniques required of a fighter pilot. Bruce's logbook charts the daily practice which intriguingly included between 17 and 20 June, aircraft carrier deck landings at the land-based practice strip at RAF Dunsfold.

On 17 June Bruce and the squadron took off in the early afternoon on a Rodeo mission over Belgian territory, specifically the Nieuwport area. They flew in at around 10,500 feet and orbited between Nieuwport and Ostend. Although no enemy fighters were sighted, the squadron was subject to medium intense flak which was reported as being in four-gun salvoes, all in all, an uncomfortable experience and one Bruce and his kite got through unscathed. He reported the mission in his logbook and as so many pilots seemed to do he treated the flak and danger as it were inconsequential, "Nothing doing. Very accurate flak."

It is important not to underestimate the deadly risks the Roaring Boys faced in flying through this flak. There were sometimes referred to as "milk runs," but were anything of the sort. The green tracer rounds, arcing their way skywards in a seemingly lazy convoy, but a with deadly intent. Mixed in with this menace were the artillery shells, which incorporated a time delay fuse so that they could explode at set altitudes. The puffs of the explosions sent forth deadly shards of shrapnel which could easily slice through the thin fuselage of a Spitfire. The Germans legendary 88 mm artillery piece, known as a tank destroyer, was also employed as a flak weapon and had an effective range of up to 25,000 feet. In the 1980's I recall meeting an acquaintance of my grandfather, Battle of Britain Spitfire pilot Jimmy Corbin DFC, who like me was born and bred in the Maidstone area. In the winter of 1940, Jimmy was flying his Spitfire from Biggin Hill on a patrol with 66 squadron and on the return leg as he passed over Calais to return to England, he experienced a "terrific jolt" which lifted him up in his seat. Jimmy knew immediately from the smell of cordite drifting around his cockpit that he had been hit by a flak shell. As he wrestled with the controls he wondered how he could have been hit when, "I was 5 miles up in the air." Jimmy had had a lucky escape and managed to nurse his damaged Spitfire back to Biggin Hill where upon landing he and his ground crew inspected a large gaping hole in his fuselage.

During this period, the other Spitfire Elizabeth pilots serving with Bruce were Tommy, Len, and Charlie which explains why they are often seen together in photos. On 23 June Bruce was sitting in his cockpit ready for takeoff at 17.00 pm for a Ramrod escort of 12 Boston bombers. As they lifted off Bruce performed his 'top of the climb' checks on Spitfire

BL897, studying the aircraft's temperature and pressure gauges were normal and that he was ready in case they suddenly got into action with the enemy. The Bostons were picked up near the Kent coast and as Bruce later wrote this was a, "fairly deep penetration" to Albert, northern France where although not stated, the likely target was the railway marshalling yards. All seemed to be going well until Bruce experienced his first close encounter with enemy fighters in the shape of 12 FW 190s which attacked 411 and 401 squadrons. He watched on as P/O Matheson and F/S MacDougall managed to fire on the 190s as did 401 squadron but no hits or damage were reported. Bruce commented later: "Four or five FW 190s had a go but bogged off right away." His first taste of air combat, that feeling of fear and tension that would forever be seared into his memory. With the FW 190s chased away the 12 Bostons started their bombing run. The ORB noted: "No bombing results over the target Albert were observed." At 18.40 pm Bruce guided BL897 into the circuit at Redhill and into land. It felt good to see the enemy at close quarters and to know how he would react in the situation. The fear wouldn't go away, like the more experienced pilots had told him, but the training took over and that had paid off. He was confident in his ability and in his aircraft. During June Bruce increased his operational flying in Spitfires to 7 hours and 30 minutes.

The Focke Wulf 190 or "butcher bird" that Bruce saw on the 23 June mission was a fearsome fighter, fast and manoeuverable, it was more than a match for the Spitfire Mark Vb. The arms race gathered pace as designers tried to develop faster, better armed and more agile fighters. In late 1941 when the FW 190 appeared, Spitfire pilots used to outrun Me 109s but were struggling to shake off the butcher bird. The legendary J E "Johnnie Johnson stated that, "it completely outclassed our Spitfire Vs." With the appearance of the more powerful Spitfire Mark IX, Johnnie was eager to engage the 190 again and judge, what he confidently thought would be a different outcome. Through the summer of 1943, he described how the dive bombing Typhoons, the Bomphoons would flush the 190s into the air where 126 and 127 Wings, amongst others, would be waiting to pounce. As Johnson said: "we were ready and waiting and smacked them down with our superior IXs." During the month of June Bruce flew 4 hours and 30 minutes on combat operations for a tour total of 7 hours and 20 minutes.

Amongst all the combat flying, Bruce did manage to find time for some entertainment when on the evening of 23 July, he piloted an Oxford aircraft with Squadron Leader Charlie Semple and P/O Russ Orr from RAF Redhill to RAF Digby for a party at the airfield. The ORB suggested that all three had thoroughly enjoyed themselves! With the party well and truly over it was back to the business of combat flying on 25 July as 411 and 412 squadrons undertook a Rodeo operation to Saint-Omer. Despite the thick cloud as the wing passed over Dunkirk, they were greeted by heavy, accurate flak. With little visibility in the air and to the ground the sweep returned to England without further incident. On 27 July, Bruce and Charlie's next Rodeo was to Poix with its nearby Luftwaffe aerodrome, the visibility was unlimited. The Spitfires tore across the Sussex countryside with the Rolls Royce Merlins of their Spitfire Vbs going full chat, reaching Beachy Head flying in the weeds at zero feet before crossing the French coast at Ault. Bruce pushed his Mark Vb Spitfire BL727 to climb power and she responded eagerly taking him quickly to 10,000 feet where the formation levelled out. Over the R/T S/L Semple announced enemy fighters had been spotted and were orbiting the Somme estuary. As one the Roaring Boys gave their Spitfires full throttle. The chase was on and Bruce asked his aircraft for everything she had but they were unable to catch the enemy and engage them in combat. The ORB gave an assessment of the mission. "No flak was encountered. Visibility was unlimited. No shipping was seen and all our aircraft returned safely." During July Bruce steadily built his combat flying times, logging 4 hours and 50 minutes for a grand tour total of 12 hours 10 minutes.

Bruce's Ramrod missions continued at regular intervals along with practice attacks, the bouncing exercises, and local formation flying. The operation on 2 August to escort 21 Marauder bombers was led by Wing Commander B D Russel DFC with 411, 401 and 412 squadrons taking part. The formation picked up the 21 Martin B-26 Marauders over North Foreland at 12,000 feet. Bruce was concentrating on his instruments at the maximum level as they pushed through the dense 10/10 cloud. With the bombers in tow in the bright sunshine Bruce's Spitfire was gently buffeted by the wind, but with his controls trimmed he barely needed to touch the stick, his aircraft rode the wind and slipped along towards the French coast which was crossed at Mardyk. The target for the raid was the aerodrome at Saint-Omer. Bruce expected heavy defence from 88 mm artillery and other heavy weapons. He hunkered down, weaving along with the others as the barrage began. The flak was uncomfortable and described as, "heavy and accurate." The ORB scored the bombing results as "fair." As they turned for the coast Bruce knew the Germans would have a parting gift of more flak waiting, which duly arrived as they exited near Hardelot. He was sweating now and willing his Spitfire to claw its way out over the sea where the flak couldn't reach them. As Bruce looked down he saw two medium tonnage merchant vessels in Boulogne harbour. He could breathe a little easier as the flak petered out and as he turned his head around to look back only thin trails of smoke remained from the barrage. Fortunately, all the aircraft were unscathed as Bruce made his descent across the Kent countryside towards Redhill. As he felt the welcome bump of his wheels touching down on the runway he did not know it would be his and 411's last operation from RAF Redhill. Bruce taxied in and checked his watch, 09.45 am. After shutting down his Spitfire Bruce quickly hopped down and made his way smartly to the debrief. He wiped his brow as he replayed the mission in his mind. A hot and heavy reception from the aerodrome flak batteries had certainly got his attention. He noted in his logbook. "Bags of flak. No E/A."

With the move to RAF Staplehurst, Kent on 6 August, operations were put on hold until 126 Airfield, including 411 Squadron was fully settled in. On occasions, operations were mounted from other bases and on 15 August W/C Russel led the 3 squadrons to RAF Predannack, near Mullion, Cornwall which today is a satellite aerodrome for the nearby Royal Naval Air station at Culdrose. Bruce was able to fly over the whole of southern England on his way to the far southwest. The mission required a long flight of approximately 100 miles across the English Channel to France. There's was to be a Rodeo operation, in support of a Ramrod mission to Guipavas airfield, which is close to Brest in the northwest tip of France. All the pilots were anxious about the distance over the sea, and their fate should they have to ditch. At least they had their Spitfire's speed to minimise the time over water and they weren't slowed by a having a to escort a beehive of bombers. The Luftwaffe launched several attacks with FW 190s against the Roaring Boys to no effect and in that sense, the operation was a success as it allowed the bombers to do their job. A German Navy destroyer was also spotted entering the harbour. Bruce later wrote: "Forward support to 8 Whirrli bombers on Brest aerodrome. Bounced once. 3 Typhs missing." The aircraft were "Whirrli" bombers, the Westland Whirlwinds from 263 squadron and Typhoons from 266 squadron. During the mission, 3 Typhoons, including the squadron CO S/L A S McIntyre, were shot down by FW 190s from 8/JG 2 and 1/128 west of Brest. Bruce returned to Predannack at 17.00 pm for fuel and refreshments before the flight back to Staplehurst.

On 26 August, Bruce and Bob Hyndman's evening mission was a Ramrod to Caen, a city which will feature heavily later in this story. The wing first made a transit flight from Staplehurst to RAF Tangmere where the mission would commence. The plan was to join up with 36 Marauders at 12,000 feet over Selsey Bill, before crossing the French coast north of Cabourg. Over the target, which was bombed accurately according to the ORB, flak streamed up and one of the Marauders was hit in the starboard engine and returned to Shoreham accompanied by a group of Spitfires from 401 squadron. The Luftwaffe was spotted in the area but did not mount any attacks on the formation which returned after 1 hour and 40 minutes. During the month of August Bruce built up a further 8 hours and 15 minutes of operational flying time for a tour total on Spitfires of 20 hours and 25 minutes.

To continue the general disruption to the German military machine and operations, bombing raids were regularly undertaken to infrastructure targets such as rail marshalling yards. The effect of delaying travel and making it generally longer and more difficult for men and equipment to move was part of the strategy of slow strangulation. The Allies knew they had to employ this approach to give the planned landings in 1944 every possible chance of success.

The squadron, including Bruce and Tommy, were involved in such an operation with Ramrod S.29 which was launched on 4 September to the rail marshalling yards at Amiens. To give an idea of the scale of this Ramrod, there were 29 Spitfire squadrons involved, escorting bombers including, Mitchells, Venturas, and Bostons to a range of targets. The Roaring Boys rendezvous with 24 Boston bombers was executed over Hastings, East Sussex at zero feet. Bruce's love of speed and all the sensations that went with it found full expression as his Spitfire hurtled across Kent at zero feet, lifting occasionally for higher ground and obstacles in sync with the formation of Spitfires strung out around him. He'd occasionally catch sight of farm workers leaping onto their tractors to wave as the thunderous noise of the formation flashed past them. As the cliffs of Sussex disappeared they flew out across the sea, wave hopping. Bruce found comfort in the pulsing roar of the Merlin engine. In Canada, Elizabeth and baby Anne were physically a long way from Bruce as he sat in the confines of his fighter's cockpit, putting his life on the line. However, they were always in his thoughts as were his wife's words: "don't come home a hero, just come home." The French coast was soon in view and they crossed it at Le Crotoy, which is around 12 miles north-west of Abbeville, climbing to 12,000 feet to bomb the target area. The welcome committee of flak attempted to knock down the attackers. It was documented as being at medium intensity over the target area and on the French coast, both emplacements of gunners being helped by the clear visibility. Tommy later gave his impression of the raid: "Light flak. Good bombing. Escort cover behind had a go with a few huns." The mission was a success and they crossed back across the French coast at Ault, Bruce drinking in the view which was unlimited at 10,000 feet. In short order, the Bostons changed course for their bases and Bruce and Tommy throttled back before touching down at RAF Staplehurst at 09.55 am. As Bruce ran through his shut down procedure he noticed the black-gloved hand of a pilot resting on his wing. It was his friend Tommy Wheler, standing with a big grin. He invited Bruce out for a drive, an offer which Bruce accepted whilst wondering how, despite the rationing, Tommy always seemed to have petrol!

The Ramrod S.38 on 7 September to the rail marshalling yards at Lille involved Bruce, Charlie and the Roaring Boys joining up with 72 Marauders from the USAAF VIII Air Support Command and two other Spitfire fighter wings, that took off from RAF West Malling, Kent. The formation met over Hastings, East Sussex before crossing the channel and the French coast at Le Touquet. Bruce put pen to paper later, writing that 411 Squadron led by F/L McFarlane, "picked up the wrong bombers." Despite the error, the mission continued and they crossed the French coast at Le Touquet before flying on to the rail marshalling yards at St Pol. The ORB provided details of the operation: "No flak was experienced during the entire operation and no enemy aircraft were seen. The formation turned left over the target and returned to base, crossing the French coast at Berck-sur-Mer and touching down at 09.30 hours. No shipping was seen."

The scale and complexity of these Ramrods are fascinating, with diversionary attacks, separate fighter sweeps and feints all designed to keep the German's defensive network off balance and second-guessing the location of the intended targets. The enemy was forced to split their forces and were unable to coordinate their resources to inflict a heavy blow on the attackers.

The Roaring Boys and the 72 Marauders they were escorting were only one element of the 7 September mission. At the same time as the raid on St Pol, the Eighth Air Force sent 114 Flying Fortresses to bomb Evere aerodrome near Brussels, which in the following year 126 Wing would make their base. The airfield at Bergan/Alkmaar in The Netherlands was visited by 29 Mitchells, whilst 147 Fortresses were sent to bomb the V weapon site at Watton, France. In addition, bomb-carrying Hawker Typhoons, the bombphoons were attacking Abbeville aerodrome.

The target for Ramrod 228, part of four Ramrods, on 18 September was the marshalling yards at Rouen. Bruce, Bob, and the Roaring Boys were led off at 09.20 am by F/L Doug Matheson and they linked up with the 18 Mitchell bombers from the USAAF over Hastings, at 12,000 feet, before crossing the French coast at Étretat. The mission planners varied the coastal entry and exit points for these missions to keep German defences off guard. The run into the target saw the formation fly close to some fairly intense flak and around 10 enemy aircraft were spotted above the formation but not engaged in combat. The broken cloud helped the flak gunners to find their range but luckily all aircraft on the raid returned safely to England, landing back at Staplehurst at 10.45 am.

Things didn't always go to plan and the weather played its part in Bruce's mission of 22 September, Ramrod 237. The squadron planned to join up with 72 Marauders whose target was the Beauvais Tillé aerodrome which at the time was the base of the Luftwaffe wing II/JG 26. With terrible weather over the channel, the formation was forced to abort the mission and return to England. Bruce limited his comments in his log to "10/10 cloud." He was back in action the next day, 23 September when he attended a briefing in the open-sided tent at 07.00 am. The pilots rushed around looking to seize the last of the available seating as the losers glumly slumped cross-legged on the ground or stood at the back. Their hands were swiftly removed from their trouser pockets as W/C Russel walked purposefully to the front with the intelligence team to begin his detailed briefing of the plan. It was to be an attack by 12 Mitchell bombers as part of Ramrod 239 and the intended target was the power station at Grand Quevilly, Rouen. With the briefing completed Russel called for watches to be synchronised after which they all headed off, in a low hum of conversation to collect their flying gear and to answer any last minute nervous calls of nature. At 07.20 am Bruce had Spitfire AD 557 turning over and warming up ready for the off which took place at 07.35 am. He climbed out and away from the base, and Staplehurst quickly grew smaller beneath him. With the wing formed up and ready over the airfield, they headed due south for the rendezvous over Hastings before crossing the channel and making landfall just west of Dieppe. As they closed in on Rouen the flak began to appear, slowly at first but with increasing intensity. Bruce was getting used to it, but the fear was still there and they knew there was little they could do other than repeatedly adjust their course by small degrees and keep weaving their aircraft. This need was brought sharply home to Bruce as one shell exploded uncomfortably close by. Fortunately, the flak was mostly inaccurate and soon, as Bruce watched on, the Mitchells dropped their bombs. He thought the results looked marginal from his lofty position but the ORB provided a less than complementary roundup saying, "bombing results were poor." The formation then made a dash for the coast, recrossing just west of Saint-Valery-en-Caux. Bruce had completed another mission and was relieved that the anti-aircraft fire was over and the remaining flight to Staplehurst could continue without interference from the enemy.

As the missions came thick and fast Bruce took the well-travelled path of a fighter pilot, building his experience, swopping notes, and tips with his fellow Roaring Boys. He put his nonoperational flying time to good use with mock air combat 'tail chase' exercises, all designed to sharpen the flying skills that might one day save his life. On 23 September, he also undertook some air firing practice locally at RAF Detling, near Maidstone, Kent.

Ramrod 242 at 10.20 am on 24 September was another aerodrome raid to Amiens with Spitfires accompanying 12 Mitchells. The Roaring Boys and 401 and 412 squadrons joined up with them over Rye, East Sussex. Crossing the channel, they climbed to 10,000 feet before making landfall in France near Cayeux. The incoming flak was accurate and heavy, and one bomber had its engine knocked out. It was escorted back to England by 412 squadron but the Luftwaffe wolves scented a wounded prey and 4 FW 190s launched an unsuccessful attack. Bruce later commented: "fighter opposition to 412 bringing out a lame duck. A little heavy flak." The mission achieved moderate success as one stick of bombs was seen to be on target and landed directly on the aerodrome itself. The formation of bombers then split in two with one box being accompanied by 411 whilst 401 took the other box back across the channel to England. The surreal existence of a fighter pilot once again played out as having landed at 11.50 am, surviving the flak barrage and an attack by the Luftwaffe, Bruce, and the others enjoyed a quiet lunch before saddling up their trusty steeds and heading off into the danger zone in the afternoon.

Bruce's mission of 26 September to escort 18 Mitchells to bomb the marshalling yards at Rouen, Ramrod 247, was once again rain interrupted. As a result, the leader of the beehive of bombers decided to turn back. It was also a notable mission as S/L Ian Ormston had taken over command of 411 Squadron from S/L Semple only that day. And, on his first mission, his Spitfire had an engine failure and he was forced to descend by parachute into the freezing English Channel some five miles off the French coast. With all the inherent dangers of being a fighter pilot, he must have had a deep sense of foreboding as the sea rushed up to meet him, the thought that he might drown, or not be rescued and freeze to death. His misfortune did qualify him for membership of both the Goldfish and Caterpillar clubs, although it is reasonable to conclude that this was the last thing on his mind at the time! The Caterpillar Club is an unofficial club started in 1922 by Leslie Irvin of Irvin Airchute of Canada who were parachute manufacturers. Membership is given to anyone whose life had been saved by a parachute upon leaving a disabled aircraft. The name originates from the silk caterpillar and the threads used from them to make the first silk parachutes.

Fortunately, the air-sea rescue boys in their Supermarine Walrus did their job and Ormston was picked up safely. If he thought his troubles were over then he was somewhat premature in that assumption. The Walrus developed a problem, couldn't takeoff due to the high seas and was forced to tow Ormston in his survival dinghy for 2 ½ hours back to England whereupon they ended up in a minefield! Having been transferred to a rescue boat he was given a warming cup of soup which he promptly threw up over the deck, much to the skipper's displeasure. His spirits were lifted somewhat when he was met in Dover harbour by a very pleasant naval WREN who happened to be the daughter of English novelist JP Priestly. Ormston made it back to Staplehurst the next day with quite a tale to tell.

The RAF's 276 Squadron specialised in air-sea rescue, and as well as the Walrus, a single-engine float plane, they operated Ansons and several Spitfires. In the Channel, the Walrus was used in conjunction with a Spitfire. Both aircraft would be vectored onto the downed airmen and the Spitfire with its greater speed would arrive first. It carried underneath the fuselage a chute containing a dinghy and a cylinder with food and rescue equipment joined by 75 yards of rope. After dropping flares to check the wind direction the Spitfire would be slowed to 100 mph, and with its flaps down the two packages would be catapulted out from underneath the aircraft, straddling the pilot. Smoke bombs were also dropped to mark the pilot's position as he awaited pick up by the Walrus.

Bruce and the Roaring Boys next mission on 27 September, Ramrod 250 involved targeting the marshalling yards at Rouen. Bruce climbed into Spitfire AB209 and completed his pre-flight checks. He looked down at his watch, which showed 09.00 am. They were scheduled to take off at 09.20 am and the good news for Bruce was that F/L Doug Matheson would lead them to the rendezvous at zero feet. Down in the weeds and hedge hopping was always a thrill in a Spitfire, especially for someone like Bruce who adored speed. As he took off Bruce was expectant as the Luftwaffe was frequently making its presence felt during these raids, although he felt increasingly confident of his ability to come out as the winner in a dog fight. The pilots were told to maintain a healthy respect for the enemy but cockiness went with the territory of being a fighter pilots. For now, as he launched his Spitfire along the runway such thoughts must be put to the back of his mind. The 10-minute flight was thrilling, a gaggle of Spitfires on the wing, slicing through the air as the small villages and towns passed by. The orchards and fields of Kent with livestock grazing and seemingly unconcerned by the passing of these large noisy birds. Ironic that they should be on their way into battle and would pass close by the market town of Battle, East Sussex where in 1066 at the Battle of Hastings the Norman invaders had beaten the Anglo Saxons and King Harold was famously slain. In 1940, the German invaders might have been thwarted, but the threat remained and these Canucks were standing firm with Britain. Centuries later after 1066 these were the modern warriors, still taking part in a man on man, blood and guts battle.

At Hastings, the 18 Mitchell bombers arrived as scheduled and the formation climbed up high above the channel until they levelled out at 10,000 feet. On this occasion, the bombers were spot on and the yards below received many direct hits. Bruce was impressed, and it made the mission and risks worthwhile when the bomber boys got it right. His R/T came alive as Doug Matheson alerted the Roaring Boys to the presence of fighters stationed above them. Bruce looked across and up and saw everyone's heads turn in unison and look at the formation of tiny black dots above them. Fighters from I and III/JG 26 were sitting high above the beehive. The anxiety levels increased as each man prepared himself and his aircraft for combat. As happened from time to time the Luftwaffe sat on their lofty perch and did not intervene.

Spitfire AB209 growled as Bruce opened the throttle for the channel dash. He and the others wished they could peel away to take on those Huns. Leaving the bombers unguarded wasn't their job and if the enemy fighters were FW 190s they might just bite off more than they could chew, outclassed as the Spitfire Mark Vb was by the butcher bird.

In the dazzling blue sky and unlimited visibility, the formation made its way back across the sea to base. Bruce let the flaps down and watched as AB209's speed bled away. Having flown downwind from the runway in the opposite direction to landing, Bruce turned his Spitfire onto the base leg and then with a curved approach turned finals to land. He took his last glimpse at the grass landing strip at Staplehurst, confident he would land smack in the middle. After taxiing in and shutting down he checked his watch. It showed 10.35 am. It was time to report in and on this beautiful day escape by taking his motorcycle on a race around some of the long straight roads and lanes. Before Bruce could set off he needed to total his monthly operational hours which for September was 16 hours 35 minutes for a tour total of 37 hours. He had now spent 126 hours flying Spitfires.

Bruce with the Roaring Boys mascot 'Joskins'

The mix of foggy weather and the move to Biggin Hill limited Bruce's flying in October to the usual bouncing drills, cine gun camera and tail chases. On 5 November Bruce, this time flying with Tommy resumed operations with the squadron as they took off at 12.50 pm to escort a beehive of 36 bombers. It was one of 6 bomber formations on a mission to the underground military Fortress of Mimoyeques, located around 8 miles southwest of Calais. This was one of the so-called "heavy crossbow" targets of Operation Crossbow and this marked the first day of that operation. The Germans were trying to develop their long-range V3 cannons, the *Vergeltungswaffe* (Vengeance weapon) with a maximum range of 165 km which were intended to launch explosive projectiles, each weighing 140 kg on London.

As they crossed the French coast a few miles north of Boulogne, the Fortress of Mimoyeques was a short flight inland. With the target in sight, the flak barrage commence. It was heavy and uncomfortably close to the formation. Bruce thought to himself, whatever this site is for the Germans seem rather keen to defend it. Just then one of the bombers took a hit and immediately dropped out of the formation. Tommy wrote about it later: "One big boy shot down by flak their lads bailed out OK." The squadron ORB recorded excellent bombing results and the mission was deemed a success. In his Spitfire, Bruce was alerted to Tommy's voice over the R/T. His friend had engine trouble. Bruce watched on as Tommy and another Spitfire peeled away. Tommy later said: "My engine started to act up over the French coast so I returned with P/O Cam McDougall Y4." After a nervy flight over the sea, Tommy successfully landed back at Biggin Hill at 13.45 pm, around half an hour ahead of the rest of the squadron.

The so-called No Ball vengeance weapon sites would feature heavily in the mission list for the Roaring Boys going forward. On 11 November, Bruce, Tommy, Len, and the Roaring Boys were providing escort to 2nd TAF Typhoons and 157 Marauders of the Ninth Air Force for Ramrod 311 which would be bombing the underground bunkers at Martinvast near Cherbourg. The site, which was originally a French naval oil storage facility, was a construction site for a planned V2 rocket launch facility. In 1944 it would be converted to fire V1 doodle bugs. It is interesting to note that Tommy only refers to it as "a construction site," in his logbook so it's clear that the pilots weren't fully aware at this stage of the threat posed by the V1. British intelligence itself was still trying to assess the potential threat. Ramrod 311 was a two-stage mission with the initial part being a short flight to RAF Ford, near Littlehampton Sussex where Bruce and the others refuelled before setting off for France at 12.00 pm for a mission that would last 1 hour 45 minutes. Tommy wrote up more details of the mission: "Escort to 36 Marauders bombing construction site works at Cherbourg. No huns about, quite a bit of flak. P/O McDougall Y3. B2 F/S St Denis hit by flak. No harm done. Cheers."

On 23 November Bruce, Bob, and Len took part in a squadron Rodeo mission over France which was briefed to the pilots by S/L Ian Ormston but led by F/L Doug Matheson. The Roaring Boys were all aware that earlier on that day Stan Kent's aircraft had suffered an engine failure and he was killed when his Spitfire crashed into the sea. There was a solemn atmosphere at the mission briefing but everyone knew Stan Kent would have expected them to press on. Those were the rules of the daily high stakes game they played with their lives. At 14.40 pm they launched forth and crossed the channel making landfall at Calais and sweeping in over the surrounding area. No enemy aircraft were encountered, and all the squadron returned safely to Biggin Hill, landing back at 16.05 pm. The next day Bruce noted that they undertook tests switching from the auxiliary to main fuel tanks as this was proven to be the cause of Stan Kent's engine failure.

As mentioned elsewhere despite being fighter pilots, the Roaring Boys were always up for some mischief-making and during the time at Biggin Hill Bruce found himself on the receiving end of this. Norm gave me the details:

"Dad had two "injuries" whilst serving with 411 that I'm aware of. One was while returning from the pub during the blackout on one of his motorcycles. He went into a corner a bit "hot" and injured his ankle in the subsequent off-road excursion. No flying time lost in the accident apparently. The other incident was the result of a "prank" (oh, those fly boys!). When in barracks, as an officer dad had his own room (and a batman of sorts, apparently). He told me that his preferred method of entry to his room was to pass through the doorway at speed and launch himself towards the target, his bed, perform a half-roll while airborne and land on his back on his bed. Some of his squadron mates, viewing this as a grand opportunity for some mirth-making, put the percussion end of a rimfire cartridge between 2 of the spring coils. When dad returned from a sortie and executed his Standard Approach and Landing, the cartridge detonated as planned. The unplanned result was that the bullet tore through the mattress and hit him in his left index finger! No bone was broken, but I remember seeing the scar which was referenced on his RCAF identity card in the 1950s. He thought the whole deal was pretty funny apparently."

On 30 November Bruce, Bob, and the Roaring Boys provided escort duties to Ramrod 341. Their outward journey saw them pass Bradwell Bay, crossing the Dutch coast at Walcheren Island which is located at the mouth of the Scheldt estuary. Their task was to provide withdrawal cover for B17 Flying Fortresses returning from bombing industrial areas in Solingen, Germany and escort them back to England. The journey across the North Sea was completed without interference from the Luftwaffe and flak defences and they landed back at Biggin on the bump 14.15 pm after flying for 2 hours. Bruce totalled up his flying time and entered it in his logbook. During the month of November, he had completed 8 hours and 40 minutes of operational flying and overall had completed 45 hours and 40 minutes since joining 411 Squadron.

On 1 December Bruce and the Roaring Boys assembled for a briefing at around 11.30 am with the news already swirling around Biggin Hill that F/L Doug Matheson and P/O J A St Denis had been shot down in the morning mission. It sharpened everyone's focus on the mission to come. W/C Buck McNair led the briefing and gave details of Ramrod 344 in which they would join up with Flying Fortresses over Knokke, Belgium. The 'heavies' would be given escort cover back to England after their raid on the industrial areas of Solingen, and Leverkusen in Germany. After lifting off from Biggin Hill at 12.20 pm the 'heavies' were picked up as planned, and for Bruce and the others, it turned into routine operation with no flak or sign of the enemy.

Throughout the majority of December, Bruce wasn't flying on operations and it is tempting to wonder if the practical joke with his exploding bed and resulting hand injury had necessitated an enforced break. Certainly, the weather wasn't good for flying either. Following the Christmas period, Bruce tested an auxiliary fuel tank drop on 30 December, a vital action requirement should they be required to enter a dog fight. On the last day of 1943, Bruce, Gibby Gibson, and Bob were rostered to fly together on a wing strength fighter sweep with 401 and 412 squadrons as part of Ramrod 403. The mission was to cover the airfields around Brussels whilst bombers were attacking No Ball targets. Should the Luftwaffe decide to scramble and try to attack the bombers then the

Spitfires were waiting as the reception committee. After taking off and forming up the 3 squadrons headed across the sea and making landfall flew a direct course for Brussels. With nothing seen, they promptly turned 180 degrees and flew back again. The 411 ORB noted: "Nearing the coast 401 squadron flying at 10,000 feet experienced some light flak and climbed to 14,000 feet. The wing landed back at Biggin after an uneventful trip." They had been in the air for 2 hours and were glad to warm up after the freezing conditions of their Spitfire cockpits.

In 1944 Bruce started the year with a mission which took place on 3 January. It was a Ranger and he was flying with Charlie Trainor and three other Spitfire pilots. The Ranger was a free-lance incursion into enemy territory in which the Roaring Boys sought out targets of opportunity. The four Spitfires crossed the channel "on the deck" with Bruce noting, "cloud base at 1,000 feet." They emerged at Knokke, Belgium where they climbed to 9,000 feet in the cloud, remaining there for 35 minutes. With no break in the cloud, the four pilots returned to Biggin Hill. Flying on instruments in the cloud is no easy task as I found out the first time I attempted it. It requires concentration and aside from the obvious hazards of flying blind in formation you must factor in that this was being carried out with 1940s technology. Bruce wrote that they, "let down coming out" and after losing altitude they crossed the channel at zero feet once again, landing after 2 hours airborne.

On 6 January Bruce was joined by Bob, Charlie, and Gibby for Ramrod 428. The patrol involved escorting four waves of 2 Group Mitchell and Mosquito bombers of the 2nd TAF, to raid No Ball targets in the Rouen area. Bruce was patrolling at 20,000 feet in yellow section flying as yellow 3, and they were led by A Flight Commander, Russ Orr. Without warning 4 FW 190s jumped yellow section. Bruce could see the butcher birds screaming down towards them and instantly Russ Orr called out, "Yellow break port." The 190s were only around 600 yards away before they flick rolled and dived for the deck whereupon yellow section set off in pursuit of their targets. Russ Orr managed to close to 150 yards and opened fire, his cannon shells ripped into one of the attackers who smoked, lost height before crashing into the deck. Meanwhile, Bruce was finally bringing all his training and practice to bear as with adrenalin coursing through his veins he pursued one of the other FW 190s, ragging his Spitfire JK795 for every ounce of power she could give him. He wanted to shoot down that German and get his first kill. Meanwhile, F/L H Russel, Yellow 4 pursued two other 190s. Bruce later wrote, "I couldn't close. Fired from 900 yards" instantly feeling the enormous vibrations within his Spitfire as the 20 mm Hispano cannons belched smoke and shells. His 50 cal machine gun bullets also poured out from his wings, the tracer rounds streaking out towards the enemy fighter. With a muzzle velocity of around 2,700 feet per second, the 20 mm shells reached the FW 190 in less than a second. Watching a live firing Hispano cannon the noise, power and recoil are enormous. Reports at the time indicated that if one cannon jammed the action of the other one firing was enough to cause the Spitfire to yaw.

Bruce was not able to witness any strikes on his opponent, but there was a sense of satisfaction at locking horns with the enemy, especially after the loss of Matheson and St Denis. At least Russ Orr had got one kill and Bruce had hopefully sent his quarry back with something to think about along, with some damage to his aircraft. He finished his entry for the mission with, "F/O Hamilton 401 destroyed one." As they turned for home Bruce could feel the residue sweat gently trickle down his face. The heat of battle had subsided and his cockpit felt markedly colder as the adrenalin seeped away. He told himself to stay alert and keep focused. There would be plenty of time to talk it over at the debrief and later more informally in the local pub with his comrades. Bruce and the others lost altitude and dropped into the circuit at Biggin, looking down at the patchwork of fields, bordered by their dark green hedges. He was soon turning finals to land and dropping down into the wide expanse of the airfield he was conscious of the rest of yellow section beside him. It was great to know that the armourers would have a job to do refilling his guns. They'd be watching and see the fabric covers covering his gun ports were gone, a clear sign of combat. A good few seconds of ammunition had been sent the enemy's way. Russ Orr's kill made for a lively debrief with Orr and F/O Hamilton roundly congratulated as the heroes of the day, the eager intelligence team waiting to wring every last detail out of them.

The strategy to attack the ever-multiplying V1 launch sites started to gather serious momentum around this time. On 21 January Ramrod 467 took off at 11.45 am with Bruce, Tommy, Len, and Bob involved in escorting 54 Marauders which were aiming to destroy No Ball targets in the Saint-Omer area. W/C G C Keefer lead all 3 squadrons in 126 Airfield.

Whilst 403 and 421 squadrons came under attack from 15 FW 190s of which they destroyed two and damaged another, the Roaring Boys saw no action from the air despite control providing a few vectors to intercept the enemy. The ORB recorded that they, "turfed around" for forty minutes and later reported very heavy and accurate flak in the target area with the result that the bombing by 54 Marauders was off target with poor results reported. In his cockpit, Bruce was shaking his head slowly from side to side listening to the chatter over the R/T as they were vectored onto potential bogeys. He vented his frustrations later: "Bags of false reporting. Too much flap by new types." This would have made for an interesting debrief session after they landed at 13.20 pm. Tommy's frustration was also thinly disguised, "Lots of turfing around. No E/A engaged."

For the Ramrod 494 on 29 January, Bruce was to fly with Tommy, Charlie, and Gibby for an 11.30 am squadron strength mission. They would be providing withdrawal cover for 675 Flying Fortresses and 124 Liberators of the Eighth Air Force returning from a bombing raid to Frankfurt. Two days earlier the Eighth Air Force and RAF had commenced their intensified bombing campaign against Germany. The squadron ORB summarised events: "The whole trip was done in 10/10 cloud and the W/Co did a very good job of leading the wing. No E/A or flak was encountered. The bombers were escorted out properly and apart from a few jet tanks cutting everything went ok." Bruce was flying Red 3 and wrote: "Climbed up through 3,000 feet of cloud to R/V with Liberators at Tirlemont." Today Tirlemont is called Tienen and is approximately 25 miles east of Brussels, Belgium. Tommy also eluded to the jet tank problems, "Bags of jet tank trouble, panic!" It was later found that grit stuck to the bottom of the Spitfire's fuselage was getting into the mechanism used to jettison the tank. In the month of January Bruce continued to accumulate his flying hours clocking up 14 hours and 5 minutes on operations. His total was now 63 hours and 25 minutes.

As a thick mist enveloped Biggin Hill on 9 February at around 8.30 am the roar of 36 Merlin engines shattered the calm and stillness. In a steady procession Bruce, Charlie, Ross, Len, Bob, and 7 other 411 pilots joined the other 2 squadrons of 126 Airfield as they took off for Ramrod 534 in which they would meet up with 72 Marauders of the USAAF's Ninth Air Force at 12,000 feet over Dungeness. The intended target was the rail marshalling yards at Tergnier, which even today are still important to the

French rail network, and which are located around 40 miles south-east of Paris. As Bruce and the Roaring Boys took up their positions, they were lined up in sections of 4, nearly line abreast on both flanks of the bomber formation. There were 4 sections each side and one flight of 4 aircraft just weaving around a few hundred feet above the big boys, ready to take any sections place which wished to dive down and attack the enemy. It was situation normal for Bruce but after 30 minutes flying the engine on Spitfire MH498 suddenly developed a different tone and cut at 2,000 feet. Bruce immediately checked everything including his supply of fuel, and magnetos trying to identify the problem. He was at 500 feet, too low to bail out as he prepared to crash land. The incident obviously stuck in Bruce's mind as Norm recalled: "Mom told me that when he related the event to her that it seemed likely it was a lot lower than 500 feet at the engine restart. Mom said she asked him why he didn't bail out. Apparently, Dad told her there was 'No goddam way' he was going to jump out of a perfectly good aircraft!" When his engine sparked into life, a much-relieved Bruce regained altitude, making his way to RAF Hawkinge, Kent where he could get his aircraft checked over before making a return flight to Biggin Hill.

Meanwhile, the Marauders proceeded to undertake a large amount of weaving which must have been disconcerting as there was the risk of collisions if concentration wasn't maintained. As they closed on Tergnier the bombers were seen to split up with the result that few bombs were recorded as hitting the target area. With reports of approaching unidentified aircraft, F/L Orr left the formation to investigate but immediately recognised the familiar elliptical wings of the bogeys as belonging to Spitfires. Meanwhile, Ross, flying Red 4 offered his views on the bombers after returning at 10.40 am, "Had to lead them home. No clue."

For Bruce's mission of 21 February, the starting base was RAF Manston, which is situated in the east of Kent. The mission was a diversionary attack to cover a mass raid on Germany which was part of the USAAF's and RAF's "Big Week" air campaign, called Operation Argument. The target for Ramrod 573's 72 Marauders was the bombing, from 12,000 feet of Soesterberg Aerodrome which is 10 miles east of Utrecht, Holland. Flying in these conditions wasn't for the faint-hearted as Bruce was lining up with snow flurries all around as he and the Roaring Boys climbed up into cloud at between 3,000 and 6,000 feet, joined shortly afterward by 401 and 412 squadrons. Their role as the top cover was to fly at 18,000 feet from which they could dive down onto any Luftwaffe fighters who decided to attack. Having met with the Marauders behind schedule over Holland, it was soon clear that the thick cloud was going to obscure the target area and the formation abandoned the mission and returned to base. From the cockpit of his Spitfire Bruce's eyes would have settled upon a sky which was literally filled with hundreds of 'heavies,' the Flying Fortresses, Liberators and their fighter escort of "little friends" made up of Mustangs, Lightnings, and Thunderbolts all returning to their bases in England. The Marauders were left over the North Sea, the squadron lost altitude and was vectored back to base where all aircraft made safe landings. Bruce commented in his logbook: "10/10 cloud. Bags of Marauders. Hell of a long way."

On 16 March 126 Airfield, Bruce, Charlie, Len, Ross, and Bob were airborne at 13.55 pm for Ramrod 661 as withdrawal support for Flying Fortresses bombing targets in southwest Germany. As the Roaring Boys flew towards their rendezvous with the Fortresses at a point northeast of Paris they were making a hazardous flight, climbing "blind" through over 17,000-25,000 feet of cloud knowing that ahead of them were hundreds of aircraft intent on leaving enemy territory for the safety of the skies over England. Within the wing, two pilots were forced to bail out due to engine failure. One, F/O Woodhouse landed in occupied France whilst the other, F/O Sanderson parachuted into "the drink" where he was rescued by one of the air-sea rescue's Walrus aircraft. Bruce returned early as he noted: "Climbed through 24,000 feet of light cloud. No E/A. Returned early from France." Technical issues were causing plenty of problems as Ross wrote, "Returned early with F/L Trainor. No oxygen." The remainder of the wing safely touched down at 15.25 pm. Throughout March Bruce only logged 2 hours 55 minutes of flying for a tour total of 79 hours and 10 minutes.

The ORB stated on 24 March that: "F/O Bruce Whiteford will be off flying for a while with a sprained ankle; it'll most likely take a week or two to heal up." This may be a separate incident to the one Norm mentioned previously, or perhaps Bruce had taken another off-road excursion on his motorbike!

Bruce flew from Biggin Hill on 6 April in a six Spitfire patrol around five miles out to sea between Portland and the Needles, Isle of Wight. The cover was required to protect an amphibious landing exercise the Army was undertaking ahead of D Day. Whilst seemingly mundane, the protection was an absolute necessity as any marauding Luftwaffe aircraft happening upon the exercise would have been presented with an array of easy, defenceless targets. The point was to be no more tragically illustrated later in the month when German E Boats of the Kriegsmarine torpedoed US Tank Landing Ships during Exercise Tiger offshore of Slapton Sands, Devon. The attack resulted in the loss of 749 US Army and Navy personnel. It was an expensive lesson and one which exercised the minds of Allied High Command planners in the lead up to the invasion of Europe.

Much of the month of April was taken up with dive bombing and strafing practice. There was also the move from Biggin Hill to RAF Tangmere on 15 April. On 23 April Bruce, Tommy, Len, and the others had the opportunity to test their bombing skills in a combat situation when they set off at 08.40 am in a squadron strength attack. W/C G C Keefer led them away as they headed for France. The target was the 1,500 foot long Merville viaduct which is situated around 35 miles southeast of Calais. The squadron ORB takes up the mission story: "S/L Fowlow flew as Red 3. We crossed the French coast at 12,000 feet." As the target came into view Bruce readied himself for the attack. Flak poured up from the ground crossing in front and behind his aircraft. There was an element of competition as each man wanted to make sure his bomb hit the target. Bruce was next in line as at 12,000 feet he throttled back and banked his aircraft over. The height disappeared in the blink of an eye as he lined up and at 4,000 feet he squeezed the bomb release button, before giving his Spitfire 'the beans' and high tailing out of the area, fast and low with the flak trailing behind him. Tommy gave his impressions: "Fair results were obtained and quite a lot of flak was tossed up. Bags of fun." The ORB added in its summary: "a lot of flak was tossed up. The C.O. found on his return he had been struck by some. Our first bombing was highly successful." The Roaring Boys were back at base at 09.45 am where techniques, successes, and failures were discussed at great length.

For Ramrod 798, one of several on 26 April Bruce flew with Ross, Len, Gibby, and Bob as they escorted 18 Boston bombers attacking the rail marshalling yards at Mons. A large flak barrage was sent up at the attackers but no hits were made during the 2 hours and 5 minutes operation. Due to the thick smoke and dust obscuring the target area the damage done by the raid was unknown. Ross commented on the effectiveness of the raid, "S.H. Bombing." And, I think we can safely say he was impressed, "SH" being shorthand for "Shit hot!" For Bruce the month of improved flying conditions allowed him to build 15 hours and 10 minutes on operations bringing his total for flying Spitfires to 94 hours and 20 minutes. He was close to completing half of his tour target as a fighter pilot.

On 1 May at 08.45 am Bruce, Gibby, Len, Ross, Bob and the Roaring Boys joined 401 squadron in a briefing for Ramrod 818. The low hum of chatter filling the briefing room was replaced by silence and concentration as the mission details were relayed by W/C G C Keefer, S/L Norm Fowlow and the intelligence boys. They would be accompanying 72 Marauders of the Ninth Air Force which would be bombing the rail marshalling yards at Charleroi. At 09.40 am they lifted off from Tangmere and Bruce angled his Spitfire skywards, pushing the throttle forward to climb out above Tangmere. In short order, the wing was formed up and heading southeast to pick up the bombers. After a period of orbiting and some inquiries by the CO over the R/T, it appeared that they had missed the bombers. Crossing the channel and into enemy territory, Bruce and the others experienced a heightened sense of expectation as well as fear. They were now over enemy territory with its ever-present danger of flak barrages. Would the Luftwaffe make an unwelcome appearance and what amount of flak was waiting for them? At least Bruce and the others presented a small target in their Spitfires versus the mass formation of Marauders which they had now joined up with near the target area. In the Spitfire Mark IX, they had one of the world's greatest fighters, nimble, agile with lethal firepower and more than a match for any FW 190s and Me 109s. As the light flak trickled its way skywards towards the formation the Marauders dropped their payload on the target area which was soon covered by a thick blanket of smoke and fire making a damage assessment difficult as the formation turned for home. The Luftwaffe stayed away, and both squadrons returned to Tangmere without loss, touching down at 11.55 am.

There was a noticeable uplift in activity in the Spring and early summer of 1944, the better weather and lighter evenings, plus the spectre of D Day looming large meant Bruce and the others were flying on operations for over 3 hours a day. Although young and fit there was a cumulative long-term effect in terms of the endless stress of these missions, the medical understanding of which was markedly improved since the First World War, but nothing in comparison with today's military.

The 8 May was a typical day for the Roaring Boys. Bruce, Tommy and the squadron were strapped into their Spitfires and airborne at 8.55 am for Ramrod 844, which was then followed at 18.35 pm by a fighter sweep. Ramrod 844 saw 4 Spitfires split off to provide close support to Boston bombers hitting targets south-east of Brussels. The remaining 8 Spitfires moved ahead to conduct a forward fighter sweep of the area, searching for the Luftwaffe. Meanwhile, over Berlin, the Germans received a visit from over 500 Flying Fortresses of the Eighth Air Force. Tommy later wrote, "10/10 – no huns or flak. Cheers!" He referenced a close shave he had had in the matter of fact way these incidents were reported by the pilots, "Nearly wrote off a Halifax." Quite what the circumstances were of Tommy's near miss with the large bomber are not known!

That day, the evening fighter sweep took off at 18.55 pm and took in the Doullens area which is located to the east of Amiens. The mission passed without incident for the Roaring Boys but Ross gave details of a lost aircraft: "Bags of flak. 1 bomber downed by flak. 3 bailed out. Bandits reported." The squadron continued its patrol before darting back across the channel where Bruce, Gibby, Bob, Dave, and Ross touched down at Tangmere after 1 hour 35 minutes.

The regular appearance in the ORBs of dive bombing missions heralded a new phase of operations for the Roaring Boys. A typical mission was undertaken on 12 May when Bruce, Dave, Gibby, Tommy, Ross, Bob, and the squadron attacked a No Ball target south of the coastal town of Le Tréport. Bruce strapped himself into Spitfire MJ237 and fired her up. Simultaneously, 11 other Spitfires also came to life. With engines warmed they all gingerly taxied out to takeoff. Each was loaded with a 500 lb bomb, and each pilot was weighed down with the thought that there was little room for error. As they got airborne and climbed out into a hazy sky the pilots manoeuvred into their sections and were soon heading southeast across the sea. By the time they reached the coast, Bruce looked at his altimeter which was showing 10,000 feet. The conditions below didn't look favourable as they readied themselves. Bruce checked over his aircraft and as they flew line astern it was soon his turn to reduce power and speed and drop his Spitfire into a steep dive. As his speed built the dust and smoke from the previous aircraft was a useful marker, overcoming the weather conditions which were making the target area difficult to view. As the height dropped away, the heavy flak seemed to converge on his diving Spitfire bisecting and crossing it from several points. Bruce had to concentrate solely on the dive and target area. As the ground loomed larger in his windscreen his thumb hovered over the release button, which he then pushed releasing the 500 pounder. Bruce levelled out and opened the throttle as he hurtled across the countryside at tree top height with tracer rounds zipping in all directions around him. Bruce weaved and pulled back the control column climbing back towards the other pilots. There was no immediate explosion from the majority of the bombs as nine of them were fitted with 20-minute delay fuses, and one with a 12-hour delay fuse. The formation headed back to Tangmere, landing after 1 hour 15 minutes. Ross and Tommy both noted that the bombing was "very good," and this information was passed on to the wing intelligence team.

The Roaring Boys moved to Hawkinge for their early evening mission of 29 May, which was a fighter sweep of the Lille area. Bruce, Tommy, and Len made the 30-minute flight to RAF Hawkinge. They made the very most of the practice time to fly their Spitfires flat out "down in the weeds." After arriving they were glad to get out of their cockpits for some fresh air. Tommy later wrote, "Bags of low flying. Too damn hot." Refreshed and refuelled they climbed back into their Spitfires ready to seek out some trouble across the sea in enemy territory. Bruce coaxed Spitfire MJ239 into the air at 11.00 am and the squadron turned south past Folkestone, pushing out across the channel. They swept inland past Calais and on towards Lille. Whilst drawing the Luftwaffe into combat was the objective of the sweep it was equally important to identify targets of opportunity and F/L Hayward did just that southwest of Cambrai. Bruce later wrote in his notes, "F/L Hayward & No 2 shot up barges." Bruce was in the box seat to watch the two Spitfires dive downwards towards a barge moored on the Canal de Saint-Quentin. The barge was heavily strafed with cannon fire, the plumes of water erupting around it. Earlier in the patrol F/O Tooley and F/L Nixon returned to England as one of their Spitfires developed engine trouble as they crossed the French coast. Tommy was less than impressed with the lack of action, "Swept Cambrai and S.F.A. No huns." All the aircraft returned to base without further incident, and there was the welcome relief of pulling back the cockpit hood and feeling the rush of fresh air as they moved into the circuit and landed at 19.30 pm. Bruce ended the month of May with a promotion to Flight Lieutenant. The lighter evenings and warm weather boosted his operational flying as he closed the month of May with 25 hours and 5 minutes of flying for a cumulative total of 119 hours and 25 minutes.

With the dawning of D Day on 6 June 1944, Bruce joined the Roaring Boys as they provided cover for the amphibious landings by patrolling Gold, Sword and Juno beaches. They will have known that below them on Juno beach their fellow Canucks were landing. They hoped and prayed that the landing was more successful than the Dieppe raid, Operation Jubilee on 19 August 1942 in which so many of their countrymen had been killed, wounded or captured.

The day before on 5 June Bruce recorded that he made a 1-hour 25-minute patrol, protecting the conveys as they formed up in the channel. This operation is not recorded in the official ORB account, perhaps to ensure there could be absolutely no breach of security where a stray official record could find its way into the hands of the enemy giving them advance notice of the colossal invasion that was heading their way. Sometime after the patrol, Bruce gave details: "Patrol Convoy. This convoy forming up for assault on France. D Day tomorrow." Being in possession of Ross Linquist's logbook it's clear he also took part in the patrol. He wrote, "Patrol. Invasion barges in Channel." Interestingly, he then gave further clues about the maximum security required at the time as he added in brackets. "(Counted with July ops)."

Bruce and the pilots were up early on D Day. There was fevered excitement around Tangmere, but also a palpable tension and every one of them felt it; the commanders, pilots, ground crews, and the wing support staff. Even Joskins the dog could tell something was in the air as he barked and raced from one place to another. All the pilots attended a wing briefing as the invasion plans for Operation Overlord were laid out before them. Each man knew what he had to do and they checked the roster eagerly to see when they were due to fly. The 08.10 am patrol pilots beamed with delight as they would be the first of the Roaring Boys over to France, where they hoped to get a crack at the hun. Those on later patrols, including Bruce, looked disconsolate and had a nervous wait before their mission was due to take off.

From my extensive research of the wartime pilots and soldiers, the fear was there and manifested itself in different ways. Most never showed it. Nearly every veteran I have spoken or listened to, including my grandfather recalling his time in the elite SAS, said everyone was scared.

Those that say they didn't feel real fear weren't being truthful in his opinion. I recall talking with Spitfire pilot Jimmy Corbin DFC about his time as a pilot waiting to go into combat and tangling with the Luftwaffe. I later found a TV interview he gave in 2007 about the Battle of Britain. He said: "We were jumped off Dover by 30 Me 109s. Now that was exciting but frightening too. It was a complete shambles but there you are we survived." He went on about the waiting to go into battle: "Some people sat and read a book; some people just dreamed. Some people played cards. We were all nervous I suppose waiting for that bloody phone to ring and praying that it wouldn't!" The interviewer then asked: "Were you ever frightened?" Jimmy replied instantly, and it was clear that the memories were still at the forefront of his mind: "Christ! Scared bloody stiff all the time! It wasn't a question of being frightened." He added with a knowing smile and a chuckle, "It was dangerous."

Bruce made his first sweep of the D Day beaches on 6 June 1944, taking off from RAF Tangmere in Spitfire MJ237 (shown as MJ237 in the ORB but there is a discrepancy with other official records and logbooks) with Tommy, Dave, Gibby, and Bob at 13.05 pm. The first patrol returned from the D Day beaches at 10.10 am with little to tell the next patrol and large welcome committee in terms of action. However, the sheer volume of aircraft in the air was a cause for concern and Bruce and his comrades were aware of the chaos that could follow if the Luftwaffe managed to break through the defensive umbrella and get in amongst the bombers and transport aircraft in particular. At around 12.30 pm W/C G C Keefer and S/L G D Robertson completed their briefing and the pilots streamed out towards their waiting aircraft. Bruce quickly located Spitfire MJ237 and stood to one side whilst he strapped on his parachute and pulled his flying helmet over his head. He made a final check of his equipment. His pistol was strapped to his side and like many of the Roaring Boys his open-topped flying boots had various items of kit stashed inside which might prove useful including; emergency rations, smokes, and a knife! He adjusted the important silk scarf around his neck which prevented the chafing from the rough service uniform. The pilots heads were constantly on the move during an operation. Bruce stepped up on to his aircraft's wing and with one foot on the door, he stepped onto the seat. He didn't carry the standard issue firearm as Norm explained to me:

"Dad was issued with a .455 Webley revolver service pistol. He didn't like it and found it bulky and uncomfortable while in the cockpit, so, he pawned it in Soho, London and bought a Belgian made .32 Fabrique Nationale Browning automatic. I still have this pistol, and fire it on occasion. He had to get a permit from Scotland Yard, which I still have. I found it somewhat amusing that they authorised him to have the pistol and 50 rounds of ammunition, while at the same time there is an authorisation in his logbook to fly a Spitfire at "Zero Feet."

Bruce's weight was supported by his hands which were firmly planted onto the top of the windscreen. As he slid down and met his seat, he shuffled to get comfortable before plugging in his R/T leads. His Spitfire started immediately with a puff of grey, white smoke and joined in with the noise of 12 others all coming up to temperature. After a short while, Keefer and Robertson led the Roaring Boys out across the airfield where they lined up and took off. The weather wasn't the best and the conditions could at best be described as "bumpy" as they formed up and moved out across the channel. There was little requirement for navigation Bruce considered, as it was mainly a case of following the endless chain of ships heading south. It looked as if you could actually walk to France, crossing deck to deck. In the air, there was a strict flight plan and flight corridors to stick to and so they slotted into their allotted altitude and course.

From the cockpit, that lasting impression was of the incredible military and logistical might on display from England across to the Normandy beachheads. Bruce reflected on the scene: "D Day 2nd front. Cheers! Patrolled left flank. Thousands of ships. Heavy armour shelling coast. Bags of troops and tanks on the beach. Looks successful." High above the fighting below the patrolling was routine. The sector control gave no vectors to enemy fighters and to Bruce and the others, it appeared as if their mission would be a repeat of the earlier one where there was no trade for them. It wasn't what they wanted but deep down they knew the work the Allied Air Forces had done in the year leading up to the invasion was designed to present the very scenario they were flying in i.e. an exclusion zone with air superiority. Over the R/T Keefer signalled the return to base and Bruce turned MJ237 northwards where after 1 hour and 55 minutes he landed back at Tangmere. The erks and armourers rushed to see if their guns had been fired which it was evident they hadn't. There was plenty to discuss at the debrief and an eager group of pilots and crews waiting for news.

The success of the Allies strategy in the months leading up to D Day meant that the Luftwaffe failed to appear in any significant numbers and complete air superiority was achieved, although the squadron ORB was sanguine about the lack of Luftwaffe aircraft for the Roaring Boys to attack, describing it as "very disappointing." As Bruce and his fellow Canadians landed back at Tangmere there was a buzz as the pilots excitedly exchanged stories with each other about what they had seen of the momentous events unfolding beneath them. As they looked down from the relative comfort of their Spitfires, they spared a thought for the troops fighting for their lives on the beaches to secure the all-important foothold in France. By coincidence one of those engaged in the battle below was Bruce's nephew Lieutenant (later Colonel) Desmond Deane-Freeman of the Lord Strathcona Horse Regiment (Royal Canadians). He went ashore with the Canadians on Juno beach in a "swimming tank," an invention which can only be described as a "skirt" wrapped around a tank which was pulled up around the sides to allow for flotation. The swimming tanks that made the beaches proved invaluable for clearing German defences but a significant proportion were launched too far out in the rough seas and promptly sank, in many cases taking their crews to the bottom with them. A quite terrifying prospect.

Bruce's work on D Day was not complete after returning from his first mission and at 21.35 pm he undertook his second patrol of the day over the same beaches. The battlefront presented a very different vista in the dusk and gathering darkness. There were eerie, silent flashes of guns and tracers streaking to and fro from the sea inland and between the front lines. The opposing armies were locked together in a titanic struggle that would ultimately decide the outcome of the war, the fate of Europe and the free world. Bruce described the scene in his logbook: "Bags of fire up to 10 miles inland. Caen burning fiercely. Yanks having problems on the western flank. Left beachhead 11.00 Dark. Night formation. Something new."

The risks of flying patrols over France at this time were brought home to the Roaring Boys during Bruce's mission of 11 June. With the Germans rushing reinforcements into the Normandy area, the number of flak units operating in theatre was multiplying. Joining Bruce on this mission were Charlie, Tommy, Ross, Jimmy Jeffrey and F/S T W Tuttle, aged 22 and on only his third mission after posting in from 83 GSU on 7 June. As their Spitfires took to the sky, they headed out across the

Channel looking down on the now familiar convoy of ships shuttling troops and supplies across to Normandy. They made land and moved south to patrol the area of Sainte-Contest in the northern suburbs of Caen. At some point over the area, F/S Tuttle's Spitfire received a direct hit from the flak defences and was seen to burst into flames, crashing down near Villons-les-Buissons. He was posted as missing, but the other pilots made no report of seeing him bail out. In Bruce's logbook, he recorded that Tuttle: "got a direct hit by flak, dived straight in and exploded." Ross added, "F/S Tuttle hit by flak. Blew up" whilst Tommy noted: "Flew over Caen at 1500 feet "twice." F/S Tuttle went for a burton hit by flak went straight in blew up – nearly written off landing." Tuttle became 411 Squadrons first fatality since the D Day invasion. F/S Thomas Weldon Tuttle is buried in Bretteville-sur-Laize Canadian War Cemetery. A few days before this fateful mission on 8 June the ORB recorded "the boys are pretty tired."

Spitfire NH341 Elizabeth
On 12 June, Bruce would have been contemplating another day of patrolling the Normandy beachhead area. His day time mission from Tangmere took off at 13.05 pm, which was recorded as uneventful. It was feeling very much like an anti-climax as Bruce recorded, "no Huns must have the twitch."

Knowing that he would be undertaking another patrol in the evening he found time to air test a newly delivered Spitfire for 15 minutes. How this flight came about is not known but it was probably due to the fact that previously Bruce flew MJ237 which carried the squadron code DB-E and therefore the opportunity to bag a factory fresh Mark IXb Spitfire NH341 with the same code as his favoured aircraft was too good to miss. Whatever the actual circumstances the connotations of what was to follow from that flight over 75 years later are incredible. Bruce, Ross, Dave, Tommy and the Roaring Boys took off at 21.30 pm for their beachhead patrol. Although it was recorded in the ORB as uneventful Bruce commented in his logbook: "night patrols are no hell. Can't see much except fires and gun flashes." Tommy limited his reflections to, "sweet Fanny Adams."

In the creeping darkness of 14 June at RAF Tangmere, Bruce, Gibby and Len were readying themselves for a nighttime mission. Bruce climbed onto the wing of his Spitfire and looked down at the engine cowling in front of him, where below the exhaust ports was the crisp newly painted white lettering spelling out the name of the love of his life, "Elizabeth." It shone out, resplendent against the dull green paintwork, a source of comfort to Bruce to know his sweetheart was flying with him. He put one foot on the cockpit door and hopped onto the seat, before clasping his hands on the windscreen and dropping down into the cockpit, where his parachute, which he was already wearing now became his seat cushion. The jack plugs for his R/T pinched between his fingers were plugged in, along with his oxygen lead. An erk passed Bruce his Sutton harness straps over his shoulders which he fastened securely. The erk had moved off next to the battery cart, or ground accumulator as its's called which was plugged into the aircraft as Bruce pulled up the cockpit door and closed the latch. The cockpit hood was open for takeoff and was locked. Bruce checked the controls for full, free and correct movement looking to see that the undercarriage indicator was on. He moved the rudder bias to the right for takeoff to counter the Spitfire's swing due to the engine torque. He reached down and made sure the fuel cut off was back. Checking the air pressure was sufficient, he put the brakes on. Next, Bruce switched on the fuel pump and heard it start to hum, as pressure built up in the carburettor. He looked down to the right and saw that the fuel pressure light was out. The light came back on and he switched the boost pump off. Bruce moved the fuel cut off forward into "run" and reaching down with his right hand he unscrewed the primer handle. As the engine was cold, he gave the Spitfire about 6 strokes of the primer, feeling the initial light resistance build as he went on. Meanwhile, his left hand was clamped to the top of the spade grip on the control column. With his right hand, he uncaged the two-engine switch covers, changed hands and set the throttle to ½ an inch open. He then placed two fingers of his left hand on the Magneto switches which were switched on whilst clamping the stick between his legs. Bruce made a whirling motion with his finger to show the erk he was about to start up and shouted a warning "clear prop." The right of the 2 buttons was the boost button that sents a spark to the engine, whilst the left, the start button turned the engine over. His middle finger pushed down on the boost and he followed this with the start button. The prop turned clockwise like a windmill and as the engine fired, a cloud of smoke from the exhausts passed quickly over the cockpit. Both hands left their buttons with the left reaching for the throttle and the right grabbing the spade grip. He reached down and snapped the switch covers shut and locked the primer pump.

The power and noise of the engine shook the aircraft as Bruce watched his gauges react to the warming engine. He was ready, and so was Spitfire Elizabeth.

Aside from the transit flight to Tangmere made by the Air Transport Auxiliary Bruce had only made an initial 15-minute test flight to settle his mind that this new Spitfire was ready for her first operational flight. He hoped the manufacturing staff at Castle Bromwich had assembled and delivered the very best Mark IX they could because this mission, Ramrod 1000 would be a severe test for him and his aircraft, flying in the dark at 25,000 feet. At around 22.00 pm the peace and quiet of the Sussex countryside was rudely interrupted by the coughs and angry roars of 12 Mighty Merlin engines. At 22.10 pm the Roaring Boys took off and turned their Spitfires south where they would join other squadrons escorting 220 Lancaster bombers from 1 Group on their mission to bomb the docks at Le Havre. This was the base of the feared E boats and their torpedoes which presented a serious threat to the battleships and supply convoys crisscrossing the channel to France. On approach to Le Havre, the large formation was subject to intense flak but as the Lancasters dropped their huge payloads, the flak petered out. Good results were reported and although the Roaring Boys saw no air combat, 2 Dorniers and a Me 410 were shot down by other squadrons.

In an interesting postscript to the mission, Bruce and Len returned early from the mission at 23.00 pm with one aircraft having engine trouble. It is not known whether Spitfire Elizabeth was the source of the problem, or if it was Len's aircraft as there is no mention in Bruce's logbook. He did however, comment on the deadly majesty of the sky surrounding him: "Escorted 220 Lancasters dropping blockbusters on E boat pens. Bags of flak and fire." The blockbuster was one of a series of RAF bomb types. During the raid, the Lancasters dropped Tallboy bombs each weighing an incredible 12,000 lb. They were designed to destroy the concrete docks and boat pens. The ORB reported on the raid: "Intense flak encountered at first but gradually petered out. Pilots reported a good job done to wipe out the E-boat menace. One aircraft developed engine trouble before the target and was escorted back by another."

On 15 June as ground units of 411 Squadron hurriedly continued their preparations for the squadron's move to France, the imperative of maintaining air superiority over the beachhead was uppermost in everyone's mind. The patrols would come thick and fast in the coming days. At 18.10 pm Bruce fired up Spitfire Elizabeth and prepared himself for the patrol ahead on which he would fly in squadron strength with Gibby, Len, Ross, and Bob. The Roaring Boys wouldn't just be undertaking a defensive patrol. With the Germans seeking to repel the landings and achieve the aim of pushing the Allies back into the sea German reinforcements were being rushed into the area. The Roaring Boys were keenly aware that by flying over enemy territory in this situation there would be opportunities for offensive action against vehicles on the ground.

The pattern of daily patrols continued for Bruce on 16 June. He and the squadron were all aware that change was in the air and that this routine of returning each evening to the safety of RAF Tangmere would soon be replaced by the rather more hostile surroundings of ALG B4, Bény-sur-Mer with the inherent risks of having the front line close by. This 2-hour patrol in Spitfire NH341 Elizabeth, accompanied by Gibby, Dave, and Gord Lapp was described as uneventful, although there was a VVIP on a Royal Navy battleship below who was returning to England after his visit to the front. Bruce's logbook entry read: "Escorted cruiser carrying H.M The King from the beachhead to England."

The next morning, 17 June it was back to business as usual for Bruce, Tommy, Bob and Gibby with an 06.10 am mission. The relief of a safe return was tinged with the disappointment that there was no enemy to attack on the ground or in the air. However, there was still danger as Tommy later noted the flak danger. "Bags of little red tennis balls." Putting themselves in the way of danger was the business of a mobile fighter wing. Their actions from the time show what these brave Canadians accomplished with a clear focus and fierce determination. A sign on the situation map, located on the operations tent and which showed the position of the Allied and enemy ground forces in Normandy, summed up the Roaring Boys philosophy to their offensive operations, "B4 is NEVER B – HIND."

On 20 June Bruce took off in Spitfire Elizabeth from RAF Tangmere with a mixture of fear, anticipation, and excitement to get stuck into the enemy. The break out by land forces from the coastal bridgehead and what the Luftwaffe's reaction would be occupied everyone's thoughts and discussions. If all went to plan, 126 Wing would dismantle its ALG base and follow the advancing front line eastwards towards the heartlands of Nazi Germany.

As Bruce settled into life at B4 Bény-sur-Mer aerodrome his next mission on 22 June with Charlie, Ross, Len, and Dave would test Spitfire Elizabeth's capabilities and his skill as a dive bomber. With all 12 Spitfires fitted with two 250 lb and one 500 lb bomb, the target was to be two bridges at Cabourg, which is situated near the coast around 10 miles northeast of the city of Caen. The relative merits of the Spitfire as a dive bomber are open to question and the topic has been explored in several books. On this occasion with no interference from flak or enemy fighters both bridges were missed by the pilots although buildings on the west and east banks of the river La Dives were hit. Light flak was experienced to the west of Caen on the flight to and from B4. Ross gave his impression of the mission, "Poor bombing. First trip from strip." After a mission debrief Bruce had time to continue his settling in process to the new home at B4, no doubt looking to sure up his accommodation against the "rain of ordnance" that was constantly falling from the sky at the time as both sides exchanged heavy fire.

At the briefing for Bruce's next operation on 22 June, he was joined by Bob, Len, Charlie, Dave, and Ross. The briefing confirmed that they would carry out a fighter sweep which would follow an easterly route to Caen and beyond to Lisieux. The sweep would then head south to L'Aigle before turning west to Argentan and then onto the final leg back to ALG B4. The Roaring Boys saw the opportunity to ground attack German military vehicles. Watching actual 411 Squadron gun camera footage from the time brings home starkly the enemy's predicament as roving hunting packs of Allied fighter bombers dived down upon their transports. In the case of the Spitfire Mark IXb's like Elizabeth, they would unleash, bombs along with a deadly volley of 20 mm Hispano cannon and machine gun fire. Watching the original 411 Squadron gun camera footage you can see trucks and mechanised vehicles such as tanks and armoured personnel carriers being chased by a deadly twisting snake of metal which neatly bisects them, the strike of the rounds lifting clouds of dust and debris into the air. Many drivers seemed unaware of their impending fate whilst others take drastic avoidance measures, including on one occasion reversing their truck rapidly under a bridge. The low level of the attacks and the flying skills required to execute them is a testament to the pilots skill, determination, and courage. On this occasion, 411 squadron destroyed two trucks and a bus. After landing at B4 at 22.20 pm they took the time to report the movement of German transports and convoys spotted during the sweep. Bruce's mission took on a different complexion as mechanical issues beset Spitfire Elizabeth. Ross wrote about the problem in his logbook: "Returned early with F/L Whiteford. Boys shot up trucks." They landed at 21.45 pm whereupon an army of ground crew set about trying to sort out Spitfire Elizabeth's gremlins.

On 23 June there were a series of aircraft scrambles in response to reported Luftwaffe incursions into the area. At 16.55 pm another squadron scramble saw Tommy replace Charlie and join Bruce and four other pilots who launched their Spitfires skywards towards the unseen enemy. Unable to locate the enemy aircraft the Roaring Boys instead set course for a sweep of the Caen area. As they flew a track along the L'Aigle to Argentan road they spotted traffic in the form of a 3-ton truck and a light van and dived down and attacked the vehicles leaving them damaged. On the return leg flying north towards Caen, two staff cars were seen north of Falaise and damaged. In what the ORB reported as stray .303 rounds, F/L G W Johnson's Spitfire was struck on the starboard side of the engine. These bullets could well have come from Allied ground fire. Either way, the fact that the round was .303 calibre confirmed it was from an Allied weapon, so it was a blue on blue incident. As Johnson struggled to maintain altitude, it became clear that his ailing Spitfire was not going to make B4 Bény-sur-Mer. Tommy noted in his logbook: "swept south of Caen at 1,000 feet. Shot up trucks. F/L Johnnie Johnson hit by flak. Crash landed ¼ mile from aerodrome– OK. Good show." Tommy's explanation of the mission being flown at 1,000 feet vindicates Johnson's decision to stay with his Spitfire rather than bail out. He was probably well under 1,000 feet after being hit and quickly concluded that his only option was to crash land. Bruce wrote, "Squadron separated by multiple targets."

As dawn broke on 25 June, Bruce made an early start, realising that he and the other Roaring Boys needed to be fully functioning and alert before the planned takeoff at 04.40 am. For some early birds, this came naturally whilst for others no doubt a shot of coffee to kick start their system was the order of the day. The pre-flight checks and start-up procedures for the Spitfire were familiar enough to all by now and it was certainly not just a case of "kick the tyres and light the fires." There was mental preparation to be done before taking off on the serious business of an armed reconnaissance patrol over enemy territory. Perhaps, somewhere a short flight away a similar process was underway, and a Luftwaffe pilot was about to strap into his Me 109 or FW 190 hoping to catch a Spitfire pilot who was not concentrating fully. As any fighter pilot will attest it's dangerous to "knock-off" for a second in the combat area, that one momentary loss of concentration could be your last.

As the Spitfires raced down B4's runway, Charlie had already preceded them by 20 minutes flying solo ahead of the main force. For Bruce, this early morning start led to an unfortunate incident as he recorded in his logbook, "Took off in dark, banged up my prop." Bruce must have given Spitfire Elizabeth too much throttle, throwing a cloud of dust and dirt into the air as the tips of his propeller hit the ground. There's no indication of what he did next, but a full mission was completed in NH341. He may have aborted the takeoff and performed some checks before lifting off again. Although the mission was a relatively quiet one German truck and passengers welcomed in the new day in the worst way possible as the Spitfires swooped down for a strafing run leaving the vehicle badly damaged. The rest of the patrol was recorded as uneventful and a staggered return was made by the sections, with Bruce perhaps deciding the stresses of a dive and strafing run were not the best idea after his propeller grounding incident. He touched down early at 5.10 am in the damaged Spitfire Elizabeth, escorted by Gord Lapp in MJ313. There was time for both the pilots and planes to refuel before the day's next operations got underway. For Bruce, Spitfire Elizabeth was handed over to Herb Strutt and the other erks for a check over, with the likely outcome being at the very least a new propeller!

With Spitfire Elizabeth fully operational again on 26 June Bruce's next mission was in squadron strength for a patrol of the beachhead offering protection to destroyers like HMS Rodney. The ship was shelling the front near Caen in support of British Army units. In addition, the patrol was overflying and protecting the resupply convoys of shipping feeding the cavernous appetite of the Allied war machine which was in overdrive in the build-up to the big British offensive, Operation Epsom. Tommy, flying together with Bruce recorded in his logbook, "the big push for Caen has started. Cheers." Whilst the Roaring Boys saw no action with the Luftwaffe Tommy noted: "No joy for us. 403 squadron destroyed 3 Me 109s."

A change was coming in terms of the Luftwaffe presence in the sectors of Normandy occupied by the British and Canadians. This was in response to Operation Epsom and the Americans capturing Cherbourg, where there were now no German ground forces left to support. The

Luftwaffe was about to enter the battle in the same sector as the Roaring Boys, covering their Canadian brethren. On 27 June a squadron strength formation of fifteen FW 190s had engaged an earlier patrol of the Roaring Boys. Bruce and the others were now eager and ready to get into the fight; the dispersal hut was alive with the chatter from the earlier patrol describing the action. At 16.45 pm Bruce throttled up Spitfire Elizabeth and formed up quickly with a familiar group including; Tommy, Dave, Ross, and Len. Their planned front line patrol would see the squadron fly from B4 Bény-sur-Mer due east to the coastal town of Cabourg before turning southwest to Bayeux where they would patrol north and south of the city. The patrol also included a further leg back to Cabourg. Suddenly, south of Bayeux the Roaring Boys were bounced and 5 FW 190s swooped down to attack. As the Roaring Boys responded Bruce turned Spitfire Elizabeth towards the enemy and opened the throttle, feeling the surge of power from the growling Merlin engine. Breathing hard, and with all his senses alive Bruce had the enemy where he wanted them, in his sights, as he asked everything of his Spitfire. Would this be his day to bag a Jerry? The Luftwaffe had other ideas about engaging in combat. This was a hit and run opportunity and engaging in combat with a numerically superior force was not on the cards. With an easily discernible sense of frustration, Bruce wrote about the action in his logbook: "Chased 5 FW 190s around but the buggers ducked into cloud." Bruce also recorded the fate of his fellow 411 pilot on this patrol, "F/L Nixon baled out." Ross was also focussed on bagging an enemy fighter and wrote: "Got into 4 FW 190s. Wheler and Harrison fired. No results." Echoing Bruce's sentiment, he went on: "Lost the buggers in cloud. W/C destroyed ME 109 on previous show." Tommy was where he wanted to be, in the thick of the action. He described the action: "Got into 4 FW 190s southwest of Caen. 5,000 feet. Fired two long bursts at FW 190 up the C. O's rear, range 4 to 500 yards about 70-80 degrees angle. Missed the son of a b - - - -. He got away in cloud. F/L Nick Nixon bailed out south of Bayeux. Hit by flak. He is OK. This morning S/L Robertson Destroyed Me 109. P/O Phil Wallace is missing. Here's luck to you Phil. A hell of a good type." H J Nixon had been hit by the heavy curtain of flak that was being thrown skywards from the area south of Caen. Having taken to the silk and parachuted to the ground safely, Nixon evaded capture and returned to the squadron as a new member of the Caterpillar Club. He returned to flying duties again on 28 June.

The early days of June and the uneventful patrols around D Day must have seemed a lifetime ago to Bruce and the Roaring Boys. For Spitfire Elizabeth, 28 June would be a day of days and her cannons and machine guns would be in action several times as 411 Squadron lived up to its "hostile to an enemy" motto. Earlier in the day, Dave had taken Elizabeth for a morning patrol, described in his chapter. At 12.25 pm Bruce prepared himself and Elizabeth for an armed reconnaissance patrol to the area occupied by the enemy south of Caen. This was a "hot" area for activity and of the 12 Spitfires pilots on this mission 6; Bruce, Gibby, Len, Tommy, Jimmy, and Bob would all fly Elizabeth in combat. As the aircraft thundered down the runway and into the air they orbited B4 to settle into their battle formation and prepare themselves. It was only a short flight to the patrol area south of Caen and everyone needed to be ready for potential action almost immediately. Sure enough, they were soon engaged in attacking enemy units on the ground. Charlie Trainor was leading the formation and over the R/T he confirmed the attack, leading the first section himself. Bruce waited above. Flak and tracer rounds were zinging everywhere as the convoy marshalled their defences and commenced returning fire. He was vigilant and sectioned the sky following a methodical pattern of searching the horizon for fighters. His R/T confirmed that it was his turn to attack. His gun camera was switched on the gun button was ready to fire as Spitfire Elizabeth banked over and drifted almost lazily into a dive. Bruce put in some small changes of direction to confuse the enemy gunners until at around 2,000 feet he lined up his gun sight on the road and pressed "the tit." His aim was true and rounds smashed into the road and trucks sending up clouds of dust and smoke. Bruce fired for around 2 seconds before breaking hard to port. He clenched all the muscles in his lower body and tilted his head to one side to stop the blood draining from his brain as the G forces kicked in. The power of Elizabeth's 27 litre Merlin engine quickly put enough distance between Bruce and the ground fire as he skimmed over the treetops. He then climbed at full power, whilst searching behind and around him, in case a fighter had latched onto his "six."

The results of the strafing attack were significant with 3 vehicles left in flames and another 4 damaged. Watching the actual gun camera footage of the attack, it's as if the Roaring Boys Spitfires are moving in slow motion as they dive down towards their targets, sometimes pulling out at perilously low altitudes as their bullets raked the area. Following the attack they regrouped but the action had only just begun as a sizeable force of Me 109s and FW 190s entered the fray. The drama of what happened next is described in Tommy and Charlie's chapters as they played a central role in events. Following what had been an incident-packed patrol the squadron returned to base at 13.55 pm with quite a story to tell. It would be a busy few hours for the intelligence team as the mission events and scores were passed on by the pilots.

With the much-improved weather situation and the offensive on Caen struggling onwards, Bruce was up flying again on 29 June at 05.30 am for an armed reconnaissance patrol along with Tommy, Gibby, Jimmy, Len, Bob, and 5 others. In the gathering light, they took off in squadron strength flying on a patrol area tracking to Flers before turning to Sées, which is around 45 miles to the southeast of Caen and then flying on a track northeastwards towards L'Aigle. The Roaring Boys, aside from Gibby who returned early possibly with mechanical trouble, found a considerable number of transports and set about the convoy. Having flown unscathed through light accurate flak in the Flers area they made impressive work of the available targets leaving a considerable and unwelcome calling card for the Germans. These missions are quite remarkable, available as they are to watch first-hand. You can see the destructive force of the Spitfire Mark IXb through the eyes of the pilots and their gun cameras as the attack unfolds. As a viewer, you are literally transported back in time to the cockpit. The footage records the actual time of the attack as 06.30 am. As each section took turns to dive in on the enemy, the others provided top cover against fighter attack. From the camera footage of F/O Ireland's attack, the area appears to be an isolated hamlet with a single-track road. There are already clouds of smoke, dust, and debris from another Spitfire's attack swirling around the vehicles, which are next to a small roadside house as Ireland's 20 mm cannon shells impact the ground. A few seconds later short clips show flashes and impacts of his rounds on the vehicles below including those located close to some orchards and a small crossroads. A later attack made by Len in Spitfire Elizabeth is also recorded along with F/L Hayward's. On a cloudy day, Hayward's attack on a vehicle results in a small flash and explosion, accentuated by the dark background of the surrounding trees. With the mission and debrief completed at 06.55 am the ORB provided details of the damage: "13 flamers, 5 smokers, and 10 damaged. One armoured vehicle damaged, and ammo truck was seen to explode." Tommy gave his personal score: "3 trucks damaged and 1 staff car in the area south of Caen." With so many targets to choose from the Roaring Boys were getting a real sense of how their attacks were degrading and destroying the enemy's transport and communications.

There was no let up from the squadron commanders or the pilots who in equal measure were pushing to continue the pace of operations. They would literally be off again all guns blazing on 29 June at 08.25 am, when Bruce piloted Spitfire Elizabeth for her second armed reconnaissance of the day with Tommy, Len, and Gibby. The patrol area on this occasion would take them around 20 miles to the southwest of Caen to Vire and Aunay-sur-Odon. The squadron experienced heavy and accurate flak as they passed Villers-Bocage. At 09.00 am enemy vehicles were identified and watching F/O Ireland's gun camera footage of his strafing attack he was not shooting at his best as the bulk of his cannon shells peppered an adjoining field, to the side of the enemy truck. I would estimate that Ireland pulled his Spitfire up at under 200 feet and over 300 mph. It's clear to see from his closing speed that these pilots needed the sharpest reflexes and skills to execute these manoeuvres, which they developed from endless practice and combat flying. The ORB provided a summary of the scores: "four flamers and six damaged Met were scored." Tommy completed his log: "destroyed 2 trucks, damaged 2 trucks, and a tank in the Vire area. No huns. F/L Charlie Trainor got another Me 109. This makes three in three days. He also takes over command of A Flight. Bloody good show." Bruce had accelerated his flying time during the month of June and he spent 40 hours and 45 minutes flying in combat. His tour total of combat flying was now 160 hours and 10 minutes.

With the start of July, it was flying as usual for Bruce in Spitfire Elizabeth. On 1 July at 07.50 am he was joined by Tommy, Gibby, and Len for an 11 Spitfire armed reconnaissance patrol which he wrote later was hampered in its effectiveness as it was undertaken "in 10/10 cloud." As they taxied out, lined up and then powered along the runway the low cloud base meant that they stayed low and formed up turning to starboard and back 180 degrees on themselves. The R/T suddenly exploded into life, "Bandits downwind." Bruce, Tommy and the others as one unit turned towards the enemy who were hugging the lower cloud. Tommy takes up the story: "Huns in the circuit. Tore after them right after takeoff. Lost them in cloud. 10/10ths at 1500 feet – very duff." It was a scare and reinforced the need for constant vigilance at all times. With the enemy lost the armed recce got underway. The patrol area saw the Roaring Boys fly a track which started southeast of Caen, at Falaise, before turning southwest for a 20-mile flight to Flers. The final leg saw them turn north for two 15-mile legs to Condé-sur-Noireau and onto Thury-Harcourt.

Having landed after the 50-minute flight the erks were quickly at work checking over some of the returning aircraft as they and some of the pilots would be back in action again at 09.10 am with a patrol of the William and Easy sectors of the bridgehead. Bruce reported that the cloud base was very low at 600 feet, so the patrol was conducted in 10/10 cloud. He also reported that there were barrage balloons in the cloud positioned as a barrier to the enemy bombing of the bridgehead sector, but also a significant potential hazard to allied aircraft.

The 2 July was a day of difficult emotions for the squadron and for Bruce. One of their fellow pilots was shot down and his situation was unknown. The Roaring Boys felt the loss of any of their fellow fighter pilots with regret, but also the resignation that this was the game they were in and that they couldn't dwell on such bad news. For Bruce, it was especially unwelcome as his favourite aircraft, Spitfire NH341 Elizabeth was also lost and he would not get to fly in her again. The details of this action are covered later in the book. He flew other Spitfires, but painted Elizabeth onto NH174, which replaced NH341.

Armed with the update that the enemy was active in the area there was a palpable increase in anticipation and nervousness for Bruce as he strapped himself into a new steed, Spitfire MK423. He and three others, including Tommy and Len prepared themselves for a 1 hour and 10-minute morning patrol of the eastern end of the beachhead, which was recorded as uneventful. After a few hours rest and recuperation at 13.30 pm, Bruce and the same trio were once again airborne patrolling Easy sector of the beachhead. The Luftwaffe did not appear, although earlier 6 FW 190s had appeared in this sector and were chased for 30 miles but could not be caught. A few hours later after Bruce's patrol landed a force of 15 FW 190s engaged the Roaring Boys in combat but no claims were made. During his patrol, Bruce did report some unusual air activity in the form of a solitary parachute with a white bundle suspended beneath it, which was seen north of Bayeux. Unlike Spitfire Elizabeth, one of Bruce's newly adopted Spitfire's, MK423, would survive the end of hostilities only to suffer engine failure on 29 July 1945 whilst being flown on a cross country flight to Naples, Italy by Squadron Leader Bob W Turkington DSO DFC and Bar. As he turned back towards the aerodrome witnesses reported that the Spitfire crashed landed and burst into flames, killing him instantly.

On 4 July, Bruce taxied his Spitfire out onto the runway of B4 Bény-sur-Mer. He was in familiar company as he looked across at Bob, Charlie, Dave, Len, Gibby, and 6 other Roaring Boys. Their mission was to be a front line patrol, taking off at 18.00 pm. This patrol was going to be far from uneventful and would be one in which they would see considerable action. As the patrol moved into the area southeast of Caen, they were engaged by several enemy aircraft at between six and nine thousand feet. The sky quickly became a melee of dogfighting aircraft, the Spitfires exploiting their ability to outturn their opponent whilst their adversaries in their Me 109s used their superior diving speed. As the pilots continued their deadly dance, fear gripped them all, their stress and adrenaline levels rocketed, breathing heavily and with sweat pouring from their foreheads as they fought for their lives. The pilots were ever vigilant, constantly flicking their heads in all directions as they searched the sky checking the enemy hadn't locked onto them. Bruce twisted and turned looking for a target and then he spotted a solitary Me 109. Ramming the throttle forward he flew after his quarry. The German pilot hadn't seen his attacker and as Bruce closed to around 500 yards he opened fire. The shells and rounds streamed forwards from his Spitfire, visible in his peripheral vision as smoke and flames burst forth. Bruce only had eyes for the strike of his rounds which bracketed the 109. The flak was becoming very heavy, the gunners had latched onto him and their fire was deadly accurate. He had to evade them and forget the enemy fighter. Fearing he might be shot down himself he was forced to break off the attack

Bruce later wrote about his own role in the combat: "Ran into Huns. Chased one and firing observed strikes and glycol poured out. Had to pull up into cloud to evade heavy flak. 1 Me 109 damaged." Meanwhile, Bob and Charlie were also in the thick of the action. Their combat is described in their own chapters. Based upon the fact that Bruce saw glycol pouring out of the Me 109 is a sure sign that the engine would shortly seize, with the likelihood it would also to catch fire. The pilot would be forced to either bail out or crash land. Bruce was officially credited with damaging the enemy aircraft, and with no witnesses or evidence of the aircraft's demise, he couldn't be credited with a kill. The 411 ORB triumphantly recordedthe day's action, at the same time as welcoming in F/O R M Cook to the squadron stating: "he came on a good day because the Squadron was again "hot."

With the battle raging for Caen, on 7 July at 21.40 pm Bruce, Tommy, Len, Gibby, Dave, and Bob took off in squadron strength for an armed reconnaissance of the Lisieux area, east of Caen. The Roaring Boys were expecting the area to be active with both Luftwaffe and flak defences as during the patrol 443 Lancaster and Halifax bombers, with escorts, were dropping 2,276 tons of munitions on the Caen area. The raid also inflicted heavy losses on the local French population, with minimal casualties inflicted on the defending Germans. An unintended consequence of the raid was the destruction of several of the city's bridges which prevented the Germans resupplying their forces in the north of Caen. The 12 Spitfires would have been able to see the unfolding raid as they progressed on their patrol. Despite the devastation and carnage in the Caen area during the patrol, the Roaring Boys were unmolested by the Luftwaffe or flak and they landed back at base at 22.40 pm. The raid on Caen made an impression on the pilots. Bruce wrote: "450 Lancs bombed Caen. Wonderful sight but no huns came up." Tommy was equally enthusiastic: "Cover for 700 'heavies' knocking out Caen strong point. No huns about. 'heavies' did a real job - Good show."

On 11 July the Roaring Boys were tasked with a long day of patrols in what was described as, "dull and threatening weather." They were split into sections of four Spitfires. Bruce was joined in his section by Gibby, Dave and Cliff Cross. The four Spitfire patrol was a much easier and flexible formation to organise and fly with versus the normal squadron strength of 12 aircraft. I can recall from my conversations with Tommy Wheler that he was a fan of this approach, which the Luftwaffe had originally developed and perfected. This finger-four formation contained a flight of four aircraft and was organised into 2 elements, a lead and second element which each contained two Spitfires. As the name suggests the formation resembles the tips of the four fingers of the human right hand, minus the thumb! The flight leader is at the front of the formation with a wingman behind him to his left. Behind the flight leader and opposite to the wingman is the element leader and his wingman who sits to his right and further back, effectively as "tail-end Charlie" covering the rear of the formation. The flight and element leaders are the offensive leaders as it would be their Spitfires that would open fire on any enemy aircraft with the flight staying intact as a formation. Their wingmen have a defensive role — the flight wingman covers the rear of the second element and the element wingman covers the rear of the lead element. Four of these flights can be assembled to form a squadron formation which consists of two staggered lines of fighters, one in front of the other. Each flight section is usually designated by colours e.g. Red, Blue, Yellow, and Green.

On 11 July, each patrol lasted for around 40 minutes to 1 hour in duration. Bruce's section flew two patrols in the morning, starting at 7.00 am and then with a break during the day they were airborne again in the early evening, followed by a final patrol with wheels up at 21.55 pm. None of the patrols undertaken by the Roaring Boys that day resulted in any air combat. In fact, although the Luftwaffe was active elsewhere, there was no sign of them in 411's sector.

Due to the previous night's patrolling and the poor weather, Bruce was not airborne on 12 July until 15.00 pm when he joined a 10 Spitfire strength patrol flying Spitfire MK423. This was to be Bruce's last operational mission with 411 Squadron. He was in good, and familiar company with pilots he knew and trusted, living cheek by jowl with them in the tented quarters of B4 Bény-sur-Mer; Len, Tommy, Gibby, and Bob. The former officer commanding 411 Squadron Dal Russel DFC who was now 126 Wing's commander led his old squadron on this patrol. The area covered on this occasion was wide-ranging and would take in the south of Caen, Flers, Falaise, and Argentan, before sweeping northeast to the coastal towns of Cabourg and Trouville-sur-Mer. No attacks were made on the ground or in the air but intelligence gathering, and "eyes in the sky" observation were also an important element of these patrols. A German radar station was detected and pinpointed near Argentan. This information would later be fed into the intelligence machinery and listed as a possible target for bombing or attack by ground forces. The mission was not completely without hostile fire as the ORB reported the pilots seeing: "slight, accurate heavy flak north of Mezidon" which is to the southeast of Caen. Fortunately, the patrol was completed without any damage and the mission was ended at 16.20 pm. Bruce made no comment on the mission in his logbook.

It is not clear if Bruce knew that this was to be his last mission as one of the Roaring Boys. It would seem likely that he was told a couple of days later as he wrote in his logbook, "Turfed on 14.7.44."

Bruce's final logbook entry is the total of his operational hours for July which were 15 hours. In Bruce's tour of duty, he had spent 175 hours and 10 minutes on combat operations. The figures are signed by A Flight Commander Charlie Trainor, and by S/L G D Robertson, who added, "Best of luck Bruce!"

Bruce had seen it all as a fighter pilot and had been in the thick of the action before, during and after the momentous events of D Day. Now it was over. He took some time out, visited some of the local Normandy area, passing the time with all the pilots and other personnel he had flown into danger with and for whom the war still continued. They had an unbreakable bond forged in combat where lives were lost and taken. The job had to be done and these players knew the rules.

Bruce's next posting was recorded in the squadron ORB: "J.10727 F/L A B Whiteford to RCAF "R" Depot 29.7.44."

The RCAF's "R" Deport was the Repatriation Unit for pilots and crew who would be returning home to Canada. Bruce was desperate to return to his wife Elizabeth, and baby Anne whom he had never seen or held having left Canada to join the war in December 1942. Bruce had fulfilled the request Elizabeth had asked of him before he left: "Don't come home a hero, just come home." He had most certainly accomplished both.

After returning to Canada Bruce found employment with Home Oil Company Limited at Turner Valley, Calgary. They were engaged in the exploration and production of petroleum and natural gas. When the Korean War started on 25 June 1950, perhaps Bruce's thoughts turned back to his days as a fighter pilot. He may have yearned once more to reprise his former role, albeit technology had moved fighter aircraft into the jet age. Whatever his thoughts, daily life continued for the Whiteford's, a family living their lives and raising their daughter. Tragically, Anne died on 12 July 1951, an unimaginably painful loss for Bruce and Elizabeth, as well as for their family. Norm Whiteford reflected on the confluence of these two events and wrote the following passage about his father's post-war life:

"Dad re-joined the RCAF and started PRTS (Pilot Refresher Training School) in Calgary on 31 December 1951. He was fully prepared to go back to Korea as a fighter pilot, but he was deemed more valuable as a flying instructor, and so after PRTS, he was sent to FIS (Flying Instructor's School) Trenton. From there, in April 1952 he was posted to 4 FTS Calgary, followed in April 1953, by a posting to 1 IFS Centralia for advanced training. A few months later in July 1953, he was posted to 4 FTS Penhold.

"Dad remained with 4 FTS until October 1954, after which he took a Supervisory Instructors course covering Harvards, B-25 Mitchell bombers, and the T-33 Shooting Star jet fighter. He instructed on these aircraft at RCAF Stations, London and Centralia between 1956 and 1960 before attending 4(T) OUT Trenton for training on the C-47 Dakota. On 1 June 1960, he was then posted to his final unit, 435 Squadron, Namao, Alberta flying the C47."

Bruce receiving the Canadian Forces Decoration, Namao, Canada 1963.

When Norm relayed details of Bruce's service to me I immediately thought about 435 Squadron knowing that in 2017 Keith Perkins had acquired C-47 "Drag 'em oot" which was transferred from the RAF to the RCAF's 435 Squadron in August 1945, retaining her RAF serial number TS422. Surely, it would be too remote a possibility that Aero Legends would own two completely different wartime aircraft, one a fighter and the other a transport aircraft that were flown by the same pilot? After an email exchange with Norm asking him for a copy of Bruce's logbook I was amazed to see three pilot logbook entries for 23 and 24 August 1960 showing him as C-47 TS422 Drag 'em oot's pilot. A remarkable coincidence!

Norm provided further details of Bruce's later life: "Prior to the war dad enjoyed hunting and was good at it. Of course in Canada, then as well as now, the opportunities for game hunting are much greater than in England, and dad became a good shot at a fairly young age (we always had firearms in the house while I was growing up, and dad drilled gun safety into us boys from the first days I can remember). Dad liked firearms and looked after them well - one of my earlier memories is of the smell of gun oil and cleaning solvents when dad routinely serviced his rifles and shotguns. I still have a couple of his favourite long guns. Although he had the rifles, after the war dad no longer favoured game hunting; he loved to go out into the wild, make camp and stalk, but he no longer had the appetite for shooting warm-blooded mammals. He had been an excellent wing shot and enjoyed hunting ducks and geese in the fall, but the enjoyment of this, too, faded. He enjoyed preparing for the hunt, setting blinds, the camaraderie of the excursion, but, not the killing, apparently. He pursued his enjoyment of shooting through his involvement with both Trap and Skeet shooting and achieved a "50 out of 50" badge in each. I was given to understand from mom that his war experiences had undermined his enjoyment of hunting in general.

"On 15 March 1962 dad landed a C-47 after dropping paratroopers. This was to be his final flight as a pilot. His most recent ECG showed he had suffered a heart attack. He finished his RCAF career as the squadron CadO (Chief Administrative Officer) on 22 October 1963. He died of a subsequent heart attack, a few days short of his 47th birthday on 29 January 1965, whilst living in Red Deer, Alberta.

Dad's former 435 Squadron mates "liberated" the last C47 he flew (putative "training" flight) and landed in Penhold to attend his funeral. Afterwards, they took Elizabeth and my older brother, Trevor, in the C47 to do low-level air work (i.e. spreading Dad's ashes) over the Highwood River area in the Rocky Mountain foothills west of Calgary. This was the area where Elizabeth was raised and where she and Bruce loved to ride horses."

A fitting end to a professional aviator who bravely served his country and the cause of freedom. Norm wrote: "My mother had never worked outside the home, but within a short time of Dad dying she started working as an Occupational Therapist at a local institution – she had three sons to raise and a mortgage to pay on an RCAF survivor's pension. She did a grand job, despite us boys being a bit of a handful! I never realised how hard it must have been for her until I had my own family. I am the only surviving child. My sister Ann died in 1951, my elder brother Trevor in

1973, and my younger brother Richard in 1980. My wife Terry and I have two children, our son Deane (the eldest) and our daughter Lindsey. Both are extremely proud of their grandfather's service and legacy and are keenly interested in, and very supportive of the whole "Elizabeth" project. They were both very close with their grandmother and often say how much they wished she had been here to share in this and how thrilled she would have been.

"My father was proud of both his service and the RCAF. Both he and my mother were very sociable and made good friends wherever they went - our homes (wherever we were) were often filled with friends and family. My father set high standards, but none so high as for himself. He was extremely honest and ethical, but not moralizing. I would often think of him during challenging times in my aviation career and would use him as an unseen "performance standard," and I was never wrong or lacking when I did. As an Air Traffic Controller I would reflect upon the high level he attained both as a flying instructor and pilot, and make sure I always held myself to that kind of technical standard. Finally, dad loved and was extremely protective and supportive of his family. As for myself, obviously, I am very proud of my father's service in the RCAF, both in wartime and peacetime. I am also very fortunate that in the relatively short time he was here with me I was (unknowingly) absorbing in some small measure some of the traits I find so admirable in him. He wasn't perfect, but he was a damn fine father.

"I think the Aero Legends team, with regards to Bruce and Elizabeth, can be proud of the attachments of their names and actions as they pertain to Spitfire NH341 – I know I am." Norm Whiteford.

CHAPTER THREE

CHARLIE TRAINOR

Hugh Charles Trainor, known as Charlie, was born in Charlottetown, Prince Edward Island, Canada on 17 July 1916. He was the son of a railway worker. Following school, Charlie attended St Dunstan's University, Charlottetown and after five years of study, he obtained a Bachelor of Arts degree. Following university, Charlie worked as a law student for a year before enlisting in the RCAF in Moncton, New Brunswick on 16 February 1940. Charlie Trainor was enrolled in No 1 Service Flying Training School (SFTS), Camp Borden, Ontario and attended this course between 17 June and 5 October 1940. On the same course as Charlie were Bob Hyndman and R M Stayner, pilots he would go on to share many experiences with at military flight training, and in combat with 411 Squadron.

At Charlie Trainor's graduation ceremony, Group Captain ATN Cowley, Officer Commanding spoke to the graduates and told them that they would be the sixth and last class to join the training course as pilot officers. From that point trainee pilots would join the RCAF as aircraftmen under the joint air training plan, formerly known as the Commonwealth Air Training Plan (BCATP). Captain Cowley said: "We knew you would be the last class, and so you were hand-picked. You are our choice, and anything you do will reflect to the credit or otherwise of the Royal Canadian Air Force."

Following the completion of this course, Charlie was retained as an instructor serving in several SFTS units from 1940 to 1942. After repeatedly badgering the top brass for an overseas posting he eventually sailed to Britain and arrived on 6 November 1942. The process of becoming a fully-fledged fighter pilot commenced in earnest for Charlie with a training course at No.17 Pilot Advanced Flying Unit (P) AFU from 17 November 1942 to 4 January 1943. Based at RAF Watton, Norfolk they flew the Miles M.9 Master, a two-seat monoplane used for advanced flying training. With a top speed of nearly 300 mph, manoeuverable and able to undertake full aerobatics, the Master was an ideal intermediate step for trainee pilots before they moved onto cutting edge fighters like the Hawker Hurricane and Supermarine Spitfire.

On 5 January 1943, Charlie joined No 57 Operational Training Unit (OTU) based at RAF Eshott, Northumberland where he progressed to flying the Spitfire, an aircraft in which he would achieve legendary status as a pilot and leader. Charlie's first posting to a fighter squadron was on 23 March 1943 to the RCAF's No 402 City of Winnipeg Squadron where he remained until 5 May 1943. The main role of this Spitfire squadron was bomber escorts and fighter sweeps over occupied Europe.

On 5 May 1943, Charlie was posted to 411 Grizzly Bear Squadron, the Roaring Boys, based at RAF Redhill, Surrey. His posting coincided with those of three others who would go on to fly Spitfire Elizabeth, Bruce, Len, and Tommy.

Charlie didn't have too long to wait for his first mission. On 17 May 1943, the Roaring Boys were tasked with a bomber escort mission, Circus 299, with 6 B-25 Mitchells that were attacking the German aerodrome at Caen. As Charlie looked out from his Spitfire his heart must have quickened at the sight of 22 Me 109s that came into view in the airfield area. Despite the contact, the Luftwaffe declined to engage the Spitfire formation and the mission was completed without loss.

It was important for new pilots to gain experience and learn the ropes as quickly as possible flying a variety of missions. On 19 May, Charlie teamed up with P/O RFM Walker for a two Spitfire early morning convoy patrol over the channel which was completed without any sighting of enemy aircraft.

With the Roaring Boys engaged in air to air firing exercises at RAF Martlesham Heath in early June, Charlie could take his time settling into squadron life. On 13 June at 18.40 pm he undertook his biggest mission to date which was an escort to 12 Ventura bombers attacking Caen aerodrome. It was his first taste of ground fire with 411. A stream of deadly flak was observed exploding in and around the formation at 13,000 feet over the aerodrome. His eyes searched the horizon for enemy fighters, hoping that his Spitfire Mark Vb would get through the barrage. The much-feared 88 mm artillery defences had found their range. As the Venturas released their bombs, good strikes were seen around the aerodrome and the Spitfires turned for home, relieved that all the aircraft had made it through safely.

At this stage of the war the Luftwaffe defeated had been defeated in its attempt to destroy the RAF and the planned invasion of Britain was cancelled. Patrols of UK air space were still undertaken as occasional hit and run raids on south coast towns were still being made by the enemy. Charlie could practice the discipline of formation flying and general operational procedures in the relatively peaceful skies of southern England.

On 17 June his early morning mission was a Circus bomber escort that saw him flying across the North Sea to Flushing, Vlissingen, in The Netherlands. His fellow SFTS trainee R M Stayner flew with him on that day. It's possible to watch Pathé News footage of similar raids to The Netherlands undertaken by RAF Venturas. The formation flying is skillful, incredible, and quite literally at zero feet, as the cameraman perched in the front of the Ventura pans out to show the rapidly approaching Dutch coastline. The low flying wasn't without hazards and in this mission, some of the returning Venturas were filmed with parts of their fuselage missing from collisions with telegraph wires and roofs of buildings. The objective for Charlie's raid was to attack the docks at Flushing, which was the headquarters of the German Kriegsmarine. As well as bombing this target, the presence of a force of Spitfires was intended to lure the Luftwaffe into aerial combat. The results of the bombing were not recorded, and the ORB reported that the Luftwaffe was not seen.

When Charlie landed back at RAF Redhill that day there were other distractions on offer in the form of the RAF Redhill sports day. This event underlines the surreal daily experience of a fighter pilot, flying on active service in the morning with an enemy who was trying to knock them out of the sky, followed in the afternoon by watching or taking part in sports day competitions.

On 22 June at 15.40 pm, Charlie climbed into his Spitfire fully briefed and ready for Circus 314, a squadron strength escort to 12 Venturas bombing the aerodrome at Abbeville. Linking up with the Venturas in perfect weather over the Channel the formation made landfall at Saint Valery sur Somme on the coast. The navigation to Abbeville was straight forward as the Canal Maritime d'Abbeville à Saint-Valery runs on a dead straight course from the coast to Abbeville. Light flak was experienced as the formation flew down the canal with the flak intensity increasing to heavy levels over the aerodrome. The bombs were dropped on the northeast corner of the airfield. Although no enemy aircraft were seen for Charlie and the Roaring Boys to engage with, the aerodrome flak batteries claimed one of the Venturas.

Charlie's last mission for the month was 29 June and it was to be a take-off at 20.00 pm in squadron strength escorting 84 Eighth Air Force B-17 Flying Fortresses on the withdrawal phase of Ramrod No 114 where they had been bombing targets at Le Mans aeroplane engine works. Meanwhile, in a huge display of air power 108 Fortresses were bombing Villacoublay's air depot, and 40 Fortresses attacked Tricqueville airfield. After orbiting the area in their Spitfires, the formation of Fortresses was spotted near Cabourg, and although light flak was sent up near Le Havre, described in the ORB as, "ineffective and inaccurate," the Roaring Boys escort successfully completed the mission with no losses or sign of the Luftwaffe. Two ME 109s and an FW 190 were claimed by USAAF P-47 Thunderbolts.

Charlie kicked off the month of July with formation flying drills as well as practice with the cine gun camera and a tail-chasing mock combat exercise. The Roaring Boys were polishing their skills for the time when they would be locked in mortal combat with the Luftwaffe, something Charlie and the others were eager to do. On 2 July the formation flying was put into practice for a more peaceful purpose, a distinguished visitor, the UK Secretary of State for Air The Right Honourable Sir Archibald Sinclair Bt KG CMG who watched a display.

When Charlie strapped himself into Spitfire BM355 on 6 July for a Rodeo mission he was all too aware that one of the Roaring Boys, F/O JR Spaetzel had been shot down and killed over Amiens 2 days before by a Me 109. As he opened the throttle and felt the power of the Rolls Royce Merlin engine surge through his aircraft thoughts of a fallen colleague were left behind. He had to stay concentrated on the job in hand. With wheels up and airspeed building, Charlie was settling into the formation and completing his instrument checks. All were operating and showing as normal. Then, suddenly and without warning his cockpit was filled with rushing air. The relative calm was shattered as his cockpit hood blew off and fell back towards the fields below. He had no choice but to call in the malfunction and turn back for the aerodrome, no doubt frustrated and with some questions for the waiting erks after executing a safe landing. Charlie was followed into land at RAF Redhill around an hour later by the rest of the squadron who had successfully completed their mission to the Gravelines and Saint-Omer areas.

Ramrod No 134 on 14 July saw Charlie and the Roaring Boys joined by 401 Squadron Spitfires flying escort to 18 Bostons which were attacking the aerodrome at Abbeville Drucat. After taking off at 08.10 am the first part of the mission was a rendezvous with the bombers over Rye, East Sussex, at 08.23 am. The formation then crossed the French coast 2 miles south of Le Touquet at 14,000 feet. The target at Abbeville was reached at 08.45 am and very accurate bombing was made on the dispersal areas to the east and northeast of the aerodrome. Turning for home Charlie looked out across the sky, anticipating any second a formation of approaching enemy fighters. At this stage, the Luftwaffe had withdrawn from the coastal areas of France. It was just too dangerous for them to operate with the presence of overwhelming numbers of Allied bomber and fighters ranging at will. After completion of the bombing, the formation crossed the French coast at Bayeux before beginning a slow descent towards Dungeness which was crossed at 4,000 feet. Landing back at base at 9.20 am Charlie and the Roaring Boys had completed their missions for the day.

Charlie would return to action on the evening of 16 July in Ramrod No 144 in which 16 Marauders were targeting the rail marshalling yards in Abbeville. All 3 squadrons of 126 Airfield were in action, led by Wing Commander Dal Russel DFC as they linked up with the bombers over Beachy Head. After crossing the channel, the formation made landfall on the French coast at the Somme estuary. Charlie was growing familiar with the landscape and landmarks of northern France below him and in the cockpit of his Spitfire, he gazed down on the Canal Maritime d'Abbeville à Saint-Valery stretching out towards the target in Abbeville. As the flak opened fire and was recorded as being, "accurate and at a medium level", the pilots hoped that one of the projectiles hurtling towards them didn't have their name on it. At around 5 miles south of Bayeux, 2 FW 190s broke away from a formation of around 15 to 20 aircraft in the area and made a long distance hit and run raid on 412 Squadron. The firing was ineffective, and the enemy aircraft offered no further resistance as they sped away. With the mission complete, the bombing results were not recorded but the formation returned to England without incident.

After a period of bad weather, on 28 July Charlie was once again ready for another Ramrod mission, this time to Zeebrugge, Belgium. Wing Commander Dal Russel led the Roaring Boys along with 412 Squadron, a formidable force of 24 Spitfires and more than a match for any Luftwaffe force that chose to engage them. After leaving Redhill a course was set to North Foreland, on the northeastern coast of Kent to link up with 18 Marauders at 12,000 feet. The formation then set course for the Zeebrugge, crossing the coastline at 11.45 am. Upon reaching the coke ovens and Benzol factory the bombers dropped their payload from 10,000 feet. As Charlie and the escort looked down flames and heavy smoke were seen from the target area. The return leg was completed successfully, and the Roaring Boys recorded wheels down at 12.00 pm.

There was little time for Charlie to settle down for a break as an urgent job cropped up. One of 411 Squadron's former pilots, now Squadron Leader Bob Wendell "Buck" McNair of 421 squadron had suffered an engine failure and had bailed out into the sea off the French coast. It later transpired that McNair had suffered the same fate as many others on two previous occasions with the Spitfire Mark IXa but had managed to crash land back in England. A fault, not yet rectified, was causing engine failures and in some cases claiming the lives of experienced pilots. On the third occasion, with his Spitfire on fire and suffering burns to his face Buck McNair bailed out and reportedly opened his parachute at around 2,000 feet. His eyes closed shut due to swelling from the burns and thinking he was close to the water he jettisoned his parachute to avoid being dragged underwater and drowned. In fact, he was still at around 300 feet and hit the sea extremely hard, suffering further injury. The Roaring Boys refuelled at Manston before flying to the area as quickly as possible where they relieved P/O Parks who was circling and had marked McNair's position. They circled the area as the ASR Walrus flew in to affect the rescue. Despite his injuries, he was thankful as he floated in the cold sea to hear those guardian angels circling above him. Buck McNair would now somewhat reluctantly become a member of both the Caterpillar and Goldfish Clubs.

The daily routine of Ramrods was now a feature of life for Charlie and his comrades. On the last day of July at 11.45 am RAF Redhill resonated to the sound of 24 Spitfire Vbs as 411 and 412 Squadrons readied themselves for their mission which was led by their leader Wing Commander Dal Russel DFC. Flying at zero feet to Beachy Head they linked up with 12 Mitchells which would be bombing the aerodrome at Saint-Omer. The channel crossing was used to gain altitude and the beehive crossed the coast at Hardelot before starting their attack run at 13.55 pm. The flak batteries began firing, sending their deadly welcome skywards towards the oncoming Spitfires and Mitchells. It was accurate and at medium intensity. This was a game of chance to which they were all equal players. The bombing from 10,000 feet was recorded as achieving good results. After the flak barrage at the aerodrome passed, a small number of Luftwaffe fighters appeared but, in all probability, having assessed the scale of the fighter escort decided did not offer any resistance. As the formation passed back over the French coast at Mardyck, the flak batteries there sent them home with a final "auf wiedersehen" barrage. Fortunately, the beehive returned to their home airfields with no losses.

With the unseasonal early August weather causing several Ramrods to be aborted, the weather improved and on 19th August Charlie started up his Spitfire and taxied out with Len and Bruce for a 3-squadron strength Ramrod 209. As was often the case, these ramrods contained multiple elements. The first phase comprised 36 Mitchells, escorted by 10 Spitfire and 9 Typhoon squadrons attacking Glisy airfield, near Amiens. Part 2 of the Ramrod attacked Poix aerodrome, with the final part of the operation seeing the Roaring Boys and 401 and 412 Squadrons escorting 12 Mitchells return and bomb Poix aerodrome again. The Wing picked up their 12 Mitchells at Rye, their 36 Spitfires flashing across the Kent and Sussex countryside at zero feet. As they set out across the channel four minutes later the beehive was cruising over the French coast at 11,500 feet. Enemy territory. The pilots and bomber crews felt a knot of tension in their stomachs. What reception would be awaiting them? Their concentration was heightened, and senses primed as the unwelcome sight of light flak homed in on the formation from batteries based in the Abbeville area. The Mitchells payload was delivered on the southern end of the aerodrome with one stick falling on the fields nearby. No flak or enemy aircraft were seen on the way back as they crossed the coast at Cayeux for a landing at RAF Staplehurst at 14.05 pm.

For Ramrod S.33 Charlie would be flying his Spitfire in escort to 72 Marauders bombing the rail marshalling yards at Ghent. The Roaring Boys followed a familiar route from Staplehurst to North Foreland, arriving at 12,000 feet to rendezvous with the bombers. From here, they crossed the Belgian coast at Blankenberg, near Zeebrugge. As the flak batteries began their barrage the formation headed towards the target and arrived there at 8.29 am where the bombing results were recorded as fair. The worrying sign for the beehive was the presence of 50 enemy fighters around the Ghent area but they made no attempt to attack, and the formation was able to recross the Belgium coast Nieuwpoort.

Then, suddenly for Charlie, his mission took an unexpected turn for the worst as his Rolls Merlin engine, the beating heart of his Spitfire misfired and seemed in imminent danger of cutting out. His mind was racing, and he could feel the adrenaline pumping as the potential implications of the next few minutes sunk in. Would he have to bail out and take his chance of being captured, with the prospect of spending the rest of the war in captivity? Or worse, if he attempted the crossing back to England and was then forced to bail out or, perhaps at too low an altitude for parachuting be forced to ditch into the sea, would he be rescued or face the prospect of being lost? At least S/L Semple was there to accompany him and if necessary, pinpoint his position for the ASR boys. With his engine still running, albeit roughly, he and S/L Semple made for England, Charlie had everything crossed that his Spitfire would keep running. He tried to stay calm and remember the training and procedures he had practiced countless times. With altitude in his favour there came a point where the two pilots knew he could, if necessary, glide his ailing aircraft back to land and make a dead stick landing in Kent. Fortune was on his side, as under the watchful gaze of S/L Semple they both made it back to Staplehurst. As Charlie shut down his aircraft, he breathed a big sigh of relief. He hoped that this would not be an experience he would have to repeat any time soon.

The daily routine of Ramrod operations moved on through September with Charlie gathering experience each day. By now he was no longer a rookie but was aware he had yet to face the ultimate test of air combat with the Luftwaffe. Charlie's mission on 14 September was Ramrod 218 to Lille-Nord aerodrome where the bombing would be carried out by 72 Marauders. The raid was planned as a diversion for B17s attacking several airfields including Paris, Rheims, and Romilly. All 3 squadrons of 126 Airfield took part, meeting the bombers at 12,000 feet over South Foreland. The formation crossed the French coast at Gravelines and turned back around 15 miles inland due to the weather. Very heavy flak came their way from the Dunkirk area to unsettle everyone and set their nerves jangling. The lack of air combat may have crossed the mind of all the Spitfire pilots as more than 100 enemy aircraft were seen in the area but declined to attack the formation.

On occasion, the Roaring Boys role included fighter sweeps over enemy territory in the hope of drawing the enemy into combat by their presence, or perhaps by German radar directing the Luftwaffe onto to the formation. Charlie and Bob undertook such a mission on 23 September at 14.45 pm when 411 took off in squadron strength for a sweep in support of Ramrod No 240. The patrol area included Lille-Nord and Merville, both locations of Luftwaffe airfields, the former of which would be bombed by RAF "Bomphoons" during this operation. The Luftwaffe decided to engage the bomber formation and 6 of their attacking fighters were shot down and several others damaged. For the Roaring Boys, it was not such good hunting and having completed their patrol with no enemy sighted, but with the inevitable flak batteries harassing them intensely at Saint-Omer, they returned to Staplehurst at 16.00 pm.

There was no let up by the Allies and their desire to keep up the pressure on the Luftwaffe. And so, with improved weather conditions over northern France, Charlie strapped himself into his Mark VB Spitfire BL780. It was 25 September at 16.45 pm and once again he taxied out to the runway with 11 other Spitfires all weaving from side to side. They looked and felt nothing like the graceful beauties they would turn into once airborne the rattling and bouncing around all looked inelegant. Once Charlie opened the throttle, he felt the reassuring thump of being pushed back into his seat as his Spitfire roared into life, followed as he left the ground by the low hum and mechanical whirr as his wheels came up. To any local observers who happened to be nearby, it would have looked as if the 12 Spitfires had magically appeared from underground as they suddenly roared above the treetops.

Charlie could see the green fields of the Weald of Kent in all their splendour stretching out before him. It was time to switch on his concentration, run through the instrument checks, oil pressure, temperature, altimeter, airspeed indicator, direction indicator. All were operating normally, so he could settle down to some formation flying as the Roaring Boys pointed their Spitfires to the south and climbed steadily towards 12,000 feet where they would meet up and position themselves next to 72 Marauders over Hastings. After the brief flight across the channel, the pilots became more vigilant of the surrounding sky. Would today be the day the Luftwaffe would choose to bounce them? As they crossed the coast at Hardelot they steered a course for Saint-Omer aerodrome where the flak batteries duly put up an intense and heavy barrage. The bombs were dropped and quickly disappeared like black arrows through the bank of clouds below as the beehives made for the coast and the relative safety of England. The results of the bombing were not observed due to the heavy cloud around the target area, but it was a successful mission with no losses and Charlie and Roaring Boys could consider it a job well done as their Spitfires dropped below the trees to the runway at Staplehurst.

For Charlie, his time with 411 had temporarily come to an end. In August he had been identified by the top brass as, "good flight commander material." On 22 September S/L Semple had described Charlie as, "a definite asset to our squadron." As a result, the wheels turned quickly and on 28 September he was posted to 43 Operational Training Unit for 83 Course as an instructor.

Charlie was posted back to 411 Squadron at Biggin Hill on 1 December 1943. He spent some time assimilating himself back into the daily life of the squadron, meeting up with fellow pilots, Bruce, Bob, Tommy, Len, Ross, and Gibby. The weather played its part in stopping Charlie returning to combat operations. On 20 December, he was back in a Spitfire with Tommy, Len, and Bob for Ramrod 374 which involved 211 Marauders, 60 Mitchells, 37 Bostons, 415 Spitfires, 155 Typhoons and 20 Hurricanes taking part in a raid on Bremen. For their part, the Roaring Boys were providing a diversionary fighter sweep over Rijen-Brussels and Eindhoven areas. From Biggin Hill the Roaring Boys joined 401 and 402 squadrons for a short flight to RAF Bradwell Bay in East Essex. Here they refuelled before setting off across the North Sea, making landfall ten miles northeast of Knokke, Belgium. Over Brussels, Roaring Boys pilots Blue 1 and Blue 2, F/O D J Givens and P/O L A Dunn shot down a Dornier Do217. The pilots bailed out and the aircraft crashed into the city below. Tommy saw the action and wrote later: "S/L Ormston pranged after takeoff! Blue 1 & 2 destroyed a Do 2017 over Brussels. I was going to have a go, but it was already out of control." Elsewhere in the Wing, L M Cameron of 401 Squadron shot down a Junkers Ju 88, but they paid a heavy price as the Ju 88 shot down P/O Buckles, and, whilst avoiding fire from the same aircraft, P/O Maybee and F/Sgt Morrisey collided with each other and with their Spitfires severely damaged they were forced to bail out. All 3 were captured by the Germans. The rest of the mission passed without incident and Charlie landed back at Biggin Hill at 12.10 pm. It had been an eventful first mission, and he was able to fit in one more, a fighter sweep on 23 December, before the Christmas festivities. There would be plenty of days like these during the momentous events of 1944.

Into the new year and Charlie's profile and prominence was growing within the squadron. On 3 January 1944 at 13.50 pm, he took part in a four Spitfire Ranger to Belgium, flying with his comrade and friend, Bruce. The flew on the deck due to the low cloud and climbed to 9,000 feet still in the cloud as they passed over the coast at Knokke. With no break in the conditions, they returned to Biggin Hill flying in the cloud for over 35 minutes.

With the commencement of the German vengeance weapon offensive, destruction of the launch sites was a priority for Charlie and Gibby flying on Ramrod No 456 on 14 January. Wrapped up against the cold the layers would have made the Spitfire cockpit a relatively tight fit as Charlie strapped himself in. The Roaring Boys would be joined by fellow No 126 Airfield squadron 401, The Rams. With wheels up at 15.00pm, the formation crossed the channel and made the French coast at Hardelot, joining up with 73 Marauders for which they would be providing umbrella cover. The ORB reported the Spitfires: "stooged around at 17 and 18,000 feet after bouncing a few Spitfires." It went on: "Squadron Leader L M Cameron DFC leading 401 got into 3 FW 190s and fired head on but was unable to close in on the others. Quite a few of the big boys were pranging different targets." Charlie and the others had an uneasy sense the Luftwaffe were about to bounce them and crash the party as unwelcome guests. Although enemy aircraft were seen at high altitude, they did not attack the beehive. The ORB further noted: "the Wing returned and landed at base safe and sound."

On 31 January Charlie was made A Flight Commander of 411 Squadron leading 2 sections each containing 3 Spitfires, while B flight would be headed up by F/L D J Givens. Charlie was soon in action with Ross on 3 February leading A Flight on Ramrod 505, one of 3 on that day targeting No Ball sites. The Roaring Boys were airborne at 12.30 pm and they crossed the French coast near Le Touquet. The Marauders sought out the No Ball launch sites which were hidden in the forested areas inland from Boulogne. Meanwhile, Charlie and the squadron patrolled above a blanket of cloud in an area from St Pol sur Mer, Dunkirk on the coast inland to Saint-Omer. As a result of the blanket of cloud, no enemy aircraft or flak was encountered. Charlie's mission of 13 February with

Ross and Len, Ramrod 550, followed a similar pattern to that of 3 February as a formation of 36 Marauders were escorted to No Ball targets in the Dieppe area, a mission that was completed successfully, albeit one section of Spitfires was assigned to escort a box of Marauders that had become separated from the main formation. Ross had his own thoughts on the success of the mission. He noted down in his logbook with reference to the Marauders, "Clueless. Only a few bombed."

At the end of February Charlie and A and B flights were sent on a week-long air firing course at RAF Peterhead, Scotland, designed to hone their skills in the offensive capabilities of the Spitfire. As A Flight Commander Charlie oversaw the party in more ways than one. With the boys sampling the delights of Edinburgh's nightlife, the ORB reported with a sense of foreboding on the evening's shenanigans: "here's hoping they all catch the train for London tomorrow." All did, and no embarrassing incidents came to light!

On 6 March, Charlie and Len fired their Spitfire Mark IXs and taxied out across Biggin Hill, lifting off at 11.55 am for a wing strength bomber escort, Ramrod No 630. The beehive containing 108 Marauders made this a large-scale operation and amongst the targets were the rail marshalling yards at Creil, located to the northeast of Paris. For reasons not explained in the ORB, but possibly due to the main target being obscured, the bombers dropped their payloads on the aerodrome at Creil, which was a secondary target before returning with their escort to England. Charlie landed back at Biggin Hill at 14.00 pm.

For Ramrod 655 on 15 March, Charlie led A flight, with Ross, and Bob as they joined all of 126 and 127 Airfields. The 6 squadrons provided close escort to 72 Marauders bombing the marshalling yards at Aulnoye-Aymeries which is in northern France, near the Belgium border. Looking at this area on a map its strategic importance is not immediately obvious but back in 1944 it was a major junction for railway connections between Paris, Brussels, Calais, Lille, and Thionville and therefore it's destruction could hamper enemy movements of troops and supplies back and forth from the east towards Germany. On this mission, the Roaring Boys comrades in 401 Squadron spotted the opportunity to attack 12 FW 190s of 7 Staffel JG 26 which were lazily circling Epinoy aerodrome near Cambrai, which lies to the west of Aulnoye-Aymeries. They dived down to attack and caught the enemy napping. It was the first time for a while that the Luftwaffe had been seen by the Canadian Spitfires and the Rams weren't about to waste this opportunity. With 4 FW 190s hitting the ground in quick succession F/O D D Ashleigh and F/L A F Halcrow spotted a Me 410 on the runway and braving the incoming flak barrage strafed the aircraft, recording it as damaged before escaping. Only P/O R J F Sherk crash-landed near Achiet after being hit by FW 190 cannon fire. He successfully evaded capture and eventually returned to his squadron. The 411 ORB recorded, "very good show boys" albeit Charlie and the others were no doubt wishing they had been able to mix it up in such a target-rich environment. With senses heightened and anticipation in the air, Charlie might have expected the Luftwaffe to put in another appearance, but after the mauling they received at Cambrai the formation continued past Dunkirk with what the ORB described as, "no further excitement." The Roaring Boys were back on the ground at Biggin Hill at 12.10 pm. It had been a busy 2 hours 10-minute mission, but aside from Sherk, they had all returned unscathed.

Despite the weather in early April 1944, stopping several operations, the Roaring Boys kept up their nonflying activities with games of volleyball. Physical fitness and mental welfare were important, and volleyball helped, along with the obvious eye-hand coordination. S/L Semple found out that it also had its dangers as he was crocked after tangling with Tommy in one lively game. Charlie's A flight seemed to be the dominant force as the ORB of 9th April described: "A Flight as usual trounced B Flighters in four games of volleyball." Charlie was very much involved as I have picked him out in a photograph of a game during his time at Staplehurst.

As 411 Squadron busied itself for the move to RAF Tangmere, there was no letup in the pressure on the enemy. On 13 April Charlie led A Flight on Ramrod 730 with Len, Bob, Dave, and Gibby. Happily asleep, Charlie and the squadron were awoken at 5.30 am and sent down to the Intelligence area at 5.50 am. They were briefed that a force of Marauders was going to bomb Namur marshalling yards. From a high-altitude reconnaissance photo taken of a mission in the following month by the Eighth Air Force, it's possible to see the scale of the complex with its curved spaghetti of railway lines snaking around a large storage area of rolling stock. The before and after photos show that the Mighty Eighth gave it a good pasting. Namur was of importance as a transportation hub because the rail lines ran to Brussels but also to the northeast and into Germany.

At 08.25 am, and perhaps with some grumbling as there was no time for breakfast, the Roaring Boys were soon airborne for the short hop to RAF Manston where they would land, refuel their Spitfires and themselves with a hearty breakfast. After this short interlude, they were soon airborne and immediately heading out to sea. The choppy grey waters below looked uninviting on that day. As an illustration of the dangers, on the same day as Charlie's mission, Group Captain P L Donkin DSO Commanding Officer of 35 (Recce) Wing was hit by flak in his Mustang near Ostend, and was forced to bail out into the sea where he spent the next 6 days and 5 nights before being picked by a Royal Navy minesweeper, just as all hope was fading. After a month's recuperation, he was back in command. Meanwhile, as Charlie and the formation made landfall the Marauders bombing run was made without ground or air interference by the Germans and the squadron recorded wheels down at 10.35 am.

The mission of 13 April was to be Charlie's last for the time being. He was posted to an Officers Training course and would rejoin the Roaring Boys on 11 May. With D Day looming large it was vital for a mobile fighting wing to have strength in depth when it came to leadership, and Charlie was certainly being fast-tracked for this role.

When Charlie returned from his training course, there was little time for him to adjust. On 12 May, he was on the roster to fly with Len and Bruce on a dive bombing mission, which was to become a regular feature of the Roaring Boys offensive operations. Charlie's mission commenced from RAF Tangmere at 15.15 pm and involved the bombing of a No Ball target south of Le Treport, which is situated on the French coast around 10 miles northeast of Dieppe. The bombs that were dropped weren't all designed to detonate on impact. In fact, on this mission the ORB details that nine bombs had a 15-minute delay fuse whilst one 500 lb bomb was timed to explode after 12 hours, catching repair and launch crews who might be back on site attending to the damage. The target area was heavily defended so whilst Charlie was concentrating on lining his Spitfire up on its steep dive from around 12,000 feet, he had to try not to focus on the flak which was described as intense and heavy in the area but light over the actual target. The effectiveness of the bombing was hampered by the hazy conditions which extended up to 8,000 feet. Despite this, 9 hits were recorded in the target area. After a dash back across the channel, the Roaring Boys touched down at Tangmere at 16.40 pm with no losses or damaged recorded.

On 28 May Charlie, Bob, Len, and Gibby were once again engaged in dive bombing a V1 doodlebug site at Arques La Bataille which is a couple of miles south of Dieppe. Of the eleven 500 lb bombs that were dropped, 2 were seen to burst to the northeast of the target. A building near the railway lines exploded, whilst on the return leg west of Greges, located to the east of Dieppe, the Roaring Boys identified a target of opportunity in the form of an army hut which despite the heavy flak they peppered with machine gun fire. Only light flak was thrown up around the target area, and all the Spitfires returned to Tangmere completing their 1-hour mission with wheels down at 16.30 pm.

The tension was palpable as the "big show" was drawing ever closer. Everyone knew it, and no one could speak about it outside of the base. In the run-up to D Day, 411 Squadron was a hive of activity as pilots prepared themselves and their ground crews, the erks, readied their assigned aircraft, the Mark IX Spitfires for the challenge ahead. On Charlie's mind would have been what these coming days held for him and his fellow pilots. Lives were on the line. Would they finally get to grip with the elusive Luftwaffe, or would it be a cakewalk? Each pilot dealt with the growing tension in their own way, perhaps playing cards, reading, writing letters home, or tentatively taking to the popular volleyball court. No one wanted to be crocked for the show on 6 June. Charlie's preparations involved a Ramrod on 2 June which is described in Tommy chapter.

As D Day dawned, Charlie got himself dressed and ready, checking his kit including his parachute, mae west, pistol, and escape kit. This was it. The first waves of troops were already ashore on the beaches, into the mayhem of spitting bullets and deadly fizzing shrapnel. For as far as the eye could see the sea presented a panorama of ships stretching from Normandy in an almost unbroken line back to England. Soon enough, Charlie and the Roaring Boys would view that sight for themselves and form their own unique memories. With his pre-flight checks done and the Rolls Royce Merlin engine on his Spitfire MJ125 warming up nicely he taxied out and readied himself. The familiar power and noise grew as he wound up the throttle and felt his wheels leave the grass of Tangmere at 08.10 am. The Spitfire, no longer rattling along but slipping through the air with ease as the formation of 12 gained height and turned south for France.

As Charlie and Len surveyed the spectacle beneath them, they were all too aware of their role, top cover fighter protection, which meant methodically scanning the horizon for any signs of enemy aircraft. The patrol sweep started over the British sector at Gold beach before they flew east, passing over their fellow Canadian countrymen on Juno beach. The final part of the patrol line was completed over the easternmost sector, sweeping over the British who were ashore at Sword beach. With the air space choked with aircraft, it was no place for the squadron to hang around for too long and with their sweeps completed they turned north for England, landing at 10.00 am to debrief and chat about what they had witnessed. Charlie had the rest of the day to ready himself, watching successive patrols of the Roaring Boys heading off and returning to Normandy before he repeated his early day patrol with the same sweep at 18.10 pm.

The Roaring Boys were to be disappointed. The Luftwaffe was conspicuous by its absence. Charlie's time to test himself and his mighty Spitfire would soon come against the best the Nazi war machine had to offer. On D Day + 2, at 13.10 pm Charlie was once again on a 1 hour 50-minute fighter sweep over the beachhead which was completed without incident. I mentioned before that these patrol sound routine, and in some sense they were, but the danger was ever present. Aside from the enemy fighters and flak, there were dozens of nervous, young gunners on Allied destroyers who, just for a second, might mistake a Spitfire for a Me 109, get a rush of blood, before opening fire and sending the pilot crashing to his doom. The Roaring Boys had to block out any such thoughts and not dwell on things they couldn't control.

The pattern of daily patrols continued into June. On one patrol on 12 June at 08.05 am Charlie was teamed up with Len, Gibby Gibson, and Bob. They returned at 09.55 am with nothing to report. The umbrella of air cover was total and proving highly effective.

Spitfire NH341 Elizabeth
Charlie's first flight in Spitfire Elizabeth was on 17 June. The routine of beachhead patrols was unending he must have thought as he stepped up onto Elizabeth's wing and settled down into the cockpit. At 13.35 pm as Charlie's eased the stick back, Spitfire Elizabeth sprung up from B4 Bény-sur-Mer's runway and climbed into the Normandy sky. He was in the company of fellow Elizabeth pilots, Len, Dave, and Ross, all unaware 75 years on how they would be connected with this aircraft. Charlie quickly got the feel of Elizabeth and he may have noticed some difference

about her. She was a newer factory fresh model somewhat unlike the other Mark IXs he was flying. The paintwork was clean, unchipped and not worn away by a succession of pilots and crew sliding off her wing. The dull brown oil trail from the exhaust manifolds had yet to blemish the sides of the fuselage. Perhaps the rudder pedals were a little stiffer and she seemed a touch quicker through the air, albeit the engine had a discernibly different, newer tone. He would become very familiar with Spitfire Elizabeth, and she would play a part in cementing his status as an ace and much respected fighter pilot. Jimmy Jeffrey's son Lawrie said his father had told him: "the younger pilots really looked up to Charlie Trainor."

Having returned to the B4 base from his beachhead patrol with wheels down at 15.30 pm, Charlie was debriefed before he returned to readiness, perhaps walking away with an admiring glance backward at NH341. He was rostered to be on a beachhead patrol which was scheduled to takeoff at 21.00 pm. He would once again be at the controls of Spitfire Elizabeth and after completion of the mission, he and the squadron would return as normal to RAF Tangmere for the night, touching down at 22.55 pm. Little did Charlie know as he settled down for a night's sleep, that on the 18 June the Roaring Boys would get the order to pack up ready for a permanent move to Normandy, France.

The settling in process had to be swift. As 411 Squadron was part of a mobile fighter wing, the planning and procedures were designed to allow for a short, sharp breakdown, with readiness to move at very short notice. The redeployment to a newly liberated aerodrome or ALG would depend to a large extent to how quickly the Allied Armies advanced forward and broke out of the bridgehead. For the time being the Germans were providing fierce resistance, so for Charlie B4 was going to be home for the foreseeable future. On the 18 June, he readied himself for his 14.55 pm patrol from Tangmere, comprising 6 Spitfires and which would include, Tommy, Len, and Gibby. This was to be Charlie's third combat patrol in Spitfire Elizabeth, which had been flown earlier in the day by Ross.

For Charlie, like all the others, B4 was a noisy, hectic place that left everyone with a sense of unease about how the situation would develop. The distant noise of battle was constant throughout the day and night and was coupled with scant news to back up the fevered speculation about the progress of the advance. Like the others, Charlie dug his so-called "funk hole" to escape the metal and bullet showers raining down in the area.

Charlie, Gibby, and Bruce undertook a squadron strength armed reconnaissance around Caen on 25 June at 08.00 am. These operations were typically undertaken at around 1,000 feet. As the squadron lifted off from the flat fields of B4 they set a course of 180 degrees on their direction indicators, due south towards Caen. Within 15 minutes, F/L Nixon returned to base with mechanical problems. There were plenty of enemy transports moving up and back from the front lines. It did not take long for Charlie's R/T to pick up a crackle of activity. The voice calmly fixed the position of several targets ahead. Tally ho, the Roaring Boys were going into action. Charlie readied himself, his gun button was switched to fire, straps tightened, gauges showing normal operating temperatures. His heartbeat quickened as he lined up his Mark IX Spitfire on the convoy of 21 vehicles. His whole aircraft reverberated from the recoil of his 20 mm Hispano cannons and machine guns that spewed a cascade of rounds which seemed to almost stop the aircraft in its tracks. In an instant, the ground ahead erupted in smoke, flames, and dust. Those in the vehicles who could dived for whatever cover they could find. The destruction was wholesale, as each Spitfire blasted the trucks and tanks spreading the smoke and flames amongst the convoy. As the pilots tallied up the carnage below the ORB reported: "6 flamers, 8 smokers, and 7 damaged. 2 tanks were also damaged. Concentration of armoured vehicles spotted in woods south of Caen." A significant result from a 1 hour and 15-minute mission, which was also being repeated along the battlefront by the British and Americans. As the 11 Spitfires touched down at B4 and debriefed, the pilots compared notes and talked excitedly about how they had fared. It felt good to get to grips with the enemy and contribute. And there was the added bonus that they had all made it back to base.

Around this time in June, the Luftwaffe were making their presence felt in the Roaring Boys sector and on 28 June they would pay a heavy price when they engaged with the fearsome Canucks. This was to be Charlie's time and he was heading very much to the fore of an extraordinary series of actions. He was soon into action as at 12.25 pm as he, Tommy, Gibby, Bruce (at the controls of Spitfire Elizabeth), Len, Bob, and 6 others lifted their Spitfires into the air for a squadron strength armed reconnaissance of the area south of Caen. On the ground, the attack resulted in damage to enemy transports which were recorded as, "3 flamers and 4 damaged." At some point in the mission, Blue 2 of the Roaring Boys reported bandits south of Le Havre and each pilot snapped to a heightened sense of anticipation as the information was relayed via their R/T. In an instant, as the battle was joined the 4 sections of Spitfires split left and right, The fight was on. The ORB detailed that the attackers were: "more than 15 Me 109s and FW 190s which were engaged south of Le Havre."

Charlie's own words in the official 411 records take up the action 20 miles south of Le Havre. These words don't come anywhere near to portraying the combat that was unfolding around him. One can only imagine the combination of stress, excitement, and fear he felt:

"I was Yellow 1 in 411 Squadron on patrol SOUTH and EAST of CAEN. Approximately 15 German fighters were sighted south of CABOURG, travelling EAST. I singled out a FW 190 and chased him through cloud but I had to brake off chase when fired on by two ME 109s behind me. I broke starboard then back port behind latter pair. Tried half second burst on one from astern at 300 yards, he was taking evasive action and no hits observed, closed to 200 yards and tried a 1 to 2 second burst. Numerous hits observed and many large pieces flew on E/A. He spun down and hit the ground. Had to return here on account of petrol shortage, without attacking other aircraft.

I claim 1 ME 109 destroyed. (An additional note was added, probably by the 126 Wing Senior Intelligence Officer Monty Berger: "Cine gun used."). The signature of another member of the Intelligence/operations section P/O Gord Panchuk is shown on behalf of Berger.

(HC Trainor) Flight Lieutenant 411 (R.C.A.F) Squadron"

This was a mission of 'firsts' for Charlie. It was his first air victory, or "kill" as it was universally known at the time. He also had the alarming experience of peeling away from his initial attack on the FW 190 as silver streaks tore past his own cockpit from the pair of Me 109s on his tail, one of which would not survive the encounter. He would have an excited ground crew waiting for news with the typical inquiry, "Any luck sir?" Other pilots also enjoyed success, including Tommy which is described in his chapter. F/L Hayward also damaged one of the attacking FW 190s.

At 19.20 pm Charlie was airborne for his third mission of the day in a 7 Spitfire patrol south of Caen. Fellow pilots Dave and Ross joined him. At 20.00 pm as they patrolled at 9,000 feet to the west of Caen 10 to 15 FW 190s were seen flying at 6,000 feet and engaged. The sky soon became a mass of aircraft, turning, tumbling, climbing and diving as each side sought a target, or to shake off a pursuer. The Roaring Boys soon had the advantage as F/L Hayward shot down two FW 190s. I have watched the gun camera footage of Hayward's attack and he was able to close in on one of the FW 190s which tries in vain to evade his approaching Spitfire. The FW 190 soon flick rolled, trailing smoke and heading earthward in a steep dive.

Meanwhile, Charlie and F/L Johnson were engaged in their own battle. Charlie was initially in peril as one of the FW 190s locked onto his "6." He described the action in a handwritten record in the 411 Squadron records: "I was flying Yellow 1 in 411 Squadron. We were flying north east when we sighted a flock of 190s and 109s coming towards us flying south. I half rolled to attack one pair and was doing a very tight turn to port when I was hit in the tail." The rounds fired by the 190 hit the tail wheel and rear fuselage of Charlie's Spitfire as he observed, "at 45 degrees deflection." Having shaken off his attacker he had regrouped and was alert to his offensive and defensive position. As Battle of Britain pilot Geoffrey Wellum DFC remarked during one of my meetings with him: "never fly straight and level in the combat area for more than 30 seconds." Charlie flicked his head behind him routinely. He wasn't about to allow another enemy aircraft to fix a beam. He takes up the story of his next action which took place 2 miles northeast of Lisieux:

"I spotted a single FW 190 who was just entering cloud at 4,000 feet. I chased him through cloud and lined up my sights on him in brief glimpses. I fired twice, from 800 yards and 600 hundred yards astern in a chase 20 miles eastward. At the end of the second burst, although I had not seen strikes through the cloud, I flew through a lot of debris. About 30 seconds later I emerged from cloud completely and there was no A/C in sight. I did complete orbits and observed an aircraft burning fiercely on the ground below. Because of the additional intelligence information hereunder, I claim this FW 190 as destroyed."

The additional intelligence was the fact that 411 suffered no casualties in the engagement and it was established that no other aircraft were operating in the area just northeast of Lisieux at the time of Charlie's combat. The conclusion of 126 Wing was that this was the FW 190 shot down by Charlie and he was duly credited with the victory.

F/L Givens was credited with damaging another FW 190 and his gun camera footage shows deflection shots at 400 to 500 yards distance as the FW 190 climbs in front of his Spitfire. The FW 190 is then seen disappearing into the cloud. The Luftwaffe had met their match and came off much the worse in this encounter. The 28 June was the most successful day in 411 Squadron's history with 6 enemy aircraft destroyed and 3 damaged, with no losses.

Spitfire NH341 Elizabeth
The Roaring Boys were full of anticipation as the previous few days showed the Luftwaffe was very much in their sector, so every patrol took off with the expectation of engaging in air combat. Albeit, there was also fear too, no doubt. At 15.30 pm, the eight Spitfires lifted off from B4 with Charlie at the controls of Spitfire Elizabeth. Within 10 minutes F/S Le Blanc had returned to base with a technical problem. As they patrolled and moved on to the front line around Caen they spotted and attacked two mechanised transports which were strafed by 20 mm cannon fire and left damaged. Watching gun camera footage of the attack by F/Os Hogg and Eskow a truck can be seen moving slowly along a single-track country lane with an orchard on either side. As Hogg's Spitfire lets loose its cannons the rounds start hitting the ground behind the truck, which is clearly unaware of the impending danger as it takes no evasive action. The round strikes slam into the defenceless vehicle which is enveloped in a cloud of smoke and dust.

The formation was right to be alert and ready for action in the air because as they turned for the return leg and climbed to 6,000 feet bandits appeared at 7,000 feet flying in the opposite direction. Charlie takes up the story in his official account of the action: "I was leading 411 sqn on a front-line patrol and was returning with 5 aircraft 5 miles east of Caen. About 15 109s came out of cloud at 11 o'clock above us. When they passed over us, I broke squadron port and got on the tail of one."

Whilst referring to Ross's logbook I checked his entry for this mission. Clearly, the 109s spotted the incoming attack. Ross wrote: "15 Me 109s came at us. One fired at me – missed."

Charlie locked onto Ross's attacker: "I fired a short burst about 150 yards from astern. Many strikes, pieces flying off including whole tail unit. Later fired on another but no strikes observed before he entered cloud. I claim 1 Me 109 destroyed."

This was Spitfire Elizabeth's first victory over enemy aircraft. Watching the gun camera footage it's possible to see a large piece fly off the 109, which Charlie reported was the tailplane, but from observation, it could also have been the engine canopy. After many replays, it's hard to conclude either way but Charlie saw it first hand and as the gun camera stopped filming, he would have had a clear view. Either way, as glycol and smoke are emitted from the 109 its trajectory becomes a steep dive towards the ground. This footage makes it conclusive as a combat victory. You can see a still frame from Charlie's actual gun camera footage of the Me 109 trailing smoke in the photo section.

To corroborate Charlie's claim, other pilots who witnessed the combat submitted their evidence. F/O R W Hogg wrote: "Shortly after the combat, I saw a parachute at 2-3,000 feet apparently from E/A attacked by F/Lt Trainor." Ross added in his logbook about his Me 109 attacker: "F/L Trainor shot him down. We chased some more. Trainor fired again. Saw no results." The ORB documented that: "our pilots broke off the engagement due to our ammunition being expended." This was Charlie's second combat victory, on consecutive days and as he touched down at B4 at 16.45 pm it's not difficult to imagine the erks showering him with praise. His fellow Roaring Boys stepped down from their Spitfires and greeted Charlie with much back-slapping, laughter, and congratulations. All the training and practice had paid off. Perhaps, Charlie allowed himself a moment of contemplation and his mind may have gone back to his graduation ceremony in Canada four years earlier. Captain Cowley said: "You are our choice, and anything you do will reflect to the credit or otherwise of the Royal Canadian Air Force." Charlie was now fulfilling the leadership and potential identified in him early on in his RCAF career.

On 30 June Charlie stepped up onto Spitfire Elizabeth's wing once again, perhaps thinking she was a lucky charm for him. The aircraft had done everything he had wanted it to do the day before and now with another front-line patrol planned he was eager to add to his tally. At 20.30 pm he pushed the throttle forward on Spitfire Elizabeth, lifting up into the Normandy sky. Amongst the 12 Spitfires who quickly formed up into their patrol formation at 7,000 feet were others who had or would soon occupy the cockpit of this Spitfire; Dave, Jimmy, and Ross.

Suddenly, there was the simultaneous crackle in the headphones of each pilot as they flew near Thury-Harcourt, around 10 miles southwest of Caen. Charlie spoke, "Bandits ahead. Tally ho Yellow section!" Charlie was soon turning onto the tail of the enemy aircraft, his left hand pushed Spitfire Elizabeth's throttle to its limit and the Rolls Merlin reacted instantly to his command with a throaty roar, pushing Charlie back in his seat as he closed on the Me 109, without thinking flicking his gun button to fire. He later reported on the combat that followed:

"I was flying Yellow 1 in 411 Squadron and flying East over Thury Harcourt when an Me 109 dived in front of us going South East. Gave chase, overtaking him as he turned port. Fired at burst at 30 degrees deflection from about 300 yards and saw strikes. He slowed up his turn and I gave him another couple of bursts at 10 degrees as I closed from 200 to 190 yards. Many strikes and lots of stuff falling off. E/A dived down and hit the ground. Pilot baled out.

I claim 1 Me 109 destroyed."

Charlie's written account also included the following additional statement: "This claim is confirmed by members of the squadron who saw the pilot bail out and the A/C crash in flames." Charlie Trainor, the "whizz" from Prince Edward Island as the Canadian press called him, was on an incredible run and his name was the one on everyone's lips around the squadron and across the wider 126 Wing.

The month had hardly lived up to its reputation as "flaming June." Nothing was changing as July came along. Flying on the first day of the month was restricted due to rain but some patrols were managed. At lunchtime the weather was flyable as Charlie, Tommy, Bob, Ross, and Gibby joined 6 fellow Roaring Boys on an armed reconnaissance. They were expectant as their Spitfires gunned down B4's runway and into the air. There was a very good chance of encountering the enemy, and the prospect of combat was exciting but also fear-inducing. Each pilot hoped he would perform well and not let his mates down. The mission was to cover an area encompassing Bernay, Alers, Villers Bocage, Condé, and Thury-Harcourt. Suddenly, 12 Me 109s came into view orbiting Caen and battle was joined. Charlie locked onto the tail of a 109 and watched intently as cannon and machine gun fire from his Spitfire ripped into the fuselage of the enemy aircraft. The 411 ORB observed: "The squadron started the month in good style when F/L Trainor destroyed a Me 109 and S/L G D Robertson and F/L R K Hayward scored one damaged each."

Other accounts of the time suggest that Charlie's victory was a "probably destroyed" versus a destroyed, as corroborated by Charlie and witnesses. Ross, who was on the mission, recorded in his logbook: "S/L Robertson destroyed an FW 190 in the afternoon. F/L Trainor destroyed an Me 109 – his 4th in 3 days." Meanwhile, Tommy wrote: "Ran into 8 Me 109s south of Caen. I chased one lost him in cloud. Charlie Trainor got an Me 109 his 5th in 4 days. CHEERS!" After landing, the potent force that was Charlie Trainor was given a hero's welcome. One can imagine the buzz as he taxied back in at 14.30 pm. Had he scored again? Did anyone else "bag one?" This was the Roaring Boys doing what all those months of training and drills had prepared them for. A mobile fighting unit taking it to the Germans and giving them a bloody nose. The almost routine ramrod missions and sweeps seemed a long time ago now.

For Charlie, a late afternoon patrol of 4 Spitfires he was leading was recalled due to bad weather. He did manage an evening front line patrol on 3 July with Tommy and Ross which was described as "uneventful." Ross wrote in his logbook that during the patrol they had observed a squadron of P51 Mustangs dive bombing ground targets. Tommy wrote, "Turfed around. No joy at all. No huns." No doubt the evening festivities at B4 were welcomed with particular relish as a steak and wine dinner had been laid on by the squadron: "as a real treat after so long a period of iron rations. The scarcity of speeches showed that the boys are quite an experienced group of after-dinner drinkers."

With the dawn of the 4th July came a significant improvement in the weather and offensive operations. The patrols and armed reconnaissance missions could be lined up and men and machines would be pushed to the limit of their endurance. The planners were keen to keep pilots like Charlie, who was on a "hot streak" in the air. His confidence, as well as those around him, was high. The Roaring Boys believed they were the best and the Spitfire was "the thing to fly" as Tommy once remarked. After his morning patrol, described in Tommy's chapter, Charlie rested up. He knew he was rostered to undertake a front-line patrol at 18.00 pm with, Bob, Gibby, Len, Bruce, Dave, and 6 other Roaring Boys. There was a good chance he could add to his tally and push well beyond the mark of "Ace" status which was set at 5 air combat victories.

As the Roaring Boys lifted off at 18.00 pm, they set course for a patrol of the productive area around Caen. Within 15 minutes Dave would return to B4 with mechanical issues. Whilst flying to the southeast of the city, within a few minutes the squadron came across several Me 109 and FW 190 bandits from 5 Staffel Jagdgeschwader 2 "Richthofen." They were engaged at between 6,000 and 9,000 feet and the Roaring Boys broke and scattered. Charlie got set in Spitfire MJ944 to engage. He managed to get onto the tail of 2 Me 109s both of which he despatched with clinical efficiency. The pilots of the 109s were Feldwebel Gustav Sens and Gefreiter Richard Koberger. Tommy summed up Charlie's effectiveness as a fighter pilot in his logbook, "Brother pin a gong on him!" Tommy also wrote about his friends Bob and Bruce saying: "Bob Hyndman and Bruce Whiteford got a damaged on 2 Me 109s. What a go!" F/L R K Hayward helped himself to an FW 190, which was destroyed along with another and a Me 109 both of which he damaged. On this day both Charlie and Hayward became "aces," and would go on to distinguish themselves as leaders and fighter pilots. Bob Hayward later became squadron leader of 411 and the squadron's only commanding officer who received both the DSO and DFC.

The Roaring Boys had been splintered into their own air battles and as a result, there were a number of Spitfires returning to B4 at staggered times. They also had to endure heavy and intense flak on the outward and return legs around Caen. By 19.05 pm all had touched down and were soon animatedly discussing the action.

The 4 July was not yet done for the Roaring Boys. Their stamina and determination are to be admired. Although in their early 20's, flying missions was intense, pressurised and required long periods of extreme concentration with no "switching off." As the Battle of Britain progressed there are numerous photos of the pilots taking the opportunity to rest and catch up on their sleep whilst fully clothed and ready to scramble. The Roaring Boys were rattling through their allotted tour time as fighter pilots which would mean a succession of new pilots being drafted in to replace them as they completed their 200 hours of combat operations. A full fourteen hours after his early morning mission, Charlie once again readied himself with his wingman Ross. At 22.00 pm the squadron lifted off into the fading light for a patrol of the frontline. They were soon vectored by control onto a potential bogey near Falaise. As they raced to intercept, they came across a Do 217 which was flying from Lisieux area, crossing the French coast two miles northeast of Cabourg. Both Charlie and S/L G D Robertson set about its destruction sharing the claim. The Dornier exploded in the air crashing to the ground near B4, a sight witnessed by 411's personnel. At 22.45 pm the squadron touched down. The day had concluded with more success and two new aces were now to be found amongst the Roaring Boys roster of pilots.

After his exploits the day before, the higher command afford Charlie a late start on 5 July. It was important to keep him flying. He was respected and filled the other pilots with confidence. He led a 4 Spitfire patrol at 10.25 am which returned without incident with wheels down at 11.40 am.

Charlie's mission 7 July was led by S/L Robertson and would be an armed reconnaissance mission around the Caen area. The squadron came across 8 to 10 FW 190s which were engaged. On this occasion F/L G W Johnnie Johnson managed to shoot down one, the third of his 8 air victories whilst F/L H J Nixon damaged another. With so much activity around the battlefront of Caen, the pilots also had their eyes on the ground for any transport movements and soon they strafed a mechanised transport and left it in flames. By 17.40 pm they had touched down. Charlie's flying was finished for the day. If he was expecting a quiet evening, he was to be disappointed as 700 Lancasters pounded the city of Caen. The ground at B4 was literally shaking and on the horizon, the assembled personnel looked southeast towards the glow and the growing tower of smoke curling high into the atmosphere.

On 10 July, Charlie was up with the larks for a dawn armed reconnaissance mission, joined by Ross and 10 other Roaring Boys. He settled into the cockpit of his Spitfire and felt the chill of the Normandy air wash over him as NH174 kicked into life with a few gentle puffs of smoke. He felt the vibrations through his feet resting on the rudder pedals as he taxied out and took off at 05.45 am. He mapped out in his mind the route for this early morning mission. The reconnaissance would take in a patrol area covering Cabourg, Lisieux, Falaise, and Caen, where the land battle still raged below. The formation moved steadily around their patrol area and identified a few scattered German vehicles which were attacked. There were enemy aircraft in the area as Ross recorded in his log, "chased 1 bogey" but no claims were made. The Spitfires arrived back at B4 with wheels down in time for breakfast at 06.50 am. The squadron ORB gave the score: "one flamer and three damaged were scored. Five plus 3-tonners were attacked on the road into Dosule from the east. Results were not observed." As I frequently found during my research, the 411 Squadron diarist often used the literal pronunciation of towns and villages when typing up the ORB. In fact, the location of the 3 tonners was Dozulé which is approximately 2 miles south of the coastal town Cabourg.

At this time the tactics for armed reconnaissance required that squadrons be broken down into patrols containing a single section of 4 Spitfires. On 11 July at 13.55 pm and 15.55 pm, Charlie led patrols with flying times ranging from around 1 hour to 1 hour 15 minutes. Throughout the day from early on at each hour, sections would be taking off and landing for across multiple wings, a nightmare of coordination for the flight planners. It was also noticeable that to beef up the effectiveness of these patrols 2 of the Spitfires would carry bombs, effectively increasing the firepower available to deploy on any targets along the German lines of communication. It was also anticipated that the practicing of bombing, as well as strafing, would be of strategic value once the break out from Caen was actioned and the front moved east and became more fluid. At the time it was also common practice for returning aircraft not to return to land with any bombs on board. The interruption to the normal operations of the fighting wings by the accidental detonation of a 500-pounder is obvious.

With the new modus operandi in place, on 12 July Charlie strapped into Spitfire MK423 for a bombing and armed reconnaissance mission. As frequently was the case, he had Ross alongside him. Soon after leaving B4 they were passing through the cloud before emerging and settling down at around 5,000 feet. It was going to be impossible to reconnoiter anything from here, albeit the sun warmed the cockpit of each Spitfire and all felt relaxed and calm. The Roaring Boys were always seeking to take the fight to the enemy at every opportunity and were reported as badgering the intelligence team for targets they could attack. Everyone's headphones became active as Charlie spotted a gap in the veil of white cloud that blanketed the countryside below, conditions that Ross described as, "very hazy." The rail marshalling yards at Argentan were pinpointed and bombs dropped. The ORB detailed the scores: "two near misses. Flak was intense, heavy and accurate over target area." At 20.30 pm the squadron touched down at B4, all intact. Charlie would follow a similar pattern of patrols with sections of 4 Spitfires over the coming days, all were a risk, none routine. On 14 July the ORB described, "14 patrols of the Low Eastern sector were carried out." Of these 13 were uneventful, 1 was the exact opposite and is described in Tommy's chapter. Charlie's section of 4 Spitfires included his regular flying partner Ross.

Things were not going well for the Germans on 17 July. The American thrust to take St Lô was finally successful and for the enemy high command, another considerable blow was the wounding of Field Marshall Irwin Rommel whose staff car was strafed by the Spitfire of Squadron Leader JJ Le Roux DFC of 602 squadron. Rommel's aid was killed, and his driver wounded. Whilst recovering from his injuries Rommel would become implicated in the plot to assassinate Adolf Hitler. He was left with no choice by the Nazis than to commit suicide which he did by taking a cyanide capsule on 14 October 1944. He was given a state funeral by the Nazi leadership. The debate about who strafed Rommel is still ongoing today. F/O Charles Fox of 412 Squadron, 126 Wing was also believed to have fired the shots that hit Rommel's car.

Charlie had another busy day ahead. On 17 July he stepped onto the wing of Spitfire MK423 and strapped himself into the cockpit. The Wing's intelligence boys reckoned there was ground activity around the Caen area. Word was also coming back from other squadrons that they were encountering massed formations of Luftwaffe fighters. Not that anyone needed their minds focused more than normal but the prospect of encountering the enemy in the air added an edge, as well as a degree of extra tension. The armed reconnaissance patrol area would cover Falaise, Caen, and Lisieux. The intelligence boys were correct as the formation of Spitfires cruised at around 5,000 feet. The ORB later said: "considerable road movements were observed and attacked. Four flamers and 9 Mets damaged." The damage inflicted by these 12 Spitfires was substantial as they followed each other into a dive towards the targets, unleashing their cannons and machine guns. The graceful Spitfire almost felt as if it would shake itself to pieces as flames spat out from the wings and rounds instantaneously ripped into the transports below. The enemy soldiers scattered in all directions, putting as much distance as they could between themselves and the hell unfolding in front of them. Some offered light small arms fire in return, but their main objective was self-preservation. As Charlie and the others regained height and formation at 7,000 feet, he could see everyone was in one piece with no hits received. It was time to take a few deep breaths, as Charlie methodically looked around the sky, a procedure repeated across the formation of Spitfires. Had their attack alerted the Luftwaffe to their presence? No massed formation of enemy aircraft was spotted. Suddenly everyone's headphones were filled with S/L Robertson's voice as he reported sighting an enemy aircraft at zero feet, most likely returning to Tricqueville airfield. They were around 6 miles northeast of Lisieux. Robertson broke away to starboard and his Spitfire swept rapidly downwards towards the bandit, an Me 109. He opened fire at around 600 yards and with the dive speed that he had built up, he soon closed to 400 yards where he could see the strike of his cannon rounds on the tail assembly. As the aircraft rose up sharply the tail unit broke off and the 109 caught fire, crashing around 1 mile south of the airfield. The squadron was there to corroborate the claim and Robertson recorded that he had used the new gyro gun sight in the attack.

In a postscript to the attack, it was established that Robertson's downed Me 109 was from III/Jagdgeschwader 26 "Schlageter." Flight Lieutenant L P Comerford was slightly wounded by his attacker Hauptman Klaus Mietusch who was flying the 109 that was bounced and shot down by Robertson. Mietusch was wounded and despite the low altitude was able to bail out. He had 75 air victories to his name but shortly after recovering from the engagement with Robertson on 17 September he was shot down and killed by an American P51 Mustang.

The 18 July saw the start of the British offensive on Caen, Operation Goodwood. The front line on both sides was a log jam of troops and vehicles moving back and forth. Charlie and the Roaring Boys left B4 for a low cover patrol of the battlefront. S/L Robertson led the 8 Spitfires across the green pastures and woods of Normandy. Charlie looked around him and saw each Spitfire in the formation making almost rhythmic movements up and down as the pilots instinctively responded to the stiff breeze and made small correctional inputs to the throttle, joystick, rudder pedals and trim wheels. Seeing the pilot's head benignly framed by the canopy he knew that in the cockpit below they were all working to maintain formation, whilst checking their instruments to see that the aircraft and its mighty Merlin engine were operating normally. Each pilot scoured the sky for bandits who might be planning to drop down and deliver a deadly surprise attack. "Beware of the hun in the sun," was an expression forged in the Battle of Britain. On the horizon, the small town of Pont L'Eveque came into view. To the east of Caen, this small town has kept its historic feel despite being devasted in the following month. Pont L'Eveque has the main east to west supply route which passes directly through the town centre and which leads directly to Caen, located around 30 miles to the west. The formation could see a large convoy of over 25 vehicles, steadily moving along the main road. This convoy had also caught the attention of a squadron of RAF

Typhoons, intent on stopping them delivering their supplies to the front. The Roaring Boys were vectored to provide cover for the "Tiffies" as they began hammering the enemy vehicles. Charlie watched on as in turn the wings of each "Tiffie," framed again the clouds, seemed to erupt as rockets and cannon fire streaked downwards. The aim was to cause destruction and chaos, and this was a well-coordinated and practiced procedure. These pilots could deliver their rockets with pinpoint accuracy. The front and rear vehicles of the convoy were quickly disabled trapping the remainder in a killing ground. Those who weren't manning flak defences or were locked down in armoured vehicles leapt to the ground and ran for their lives. Watching gun camera footage it's possible to see how these attacks would unfold. In one sequence a soldier emerged from the clouds of dust and smoke and quickly disappeared into the roadside ditch. The diving "Tiffies" weren't having it all their own way and during the day several were lost to flak across the front.

With the attack completed the Roaring Boys turned their Spitfires for home. F/S D J Le Blanc was relieved as his wheels touched down on the grass of B4 at 10.45 am, 15 minutes before Charlie and the others. His Spitfire had developed engine trouble. A swarm of erks were soon feverishly at work diagnosing the issue.

The Roaring Boys were spending a considerable amount of time in and around the front line. For Charlie's evening mission of 24 July, he was accompanied by Ross, Gibby, and 10 others for a full squadron strength patrol. At 21.25 pm they left the base and climbed into the early evening sky for patrol that would turn out to be far from routine. Of the 12 Spitfires, those flown by P/O L A Dunn, and F/L Gibby Gibson would return early after being hit by flak. It's not clear whose Spitfire this was but it was routine to send the damaged aircraft back to base with a buddy who could defend his colleague if enemy aircraft sensed the opportunity for an easy kill. They could also note the location and record the outcome of any forced landing or if the pilot bailed out and "took to the silk." Neither happened, Dunn and Gibson touched down at B4 at 21.55 pm. They were followed shortly after at 22.00 pm by F/O H W Kramer who returned with nonspecified "technical trouble." Charlie and the remainder of the squadron, as Ross noted, "landed at dark" at 22.40 pm. This day was also a landmark for No 126 Wing as F/O W Banks of 412 Squadron shot down the 100th German aircraft since 126's inception. He also received a handsome reward of French Francs to mark the occasion.

The 26 July was to be Charlie's last day flying with the Roaring Boys. He took part in 4 patrols on this day, all uneventful. His first operation took off at 06.25 am and the final patrol landed at 22.40 pm. He was combat flying for a total of 4 hours and 35 minutes, leading from the front. The preparation for a leadership role was over. He was ready to step up to the role of squadron leader at 401 Squadron, the Rams. Charlie would be taking over from S/L Hap Kennedy who on this day was shot down by flak. Kennedy bailed out, successfully evaded capture, before returning to Allied lines on 24 August. Charlie would stay as part of 126 Wing and being based at B4, could catch up with the Roaring Boys around the airfield. Best wishes were passed on by 411 accompanied no doubt by along a degree of banter and good-natured joshing for his promotion.

There was no bedding in process for Charlie. He was airborne and leading from the front on 27 July as 401's new CO. It turned into their most successful day of the war with the squadron shooting down 9 aircraft during 45 sorties. Charlie was amongst the successful pilots shooting down a Me 109. He would follow that up by downing an FW 190 on 31 July. On 8 August Charlie was awarded a DFC: "in recognition of his skills and fighting qualities." During the battles around Falaise on 18 August, Charlie was hit by flak and crash-landed near Lisieux. He managed to evade capture and returned to the squadron on 24 August. During the Allied airborne operation in Holland, Operation Market Garden, Charlie was leading No 401 and providing air support when on 19 September he suffered an engine failure, forcing him to bail out over enemy territory. He was captured and spent the rest of the war as a prisoner. Charlie was awarded a Bar to his DFC in recognition of his, "leadership, tactical ability and resolution." In December 1944 Charlie was awarded a Distinguished Service Order in recognition of his: "magnificent leadership, great determination, and devotion to duty." In April 1945, at the end the war Charlie was liberated from a prisoner of war camp and released from service on 4 October 1945.

Upon returning to Canada, Charlie continued his aviation career when he joined Central Maritime Airways as a pilot. He stayed with this Company and with its successor Eastern Provincial Airways for the next thirty years where he would fly Boeing 737s. After his flying career, he became the Regional Sales and Promotions Manager for Eastern Provincial Airways. Charlie passed away on 4 July 2004.

CHAPTER FOUR

ROSS LINQUIST

Ross with a captured Me 109 in 1944

Stewart Ross Linquist, known as Ross, was born 28 October 1922 in Emo, Ontario. He was the youngest of 2 brothers and 3 sisters. His father had emigrated to Canada from Sweden as a young man, following his career as a dairy farmer and milkman. Ross's parents died within 6 months of each other whilst he was training to become a pilot. Ross was asked in a TV interview why he joined up and said: "I have always had an interest in aircraft and I had some friends from home who came home in uniform. I was fortunate that I went to Winnipeg to join the air force. I was accepted, and doubly fortunate that I was accepted for aircrew. I joined up because it was the thing to do and when you're young you're looking for adventure." He enrolled in the RCAF Reserve as a Leading Aircraftsman on 1 June 1942, joining No 4 Elementary Flying Training School (EFTS) at Windsor Mills. There's an interesting film called

Knights of the Air which describes the RCAF's initial training at Windsor Mills, flying the Finch on first solos just as Ross and many of the Roaring Boys would have done. Watching the first fresh-faced pilot ballooning his aircraft upon landing on his first solo flight it was amusing to then see his classmates welcome the unscathed trainee back by rolling him in the snow, whilst the straight-faced instructor removed his service cap and theatrically wiped his brow in mock relief!

After completing his initial training at Windsor Mills, Ross was enrolled onto Course 64, No 6 Service Flying Training School (SFTS), based at RCAF Dunnville, Ontario on 12 September 1942. As he moved through his initial training, flying the Tiger Moth and Harvard he was promoted from Sergeant to Pilot Officer on 1 December 1942, eventually graduating on 29 December 1942.

Ross's next posting in early 1943 was to No 1 "Y" Depot for Embarkation Proceedings and No 2 Personnel Reception Centre awaiting the next move. When his next posting came through Ross knew he was going to get into the action as he made the long voyage across the Atlantic from Canada to England. Here, he would join No 6 EFTS at RAF Sywell. It is amazing to think that all these years later Spitfire Elizabeth would be touching down on the very aerodrome that one of her pilots did all those years before.

There followed for Ross a few advanced flight training courses throughout 1943, commencing with No 7 (Pilot's) Advanced Flying Unit Course. On 1 June 1943 Ross was promoted to Flying Officer for the RCAF. Although he was a qualified pilot wearing his "wings" with pride, there was a big difference for these Commonwealth pilots when they started flying in England. In Canada, the skies were uncluttered with no hostile forces, whereas in England there were Allied and Luftwaffe aircraft flying on missions and in combat, barrage balloons, as well as the risk that a jumpy "ack-ack" battery might try to shoot down any aircraft flying over their guns. This was a war zone and operationally things needed to be approached very differently.

Ross was moving onwards towards his posting to an operational fighter squadron. He was next posted to No 58 Operation Training Unit Course at RAF Grangemouth, Falkirk Scotland where he would develop his skills as a day fighter pilot. A full-size replica Mk 1 Spitfire is still displayed there today as a memorial and "gate guardian" honouring all those who flew from the airfield.

Ross was posted into 411 Squadron, at RAF Staplehurst and recorded in capitals in his logbook "RCAF 411 Squadron 126 AERODROME #83 GROUP." His first flight at Staplehurst on 10 October 1943 was in an older Spitfire loaned by 412 Squadron, a Mark Vb coded DB – X. New pilots wouldn't be trusted with a newly produced Mark IX in case they "pranged" it. Ross undertook 50 minutes of what is often referred to in aviation as "circuit bashing." Basically, the idea is to perform a continuous set of takeoffs and landings, effectively a "touch and go" where the aircraft is briefly landed and then immediately after the throttle is opened, and the aircraft is put back into the air. The circuit is effectively a rectangular aerodrome traffic pattern, typically flown at 1,000 feet in a prescribed and standard pattern to coordinate traffic and avoid collisions. The aerodrome is always kept in visual contact and the direction of the circuit pattern is dependent upon the prevailing wind direction as aircraft land and takeoff into the wind. Flying circuits is a familiarisation exercise and at a home aerodrome, new pilots can quickly understand the layout and local landmarks, all vital for landing a Spitfire, even with battle damage. Landing a Spitfire is tricky due to the undercarriage configuration, weight and that mighty Rolls Royce Merlin engine on the front which limits a pilot's forward vision, hence with the cockpit hood back, the pilot makes a curved approach before straightening up to land on the runway. It's also important to understand any aspects of an aerodrome layout or surroundings that might trip up an unwary pilot. An example could be trees that disturb the prevailing wind, disrupting the airflow over the aircraft's wing causing it to drop. Marker boards on either side of the runway aid the pilot in staying as close to the centre line as possible. In the back seat cockpit of a Spitfire landing on the grass strip at the Imperial War Museum, Duxford I could understand the skill and practice required to become proficient at landing, particularly in all weather and light conditions including darkness. On my Spitfire flight, Brian Smith executed a perfect landing, with only the slightest bump on the grass runway and as we slowed down the once graceful Spitfire took on her other ungainly "tail dragger" self as we taxied in, weaving from side to side to check the way ahead was clear.

On 10 October with plenty of the circuit bashing under his belt, Ross was soon up practicing formation flying and familiarisation with the local Kent geography. There was cine gun camera training to practice and then into the afternoon he was practicing mock dog fights, chasing a more experienced pilot around the skies, and being chased himself. Here he could find the limits of the Spitfire, her strengths and weaknesses against the opposing "enemy" forces, skills he would one day need in combat, and which could save his life. With day one complete, Ross recorded the 3 sorties, totalling 2 hours 25 minutes in his logbook.

As a thick blanket of fog gripped the Weald of Kent area, Ross joined in the volleyball, always a favourite with the Roaring Boys. Everyone was frustrated as the promised delivery of shiny new Spitfire Mark IXbs couldn't be made. There was no lounging around for the fog bound fighter pilots. The local woods were raided for wood and the aerodrome was soon a hive of activity as the Canadians sawed up logs. As the ORB observed: "this wood will be taken along with dispersal equipment on the move (to Biggin Hill)."

On 12 October Ross was able to fire up his Spitfire for some further intensive operational flying. Getting hours "under his belt" with the squadron was vital. His two flights enabled him to practice formation flying as wingman and at squadron strength, vital for the ramrod, sweeps and armed reconnaissance missions to follow. He recorded a further 1 hour 50 minutes in his logbook. The squadron was a scene of furious activity as everything was taken down and packed up ready for the move to Biggin Hill.

With the Roaring Boys settling into life at Biggin Hill, and the weather mixed, any opportunity to get airborne was undertaken. On 15 and 16 October, Ross was able to get a Mark Vb airborne for a 50-minute local map reading and exercise.

Ross's competence as a pilot was evidenced by the fact he was upgraded from the Spitfire Vb to a freshly delivered Spitfire IXb. On 21 October, he strapped himself into DB – S for a familiarisation flight around the local Biggin Hill area. It was his first opportunity to feel the extra power and speed of the Mark IX and compare its qualities with the Vb. With his first combat mission getting ever closer Ross was keen to absorb every possible piece of advice and information from those "older heads" within the squadron.

The weather around this time was described as "duff" by the squadron ORB. Ross had joined the Roaring Boys family and could spend time getting acquainted with his new colleagues in the mess, badminton court, and gymnasium as flying was limited. The weather seemed to alternate between rain and fog but where conditions allowed Ross joined in with practice formation and cine camera exercises on 24, 25 and 31 October.

With the arrival of November Ross's daily routine of training exercises continued. It was particularly important that as front-line fighter pilots the Roaring Boys practiced target estimation, range and deflection calculations, with their gun sight and cine gun camera. In combat with the enemy, they would carry this out instinctively whilst trying to stay on the tail of their opponent, who was mightily keen to remove the assailant from their tail as quickly as possible. As with other areas of life and experience the maxim "always expect the unexpected" is particularly pertinent to aviation. On 8 November, after a 2 hour 10 minutes intensive flying formation and cine camera practice Ross ran through his pre-landing routine, lowering his flaps, bleeding off his airspeed, checking his instruments, and selecting the undercarriage selector lever. He checked the electrical visual indicator which would be showing green if the landing gear was down. If red lights were showing it would have meant both undercarriage legs were still up. As Ross quickly focused on the visual indicator, he could see no lights. This immediately told him he had a problem, only one of his undercarriage legs was down. He radioed in to control who acknowledged his emergency call and cleared the surrounding air space. On the ground rescue crews responded to the alert and rushed to their rescue vehicles which were soon racing out to the runway. Ross later wrote in his logbook: "landed with one wheel down. First time ever scratched an a/c." The actual damage to the Spitfire was not recorded, although "scratches" would seem a rather optimistic damage assessment!

On 9 November, Ross was airborne for just under an hour in a squadron strength formation flying exercise. As he returned to Biggin Hill he was suddenly faced with engine issues. The normally reliable Rolls Royce Merlin engine was rough running and sounding decidedly unwell as Ross rapidly processed his options. Would he make the aerodrome or be forced to crash land? He was too low to bail out. He wrote later, "landed, engine cutting." He had got away with it and with a huge sigh of relief taxied in. Later around the officer's mess, he found himself on the receiving end of some typically good-natured ribbing from his fellow pilots.

After several more November days of practice, the fateful day duly arrived on 26 November. The waiting was over. Ross stepped up onto the wing of Spitfire EN579. He sat in the small cockpit of his aircraft and tried not to let any nerves interfere with his pre-flight procedures. As the engine fired up, he checked all was well before taxiing out with the other 11 Spitfires. The operation was Ramrod 336, led by S/L Ormston, with Tommy flying on the mission too. They were escorting 73 Marauders bombing Cambrai airfield. As Ross's wheels left Biggin at 11.40 am he settled into the formation as he had done many times in the months leading up to this day. Ross could see enemy occupied France getting ever closer. This was it; all the training and preparation didn't quite seem enough as his Spitfire quickly passed over the French coast at Saint-Omer. As the formation ran into the target Ross, Tommy and the Roaring Boys were providing "top cover" to the bombers at 20,000 feet. Suddenly Ross's headphones picked up radio traffic. He could make out that 401 Squadron had spotted 2 FW 190s taking off from Achiet airfield, a satellite of the main Cambrai airfield. So much for a quiet first mission! Some lucky fellow was about to get into a duel with the enemy and help himself to a kill. Ross concentrated on his own flying as he watched the Marauders drop their payloads. The results weren't visible as the formation passed by the target and turned towards Courcelette, situated around 15 miles to the south west of Cambrai. Word got out that F/L Shepperd of 401 Squadron had downed one of the FW 190s in low-level combat, during which the enemy pilot's desperate attempts to evade Shepperd's fire resulted in his propellers meeting the ground 3 times, throwing up clouds of dust before he eventually crashed in flames. Meanwhile, Ross and the formation crossed back over the French coast at Le Touquet. He could breathe slightly easier now, although there was always that nagging doubt about reaching "dear ole Blighty" without any mechanical issues, which would lead to an unwelcome visit to the cold grey sea below. The memories of his previous issues with malfunctioning Spitfires earlier in the month were probably still very much on his mind. At 13.20 pm a relieved Ross felt the welcoming grass of Biggin Hill beneath his wheels. He had completed his first operational mission. He taxied in, he felt that he was on his way to becoming a competent and valuable member of 411 Squadron. Tommy wrote up details of the operation in his logbook: "6 FW 190's took off from the drome as we arrived. 401 went down and destroyed one of them. Digby Vs got another, cheers! There was no rest for Ross as after a debrief on the operation, he was once again airborne for 1 hour 20 minutes of squadron formation flying, "dummy bombing attacks" and cine camera practice.

For Ross's mission of 1 December, the Roaring Boys were led by W/C Buck McNair. He also flew with Len for Ramrod 343 which involved escorting 72 Marauders from USAAF Ninth Air Force who planned to bomb Cambrai aerodrome. This was part of a much wider operation as 100 Marauders would at the same time be bombing airfields at Chievres, Belgium and Lille. As 126 Wing's Spitfires headed off from Biggin at 09.10 am they formed up as normal at 1,000 feet and once in formation headed south to pick up the bomber formations. Ross's attention alternated between his instruments, holding his position in his section, and as they crossed the coast at Berck-sur-Mer a few miles south of Le Touquet, methodically searching the sky for enemy fighters. The bombers attacked Cambrai with what was described in the ORB as, "fair results." A voice suddenly spoke, and Ross listened as information was passed that one of the other squadrons had spotted fighters taking off from Chievres aerodrome, approximately 40 miles to the northeast of Cambrai aerodrome and just across the Belgium border. The Germans air defence system had tracked the sizeable formation and anticipating an aerodrome attack and had scrambled their Staffels to intercept. Blue section of the Roaring Boys was ordered to head off the incoming bandits and Ross observed a procession of elliptical winged Spits flashed their blue undersides as they rolled away to attack. Everyone was on high full alert and Ross had an uneasy feeling, which was not helped as he felt a sudden impact on his Spitfire. It must be flak. He calmed himself and checked the vital actions of his aircraft. Everything seemed normal and his temperature and pressure gauges all showed green. He radioed in to report that he was hit and was reassured when other pilots checked over his Spitfire but could see no obvious damage. Ross later recorded in his logbook with no sense of drama, "got hit by a small piece of flak." Meanwhile, the enemy fighters would expect a reception from the escorting Spitfires, but some would move aside from the main formation and attempt to evade detection and slip in amongst and attack the main bomber formation. If they could break up a box of the Marauders and isolate some of them then there was a good opportunity to shoot them down. Down below and away from the main formation Blue 1 F/L Douglas Matheson, and his section wingman Blue 2 P/O J A Saint-Denis, engaged an FW 190 near Cambrai and Matheson shot down Hauptman Helmut Hoppe who was killed. P/O S A Mills also destroyed the FW 190 of Feldwebel Rudi Weyrich who was also killed. Matheson and St Denis regrouped and opened their throttles to return to the formation. They were not alone.

Suddenly, a group of FW 190s which had seen the unfolding combat swept down and bounced the pair. Both Spitfires twisted, jinked and weaved, in a desperate attempt to escape the attack but it was too late as the "butcher birds" pressed home their advantage. Matheson realised his Spitfire was heading into a steep dive and he successfully bailed out. Upon landing, he was captured and as described in the 411 Squadron chapter he was interred in Stalag Luft III, later helping to dig one of the escape tunnels featured in the film *The Great Escape*. Jack Saint-Denis's Spitfire was now in a steep dive and as it streaked earthwards, no parachute was observed. His Spitfire crashed near the commune of Sauly, around 15 miles southwest of Arras. He is buried in the British Cemetery of Longuenesse, near Saint-Omer. As a tribute, the Merlin engine from Saint-Denis's Spitfire is on display in the town office at Saulty and an exhibition was held to commemorate his sacrifice.

On this day both men had the misfortune to meet in combat one of the Luftwaffe's surviving *experten* Oberfeldwebel Adolf "Addi" Glunz of 5/JG 26 who had scrambled his FW 190 from Cambrai-Epinoy airfield. Matheson and St Denis would be Glunz's 48th and 49th victories, which by the end of the war would rise to 71. On 29 August 1943, Glunz became the only non-commissioned officer in JG 26 ever to receive the Knights Cross of the Iron Cross, the Ritterkreuz, to which oak leaves would later be added to recognise his distinguished service. Glunz claimed his 50th victory on 31 December and was appointed Staffelkapitän of 5/JG 26 on 15 January 1944. On 22 February 1944 Glunz achieved the incredible feat of shooting down 6 Allied aircraft in one day including 5 bombers. He became a commissioned officer with the Luftwaffe rank of Leutnant in the first week of April 1944. Addi Glunz survived the war.

The bomber formation and escort recrossed the French coast for the short trip across the channel. In Spitfire MH734 Ross was nervously preparing himself for the short channel crossing knowing his Spitfire had been damaged. Combat missions were a roll of the dice and at least he hadn't been a victim of the FW 190 butcher birds like Saint-Denis and Matheson. Ross was carefully the distance and his altitude to see if, with a sudden engine failure, he could glide back to England. He certainly didn't fancy a dip in the freezing sea below which would have meant certain death within a few minutes. As the English coast appeared and rapidly closed, the tension eased. His prospects of a safe return to Biggin were looking odds on and at 10.55 am he and the Roaring Boys once again felt the welcome grass of "Biggin on the bump" under their wheels. As the group of erks marshalled them in, Ross quickly shut down and unfastened his straps. He jumped down off the wing of his Spitfire and perhaps patted the fuselage of his Spitfire MH374. It had got him back in one piece. Now to find out where that flak had struck him.

On 13 December Ross wasn't rostered to join the day's ramrod mission. Instead, he took the opportunity to take the squadron Tiger Moth on a flight from Biggin Hill to Gatwick. As the Tiger is an open cockpit aircraft Ross wore several layers and his Irving jacket to stave off the winter cold. The flight was a round trip of 50 minutes and gave him the chance to check out the local landmarks. The cine gun camera and formation practice continued on 15 December for 1 hour 15 minutes. This was followed on 20 December with combat practice tail chasing and on 21 and 22 December by testing a new Spitfire and Hispano cannons respectively.

The weather on 22 December was good enough for 2 ramrods. Ross and Gibby were rostered to fly on the afternoon Ramrod 386 in which No 126 and 127 Airfields would be taking part. As the Roaring Boys fired up their Spitfires and lifted off at 14.50 pm the sun was already getting low in the sky. Once they had formed up over the aerodrome they turned south and flew on the deck, blasting across the Kent countryside and out over the channel, still at zero feet to deceive the enemies defences, Once in mid-channel, they climbed and gained altitude before crossing the French coast at Gravelines. Ross checked his altimeter and saw he was cruising at 10,000 feet. The ORB described it: "As part of the fourth fighter sweep in and around Cambrai at 15,000 feet. Shortly after crossing the accurate flak forced the squadron from 10 to 16,000 feet. F/L Stayner was hit in the wing but his aircraft remained quite serviceable. The wing returned and crossed the coast slightly south of Dunkirk. On the way, considerable flak was again encountered in the Saint-Omer and Foret de Crecy areas." Ross's logbook recorded, "bags of flak in and out near Dunkerque." By the time the squadron returned to Biggin Hill, it was 16.30 pm and dark. As they jumped off the wings of their Spitfires the Roaring Boys thoughts had already turned to evening dinner followed a trip down to the White Hart at Brasted for a pint, or many, and a chat about the day's mission. The pub was a pilots favourite during the Battle of Britain, which to this day still has on the wall a chalkboard signed by some of the famous aces from that time.

Ross continued to fly formation and cine gun practice. Like most of the pilots he liked to fly his regular Spitfire DB – B. On 23 December

Ross noted that his aircraft had been involved in an accident the circumstances of which are not recorded. However, he pointed the finger of blame in his logbook: "Army pranged old "B". Very ungood."

With the Christmas festivities behind him, Ross was rostered to fly with Tommy and Len on 30 December for Ramrod 396. The wing took off at 13.00 pm and formed up over the airfield. The mission was to provide withdrawal cover for 530 Flying Fortresses and 168 Liberators which were returning from an operation to Ludwigshafen, southwest Germany where they were bombing an oil refinery and docks on the River Rhine. Ross contemplated the mission ahead. The wing would link up with the Fortresses around 40 miles northeast of Paris, over Compeigne. There was an extra edge to this mission which unlike so many others was not in the coastal areas. This time, the Roaring Boys would be flying much further into France and by doing so the risks increased immeasurably. Ross later recorded, "withdrawal cover for Forts – quite deep." As the formation crossed the French coast north of Cayeux the ORB noted: "met the Forts coming out at 25,000 feet between Beauvais and Montdidier. Six FW 190s were seen to be making head-on attacks on the Forts but only one carried out the attack after firing rolled on his back and dove vertical for the deck. F/L George "Screwball" Beurling of 412 Squadron chased him down and destroyed it. All the squadrons did quite a few orbits but returned without further incident." They touched down at 14.55 pm. This was Beurling's last victory before his posting back to Canada. Ross wrote, "saw several Hun. Beurling got no. 31." Tommy put pen to paper: "Ten Huns reported making attacks on big boys. FL/LT Geo Beurling 412 shot down his 31st & landed at Friston, duff engine and no juice."

Ross started 1944 on New Year's Day writing in his logbook: "formation and cannon test. Tested brand new "B." Clearly, whatever damage the Army had done to his old "B" for beer as he referred to the aircraft, it had necessitated a new replacement aircraft. Ross spent 45 minutes giving Spitfire MJ125 DB-B a thorough workout. He was once again able to test out his new steed with some formation and cine gun practice on 2 January. All aspects of flying had to be regularly practiced and proficiency at low-level flying, whether because of operational requirements such as flying under the radar, ground attack or air combat was vital. A key skill that needed practice was the ability to navigate whilst flying at zero feet, not an easy skill to acquire, aside from the obvious dangers from obstacles.

Ross undertook a 40-minute low-level cross-country exercise on 3 January which was combined with some cine gun camera practice. He wanted to make the most of these practice days as he knew he would be flying in combat again very soon.

On 5 January, at 12.50 pm, after a quick lunch and with briefings complete from the intelligence boys Ross was ready and prepared for Ramrod 425. Both 126 and 127 Airfields, would provide top cover, for the withdrawal of Flying Fortresses of the Mighty Eighth Air Force that were bombing targets in western France. The targets were airfields in Tours and Bordeaux Merignac, which is located on the western outskirts of Bordeaux and is today the city's main airport. Ross later wrote: "Ramrod 425 to Caen. Withdrawal cover to Forts. Met them in Channel. Turned back French coast." Ross and the Roaring Boys split off from the Fortresses over southeast England as the danger of enemy attack was passed and the heavies could make their way to their East Anglian bases. Both wings returned to Biggin Hill without incident landing at 14.05 pm.

Ross's practice drills of 20 January involved a mock combat tail chase which he described as a "fine thrash." There was also the opportunity for Ross and the squadron to take place in an exercise with the army. Close cooperation would be a feature of the mobile fighter wing operations post-invasion so all services recognised the importance of these exercises. Clearly, the army would also expect to come under attack from the Luftwaffe once ashore so the sight and sounds of attacking aircraft would add to the reality of any exercise. Ross called it an, "Army beat up."

On 24 January, Ross was sent to Derby for a 5-day Rolls Royce Merlin handling course. Upon his return, he was itching to get back into action and on 30 January he joined Tommy for a Wing strength Ramrod 499 to Brussels south aerodrome, near Charleroi, Belgium. W/C Buck McNair led the Roaring Boys as 126 Airfield took to the air at 10.00 am. The low rumble of 36 Spitfire Merlins shattered the silence of Biggin Hill as McNair turned the formation south for France. Ross summarised the mission as a "sweep ahead of the Forts. Almost 10/10. Nothing doing." The thick cloud cover meant the formation had zero visibility on the ground. No Luftwaffe aircraft were enticed up to intercept them, even though their presence was probably known. The presence of so many fighters acted as a deterrent, which of course it was designed to so that the heavies could make complete their operation unhindered. Tommy provided details of the return leg route as being via: "Cap Griz Nez.

Aircraft were reported at 9 o'clock but turned out to be Spits. A little flak. No huns." The ORB recorded, their return to base at 11.30 am and "the sweep was uneventful. On landing the aircraft after the operation P/O S G Brooks pranged his machine."

For the month of January 1944, Ross recorded a total of 115 hours and 30 minutes flying Spitfires with 5 hours 25 minutes spent on combat operations. He also recorded his total time on combat operations as 17 hours 50 minutes. He was coming up to 1/5 completion of the 200 hours combat flying required to complete his tour.

The Allies were ratcheting up the pressure on the Germans to denigrate their fighting forces, communications, and infrastructure and for the Ross and the Roaring Boys, this meant plenty of combat flying. The 8 February 1944 dawned as a gloomy winter's day with a chill wind swirling around the open aerodrome. Ross was due to fly in the afternoon with Bruce for Ramrod 529, the second one of the day which was escorting Marauders to Cambrai aerodrome. It was part of a series of multi-pronged, Ramrods 526 – 532. At least Ross got to have a decent lunch and prepare himself for the mission ahead before he climbed up onto the wing of Spitfire MJ125, his old faithful DB – B for "beer."

With his pre-flight checks complete, a message came into his headset as S/L McFarlane ordered them to move off. Ross eased the throttle forward, taxiing out to the dispersal point. Soon the Spitfires were in the air and settling into their neat section and squadron formation. They headed south to link up with the bombers, passing through a thick layer of cloud. The Roaring Boys flew close to the Marauders and Ross looked across at them and wondered what lay in store. He felt his Spitfire jolt as a gust of wind hit the aircraft and noted in turn as each Spitfire did the same before they settled back into steady flight. The boys were running on low throttle as if holding back eager stallions. The Marauders cruised at around 280 mph and the Spitfire was just ticking over at that speed. He could see movement inside the closest bomber as they neared the French coast. The crews were putting on their helmets as protection against flak. Ross hoped the thick cloud would dissuade the flak crews from sending up any of their deadly fire. As they crossed into enemy territory, suddenly the bomber leader announced that due to the thick cloud the mission was being aborted. Ross summed up the Roaring Boys feelings in his logbook, and you can almost imagine the words he muttered: "close escort to clueless Marauders. Turned back 10 miles inland. Had to lead them home." No 126 Airfield eventually pushed ahead and away from the Marauder formation returning to "Biggin on the bump" at 15.35 pm. P/O Dunn landed 50 minutes earlier with engine trouble. Bruce described his feelings about the mission in his logbook: "The bombers were a colossal cock-up – didn't have a clue."

On Valentine's day, 14 February the Roaring Boys were onto a new form of offensive training, dive bombing. As close support, they would need to be proficient at this. Ahead of the exercise "the boys washed their kites." They treated this training as a competition which created a buzz as each of the Roaring Boys chipped in their money. The ORB noted: "The chap with the best score will win the pot of gold." The stakes were high and there was likely to be keen interest as to the winner. What Ross thought of his own chances is not known. The next day the ORB revealed the result: "F/O Linquist was the happy winner of the pot of gold for the highest score in the bombing operations yesterday. Good go!" There was a mix of experience amongst 411's pilots and Ross was still relatively new. By winning the pot of gold he had demonstrated an aptitude for this offensive capability, which was duly noted by his commanders for when the real missions came along. He was also probably carried physically to the pub in celebration.

The hazards of flying during the winter were always lurking in the long shadows. With the Roaring Boys moving to RAF Peterhead, Scotland for a week-long air firing course, the dangers manifested themselves as the ORB described: "The morning was spent on bombing but in the afternoon a snow blizzard came up and cancelled flying. P/O Dunn was forced to land at a drome further south and P/O Linquist tipped his kite up on its nose causing a breakage in the prop. He, unfortunately, got stuck in the mud while taxiing." Not a good day for Ross and he was forced to run the gauntlet of some serious mickey taking, most likely along the lines of paying for the damage from his "pot of gold!" They say, "you can't keep a good man down" and, so it proved with Ross. With the weather curtailing any chance of flying, lectures were undertaken and then: "a spot of skeet shooting smartened up the pilots with P/O Linquist as the best shot." Ross had now scored the highest marks with a shotgun, which was frequently used to practice deflection shooting. There's no mention of a pot of gold on this occasion, perhaps his fellow Roaring Boys were wary of any wagers with such a sharpshooter in their midst.

For the month of February Ross had recorded 130 hours and 50 minutes flying Spitfires. His operational flying hours amounted to 8 hours and 20 minutes, with his total operational flying increased to 26 hours 10 minutes.

As March came along the air campaign started to move further east as Hitler withdrew his Luftwaffe forces for home defence duties. The Allies had vast superiority and with additional units being added to the Mighty Eighth and Ninth Air Forces, the headaches for the German high command were increasing. For Spitfire pilots escorting bombers, auxiliary fuel tanks were needed for the operations into The Netherlands. To ensure maximum range, the Wing would first fly from Biggin Hill to RAF Manston on the east coast for a refuelling stopover. On 8 March at 10.05 am, Ross was joined by Charlie and Len as the Wing took off from a windswept Manston, formed up over land whilst everyone carefully checked their Spitfire's instruments. No one fancied a trip "into the drink" below, with its white caps rhythmically dancing across the horizon. Ross wrote down details of the operation in his logbook: "Ramrod 637. Volkel A/D. Close support to 108 Marauders." I was intrigued to read Ross's reaction to this Marauder operation having described their performance as "clueless" on a couple of previous occasions. Volkel aerodrome is around 15 miles to the east of Eindhoven and would later be a base for 126 Wing. To Ross, its position on the map looked an awfully long way from the safety of home. As they moved in on the target area Ross watched from his close escort position as the bombardier navigators, the "bombagators" as they were known, settled down into their goldfish bowls in the perspex domes on the front of the Marauders. They were looking carefully for visual reference points on the ground. The visibility was excellent. Ross noted the opening of the bomb doors. The run into the target had started. In each Marauder, the bombardiers were looking down through their bombsights ready to unleash their ordnance. Ross and the Roaring Boys looked out across the iridescent blue sky around them, waiting and watching for bandits and hoping Volkel was going to get a good hammering. As if on cue a cascade of bombs fell from the belly of each aircraft, neatly spaced and uniform as they dropped away in ever increasing lines. Ross observed a multitude of flashes which appeared in a grid pattern on the ground, followed by blooms of black smoke curling upwards from the aerodrome. The damage assessment indicated that 12 of the 43 aircraft shelters and 3 of the 4 repair hangers were hit as well as one of the 50-ton fuel tanks which had sent a bright orange mushroom of flame high into the sky. This was quite a show for the watching beehive who collectively started the dash back to England. This time Ross seemed impressed, "good bombing. No Huns. Little flak." The squadron ORB did record: "Tuffet Control did report 20 Huns around Rotterdam." By 12.30 pm the Wing had landed safely back at base.

As March progressed Ross's flying Ramrods was interspersed with the daily practice of formation flying, cannon testing, dive bombing tail chasing, and "beating up" the army on their manoeuvres. The boys skills were kept very sharp. The weather was poor at times and towards the end of March, Biggin Hill was shrouded in fog. Ross noted his total flying time in Spitfires at the end of March as 160 hours 45 minutes. He spent 9 hours 40 minutes on operations and his tour total of combat operations increased to 35 hours 50 minutes.

Spring was in the air and the routine of practice continued at pace. Ross took part in "bouncing" squadron formations where the various colour coded squadrons practiced their tactics, based upon the Luftwaffe's favoured modus operandi. A navigation exercise was undertaken to Ford where Ross and the Roaring Boys stayed overnight, finding time as the ORB noted to visit, "one of the nearby locals" where a few local Sussex ales were tested. It would be 10 April before the seemingly endless days of fog cleared and operations could begin once again.

At this time the squadron had tested the new 90-gallon auxiliary fuel tanks. Although they functioned well the tanks did nothing for the Spitfire's look or aerodynamics as it was noted: "it caused the aircraft to wander in turns." In combat situations, the tanks would be immediately jettisoned so that the Spitfire could exploit its air combat capabilities and prevent bullets from the attacking aircraft hitting the fuel tank and causing a catastrophic explosion.

Ramrod 713 on 10 April would be an evening "show." Ross was joined by Charlie and Gibby as at 18.30 pm and at full squadron strength they lifted off, forming up and leaving Biggin Hill behind in the gathering gloom. During the mission, the Roaring Boys struck east into Belgium and the rail marshalling yards at Charleroi. Ross later wrote: "close escort to 36 Mitchells. Monceau engine sheds." The specific target was Monceau-sur Sambre, near Charleroi. Even today it's possible to see that Monceau is still a major rail marshalling area. The Sambre river winds its way past Monceau and a canal route strikes out from the river on which goods and supplies would have been transported. The multiple rail lines and repair sheds are extensive. As the Roaring Boys looked on, each box of 6 bombers opened their bomb doors. They were flying at about 12,000 feet and the target area was visible just below. To Ross, this looked a successful operation and the results were recorded as "fairly good" in the ORB. The squadron inched its way across the black of the Channel and then Kent, shrouded in blackout darkness until they felt the welcome bump of Biggin's strip, a full 2 hours after they had left.

For much of the middle of April Ross flew several low level and dive bombing practice exercises in the lead up to the Roaring Boys opening their own offensive bombing operations from their south coast base at RAF Tangmere. This was part of the wider bombing strategy to degrade the Germans military capabilities ahead of the "big show" on 6 June. On 23 April Ross recorded in his diary, "first attempt at bombing" which was targeted at the Merville viaduct. The mission is described in Bruce's chapter.

The 27 April was a busy day of bombing for Ross, Bob, Len, Bruce, Gibby, and Dave. They were ready to take to the air at 18.30 pm as at squadron strength the Roaring Boys were heading for an oil refinery in an area on the west banks of the river Seine west of Rouen. As they crossed the French coast each man checked over his Spitfire's instruments and rehearsed in his mind the dive bombing procedure. As the target came into sight Ross followed the other Roaring Boys in line astern formation and dropped the nose on his Spitfire sending it into a steep dive. The speed built as he focused on the refinery below. At around 4,000 feet he felt the 500 pounder leave the underside of his Spitfire and at the same time he pulled back hard on the stick. Flak was evident and Ross weaved his aircraft as he made his way back to form up with the others. The ORB described the results: "a direct hit was made on the refinery. Aircraft from another unit scored a direct hit on one of the tanks. This was a very successful and effective operation." The ORB's assessment was backed up by Ross who commented: "very good bombing. Lots of smoke. Whiteford hit by flak." After his top score at dive bombing, it is only speculation that the bomb that scored a direct hit on the refinery was dropped by Ross. Despite the damage to his Spitfire, Bruce was able to make it back to Tangmere at 19.30 pm, exactly one hour after takeoff. As the Roaring Boys taxied in, they quickly gathered for a debrief and to eagerly discuss the mission and their experiences of this new form of warfare in which they were now engaged.

In the last few days of April, the daily routine of practice and tests continued unabated, interspersed with Ramrods and dive bombing of No Ball targets. On 28 April, the alarm sounded at Tangmere, local air defences had picked up incoming enemy aircraft, possibly a pair of Me 109s or FW 190s on a "tip and run" raid. The random attentions of the Luftwaffe had no strategic military purpose other than to damage morale. Either way, Ross leapt up onto the wing of DB- B. The erks had already started the Spitfire's engine as he gulped down a lungful of hot Merlin exhaust gas, adjusting his body against the prop wash. The erk reached down and passed Ross his Sutton harness straps, which without having to think were fixed and his R/T was plugged in. In an instant, the erk was gone. Ross saw him mouth a message which he could read as "good luck sir." Ross flicked both thumbs in a sideways movement to indicate "chocks away." He didn't want to open the throttle and plant her on her nose. Within a few minutes, he and the others were climbing rapidly as their Merlins made their familiar guttural roar. They were vectored on to the last known position of the bogeys. They stooged around for some time but despite everyone searching the sky as Ross later wrote: "nothing doing." After around 50 minutes airborne DB-B's wheels once again down met the grass runway at Tangmere. Ross shut down his aircraft and made off towards the intelligence centre to debrief. By this point of the day on 28 April 1944 the unfolding disaster of Operation Tiger was happening further west at Slapton Sands, where E boats wrought havoc amongst Allied shipping. Whether the enemy's presence was designed to sow further confusion and alarm or test defensive response times is not known but the Roaring Boys had to scramble. These attacks were notoriously difficult to repel, although south coast gun batteries were strengthened in an attempt to ward off the attackers. Despite the rapid response, the "tip and run" raiders were usually well on their way back across the Channel before the scrambled Spitfires appeared. For the month of April Ross was able to take advantage of the improving weather and increase his hours to 199 hours flying time in Spitfires. His operational flying for the month totalled 16 hours, bringing his tour total on ops to 51 hours and 50 minutes.

On 2 May Ross, Bob, Gibby, Len, and the squadron readied themselves for a "do" to the rail marshalling yards at Busigny, which is around 110 miles southeast of Calais. Ramrod 822 would involve the Roaring Boys escorting 72 Marauders of the Ninth Air Force. Several other strategic rail targets were bombed at the same time as the campaign to break down the transport network ahead of D Day continued. Ross and the Roaring Boys were flying much further inland and there was an extra frisson to the mission as at 15.50 pm they took off into the air and climbed out, reaching around 12,000 feet where they would meet up with Marauders. Below him, the East Sussex and Kent countryside displayed a sun-kissed handsomeness in the warm Spring sunshine. Soon the bombers were onboard as the formation made its way across the channel. Every German for miles around can see us, they must have thought nervously, as crossing the French coast a silent puff of smoke appeared around the formation. The flak batteries had indeed seen them and now plied their deadly trade. They rumbled on; eyes peeled for a bounce by the Luftwaffe. So far so good, around an hour in and the bombagators were in position as Ross watched the activity in his nearest box of Marauders. Surely with this visibility, they can't miss he must have thought. They didn't. The bombs fell earthwards and exploded in the target area. Ross peered downwards as the beehive turned to the north. The Marauders now relieved of their heavy bomb loads stepped up the pace for the sprint to the channel. Ross nudged the throttle forward on his Spitfire, happy at the increase in speed as the Merlin responded with a slightly higher tone. Ross instinctively checked the oil pressure and temperature gauges. All were normal. The flight home was going without incident so far and whilst not taking anything for granted with the French coast looming large Ross was hopeful that they would soon cross back across the English coast and could then relax, just a little. He checked his fuel and didn't like what he saw. At the same time, a voice spoke. It appeared that everyone was running low on fuel, whether by miscalculation or plan is not known. The Roaring Boys were going to need to make a "splash and dash" at RAF Manston. With the operation complete the squadron was soon back in the air heading southwest towards Tangmere. The medieval city of Canterbury caught his eye with its cathedral dominating the skyline, glowing and resplendent in the early evening sunshine. At 17.50 pm the mission was over, and Ross made for the mess hall. His logbook could wait. In the early evening, he entered the results, "very good bombing. Landed Manston."

The targeting of No Ball sites was a top priority with the threat the V1s presented to civilians in London and the southeast. The mission of 11 May as part of Ramrod 867 was at wing strength and along with Ross that day were Tommy, Len, Bob, and Bruce. The pilots were briefed and ready as trundling past them came a slow-moving truck towing a caterpillar of trailers loaded with bombs, two erks casually sitting astride them. At 11.10 am the Wing's bomb-laden Spitfires gently took off, each pilot conscious of the payload strung beneath the belly of his aircraft. At 1,000 feet the Spitfire sections of each squadron formed up and closed in tight to each other. No 126 Airfield moved south to their selected No Ball targets, starting with a sweep of Creil, Reims, and Laon. The ORB gave the official account: "Two FW 190s were detected at 6,000 feet, near Reims but were lost in haze." With the sweep complete the formation headed northwest towards the coast past Amiens as the 3 squadrons prepared to dive bomb the No Ball target south of Abbeville. As each Spitfire dived on the target a plume of smoke filled the air. With the bombing complete it was time to head for home. After landing and heading to the intelligence section to debrief, the ORB later proclaimed: "five hits made in target area with a direct hit on a large building at the side of the target. Some concentrated accurate light flak was experienced over the target. No E/A encountered and all A/C returned safely to base." Ross had a slightly different take as he noted in his logbook: "Poor bombing. Thatcher 412 baled out over France. Hamilton in drink." The 412 pilots were F/O R W Thatcher and F/O J S Hamilton and the reason they were lost was due to a collision over Pas de Calais. Thatcher ditched his aircraft and was rescued by an ASR Walrus after spending 11 hours drifting in his dinghy, whilst Hamilton "took to the silk" and was also rescued.

For much of May Ross's logbook details the endless days of practice as described previously, but there was a new element which was practice with the new Gyro gunsight which first appeared in his logbook on 26 April. It was hoped that the addition of the new Mark IID Gyro reflector gunsight would offer pilots a significant advantage in air combat. It was a modification of the non-magnifying reflector sight in which target lead (the amount of aim-off or deflection in front of a moving target) and bullet drop were calculated automatically (the further the distance from the barrel the higher the amount of bullet drop). To operate the Gyro gunsight the range was set by automatically moving the dial which adjusted the reticle size to match the wingspan of the enemy aircraft. There was a set of pre-programmed numbers to cover a range of Luftwaffe fighters and bombers, including the Me 109 and FW 190, that the Roaring Boys were most likely to encounter. The amount of lead required to hit a target is a function of the rate of turn of the attacking aircraft and the range to the target. The former is measured using a gyroscope in the sight, while the latter is estimated by the pilot by moving a dial or pointer so that a reticle in the sight matches the wingspan of the target. The pilot would point his Spitfire at the intended target and when the cross bisected the target the range was matched as the surrounding "diamonds" would match the silhouette of the enemy.

The effectiveness of this new technology versus the older non-magnifying reflector gunsight was a subject of constant discussion amongst the pilots. One of the most authoritative sources of information on the subject can be found with 127 Wing's Commander JE "Johnnie" Johnson CB CBE, DSO and Two Bars, DFC and Bar. As one of the Allies most successful fighter pilots with at least 38 kills, he felt that the new sight forced to spend too long with his: "head in the office as it were, peering into the sight and not paying enough attention to my tail. I preferred the old-fashioned simple reflector sight, which I kept installed in my personal Spitfire until the war was over."

For Ramrod 941, Ross was joined in the squadron strength dive bombing mission by Dave, Charlie, Gibby, Len, and Bob. At the intelligence briefing, the Roaring Boys were talked through their route in and out as well as details of the No Ball target which was to be attacked with 12 X 500 lb bombs. Ross looked around to the south as he climbed onto the wing of "B for beer." The visibility was in excess of 20 miles, ideal for dive bombing if conditions were the same in France. He also knew it was ideal for a "bounce out of the sun" by the Luftwaffe as well as providing an uninterrupted view for the flak batteries. As Ross fired up his Spitfire, all around it was if a series of windmills had suddenly embraced a summer breeze as the propellers of the Roaring Boys aircraft turned. Their Spitfires came alive, some instantly, others emitting a large plume of grey smoke as if in protest whilst another angrily lived up to its name by spitting fire. They taxied out and in an instant were at 1,000 feet where in turn each section of aircraft was welcomed into the growing formation which turned south and was soon heading across the Channel. The French coast was soon in sight, although their point of crossing is not recorded. There is a discrepancy, which is a common occurrence, between the pilot's logbooks and the ORB. The ORB mentions the location of the No Ball target as "Abbeville area." In previous missions, the raiders had made land at Saint Valery sur Somme and followed the Canal Maritime d'Abbeville à Saint-Valery southeast directly to Abbeville. There were flak batteries all along the canal and as Ross's logbook and the ORB make no mention of flak it is reasonable to conclude that if the target was south of Abbeville then they crossed the French coast elsewhere. For his part, Ross recorded the location of the No Ball target as Saint-Omer rather than Abbeville. He suggests the Abbeville raid was on the 28th, not the 29th May. Perhaps, Ross had his days mixed up, understandable if that was the case with the endless daily routine of missions which inevitably seemed to roll into one.

Whatever the designated target, the Roaring Boys flying line abreast, in turn, swept their Spitfires down to follow the aircraft in front from 8,000 feet, before releasing their 500 pounders at 4,000 feet. Each man then pulled back hard on his Spitfire's control column. Some of the bombs carried delay fuses which were designed to dissuade any repair activities by the Germans after the raid. With their mission completed, the Roaring Boys weren't going to hang around to admire their handiwork. A thick, rising cloud of smoke indicated they had hit something of significance and they executed their exit strategy and were soon in the relative safety of the Channel. Ross noted later: "Good bombing. Came home from Hawkinge on deck. 9 gals." He had 9 gallons of fuel remaining. With the extra drag and weight of the bomb load along with the blast along the deck from Hawkinge to Tangmere, the remaining fuel from his Mark IX's 85-gallon capacity only gave him around 20 minutes flying time, which was sufficient you might think. As every pilot knows, with aviation being what it is, just when your fuel level starts to cause concerns would be exactly the moment when the aerodrome is unexpectedly closed, and an unplanned diversion must be rapidly made. On this occasion at 12.30 pm, exactly 1 hour and 30 minutes after takeoff Ross and the others landed safely at Tangmere, satisfied with their morning's work.

By the end of May, Ross had spent 246 hours and 55 minutes flying Spitfires. He had accumulated 27 hours 15 minutes flying on operations in the month for a total of 77 hours 15 minutes altogether.

With the arrival of June, the rumour mill was in overdrive about the "the big show." Ross started the month with a 30-minute flight to Southend, the usual formation flying and continued practice with the Gyro gunsight. On 6 June at the top of the page of his logbook is emblazoned in capital letters "D" DAY INVASION OF FRANCE." Ross had a long, frustrating wait until 18.00 pm on that day before his beachhead patrol got airborne. Very unusually, and the only time it appears during Spitfire Elizabeth's pilots' operations, 14 Spitfires rather than the usual 12 launched off from

Tangmere for the short duration flight south to Normandy. No one wanted to miss out it seems! Ross had waited all day and seen several patrols go and come back with their stories of the developing landing and progress to securing a lodgement. It was expected that the Luftwaffe would throw every flyable aircraft they could muster against the invasion, particularly as the German High Command had plenty of time to absorb the news of the invasion and interpret the intelligence that was being fed back to them. A partial explanation for the lack of engagement in the air by the enemy could be the belief from Adolf Hitler and his senior commanders that the Normandy landings were a feint and a prelude to the main invasion in the Pas de Calais area. The Germans high command had taken the elaborate deception plan "bait" deployed by the Allies as readily as the wiliest chalk stream trout, deceived by an angler's well-presented artificial fly. The overwhelming air superiority and the sheer number of aircraft at Eisenhower's disposal were also a key factor. Hitler's priority was the defence of "die Fatherland."

The lack of enemy aircraft in significant numbers around the landing area increased the apprehension and anticipation amongst the Roaring Boys. Were the Luftwaffe waiting to strike in the early evening as their patrol made for the front? For Ross, Charlie, Dave, and Len this was their D Day, albeit both Charlie and Dave took part in patrols earlier in the day. W/C George Keefer led the Roaring Boys, his third patrol of the day. After 1 hour and 50 minutes, Ross and the squadron touched down at Tangmere. He collected his thoughts and talked with the others as they successively dropped down off the wings of their Spitfires. Groups of 411 pilots and erks were huddled in small groups, eager to hear from the latest returning patrol the news from the front line. After a debrief with the intelligence boys, Ross completed his logbook: "D Day landings between Le Havre – Cherbourg. Very quiet to what was expected."

The pressure was continuous on the fighter boys to carry on with patrols and maintain a presence around the ever-expanding beachhead. On 10 June, Ross, Dave, Bruce, Charlie, and Bob walked across to dispersal in the cool dawn air. Ross was now wide awake, the prospect of going into combat for Ramrod 985 spiked his adrenalin and senses. A bleary-eyed erk handed him is parachute as he jumped up onto the wing of NH195 (Spitfire NH195 would be destroyed the next day and F/S Tuttle killed after being hit by flak). Ross's Spitfire belched smoke and he felt the cool wash from the propeller over his face, accompanied by the familiar oily fumes from the mighty Merlin engine. It was wheels up at 05.20 am as the 12 Spitfires headed south where they picked up their Stirling and Halifax bombers. As the formation moved across the Normandy coast, the signs of battle were all round on the ground, the odd silent flash of an artillery piece and the curls of smoke, drifting upwards. What sights and sounds there must be down on the battlefield Ross thought, as all he could hear was the dull hum of his Spitfire. Through his headphones, he picked up word that the heavies were about to drop their supplies by parachute to the troops below. Ross watched the stream of parachutes swaying gently as they fell. The formation had awoken the enemy flak batteries who sent up an unwelcome amount of fire. The formation made their escape and Ross was pleased to pass once again over the coast as the bombers headed northeast to their bases. With wheels down at 07.10 am he made some brief notes, "Very quiet. Flak from Hun." The Roaring Boys trudged back from their Spitfires and headed off to breakfast where they could talk over the mission and catch up with Dave who turned back and landed at 06.00 am following technical problems.

Spitfire NH341 Elizabeth

On 18 June Ross was rostered to fly Spitfire Elizabeth. They were scheduled to takeoff at 06.00 am for a beachhead patrol. He was joined on the mission by Dave, Len, Gibby, and Bob. On the face of it, Spitfire NH341 looked like any other Mark IXb in 411 Squadron. She was distinguished by the large capital E painted on the cowling under the propeller, but each Spitfire was differentiated by the subtle artwork that adorned it. Some had black crosses to denote "kills" over the enemy whilst others had the names of their sweethearts painted on each time a pilot bagged his favourite Spitfire. There are many examples of this artwork from amongst the Roaring Boys, like Spitfire "Elizabeth," Tommy's "Lil Mill I, II, III," after his future wife Millie and S/L Bob Hayward's Calamity Jane VI". For Bob, it was "Sad Sack" after the wartime cartoon character. I believe "Letchy Lady" was Ross's aircraft, but who the lady in question might have been is lost in the sands of time! Ross recognised NH341 by the name Elizabeth painted on the cowling and "Eo" on the opposite side. Men, and these days ladies too, have always carried good luck charms, or personalised their weapons of war hoping that they will keep them safe from harm. Even today Parky will kiss both his hands and pat Spitfire Elizabeth saying "well done" as he jumps out.

As Ross fired up Spitfire Elizabeth, he might well have been thinking about the patrol ahead. Would it be routine, or would he get the opportunity to lock horns with the enemy? They taxied out across Tangmere and formed up. Both 126 and 127 Wings would be patrolling the skies above the front. With his power checks done he began his takeoff roll, and Spitfire Elizabeth's rear wheel was quickly up off the grass as the propeller wash blasted past his open cockpit. The first 7 of 411 Spitfires would takeoff to be followed at 06.25 am by 5 more. He hoped Spitfire Elizabeth would not let him down, she'd had a few teething troubles since delivery on 12 June. As they crossed the channel low cloud prevented any view of the sipping supply convoys. The air space was crowded, and even more attention was needed so as not to fly into a huge beehive of bombers and their escorts, or resupply aircraft. Thus far the patrol was uneventful, perhaps the weather was keeping the Luftwaffe grounded. When it was time to head back Ross checked his fuel and saw he was running low. He was experienced enough now to know that he might struggle to make it back to Tangmere. He tapped his fuel gauge to check the reading. The patrol of five 411 Spitfires which left later had already landed back at Tangmere at 07.40 am. Ross was still flying over Normandy. Each one of the Roaring Boys was thinking the same as him regarding their fuel situation. Ross thought he could make it to base without needing to land to refuel at ALG B3 St Croix-sur-Mer or B4 Bény-sur-Mer and so they pushed for home. With the south coast in view and the welcoming grass of Tangmere, they all hoped there wouldn't be trouble. Their fuel situation was by now becoming critical. They'd flown into a northeasterly wind and had burned much more fuel than anticipated. A warning message was sent to air traffic control. The field was clear, and Elizabeth touched down. Ross was relieved. He later completed his logbook with the following entry: "Quiet. Low cloud. Landed with 4 gals. P/O Pine 412 crash landed."

All of RAF Tangmere was suddenly a buzz of activity just after 11.00 am on 18 June as the order was given for 126 Wing to pack up within half an hour ready for the move to ALG B4 Bény-sur-Mer. Ross wasted no time and packed up and stowed his kit. He was ready when the order came to board one of the 10 RAF Dakotas that would ferry them and their kit to France, where they would join up with the advance party who a few days before had made the crossing by sea with the bulk of the Wing's equipment and supplies. Ross recorded the momentous day in his logbook: "Tangmere – France. Moved to France. Forced landed on B2.

1.00." The ALG B2 was located at Bazenville airfield which a few days before had become the home of 127 Wing, and their legendary commander Johnnie Johnson. The reason for the forced landing there is not recorded. It could have been aircraft technical issues, a navigation error or with B4 being close to the front line the pilot was ordered to land at B2 as the airfield was still dangerously close to the front line. The sight of so many large, vulnerable transport aircraft landings would not go unnoticed by enemy spotters who could call in artillery fire, or an air raid against such a target-rich environment. It seems all passed off without incident and like the rest of the Roaring Boys, Ross spent the day settling into his new base. He noted immediately how different it was from the quiet of Tangmere. There was a constant rumble of artillery and small arms fire. Although he had been at war for a while, he had only seen the ground conflict from high above in the relative calm of his Spitfire. There was a distinct and visceral feel to this place. It was slap bang in the middle of a war zone, and the background noise of guns and battle would take some getting used to.

As befitted their title as a mobile fighter wing, 126 was soon operational and ready for combat at B4. Ross, like everyone else, had quickly concluded that digging down into the Norman soil was the best and safest way to escape the endless shower of ordnance falling from the sky during the day and throughout the night. On 20 June at 20.40 pm he saw that he was rostered to fly his first mission, escorting 2 Dakotas back to the UK from B4. They would make up a section of 4 Spitfires, and in addition to Ross, P/O P Wallace, F/Os L A Dunn, and R W Hogg comprised the rest of the quartet. At least the poor weather had temporarily damped down the endless swirling dust as aircraft came and left, although no one was quite sure if that was worse than the glutinous quagmire that had replaced it.

At 20.40 pm the four Spitfires weaved their way out to the runway. Ross glanced over at the local church spire that once housed a deadly nest of German snipers. Thank goodness he thought someone had put several artillery rounds through it. Problem solved. The Spitfires took off ahead of the 2 Dakotas and stooged around on a mini reconnaissance mission just in case any bandits were in the area looking to help themselves to a defenceless Dakota. The coast was clear, and the four Spitfires climbed steadily as the mini formation headed for England. It was an impressive sight, the fighters looking quite insignificant against the twin propellered C47 transports. For

Ross and the 3 others, this was expected to be a routine trip until without warning after 30 minutes Ross's headphones sparked into life. The calm, clear voice of Len Dunn was speaking. He had engine trouble in MJ905 and was bailing out. Len had no time to make landfall and wanted out whilst he had plenty of altitude. Ditching in the sea was inherently riskier and was accompanied by a one-way invitation to "Davy Jones" locker. The others watched on helplessly as Len's hood slid back and he tumbled out, curling himself into a ball to avoid hitting the tail fin. MJ905 was soon in a steep dive into the dark grey sea where it hit the water with a single large splash and was instantly gone in the best traditions of a theatre magician. The others had lost sight of the tumbling Len and were desperate to see the welcoming site of his blooming silk saviour, which duly appeared. At least they could fix his position and pass it to sector control who could vector in the ASR boys. They also hoped one of many ships traversing the channel with sailors manning their observation decks eagerly watching for enemy aircraft would see Len as he continued his gentle progress towards the sea. Whilst Ross and Wallace continued with the Dakota escort, Hogg circled Len. The ORB later gave the details: "F/O L A Dunn's aircraft developed engine trouble over the Channel and he bailed out being picked up and taken to England by a destroyer. Otherwise uneventful. He qualified for membership in both the Caterpillar and Goldfish Clubs for bailing out safely and clinging on to his dinghy until helped reached him." Ross also made note of the incident, which with air combat casualties and regular technical issues was almost a matter of daily routine: "Landed Tangmere. Len Dunn baled out in drink."

The daily routine at B4 continued as the Roaring Boys "funk holes" were developed into comfortable dwellings, some of which became wonders of innovative design, construction, and innovation. There was still the odd raid by 411 pilots and crew into the local area and the abandoned German camp in a search for construction materials. Observers from the time confirmed that all personnel were banned from one such expedition as army engineers had yet to clear the site of booby trap devices left by the retreating Germans. In fact, the souvenir hunting Canucks were looking for any material that could be useful or traded for the growing supply of local Calvados, cheese and wine that was finding its way into the camp from the local French entrepreneurs, in exchange for highly prized tobacco or chocolate. On 26 June, Ross and the Roaring Boys were rostered to fly a beachhead patrol. It was obviously a slow news day in the war as the ORB triumphantly recorded the arrival of Myrtle the horse who would be helping move equipment around the base and who quickly became a favourite across the squadron. The reaction of Joskins Firkin of Scopwick, the original mascot, to the new competition for the squadron's affections, is not recorded! As the beach patrol party made their way to their Spitfires Ross walked along with, Bob, Dave, Charlie, and Gibby. They were into the air from a gloomy B4 at 12.10 pm. It was hardly flaming June Ross thought. This was his second mission of the day and so far, all was quiet in the sector. The day before Operation Epsom had got underway, and this brought the possibility of a response from the enemy. As they patrolled their area, they received warning of enemy aircraft in the sector. Everyone immediately became that little bit sharper and all began busily checking everything was running normally in the world of their Spitfire. You didn't want to have loose Sutton Harnesses whilst pulling high "G" force manoeuvres in air combat. Nothing was left to chance. Despite a search for the next hour, nothing was seen. It could have been an Allied formation, or perhaps the Germans had returned to base, especially in the appalling weather. At 13.25 pm Dave, R K Hayward, B Eskow and Ross touched down, the others following in groups of 4, protecting the vulnerable landing Spitfires in case of an attack by the enemy. As they hopped down from their aircraft and trudged back through the mud to debrief in dispersal, Ross took the opportunity to complete his own logbook, the disappointment emanating from his written words: "Several bogies reported. Unable to find any."

Despite the appalling weather, June had been a month of months. D Day had successfully taken place, and the Roaring Boys had transferred their operation to France. Ross had spent a total of 298 hours flying Spitfires, with 41 hours and 35 minutes being on operations during June. His total hours on operational missions in the Spitfire was now 120 hours and 40 minutes, so he had moved completed over half of his operational tour. His total flying on all types of aircraft now stood at 599 hours 10 minutes.

Glorious July hadn't started that way as the squadron diarist wrote: "Weather was bad major part of the day." Despite this, a full day of flying patrols and armed reconnaissance were undertaken by the Roaring Boys. Ross's 4 Spitfire patrol was to be the last of the day and he would be in the familiar company of section leader Charlie, Dave and Gord Lapp. Charlie was on a hot streak and should they meet any enemy aircraft the others knew he wouldn't miss the opportunity to increase his score. As they took off at 17.20 pm into the late afternoon gloom they immediately wondered if the enemy was thinking the same as them, a bad day for flying. Despite this, there was a patrol of the William sector of the bridgehead to conduct and it would be just like the enemy to try something when it was least expected. After several sweeps of the area and with the weather becoming progressively worse, Charlie made his decision and transmitted that to his fellow patrol members, "Return to base." At 18.05 pm the formation landed, with Dave having returned with technical issues 15 minutes after takeoff. That was Ross's day done. He'd have to see what tomorrow would bring.

Ross's day started early on the 2 July as he was on the eventful early patrol of the eastern sector of the bridgehead with Jimmy Jeffrey in Spitfire Elizabeth and Gord Lapp. At 16.00 pm Ross was once again strapped into his Spitfire and ready to lead another 4 Spitfire patrol of the William sector of the bridgehead which on their side was uneventful. The patrol was led by Charlie who left 15 minutes before them. They were soon vectored onto 15+ FW 190s and whilst the ORB stated they were engaged in combat no claims were made. Ross and the patrol landed after 50 minutes with him reporting: "F/L Trainor didn't get his (fired with no results). Ross's pattern of bridgehead patrols continued with an armed reconnaissance and a front-line patrol on 5 July. The 2nd TAF was enhancing its reputation as a fighting force, and part of the success was due to their highly successful operational control system. The endless hours of practice by the Roaring Boys and their familiarity with each other, the procedures and the ability for control to put them in the right area to attack the enemy, were key contributors to this success. At 14.20 pm Ross chatted to his fellow patrol pilots, Tommy, Len, and Gord Lapp. They talked through the briefing and who would fly where. They agreed their positions in the finger-four formation.

The ORB recorded the details of the mission as briefed by Ross and the patrol: "Eastern Low patrol. Scattered Met seen but not attacked. One aircraft became separated and returned early. One enemy tank was seen and pinpointed." The aircraft that separated from the formation was Ross. He gave the details in his logbook, "Returned early. No R/T." Tommy was also unimpressed by the lack of action as he put pen to paper, "Turfed around from Le Havre to Bayeux. S.F.A."

The 6 July was the first day in around a week that the weather was good, and no one wanted to miss out on the opportunity. B4 came to life as the intelligence section, under pressure from the eager pilots processed their reports, assigned and briefed rostered pilots for their missions. S/L Roberston gathered the 11 other Roaring Boys around him with a few final words as they prepared for their 11.55 am an armed reconnaissance mission. The sections then broke up and discussed a few final details and words with each other. Ross listened intently as A flight leader Charlie gave some words of encouragement, As his wingman, Ross would shadow "the boss" and cover him should any bandits make an appearance. An interesting note to the mission is that the Spitfire Gord Lapp is officially recorded as flying in Spitfire NH341 Elizabeth! Clearly, a clerical error as she had crashed 4 days before into a field near Orbec. As Ross dropped into the cockpit of his favoured Spitfire NH240 "DB – L", he already knew that after taking off they would form up over B4 and then swing almost due south towards Domfront, which was approximately 60 miles away, and well behind enemy lines. The return leg created a flight path that resembled an elongated letter "U." The plan was to fly over the town of Flers, which is located around 15 miles to the northeast of Domfront. The anticipation of finding ground targets of opportunity to attack was high and so it proved. The hunt was on and their blood was up. Whilst one section provided top cover Ross kept tight in behind Charlie as he watched the flashes from his Hispano cannons followed by the tell-tale smoke trails behind each wing. In an instant, the APVs were decimated and smoke and flames leapt up. Then Ross took his turn and he picked on another Met which had stopped. Through his gun sight, he could see clearly as a door swung open from the truck and a small figure bolted for cover. The truck was then enveloped and in amongst the dust and smoke, there were instantaneous flashes of bright white light as the fizzing tracer rounds found their mark. The risk of strafing attacks is of becoming fixated on a single target that creating a vignette that holds the pilot's attention as if hypnotised by what he is witnessing. During many sports 'white line fever' is a similar phenomenon where the attention of scoring a goal, or try overtakes everything else. Ross's Spitfire was losing height rapidly at speeds of around 350 mph. He was an experienced campaigner by now and wasn't about to plough into the ground or run the risk of offering an easy target to an army private spraying his Spitfire with fire from his Schmeisser MP40 machine pistol. He pulled up and kicked the rudder pedal to take his aircraft well away from the smoking convoy. At the same time, he tensed his lower body to counteract the "G" forces that were fighting to drain the blood from his head as his Spitfire banked away. There was no time to hang around. Local ground units were alerted to their presence and they weren't keen to embrace the attention of a flak battery armed with their deadly Flakvierling 38 anti-aircraft guns. This weapon consisted of a four-barrelled 20 mm weapon that was highly effective against low flying aircraft. As the formation drew back together the thunder of Merlin engines grew silent amongst the smouldering wreckage of the convoy. It was a short uneventful flight back to B4, although the apocalyptic scenes of battle, gun flashes, and rising smoke stretched out across the front, especially in the ferocious battle for Caen. The formation fell into its landing order and Ross throttled down and bumped along B4, a compact but busy metropolis seemingly never quiet, and always busy. He jumped down and spoke with Charlie and A flight. B flight did the same with S/L Robertson. Their reports to intelligence were then transcribed into the ORB: "The squadron took off on an Armed Recce in the Domfront – Flers area. Two APVs and three other Met were damaged." By the time the squadron gathered again in the evening for a further reconnaissance mission, Ross could see in the distance the distinctive form of cumulonimbus clouds forming a giant white and grey tower with an anvil shape spreading out from the top. Storms like these presented a serious hazard to the aviator, especially in a small fighter like a Spitfire. Other than the obvious dangers of a lightning strike, the biggest danger is the wind shear of the updrafts and downdrafts as warm moist air is drawn in and cools. An aircraft could suffer a structural failure, or stall as the normal passage of air over the wings is lost due to its rapid change in direction. Thunderstorms can be localised and so at 20.30 pm, Ross taxied up alongside Charlie who would this time be leading the squadron formation. They were soon airborne and at the starting gate of their patrol area. Ross surveyed the scene, the wind was picking up for sure, he could feel it as his Spitfire pitched and dropped. They were heading for the centre of the storm, and its swirling, concentric circles of torment, flashes of lightning illuminating the Normandy sky, ready to reach out and grab each plucky Spitfire in turn and spin them out in all directions. He was thinking that they should turn back, and he knew in the other cockpits everyone else was thinking the same. It was up to the boss, Charlie to decide. His R/T was filled with a calm Canadian voice and one word was uttered, "abort." The relief was palpable as the formation returned to a still sunlit B4 at 21.10 pm. It was time to batten down the hatches before the storm blew in.

Ross awoke on the morning of the 8 July. It had been a noisy night as RAF Bomber Command visited the area with 700 Lancasters which carpet-bombed the city of Caen. The cacophony of noise was supplemented by the distant thump of German flak batteries in the surrounding area, along with the familiar noise of battle. It seemed to Ross as he wandered over to breakfast that you didn't need to walk too far to find under your feet the crunch of shell fragments or rounds deposited from the heavens. At least the weather was good for the armed reconnaissance mission. At the briefing everyone was warned that the pasting given to Caen was tantamount to "poking a stick into a wasps nest" and the enemy flak boys, grumpy after a sleepless night, would be looking for revenge.

Ross with Spitfire 'Letchy Lady'

This armed reconnaissance would be a squadron strength affair and Ross would, as usual, be in position on Charlie's wing. As if the conductor had tapped his baton for the orchestra to start so in random order the extended line of Spitfires became a whirling formation of propellers and smoke, interspersed with the occasional bright set of flames, gently waving from the exhaust ports in the breeze. Some of these graceful ladies needed a little more priming with fuel before they were ready for work. The erks, as proud as any stable lad or lass of the finest thoroughbred they had turned out for The Derby, disconnected the battery cart and dived down to remove the chocks before giving the thumbs up or salute to the pilots as the 12 Spitfires made their way out to takeoff at 10.20 am. As the formation moved in close together the patrol area would take them on across an area covering Caen, Thury-Harcourt, Condé- sur-Noireau, and Falaise. On the map, Thury-Harcourt is situated around 15 miles to the southwest of Caen with Condé-sur-Noireau a further 10 miles on to the southwest. The roads passing through these towns would have been filled with German transportation moving up and back from the front around Caen. As the mission unfolded the advice about the flak batteries proved well-founded as Ross later recorded, "Bags of flak." After a short time, F/O R W Hogg and F/S D J Le Blanc peeled away from the formation reporting a hit by flak. It's not clear who was hit but the other aircraft provided cover in case any enemy fighters were in the area to pick off the ailing Spitfire. The ORB logged the incident: "One pilot returned early because he thought he was hit by flak – this later proved to be wrong. There was heavy flak from several areas." Despite the flak, the Roaring Boys weren't going to let a road busy full of transports go by without receiving some attention from them. Every truck or armoured personnel carrier they could destroy, or damage would help ease the pressure for the boys at the front. They were the aggressive Canucks of 411, and all were mindful of the squadron motto "hostile to an enemy." They were also driven by the overwhelming desire to beat their fellow 126 Wing squadrons, 401 and 412 Squadrons on the leader board of damaged enemy aircraft and ground transports. A section of the Spitfire formation rolled down onto the helpless transports, the hot reception in the area from flak intensified as the vehicles felt the full force of the Hispano cannons. With half the squadron providing aerial cover from any Luftwaffe incursion the attack was soon complete and as Ross craned his neck downwards, he could see the billowing smoke and flames drifting across the fields. They had inflicted some significant damage. As the Roaring Boys touched down at 11.25 am, they were greeted by the ground crews, who were quickly removing the aircraft's wing panels to reload with ammunition almost as soon as they shut down. With a quick inquiry about any technical issues on the aircraft to which Ross replied with a negative, he moved quickly back to dispersal to debrief. The official account of the mission listed the damage, "Three APVs and six vehicles damaged." The operation had been a success and inflicted serious damage on the enemy.

With the issuing of communique, No 17 (F) Sector HQ, RCAF tactics would have to change in respect of armed reconnaissance missions.

From 10 July, these operations had to be carried out with a proportion of the aircraft in a section carrying bombs. Despite the firepower of the cannons and machine guns, the top brass had concluded that more damage and destruction could be inflicted if bombs were also dropped on the targets. And so, for Ross's mission of 13 July, at least half of the Spitfires would carry bombs. At the briefing, it was confirmed that the formation leader would decide which target of opportunity should be bombed and if none presented themselves then they would select a "last resort" target which was preselected at the operation briefing in conjunction with the Army Liaison Coordinator.

Ross lined up next to Charlie. From his other logbook entries, and because he had some months before won the squadron "pot of gold" bombing competition it's an odds-on certainty that Ross would have been selected to carry bombs on his favoured steed, NH240 "DB – L." It was engines start at 16.35 pm as Ross pushed the starter and the Rolls Merlin 66 burst into life. In short order, he and the squadron were bouncing their way along B4's mesh runway, dirt and dust kicking up behind them. The dust cloud soon drifted across the airfield enveloping many of the tents and the dispersal area. Everyone was quite used to this now and to every item of their kit being coated. Once they had formed up, the 12 Spitfires climbed, gaining altitude rapidly as Ross looked over to the sea, still packed with ships of all shapes and sizes supplying the giant machine that was the Allied force. They were soon ready to begin the reconnaissance patrol which would cover an area bounded by the towns and villages of Évrecy, Le Bény-Bocage, Vire, Domfront, Flers, and Thury-Harcourt. At their furthest point, they would be around 60 miles southwest of Caen, well behind enemy lines and would be expected to observe and hunt down German Army transportation. As they cruised along at around 5,000 feet, over to the east of patrol area, one of the formations identified a tank which was duly strafed and left damaged. Further on and few miles to the southeast of Caen a much bigger convoy was spotted. Ross was detailed to dive-bomb the convoy and along with the other bomb carrying Spits. They were soon gaining altitude, noting carefully where on the ground the slow-moving targets were located and their direction of travel. Ross led the bombing team and eased back gently on the stick and watched his altimeter quickly rotate until at around 12,000 – 14,000 feet they could begin their attack. As Ross headed down, he didn't need his instruments to tell him his Spitfire was soon pushing nearly 400 mph as he lined up on the road. At around 4,000 feet he pulled back on the stick and a split second later pulled the bomb release. As he eased away, he could see the other Roaring Boys following him in to attack. Over the sound of his Merlin which he had throttled back to reduce speed, he saw a large mushroom cloud of earth and dust rise up as the next bombs smashed into the road adding to the destruction created by his bomb. He had certainly hit a couple of them. As the dive bombing team formed back up, they were on alert for enemy aircraft. The occasional arc of tracer fire from the ground made its way past them. Ross's attention was drawn to a section of Spitfires as they raked the convoy with cannon fire, a soundless vista of deadly bright flashes and smoke erupting from each set of elliptical wings. It seemed to be over in an instant, and all too soon the 12 Spitfires saw B4 come into sight, and with clearance to land, Ross settled NH240's wheels back on the ground. A quick comparison of notes and debrief with the others freed the flight commanders to make their reports to 411's intelligence team. The squadron diarist noted: "one tank damaged near Argentan. Two flamers and four damaged Met scored near Mezidon. Meagre inaccurate flak from St Pierre near Mezidon." Ross also completed some notes in his logbook: "Got a few trucks. F/L Trainor gets DFC." This was the earliest reference I can find to Charlie's award. He was roundly congratulated by all the Roaring Boys and wider 126 Wing pilots and crew for whom he had become a stand out leader.

The 14 July was a day of intense aircraft activity, and the aircraft dispatchers had the headache of scheduling in patrols containing 4 Spitfires for 126 Wing. Each patrol would be taking off and landing at precise intervals throughout the day. A total of 14 patrols would be undertaken by the Roaring Boys in the day. Ross's patrol, led by Charlie and including F/L K I Robb and F/O E G Gord Lapp was scheduled for 09.00 am. With their Spitfires loaded with bombs, they would patrol the Low Eastern sector in the now standard finger-four formation, a patrol that passed by without incident. On returning to B4 the formation could easily pick out the outgoing patrol lifting off and within 5 minutes they had returned to base. A quick debrief to the intelligence section and they were returned to readiness for further patrols in the day.

For 16 July Ross was rostered to fly on an evening armed reconnaissance mission which would take in Évrecy, Villers Bocage, Aunay-sur-Odon, and Thury-Harcourt. As Ross lifted off in NH240 he was once again carrying a 500 lb bomb. S/L Robertson led the formation of 12 Spitfires and he soon ordered the bomb-carrying section of their target, a set of crossroads near Évrecy. As Ross prepared to commence the dive his eyes quickly scanned the dials on his instrument panel, temperatures, pressure which all showed normal readings. He throttled back and pushed the spade grip forward and as his Spitfire reached a 45-degree angle he focused in on the crossroads and made small adjustments with his rudder pedals and stick as the speed built. Ross's thumb felt for the bomb release button located on the end of his throttle handle and as he reached around 4,000 feet, he eased the stick back and pressed the button. He knew immediately as NH240 pulled up that he had had a "hang up" and his bomb had not released. He regained altitude and checked the target area, just in time to seem a rising cloud of earth, smoke, and dust, a direct hit by the pilot behind him. The flak was heavy and continuous, and they needed to weave to stop the flak gunners getting a fix on them. It was frightening but they all had to push through the fear they felt and do their job. Ross was not the only one experiencing issues, two other Spitfires had the same problem, and on the return leg the secondary target of a quarry was located and the bombs which failed to release in the attack were eventually released there. One final bomb was dropped off in the sea off Cabourg as it needed repeated attempts before it detached itself. It would seem likely that this final bomb release was Ross's and he was escorted by S/L Robertson. The rationale for this is that if he had to land with the bomb still slung under his aircraft's belly there was an extra risk if he had an accident. A runway closure would affect the smooth running of the other 2nd TAF operations at B4. Ross and S/L Robertson were the last to land at 21.45 pm. He wrote in his pilot log: "Trouble releasing bomb. Flak too hot. F/L Robb landed 1 wheel up." The ORB reported: "Flak was 10/10 throughout with the Hun firing at anything moving through the air."

On 18 July Ross and F/L K I Robb were called in by intelligence and briefed about an urgent mission, which was different from their normal daily operations. They would be undertaking an air-sea rescue search over the channel. With every minute critical to the prospective survival of the crew they quickly made their way to their Spitfires and started up. They climbed out and turned north towards the coast, which they quickly crossed, the wide expanse of the channel filled their windscreens. Their target was an RAF Lancaster bomber crew, one of 1,000 that had bombed Caen under the cover of darkness, and which had been forced to ditch into the sea. The fate of the crew was not known and whether they have stayed with the ditching aircraft or baled out into the sea. As Ross and F/L Robb reached the last known coordinates for the downed Lancaster they began to methodically search the area. It wasn't long before they spotted bright green patches of fluorescein dye in the water. These patches had produced a vivid marking against the dark sea and from their vantage point a few thousand feet above Ross and F/L Robb could see two green patches stretching out for quite some distance. The two Spitfires descended to take a closer look at the area. As they circled there was no sign the crew or any aircraft wreckage, despite widening their search area in case the crew had drifted on the wind they could find no trace. They did see a patrol launch in the area of the dye. Ross spoke in his R/T and Robb agreed; they had done all they could. After they radioed in their discovery of the fluorescein dye, they turned south to return to B4 with wheels down at 10.10 am. Ross and Robb were debriefed and afterward, Ross completed his logbook: "Lanc in drink. Bags of fluorescein. No aircraft."

On 24 July, the S/L Robertson briefed the Roaring Boys for their squadron strength armed reconnaissance mission which would be carried out in the Domfront and Argentan areas. It was 19.05 pm as the formation rumbled down the runway, each Spitfire compromised by its large, bulbous 500 lb bomb. After gaining altitude and forming up over B4, Ross drew in close to Charlie and the formation turned to the south to start the patrol. All eyes were focused outside the cockpit searching for any aircraft formations. Their gaze then turned to the ground and finding the slow-moving enemy trucks or tanks. Ross strained his eyes; the visibility was poor, and they were struggling to pinpoint any ground forces. The patrol continued but the Roaring Boys were all starting to conclude that there would be little to report unless the Luftwaffe made an appearance. At 20.25 pm he landed back at B4. The haze had prevented any observation or offensive action against the enemy who no doubt welcomed the conditions as they could move around without fear of attack.

The 26th July Ross took part in for patrols of the low East sector. Each patrol comprised the usual 4 Spitfires. He had already been on an early morning patrol and at 9:25 am as he strapped himself once again into NH 240. He looked over at Charlie waiting for his signal to move off. Charlie raised his hand and Ross opened the throttle and taxied his Spitfire out, following his leader. Once over B4, Ross looked down at the hive of activity, it was like a colony of ants moving around the airfield which now covered a vast area. On this day, the ground crews and pilots would earn their pay with a succession of missions taking off each hour pushing the organisation to its limits. The squadron ORB describes that everyone was: "on defensive readiness all day. 17 low eastern uneventful patrols were carried out." As they swept over the front line, looking for action, none was to be found. Part of the problem for the patrol was a low cloud base, and Ross noted in his logbook the patrol area which was: "Caen, Villers Bocage. Huns reported." He also wrote, "F/L Hayward, Kiersy and Orr each get DFC." After one hour 20 minutes Ross's heard Charlie deliver the order for the patrol to return to base. The patrol had lasted one hour 20 minutes. After touching down at B4 the Roaring Boys quickly made their way to be intelligence section to debrief.

Ross's mission of 27 July would be eventful. The Roaring Boys were to be at full squadron strength for an armed reconnaissance mission with Bob joining Ross on the mission. In the briefing, they synchronised their watches and listened intently as the intelligence team and S/L Robertson outlined the patrol area. They would takeoff at 14.45 pm and head on a northeasterly course towards Rouen. The reconnaissance patrol would take in Pont-Audemer, around 40 miles to the northeast of Caen, and Yvetot which is around 20 miles northwest of Rouen. On the final leg of the mission, the formation would reconnoitre the territory around the city of Rouen.

Ross lowered himself into DB – L, NH240 and felt the warmth of the sun on his black leather RAF gloves. Not the ideal glove colour for the summer heat he thought as his hands soon became clammy. He strapped in and ran through his startup procedure, a quick prime and push of the starter and his Spitfire roared into life. Around him, the other 11 Spitfires were in the process of doing the same and soon the air was filled with sound and smell of Merlin engines. S/L Robertson moved forward and Ross signalled for his chocs to be removed. He formed up next to his leader and soon his Spitfire was bouncing along the runway of B4. With gentle back pressure on the column, his Spitfire rose into the air. His eyes flicked over his instruments, checking oil pressure and temperatures were normal. Simultaneously, he felt the reassuring clunk as the undercarriage tucked in under his wings and the greens lights illuminated. The formation was flying at 1,500 feet almost in the blink of an eye as they moved off towards Port-Audemer. It was soon clear to Ross and the formation that there was great potential for ground attack and as such, they could expect to be met by flak, which on cue duly appeared. Those unwelcome puffs of black smoke signalled mortal danger to the Roaring Boys and their Spitfires as they flew through a patchwork of exploding airburst shells. There was some evasive action taken as the Roaring Boys sought to put the flak gunners off. Very soon each section was ready and with one providing top cover the others, in turn, attacked the transports below, raking the convoy with cannon fire. The ORB provided details of the damage: "two flamers, 3 smokers. 3 damaged." The Roaring Boys weren't finished as one of the squadron spotted a formation of 5 tanks trundling along the Fleury road near Rouen. Ross joined in the attack, hammering the target area with his wing cannons. A couple of the formation radioed in that they had been hit by ground fire but were ok. For F/L H J Nixon in NH344, his day was about to take a turn for the worse and his life was in mortal danger. He was hit by return machine gun fire from one of the tanks whilst flying at only 50 feet above it. The black smoke pouring out of his cowling told the rest of the formation that he had no time to gain altitude and in an instant, his Spitfire had ploughed into a field near Fleury-sur-Andelle, around 5 miles southeast of Rouen. The ORB commented, "He was seen to run into woods." At least the Roaring Boys knew their comrade had survived. For Nixon himself, his first thought was to put as much distance as possible between himself and the wreckage of NH344. He wasn't going to hang around to see if the remaining tanks came his way. The attack had left 2 tanks smoking with an unknown number of casualties and Nixon didn't fancy facing their angry crews, especially if they members of an SS Panzer unit. As Ross and the remainder of the formation landed back at B4 at 16.15 pm, the first topic of conversation was Nixon. "Did you see him hit? It was one of the tanks. He was only at 50 feet. I saw him go in." Once the vehicle damage had been totalled up, and each section and flight had completed the debrief, everyone was ready for dinner. As they ambled over to the mess tent their minds were preoccupied with Nixon's fate. He was now on the run in enemy territory, and they hoped he had evaded the convoy they had attacked. All were thankful that they had returned safely, although the erks were busily repairing flak damage on 2 of the other Spitfires. Ross also referred in his logbook to Charlie, his former leader and comrade's first successful outing as squadron leader of 401 Squadron: "401 got 8 and 2 damaged. Huns reported 442 (squadron) had a go."

The 28 July was a busy day for Ross. He was awoken early, before Dawn and sipped a black coffee with Bob, R W Hogg, and D J Le Blanc as their mission was briefed. Ross would fill in as wingman to Bob as flight leader. With the briefing complete they walked briskly to their Spitfires, the scent of battle in their nostrils. B4 was stirring and the sound the of 4 Rolls Royce Merlins was about to shake those yet to rise from their slumbers. At 05.25 am as the Roaring Boys lifted off for their patrol it would be a high-altitude job, at heights of up to 20,000 feet. Ross wrote, "10/10 cloud. Took off at dawn." He didn't report anything else of interest from the patrol, neither does the ORB and at 06.40 am the formation settled back onto the welcoming strip of B4 in time for a quick debrief and a hearty breakfast. It wasn't long before Ross hopped up again onto the wing of Spitfire NH240 to prepare for his next high-altitude patrol on the eastern sector of the front. At 08.25 am they lifted off again as would happen every hour with another 4 Roaring Boys taking their Spitfires off into battle.

As the 4 Spitfires reached their patrol altitude Ross breathed deeply from his oxygen supply and just then in front of them loomed a huge formation of what they quickly identified as USAAF heavies. Ross later noted the meeting: "Bags of BIG BOYS." Bob's voice came over the R/T warning everyone to keep their eyes peeled for the escorts. Sure enough glints of silver suddenly appeared high above them and which alarmingly were soon diving down to attack them. The Roaring Boys watched them all the way. It was the so-called "little friends" of the heavies, the fighter escorts. This was an uncomfortable moment as the Spitfires wagged their wings and held their course. Ross wrote, "Jumped by Mustangs." Fortunately, the incoming Mustangs realised that the Spits were also "little friends" and with a waggle of their wings, Ross and the others watched the P51s climb back up to their vantage point above the beehive. Others in these situations weren't so lucky and getting too close to formations like this, especially the bombers often resulted in a hail of machine tracer arching over in response. At 09.35 am the patrol was over and the routine of debriefing and refreshments followed. There was a chance to catch up on the paperwork and relax a while in the sunshine before Ross would take his final high-altitude patrol of the day which lifted off at 10.25 am. Within 20 minutes DJ Givens had returned with a technical problem whilst Ross and the other three pressed on. There was no sign of other aircraft and as they flew on Ross detected that something was wrong as he was struggling to breathe. At this altitude, the consequences of oxygen depletion, hypoxia could be deadly. He quickly radioed the other 3 and they decided to cut the patrol short, as Ross dropped the nose of his Spitfire and quickly levelled off at under 12,000 feet where he filled his lungs with fresh air, at the same time ripping off his face mask. He later added a note with his usual brevity, "oxygen trouble" as the shortened patrol returned to B4 at 11.10 am. For Ross, his day's flying was done.

Ross would participate in another busy day of patrolling on 30 July, with his first mission in squadron strength all briefed and ready for wheels up at 07.15 am. The armed reconnaissance patrol would take in an area covering Caumont, which is around 10 miles to the southwest of Rouen and Villers Bocage, which is approximately 20 miles to the south west of Caen. Ross gently manoeuvred his Spitfire to the side and a little behind the A flight leader, Bob. Gibby was positioned elsewhere is a separate section of the formation as the patrol moved off to their start point at around 5,000 feet. The patrol's objectives, reported as "uneventful" in the 411 ORB was described in more detail by Ross: "Cover for bombers. 700 'heavies' bombed front line." From their Spitfires, there was no missing the target area which had a neat curtain of smoke rising high into the atmosphere. The formation seemed endless, the sky before them was filled with black dots in neat regular patterns, the occasional aircraft distinguished by a trail of smoke from one of its flak damaged engines. Ross and the others stared intently at the sky around. The sheer scale and power of the forces ranged again the Luftwaffe was jaw-dropping. Would the Luftwaffe take a chance on a hit and run attack on the formation? No attack materialized, and all too soon at the Roaring Boys touched back down at 08.30 am for a quick turnaround of men and machines, in readiness for the next mission.

Ross's total flying times were prepared, and he passed them to Bob as OC A flight to check before they were endorsed by Squadron Leader Hayward. For the month of July Ross had clocked 40 hours 20 minutes flying on operations. His total operational flying in Spitfires was 162 hours 25 minutes. This gave him a total time flying Spitfires of 339 hours 15 minutes. He had accumulated total flying on all aircraft of 638 hours 25 minutes. His tour completion was drawing ever closer.

On 2 August Ross and the Roaring Boys were ready for another full day of patrolling. Ross and Bob made their first 4 Spitfire patrol at 14:45 pm. The patrol area for the day was Bayeux and Cabourg. The patrol was uneventful although Ross provided further details: "412 Squadron lost Squadron Leader Sheppard and Sanderson got an FW 190." The patrol landed at 16.00 pm and Ross had a brief opportunity to relax before he was airborne again at 17:40 pm for his next hour-long patrol. He again described the patrol as uneventful but did note that: "401 Squadron got 3 FW 190s."

With the weather being described on 4 August as "duff," the ORB provided welcome news: "On 5th August leave will commence for the pilots. Seven days less one day travelling is allowed with air transportation provided from ALG B14 Amblie to England. F/Os LA Dunn and SR Linquist were the first 2 lucky fellows." We can only speculate where Ross spent his leave in England, but perhaps the bright lights of London were a draw for him. He noted in his logbook that he took a Dakota flight from B14 to RAF Northolt. He returned to 411 Squadron from Northolt on 14 August in an Avro Anson. His next mission was flown on 15 August. At around 7.00 am Ross entered the intelligence section for the operational briefing. The plan was to dive bomb barges and tugs on the river Seine. The location for the attack would be the area of Elbeuf. At 7.15 am, 12 pilots walked towards the dispersal area. Ross immediately made for NH 240; the distinctive "L" now slightly faded but still visible underneath the propeller. It was like being reacquainted with an old friend, his faithful "Letchy Lady." The wing was now situated at a new base, ALG B18 at Cristot. They had advanced in the manner of the mobile fighter wing to keep up with land forces who were breaking out across Normandy. For Ross, it was back to business and the dispersal area was soon filled with the smoke and noise of 12 Rolls Royce Merlin engines. Ross noticed how each Spitfire, laden with fuel, bombs, and ammunition seemed to take on an even more awkward appearance on the ground. At precisely 7.30 am, B18 was once again a cacophony of noise as the 12 war machines rolled down the runway and into the air. They set course for Rouen, and in turn, each section prepared itself for the upcoming bombing of barges and tugs. Sitting at an altitude of around 14,000 feet Ross watched the first section gracefully turn their Spitfires earthwards to begin their attack. From this altitude, it was difficult to see the results but a wisp of smoke began to rise from twisting river Seine. Ross was next and Spitfire NH 240 responded to his forward pressure on the control column and on the left rudder pedal that rolled his Spitfire into a steep dive. Ross pushed the bomb release button. As he gained altitude, he quickly turned his head over his shoulder to see a very large plume of water landing back into the welcoming grasp of the river. With the bombing part of his mission complete Ross and his section-maintained cover for the other sections as they attacked a succession of barges, tugs, and locks, doing their best to avoid the flak from the Rouen area. The Roaring Boys returned to B18 section by section with Ross landing at 8.40 AM. Ross commented on the mission in his logbook: "Good bombing. Bags of flak. Lost F/O Wheler." Ross obviously wanted to make mention Tommy's disappearance on 7th August whilst he was his break in England. A great comrade and a big loss to 411.

There was barely time for Ross to relax after his first operation. He would be back in action again at 11:05 am. As a skilled practitioner in the art of dive bombing, he was rostered to fly on the next mission. On this occasion, the mission would be led by S/L Hayward. The secondary objective was an armed reconnaissance of the area around Le Havre. Hayward led the formation of Spitfires out from the dispersal area. And shortly after, they were on their way towards Le Havre flying along over the sea. Ross's headphones relayed Hayward's order to attack. The pier below was prominent as Ross carefully lined up his diving Spitfire, breaking out towards the sea as the bomb fell towards its target. With this part of the mission complete, the reconnaissance was soon underway, and they scouted the area from their vantage point around 5,000 feet above the ground. In a moment a voice piped up and using a clock face directed the formation to look towards a collection of vehicles on the road below. It was time to unleash the cannons. The attackers were all too aware of the vulnerability of the Spitfire to ground fire. Nonetheless, Ross pressed home his attack. The two cars were hit hard with cannon shells, emitting a plume of smoke and flames. Ross later wrote, "Got 2 cars on recce."

The squadron ORB reported on the mission results: "Dive bombing jetty on Seine. One direct hit, 3 near misses and 4 in target area was scored. One bomb overshot and 3 others were jettisoned in enemy territory." It was wheels down for the Roaring Boys at 12.05 am and Ross could reflect on a successful day. He was now a senior pilot and as many of Spitfire Elizabeth's pilots had completed their tours or were shot down it was up to the old hands like Ross to advise and guide the new intake.

In mid-August, as the Falaise pocket closed around the retreating German Army, it is clear to see from the squadron records that there was an abundance of targets for the squadron to attack. They were eager and keen to create as much damage and chaos as they could. Ross looked out across the airfield and could see that the visibility was poor. It was 16 August, one of those hazy summer days which were operationally difficult for ground attack missions to identify their targets. S/L Hayward led the briefing and at 15.15 pm it was time to jump into the assembled Spitfires and get the armed reconnaissance underway. The ORB diarist wrote about the area they would cover: "Armed recce in the Flers/Lisieux and L'Aigle areas. Scattered Mets were sighted. Score 8 flamers, 2 smokers, 15 damaged and 2 tanks damaged. Accurate light flak was encountered." For his part, Ross noted after the 1 hour 10-minute mission: "Very poor viz. Got several vehicles."

The Germans were on the run and the shrinking pocket of land around Falaise became known as "The Shambles (an old English name for a slaughterhouse). There were men, equipment and transportation scattered across the Normandy countryside and 126 Wing was about to have the best day in its history. Against this backdrop, Ross embarked on an armed reconnaissance of the Bernay, Lisieux and Vimoutiers areas. Vimoutiers is approximately 15 miles to the east of Falaise. At precisely 7.30 am on 18 August, a squadron strength formation of Spitfires headed off into the Normandy's cloudy skies. The scale of the German retreat was evident as soon as the reconnaissance patrol commenced. There was reported to be a column of up to 400 vehicles in the Vimoutiers area. As well as Spitfires of the RCAF and RAF, there were squadrons of "Tiffies," Typhoons unleashing salvoes of rockets and bombs on the columns below along with American forces adding to the firepower that was decimating the retreating enemy. It was no time to be sentimental, albeit some pilots were reportedly reluctant to participate fully in the "turkey shoot" that the Falaise pocket was turning into by strafing the large columns of infantry and support staff that were filing east. The Roaring Boys knew that the continued destruction of enemy equipment would subsequently save the lives of Allied soldiers. The ORB recorded a big score for vehicles destroyed: "Met score 13 flamers, 6 smokers, and 6 damaged. One A/C returned early due to engine trouble." Ross himself recorded his personal tally of vehicles destroyed in the mission, "3 trucks. 1 car." The usual post-mission pattern followed after touching down at 08.35 am. Ross was debriefed and then after some refreshments, he was ready for his next mission. The top brass pushed 2nd TAF to go all out to smash the retreating Germans, especially as the weather, which been poor on and off throughout the summer, was holding for the time being.

The Roaring Boys walked with purpose towards their waiting Spitfires. The erks had cleaned, fuelled and armed them and it was an impressive sight. One of the best fighters of its time defying its sleek lines to look menacing, perhaps something it never quite managed when compared to more sinister looking Me 109 and FW 190 "butcher bird."

At 11.10 am, the squadron strength formation took off, and the flight included F/L A F Halcrow, of whom we will hear more shortly. They climbed steadily away from B18 towards the patrol area of Bernay, Louviers, Vernon, Vereux and Orbec. The armed reconnaissance would cover a sizeable area with Orbec being around 50 miles to the east of the Falaise pocket, and further east to Louviers which is approximately 20 miles south of Rouen. It wasn't long before Ross and the others were unleashing a storm of fire upon the transports below. They hammered vehicle after vehicle until some of the pilots ran out of ammunition. Ross later tallied up his score as, "3 trucks 3 RRs." The ORB recorded an extraordinary score of: "23 – 12 – 40 (effectively, flamers, smokers and damaged) Met and 3 damaged tanks." After only an hour the formation, empty of all munitions touched back down at B18.

On the afternoon of the 18th of August F/L Alexander Foch "Sandy" Halcrow was flying a squadron strength armed reconnaissance with the Roaring Boys. He was hit by flak whilst attacking a convoy on a road going south from Vimoutiers. His recollections of the event provide us with a useful insight into the fighting condition of the German army at the time of the Falaise battle and what it was like for the average German soldier who was on the receiving end of the onslaught. Sandy Halcrow takes up the story:

"I came down from 3000 feet to tree top height and gave them a 4 second burst of cannon and machine gun fire. I flew on for a bit on the deck climbed to around 1000 feet and made another low-level attack in the same direction north-south. It was on the second attack I was hit by some 20 MM shells, my propeller glycol and oil lines were hit, the engine about leapt out of its mountings. I called up my Squadron Leader (R L Hayward) telling him I was returning to base. I found this to be quite impossible, the temperature was rising rapidly and there was a great danger of fire so from 800 feet I baled out. No sooner had I landed I released my harness and called out 'Anglais.' The civilians approaching Sandy Halcrow were, in fact, Germans soldiers and he was captured. "They started to takeoff my Mae West, help themselves to the chocolate, cigarettes, and compass in the escape box; they handed the money back to me. While they were busy robbing me one of them asked in English: 'have you been shooting up Red Cross wagons? I said no."

At this time, the Allies had discovered that the Germans were using Red Cross painted trucks to ferry men and equipment to and from the front lines, rather than the wounded. The order had been given for air crews to attack them. The Germans took a dim view of this and it is a matter of speculation what might have happened if Sandy had foolishly answered "yes" to the question, or had been witnessed attacking Red Cross vehicles before he was captured. Sandy asked his fellow prisoners about the guards At this stage of the war the Germans had drafted in soldiers from other countries, both Axis nations as well as fascist sympathisers from defeated nations across Europe. He was told that the guards included Romanians, Greeks, Italians, Poles, and Russians. Sandy said: "we got the Russian and the Pole working on the other guards and with my limited French I explained to them that the Luftwaffe was finished and that they were completely surrounded. Out came the 'safe conduct' passes which had been dropped by the RAF. One of the Italians came up to me and said 'tomorrow, I your prisoner." The passes, usually signed by a senior officer like General Eisenhower, were dropped in their tens of thousands and could be given to any Allied personnel. In return for surrendering, the German soldier would be disarmed and given food and medicine. It was clear from their actions that many enemy forces knew the "game was up" for Germany and the Axis powers and were looking to surrender. This attitude certainly didn't apply amongst the elite Panzer and SS units, including the fanatical Hitler Youth. The Germans were acutely aware of this faltering morale and would post fanatical Germans amongst these troops with orders to execute any deserters.

Sandy's problems weren't over and after being loaded into a truck he was moved towards Tournay sur Dives, where his convoy was shelled. He wrote: "British shelling was amazingly accurate, piles of destroyed vehicles, dead horses and Germans littered the area. After sheltering in the basement of a house with his captors, he was then dive bombed by USAAF P-47 Thunderbolts. Having described the Roaring Boys missions at this time it is interesting to read the first-hand account of one of them who was on the receiving end of the air and land operations. Eventually, Sandy Halcrow was able to persuade his captors to let him go and he walked towards the Allied lines with one of the Germans carrying a Red Cross flag. Sandy carried a note from the Germans saying they wanted to surrender, and he soon met up with a fellow Canadian Major John Petersen of the Stormont, Dundas and Glengarry Highlanders. Major Petersen couldn't spare any men to retrieve the Germans and so from there Sandy Halcrow made his way to Battalion Headquarters and then onto Creully.

Aside from the shooting down of Sandy Halcrow, 18 August had been an extraordinary day. For 126 Wing, it had been the best day in its history in terms of the destruction of enemy transports. The ORB set out the achievement: "Slightly over 700 vehicles were accounted for, of which 411 Squadron claimed 244." To any army, the loss of so much equipment in just one day was unsustainable. For both sides, aside from Hitler and certain fanatical members of his inner circle, the senior German ranks down to the humble private soldier could see the war was lost for Germany and her allies.

On the next day, 19 August the success continued although Ross couldn't increase his personal tally, perhaps because he was providing cover against any potential bounce by fighters whilst the dive bombers and strafers carried out their deadly work. He wrote: "No go. Sad sack. Bernay area."

By 20 August the movement of enemy transports had tailed off. Those that were going to escape through the Falaise pocket had already done so and many of the roads were jammed with the smouldering wreckage of vehicles. Elements of the German 7th Army and 5th Panzer Army managed to extricate themselves from the Falaise pocket. In a reverse of the German strategic aim of territorial expansion, "drang nach osten," it was the Germans themselves who were now being 'driven to the east.'

Ross experienced the sudden evaporation of available ground targets to attack as he prepared for a fighter sweep on 20 August which would be led by W/C Dal Russel DFC. The weather early on did not look promising. At 13.10 pm, briefed and ready, Ross climbed up onto the wing of Spitfire MK885 and slid down into the cockpit, the strapping and preflight procedures were second nature and almost done by muscle memory. There were a few breaks in the cloud appearing and the Roaring Boys would be joined by the Rams of 401 Squadron. The sweep area would cover Beauvais and St Andre de L'Eure which are approximately 50 miles to the north and northwest respectively of Paris. France's capital and the garrison of German forces would soon be surrounded. As the 24 Spitfires lifted off, within a few minutes the formation was neatly spread out across the sky as the sweep commenced with a heading of southeast towards Paris. The official ORB account of the patrol area is a little different to Ross who recorded in his logbook: "St Omer 16,000 feet. Nothing doing. Nice ride." Saint-Omer is some way to the north and it's possible that within the 1 hour 10-minute sweep the formation also flew northwards towards the coast. As Ross landed, he knew he was heading towards the end of his tour of duty. His actions suggest that he was still eager for action and to press home any attack whenever the opportunity presented itself. Two days later on 22 August Ross's armed reconnaissance mission was not completed as he was one of 3 Spitfires forced to return early. He later reported, "Early return. R/T trouble" It seemed after landing back at B18 the summer rains compounded his bad fortune as he glumly noted his Spitfire was, "Stuck in mud." The remainder of the Roaring Boys returned later with a respectable score. The ORB gave the location and provided the numbers: "Met were attacked on the road leading east of Bernay. Score 13-1-12 and 2 tanks damaged. F/O Reid returned early because of his undercarriage being U/S."

On the ground, the British and Canadian divisions were making rapid progress after getting bogged down around Caen. The Roaring Boys missions were now ranging further east in support of the advance. This once again necessitated the use of external auxiliary fuel tanks that were used in the bomber escort from England in 1943 to increase the Spitfire's range. Ross's first mission on 23 August was a fighter sweep with 442 squadron. The patrol areas would be Laon and the city of Rheims which is around 50 miles from the Belgium border. It was anticipated there might be formations of Luftwaffe fighters seeking to cover the withdrawal of their forces. S/L Hayward led the formation which took off from B18 at 14.00 pm. The ORB recorded the sweep scored: "1 flamer. Overheated engine caused one aircraft's early return and R/T caused another." There was no additional activity that affected the formation albeit Ross gave further information: "45 gal tanks. Laon – Rheims. 60-80 Huns up. No go." The sweep lasted for 1 hour and 50 minutes with Ross touching down again at 15.50 pm. He taxied in, debriefed and checked the roster to confirm the time of his next mission of the day which would be an armed reconnaissance covering the river Seine to the west of Rouen. On this occasion, Ross and the Roaring Boys identified some significant targets and pressed home an attack that yielded: "5 flamers, 4 smokers and 8 damaged. One APV smoker also claimed." Ross's share of the destruction was, "1 staff car." The following day the pattern of squadron strength missions was broken as the Roaring Boys were organised into a day's worth of patrols, each containing 4 aircraft. Although uneventful for Ross he did note the return of some of his fellow pilots: "Tew, Trainor, Kennedy, Halcrow all escaped back."

The rapid pace of the Allied advance on the ground saw the Roaring Boys ranging further and further east to provide a protective umbrella for the ground forces. It seemed that they would soon be at the limit of their operational range without carrying long-range fuels tanks and a move east was soon required. It was also a matter of luck if a patrol happened to run into the enemy in the air. The days of late June and July when virtually every mission involved an air to air engagement were seemingly over. When the Luftwaffe was engaged invariably their inexperienced pilots were suffering at the hands of overwhelming numbers of Allied fighters, containing better trained and more experienced pilots.

On 27 August at 14.50 pm Ross was strapped into DB – L, NH240 and soon launched her into the air for a squadron strength armed reconnaissance mission which covered an area east of Rouen and Gournay. As a senior member of the squadron, Ross was involved in an attack on ground transports and after peppering one vehicle he later wrote, "1 car smoker." The Roaring Boys were still punching well above their weight and during the hour-long mission the ORB listed a respectable score in the usual format of "flamers, smokers and damaged. Scattered Met encountered. Score 4-2-3. One tank flamer." On 28 August Ross, Bob and the Roaring Boys returned to the same area for their reconnaissance mission. He wrote "45 gal tanks" to indicate that addition of the auxiliary tanks to enable them to extend their patrol time in the area. The mission would cover areas around 20 miles to east and southeast of Rouen, flying over the towns of Gournay-en-Bray and southeast to Gisors. Moving towards Belgium heralded new virgin territory, with rich pickings for the ever-hungry fighters. The ORB gave a situation report: "much Met was observed, and the squadron scored 17-5-15 of flamers, smokers and damaged transports." Ross and his section observed the attacks going in until it was their turn to drop their Spitfires into the attack and unleash withering fire on the convoy below. Where they could, men scattered in all directions as did the occasional vehicle that could find an escape from the area of immediate danger. Ross and the others were conscious of the dangers of flak. If hit, split-second decisions needed to be made that could save a pilot's life. Suddenly, an anxious voice came over Ross's R/T, "I'm hit." Ross saw the telltale signs as a plume of white vapour trials emitted from around the engine of Spitfire NH317, which had F/O R M Cook at the controls. One of the formations dropped down to shepherd Cook and his ailing aircraft back towards Allied lines. Ross and the rest of the formation had to continue as normal, whilst other aircraft peeled away to act as cover. At 12.10 pm Ross and half the squadron touched down and taxied back to dispersal where a gaggle of erks were waiting as if lined up for the start of a race. They were eager to greet their Spitfire and replenish her fuel and ammunition. As Ross shut down, he offered a quick word to his erks that all was well with NH240 and he quickly found Bob to talk over the mission and Cook's fate as they headed away from dispersal to debrief with intelligence team. The ORB gave details: "F/O R M Cook crash-landed behind our own lines…he was unhurt and immediately reported back to the unit." Intriguingly, a rare handwritten note has been added in the 411 ORB asking, "did he crash land or bale out?" Ross confirmed what happened to Cook. He wrote: "Got 5 flamers. Cook crash landed."

With the end of August Ross sat and calculated his flying hours, which were then signed off by OC A Flight Bob and then countersigned off by S/L Hayward. Ross had logged 22 hours 30 minutes of operational Spitfire flying in the month for a total tour total of 184 hours and 55 minutes. His total time flying Spitfires was 361 hours and 45 minutes, and his total flying time on all types of aircraft now totalled 660 hours 55 minutes. Ross was inching inexorably towards the end of his tour time as a front-line fighter pilot and one of the Roaring Boys. He hoped his final few missions didn't generate too many dangerous situations.

With the start of September, 411 Squadron and 126 Wing were on the move again. The ORB noted: "The squadron finally moved from Cristot today. The A/C left shortly before noon for St Andre because the strip at Evreux (Fauville) was not ready. Road vehicles departed at 12.30 hours." From their new base at B44 Poix, Ross and Bob, two veteran fighter pilots amongst a sea of new faces were briefed and ready to lead a 6 Spitfire forward patrol. The area covered included Brussels and Antwerp and so each pilot took the time to study the maps and familiarise themselves with key landmarks and the relative disposition of the opposing armies. If they became separated and had to select an alternative aerodrome to divert to, or worse bailed out it was important quickly assess the options and limit the chances of an incorrect decision. As Bob led the formation off at 15.00 pm, they formed up and headed northeast towards Brussels. The patrol settled in at around 15,000 feet and Ross looked either side to see Spitfires on each of his wings as they traversed the Belgian countryside. After an uneventful patrol, the formation radioed in and entered the circuit pattern to land at 16.20 pm. Ross updated his logbook: "Good ride. Nothing doing. Tanks. Army going too fast."

Ross's words were prophetic as the next day at 17.00 pm the Roaring Boys took off for a new base at B56 Evere, near Brussels, which Ross described as, "a lovely place." With its large terminal building that served the city of Brussels pre-war, it was certainly a lot different to the tented community that sprung up around B4 a few months before in Normandy. The delights of Brussels were a short ride away with a liberated people displaying an almost overwhelming level of hospitality to anyone in Allied uniform.

On 7 September Ross and Bob took part in front line patrols that would see the Roaring Boys push further east towards Hasselt and Tournhout, which are around 50 miles east and north respectively of Brussels. Ross noted that his morning mission which left B56 at 09.00 am for 1 hour and 25 minutes, was flown with "low cloud. Light flak" but was otherwise uneventful. After a debrief, he was on combat readiness for a 14.00 pm departure to the same area. After one hour, the mission was recalled. The landing was going to be a challenge as Ross described: "Terrific crosswind on landing. Doran pranged." P/O J A Doran came to no harm in the incident, aside from some dented pride, and would later shoot down an FW 190 in January 1945.

The 8 September represented a momentous day for 126 Wing. The combined fighter sweep and armed reconnaissance would see the Roaring Boys fly over the "Fatherland," Nazi Germany for the first time. For Ross, with his tour about to be completed, it was a time to reflect upon his time as a fighter pilot and how far he and the squadron had come since he joined them at RAF Staplehurst. The Germans had been falling back towards their homeland and were sure to put up a mighty defence. Despite this,

Ross was a seasoned fighter pilot who knew what his responsibilities were. To lose concentration for a moment could be disastrous for him or someone else. A flight commander, Bob was first to taxi out from dispersal and at 11.20 am, as the squadron roared into the air, they were soon followed by 412 Squadron. The 24 Spitfires formed up over the aerodrome and then set course for Aachen, Germany. Ross later summed up the reception they received as the Spitfires crossed the border into Germany. "First time over Germany. Heavy flak." Ross and the others were helpless as the flak defences unleashed their fury. Everyone was crossing everything possible, fearful that one of the artillery shells would find its target. He only needed his old faithful NH240, DB – L to carry him safely home a few more times. No one wanted to bail out and be on the run in German territory. The sweep and reconnaissance were soon complete, and the formation landed at 12.25 pm. The pilots gathered together to debrief and to reflect on what they had just taken part in. The significance of the day wasn't lost on anyone. It appeared that the end of the war may just have been coming into view.

The 9 September 1944 was a momentous day for Ross. This was to be his last day as an operational fighter pilot. It was a leisurely start, with him being rostered to fly in a 6 Spitfire patrol to the Hasselt and Tilburg areas, crossing another border into the Netherlands.

His first mission of the day was at 13.30 pm and he was joined by Bob who led the patrol. As the 6 Spitfires taxied out the area around their dispersal seemed to be bursting to the seams with aircraft, men and equipment. They were soon airborne and heading east to commence the patrol. The operation passed by without incident. Ross described it as "quiet." After 1 hour 25 minutes the formation entered the busy circuit and touched down. They would have a few hours rest after the debrief to look around their new surroundings before the next briefing. The Germans had left the airfield in a hurry, so the pilots were eager to look over some of the abandoned fighters and bombers that were scattered around, once the engineers had checked for booby traps.

After the briefing, Bob and Ross walked out to the dispersal area. This moment would soon close the chapter and story of 9 Canadian pilots, forever linked with one Spitfire, NH341 Elizabeth. They flew, fought and against overwhelming odds all survived combat during one of the most momentous periods of the Second World War. As Ross and Bob parted company and headed to their respective Spitfires. Ross jumped up on the wing of NH240. He ran his hand along the side of the fuselage of his trusty DB – L. Just one more time he thought. Just get me back and I'm finished. With his hands resting on the windscreen he slid down in the cockpit and his erk passed the Sutton harnesses over his shoulders. He settled down, turned on the battery and the magnetos, pushed the starter button and with a quick snort of smoke NH240 fired up. The familiar sound and smell of the Rolls Royce Merlin engine, that had been a part of Ross's life throughout his tour filled his senses. He checked through his instruments, and in turn checked his magnetos were functioning correctly, oil pressure and temperatures were all normal. It was time to go to war. No more thinking about the end, time to concentrate like never before. Of all his missions, this was not the one to tempt fate and make a costly mistake. Ross lined up slightly behind Bob and soon they and the other Roaring Boys were gathering speed down the runway, flashing past rows of Dakotas and Typhoons, all readying themselves for their next operations. The rattling and shaking within NH240 as she bumped and bounced her way out soon disappeared and were followed by the whirr and clunk of the retracting undercarriage. Ross angled his Spitfire upwards to begin the climb to patrol height. Just the sound of air rushing past the canopy and the roar of the Mighty Merlin as company. The patrol area was a familiar one and it was clear that the good flying weather had brought everyone out. The sky seemed to be filled aircraft crisscrossing the horizon. A voice in his ears reported a formation of fighters closing in on them with apparent deadly intent. As they anxiously watched on in his head Ross and Bob were already preparing to break before any deadly flashes began blinking on the wings of the approaching attackers. Ross wrote of his final mission: "Chased - bags of T-Bolts. Visual on 2 Hun Jets." The approaching aircraft, "T – Bolts" were USAAF P-47 Thunderbolts, also known as "the flying jug," because their side profile resembles a milk jug. The P-47s clearly thought they had come across a formation of Luftwaffe fighters to engage. The ORB later confirmed the encounter with the Luftwaffe jets: "Two Me 262 (Jerry's twin-engined jet-propelled aircraft) were seen flying in a northwesterly direction at 15,000 feet near Mol (Hasselt). They disappeared after our A/C broke into and attacked without success." The Thunderbolts, recognising the RAF roundels and the distinctive elliptical wings of the Spitfires backed off and broke to starboard on the reverse track they had just flown, disappearing into the distance. So far, so good Ross thought, and the only remaining excitement was when the word was passed that Me 262s had been spotted. Flashing across the sky the pair merely flirted with the formation and all too soon they were gone. The flak batteries were also quiet, no with the of the Allies advance they were more concerned with crossing the border back into Germany. The seconds turned into minutes and quarter hours and as Bob signalled the return to base Ross grew more confident that this last uneventful mission would close his war. He had fired at the enemy and now his duty was done. He'd faced danger on many occasions and been fired at countless times including by the Me 109 that Charlie shot down in Spitfire Elizabeth a lifetime ago at the end of June. As the formation entered the busy circuit at B56 Evere, Ross slid back the hood of NH240 and felt the rush of air as he lined up to land. He wanted to make his final Spitfire landing a "greaser." As his wheels touched down there was only the merest of delicate bumps as NH240 continued on her main two wheels, Ross eased the control column forward a fraction to compensate for the slowing speed before gently allowing the rear wheel to follow suit and kiss the runway. The graceful Spitfire was back to her old awkward, rattling self. Well, at least the erks were saved one job of reloading ammunition. They would only need to fuel her up. Ross shut down his aircraft and took one last look around the cockpit where so much had happened. The joy of stepping into one of the greatest and most famous fighters of the time and the fear and nagging doubts that he might "catch it." There was no time for sentiment as he released his harnesses and made for the debrief and a catch up with the last Elizabeth pilot still flying, Bob Hyndman. He wrote up his last mission in his logbook and in large joined up handwriting: "Completed tour with 411 RCAF squadron." The summary of his combat service was duly signed by Bob and countersigned by S/L Hayward. He had flown 136 sorties and spent 371 hours flying Spitfires. His operational flying time in September was 8 hours 20 minutes and his tour total was 193 hours and 10 minutes. He had flown 669 hours throughout his RCAF service.

There were some administrative matters to attend to, but Ross appears to have had a few days off before he is recorded as flying again. This time he was a passenger in Dakota 282 from Brussels to RAF Northolt. Whether he was then rostered to fly or volunteered is not known but on 13 September Ross was back in a Spitfire when he flew Spitfire MJ852 from RAF Bognor

Regis to Brussels. The aircraft joined 401 Squadron, shared a 1/5 kill of a Me262, shot down an FW 190 before being lost on Christmas Day 1944 after being hit by debris from a Me 109 which was being attacked by another Spitfire. The last entry in Ross's wartime logbook was a flight on 16 September in an Avro Anson 891 from Brussels to B6 Coulombs, west of Caen from where he would later return to Canada.

After the war, Ross was demobilised on 1 September 1945 and returned to Emo where for 4 years he ran a grocery store with a friend. He was then contacted by the Canadian Navy who were searching for former Second World War 2 pilots to join a new naval air division. As a frontline fighter pilot with combat experience, Ross was exactly the calibre of individual the navy was looking for. On 15 July 1949, he was offered a Short Service Appointment with the Royal Canadian Navy. Ross was soon back in the cockpit of an aircraft as he was sent to RCAF Trenton for a pilot refresher course. He eventually joined 883 squadron who flew from HMCS Magnificent. During his time in the Canadian Navy, he made 133 landings on aircraft carriers and was promoted to a Lieutenant Commander of the RCN's VU-32 squadron which flew the Grumman CS2F Tracker, which Ross also flew. He was eventually made Lieutenant Commander of Operations aboard the anti-submarine warfare carrier HMCS Bonaventure before moving on to several flying instructor roles and staff positions. In 1965 Ross was transferred to Canadian Forces HQ as Staff Commander of Northern NORAD Region Air Defence Command, North Bay. An interesting article featuring Ross appeared in the Royal Australian Navy News edition of 19 January 1968. The article compared Admiral Lord Nelson's time in the British Navy when service was conducted on the open sea. It commented on Nelson's supposed reaction to Ross's posting: "He would most likely pause at the thought of a 1967 vintage Lieutenant Commander earning his daily rum ration 600 feet below the ground!"

During his flying career, Ross accumulated a total of 6200 hours flying fixed-wing aircraft along with 1400 hours in helicopters. He was a lifelong aviator and flew an impressive list of military aircraft which included the; Tiger Moth, Harvard, North American NA-64 Yale, Supermarine Spitfire Vb, IXb, Miles Master III, P-51 Mustang, Hawker Hurricane, Avro Anson, Bristol Bolingbroke, Fairey Firefly, Hawker Sea Fury, Texan, Beechcraft C-45, Grumman TBM Avenger, HVD, Lockheed T-33, Grumman CS2F Tracker, and Douglas DC-3. Ross also flew an impressive list of civilian fixed wing aircraft and helicopters including; Cessna C-150, 152, 172, 185, Seneca, Piper Navajo, Bell 47G2, 47G4, Bell 206, Ranger III.

Ross retired from the Canadian Navy with the rank of Lieutenant-Commander on 1 April 1968. His daughters Jan and Jill take up the story of father's second career:

"Dad joined Canadore College, North Bay. Initially, he was involved with adult education and student awards before establishing a flying training programme in 1980. It offered training programmes for helicopter pilots and air maintenance technicians. He was chairman of the department when he retired aged 65. However, he was able to continue on a part-time basis teaching ground school and flying. He was still doing this when he passed away suddenly in September 1999."

Ross's daughters said their father didn't speak much about the war and anyone who has met these veterans will testify that is a very common trait. They were humble and modest about what they did. I found when talking to the veterans that stories had to be virtually levered out of them, understandable as many lost good friends and witnessed such terrible death and destruction.

Ross's daughters did manage to unearth a couple of interviews that Ross gave in 1994 and 1998 to local television in Canada, talking about his wartime experiences and what he remembered:

"When I started flying combat missions as a fighter pilot it was relatively quiet. We weren't running into much German fighter opposition because at that time the American Eighth Air Force was bombing Germany with Fortresses and Liberators. The German's had pulled most of their air force back inland farther. We didn't see too much enemy action at that point, but there was lots of flak.

Ross went on to describe a typical day in between his missions: "We had a lot of readiness time, where you were standing by on short notice calls. Other times, we were out cleaning our aircraft, that kind of thing, keeping generally busy. Mostly sitting by on readiness. Most times we knew in advance what trips we were flying on. During the evenings we did the normal things people do. We went out and had the odd pint at the local pub and so on for relaxation. The big thing was every trip you flew you didn't know whether you'd be coming back or not, so we tended to enjoy life as much as we could under the circumstances.

"One evening we were diving bombing a rail yard in Hazebrouck, France. The Germans had terrifically accurate anti-aircraft fire, and as we rolled into our dive from about 10,000 feet to dive bomb the yards, the Germans were putting up a curtain of flak. It was late in the evening and the sun was low on the horizon, and it just looked like water, like sunlight on shimmering water, the layer of flak. We flew down through that of course. But what happened on the way down, our commanding officer was leading 12 of us, got a direct hit by flak, and he blew up. So, we not only had to fly through the debris of the bomb and aircraft, but we had to fly down through the anti-aircraft fire as well. Fortunately, other than our commanding officer, we all survived."

Ross was asked what it was like to witness something like the death of your squadron leader. He said: "well it was a common thing." He added, after being asked how he dealt with it: "you just pressed on. It was war. The sight was what stuck out in my mind. The setting sun shimmering off this curtain of anti-aircraft fire.

"Often, when we were escorting bombers, we would see a bomber shot down, and if we had a chance, we'd count the parachutes to know whether the whole crew got out or not, so we had a lot of sympathy for our bomber friends. It was just one of the things of war, you tend to forget about it."

In answer to questions by both interviewers about stand out moments during the war Ross answered: "Memory tends to fade with time. D Day 6th June. We were stationed at Tangmere, in the south of England and on the eve of D Day in the later afternoon, all the ships and landing craft etc began moving out from all the ports and harbours. I was fortunate to be flying air cover that evening for the fleet moving out, and at that time of year, Britain was on double daylight-saving time. It didn't get dark until after 11 o'clock at night, so we flew air cover for the armada moving out. And then, first thing the next morning we were giving coverage for the armada over the beachhead, so between seeing the fleet moving out, and moving to the beaches it was a spectacular sight, and perhaps the beginning of the end of the war. It was a once in a lifetime sight and feeling."

Ross commented further on vivid memories he has: "The first time you were shot at. The first time you fired your guns in anger. The anti-aircraft fire was our greatest enemy. The most positive experience was achieving the air superiority that we did, particularly after D Day. It was a very positive feeling that we were part of winning the war. And then, thinking about all those people I met and flew with, some of whom weren't fortunate to survive. All in all, just being part of a winning team, you might say."

Ross described what followed after his service with 411 Squadron: "After I finished my tour of operations on Spitfires, I spent 6 months instructing back at an operational training unit and then came back to Canada for a short leave period, prior to going back for a second tour of operations. Another gentleman and I were instructing at the same time. At around that time in late March 1945, we were offered the opportunity to go back home for 30 days leave, or immediately go back to the squadron for a second tour. My friend, because he had just recently been married in England, he elected to go back for a second tour, whilst I elected to go back to Canada. Unfortunately, he was killed on the first trip of his second tour.

"Victory in Europe was rather anti-climactic for me. While I was back in Canada VE came along. I was home here when it happened. It would have been nice to have been in Europe and experienced the euphoria when it was all over there. I was with my brother in Thunder Bay, and there wasn't a great deal of jubilation. I was released from the air force in the fall of 1945. I subsequently joined the Fleet Air Arm where I became a navy pilot and spent 20 years flying with the navy."

When Ross was asked the question that considering all the death and destruction during the war would he do it all again, his answer was instant and unequivocal: "certainly. It was a feeling of achievement.

"I think we should remember all those, to use the old phrase who paid the supreme sacrifice. I don't think the young people today realise what the Canadians and all the Allied forces went through. We did a job, and I think we did a pretty good job."

It's clear from Ross's story that he maintained a lifelong passion for aviation, and service life was in his blood. As one of the Roaring Boys, flying the legendary Spitfire, and post war in the Canadian Navy he more than "did his bit" for our freedom. He also made a significant contribution to general aviation, which continues today with flight training programmes at Canadore College.

1. Bruce and Elizabeth Whiteford.

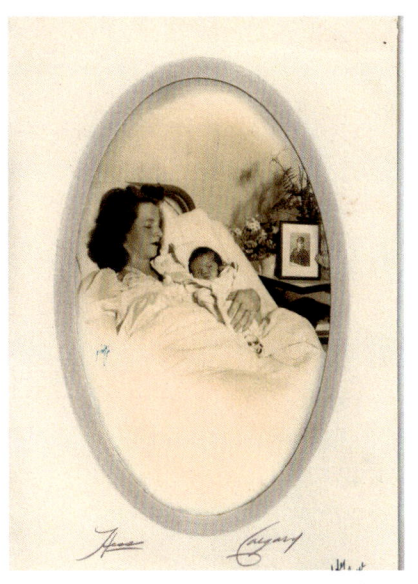

2. Elizabeth and baby Anne Elizabeth Whiteford born 26 June 1943.

3. Bruce Whiteford (front row left) at the Calgary Stampede parade 7 July 1941.

4. Bruce Whiteford on his favoured mode of transport in front of Art Tooley's car. Biggin Hill 1943.

5. Bruce with 411 Squadron's Sid Mills Mark IXb Spitfire DB-M, Biggin Hill 1943.

6. Bruce at RAF Redhill, summer 1943.

7. Bruce sketched by Bob Hyndman. Unfinished due to a squadron scramble.

8. Bruce with Spitfire Elizabeth pointing at his wife's nickname 'EO.'

9. Tommy Wheler and Bruce, England 1943.

10. Spitfire Elizabeth with D Day invasion stripes painted under the wing. (Photo by Bruce Whiteford). This Spitfire, NH174 replaced Spitfire NH341 Elizabeth on 3 July 1944.

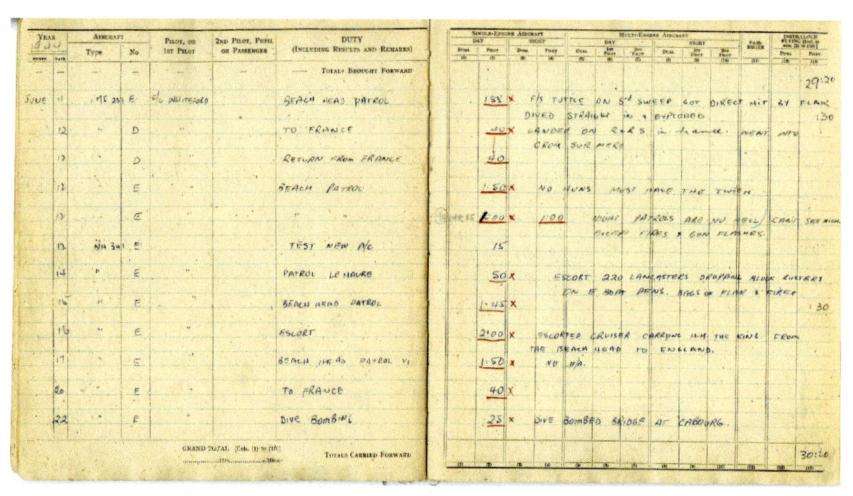

11. Bruce's log book June 1944 showing his first flight and missions in Spitfire NH341 Elizabeth 'E.'

184

12. L to R: Joe McFarlane, Bruce and Charlie Trainor Biggin Hill 1943.

13. Charlie and Bruce. Biggin Hill 1943.

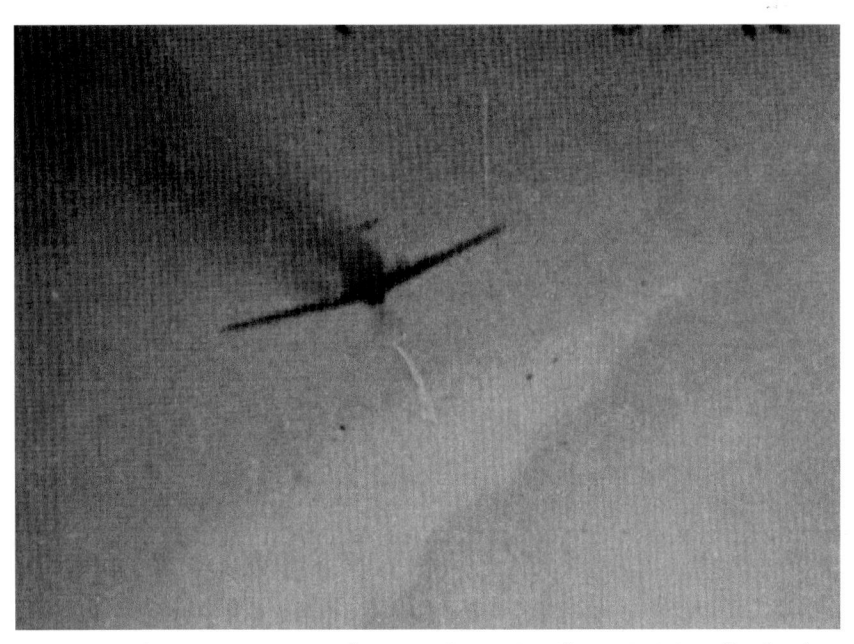

14. Combat Gun camera footage from Spitfire NH341 Elizabeth whilst being flown by Charlie. He has just shot down this Me 109 which is trailing smoke. He was credited with the 'kill.' 29 June 1944. Reproduced with permission of IWM Duxford.

15. Ross Linquist, (front row left)
England 1943.

16. Ross and Spitfire Mark Vb, Biggin Hill 1943.

17. Ross outside his tent, probably RAF Tangmere 1944.

18. Ross with his Spitfire.

19. Ross in his Mark IXb Spitfire, Biggin Hill, 1943.

20. Ross with a German Me 109. This was probably taken in Belgium, September 1944.

21. Ross with Hawker Hurricane at an air show in Victoria, British Columbia in the early 1990's.

22. Tommy Wheler at
RAF Shrewton, Wiltshire
in 1942.

23. Tommy and Ken Chandler
reunited.

24. L to R Stan Kent, Len Harrison, Syd Brooks and Tommy with
their tent in the orchard at RAF Staplehurst August 1943.

25. Tommy standing on Spitfire 'Little Mil' in England 1943.

26. Tommy's service cap with a photo of his wife Millie inside.

27. Tommy at Biggin Hill 1943.

28. Tommy and son Doug at Historic Flying in July 2015. As well as viewing Spitfire Elizabeth's restoration Tommy was able to hold an original panel from the aircraft marked with the serial number 'NH341.' Tommy flew Spitfire Elizabeth in combat on 30 June 1944.

29. Tommy painted by Bob Hyndman in 1974.

30. Tommy and Doug after his speech at the Aero Legends Air Show July 2015.

31. L to R: F/L Tooley, Dave Evans, P/O Kerr and F/L Johnson. Probably Biggin Hill 1943.

32. L to R: Doug Givens, Hal Kramer and Ron 'Gibby' Gibson Biggin Hill 1943.

33. A photo entitled 'Ron Gibson acting foolish.' Location and date unknown.

34. Photo entitled 'Gibson again' (standing right). A 411 Squadron Spitfire DB-A is in the background. Biggin Hill 1943.

35. The Roaring Boys. L to R: Gibby, Bob Hyndman, Cuff Cross, Hal Kramer, Charlie Trainor and Doug Givens Biggin Hill 1943.

36. L to R: McFarlane, Bruce (with camera which Norm Whiteford still has), Hogg and Len. Probably Biggin Hill.

37. Len with his Mark IX Spitfire. An excellent close up of the long barrel of the 20 mm Hispano cannon with 0.5 cal machine gun port to the side.

38. Bob Hyndman (left) and unknown trainees during flying training in Canada 1940.

39. Bob flying a Harvard whilst training in Canada.

40. Bob's first flight in a Hawker Hurricane, Canada 1940.

41. The Roaring Boys at Biggin Hill 1943. L to R: Charlie Trainor, unknown, Tommy Wheler and Bob Hyndman. Crouching down at the front is Ross Linquist and to his left with back to camera and hands in pockets is Len Harrison. Standing on the aircraft, far right is McFarlane.

42. A photo sent by Bob to Vic Baker in 1990. The handwriting is Bob's own.

43. Robert Hyndman. 'Above Falaise.' Date unknown. CWM 197-10261-3229 62.

44. Robert Hyndman. 'Divebombing V1 site' 1945. CWM 197-10261-6450. Both paintings with permission of the Beaverbrook Collection of War Art Canadian War Museum.

45. Bob at B56 Evere Belgium September 1944.

46. A No Ball V1 doodlebug site showing a ski launch ramp.

47. 411 Squadron Spitfire and C-47 Dakota late 1944. Location unknown.

48. A photo Bob sent to Vic Baker. The handwriting is Bob's own.

49. Course No 66 SFTS, RCAF Dunville, Ontario autumn 1942. Jimmy Jeffrey (middle row standing 4th left).

50. Jimmy back home in Toronto, winter 1944.

51. The 'four horsemen' as they nicknamed themselves. From L to R: Robert Davidson, Ross Kelly, Jimmy Jeffrey, and Robert Wallace, Bournemouth 1943. Davidson and Wallace were both killed in action flying Spitfires in 1944.

52. L to R: Bob Davidson, Ross Kelly, Jimmy Jeffrey and Bob Wallace working on a farm whilst training at 53 OTU Kirton-in-Lindsey, Lincolnshire.

53. L to R: Bob Davison, Jimmy Jeffrey, Bob Wallace, Robert Dieble and William Dunlop with a Spitfire at 53 OTU.

54. Bob Davidson, Bob Wallace, Jimmy Jeffrey and unknown in front of their accommodation, Normandy, France 1944.

55. Jimmy Jeffrey (back row 4th left) after being shot down on 2 July 1944. Standing next to Jimmy is local Resistance leader Paul Lecor and others who helped Jimmy escape.

56. Top. L to R: Jimmy, Paul Lecor's widow Henriette, and USAAF P38 pilot George Tripp who was with Jimmy in 1944 after being shot down, at Albert Soetart's house.
Bottom. L to R: Henriette, Jimmy and Paul & Henriette's son Louis at the Lecor's wartime house where Jimmy was based. Both photos taken during the Jeffrey family trip to France in 1999.

57. RAF Staplehurst Advanced Landing Ground 1944. The aircraft are shown are USAAF P51 Mustangs.

58. 411 Squadron Spitfire being run up at RAF Tangmere June 1944. All the aircraft are painted with D Day invasion stripes.

59. A 20 mm Flakvierling 38 at a captured Luftwaffe airfield. A 411 Squadron ground crew is wearing a German helmet. The weapon was deadly against low flying aircraft. The barrels show 7 rings, indicating its crew shot down 7 Allied aircraft.

60. Keith Perkins, Aero Legends and Spitfire Elizabeth owner with Martin Overall from Historic Flying who led the project team that rebuilt the aircraft.

61. Parky holding a photo of Bruce Whiteford in Spitfire Elizabeth. Taken on 29 June 2018, exactly 74 years after Charlie Trainor shot down an Me 109 in the aircraft.

62. Charlie Brown with Spitfire Elizabeth.

63. Andy Millikin joined the Aero Legends team in 2019 and flies Spitfire Elizabeth.

64. Looking through an original working Mark IX Spitfire reflector gun sight just like the Roaring Boys would have done.

65. Spitfire NH341 Elizabeth gracing the skies once more with Parky at the controls.

66. The memorial to 411 Squadron, 126 Airfield and the US Ninth Air Force at the former RAF Staplehurst, Kent.

67. Elizabeth Whitford's signature which Bruce copied onto Spitfire NH341's cowling.

68. (Back row 2nd left) Aero Legends Managing Director Ben Perkins with the ground crew at Headcorn aerodrome.

CHAPTER FIVE

TOMMY WHELER

Tommy with Spitfire 'Little Mil'

Thomas Ross "Tommy" Wheler was born on 14 February 1921 in Tignall, Georgia USA. His parents were Canadians and the family moved back to Canada in 1927. Tommy enlisted into the RCAF on 28 January 1941. During our discussions, he recalled a conversation he had had with his father about joining up. Tommy said he told his father: "Dad, I've got to get into this fight. I'll give it one more year. Next year I'll be nineteen and then I'll be gone." His father, cognisant of what had happened to his generation in the First World War pondered this news for a moment, and then delivered a response to his son's announcement: "Well, good for you... jackass!" Tommy chuckled at the memory as did his daughter Gail and me! "There's nothing like a bit of fatherly encouragement!" I replied. Once the laughter had died down, Tommy carried on saying some more about his father. It was clear that he had great respect for him as he added: "He was a wonderful man, he really was." Tommy then went on to talk about the young age of those enlisting into the RCAF at the time he joined up: "They wouldn't take them for fighter pilot above the maximum age of twenty-eight as they were considered the old buggers!" Cue more laughter.

Tommy joined RCAF and undertook his initial training at No.3 Initial Training School in Victoriaville, Quebec. I asked him if he was able to fly before joining up and he said, "No." I went on to ask if the first aircraft he flew was a Tiger Moth. He thought about it for a while before replying: "Oh, gee whizz, we had….the Finch. The first plane I flew was the Fleet Finch." His first logbook entry for this aircraft was on 22 August 1941 at No.11 Elementary Flying School, Cap-de-la-Madeline, Quebec. At the end of the course, he wrote: "A step in the right direction. So far so good." Tommy and I discussed making a first solo flight and I recalled vivid memories of my instructor, Tony de Ste Croix telling me to land early during a lesson. He then said he was going to get out. And, you need a few seconds to process what's just been said to you. Tommy laughed: "Yes, that was a trick they used to use with us too."

As we discussed my own wonderful day flying in the backseat of a Spitfire, Tommy asked about Aero Legends Spitfires Elizabeth and St George: "They're still at Duxford, aren't they?" I confirmed that they were. We talked about some of the inevitable "pranging" of aircraft that went on back then. Tommy said: "My brother in law Jack Lush, he flew Spits out of 19 squadron when he crashed. The engine quit after takeoff and he went through three stone walls, but he was alright." After a quick bit of research, I was able to establish that on 16 October 1942 Sgt Jack L Lush was flying Spitfire Mark IIa serial number P8200 from 52 OTU when his engine failed at 200 feet just after takeoff, and he landed "straight ahead." It's amazing that Tommy could recall so vividly these events that took place over 75 years before. After a slight pause, I said to Tommy about his upcoming birthday party and how I thought he was looking very well in recent photos Gail had sent to me. He quipped: "I'll be 97 and I've given up drinking! I don't drink any alcohol at all now. I usually have milk."

Once Tommy had completed the elementary part of his flight training, he moved onto No.8 Service Flying Training School, Moncton where on 15 October 1941 he first flew the Avro Anson, known as the "Annie." At the end of this course, he wrote: "That's finished with, now for some real flying." Tommy graduated on 2 January 1942 and then on 23 January 1942 he sailed to the UK onboard the SS Vollendam where he joined the

RAF. I spoke to Tommy about the initial time he spent in England. He told me that when he arrived at RAF Hurn aerodrome near Bournemouth, he saw his first Spitfire and thought they were magnificent. After this initial encounter, Tommy and his good friend Ken Chandler were asked by the RAF to complete a form indicating with a tick which aircraft they were interested in flying. They crossed out every aircraft apart from the Spitfire! To their disappointment, both men were sent to No 1 Glider School, RAF Kidlington, Oxfordshire to fly Hotspur gliders in preparation for sabotage operations in Europe. Tommy was unimpressed and put his feelings down in his logbook, "Woe is me – gliders!" The prospect of flying gliders may not have pleased Tommy or Ken but as his entry of 8 April showed once he had mastered the aircraft there was still some fun to be had: "Looped a Hotspur – won 5 beers."

As you will have gathered by now Tommy was not the sort of character to let rejection stand in his way. After completing the course flying Hotspur gliders, he wrote on the Summary of Flying Assessment Form: "This can't go on. No Spits yet." More flying followed in the Tiger Moth and Hotspur, and Tommy was progressing well being assessed as "above average" as a pilot. He tried again to be posted to a fighter squadron but instead spent time from 5 June 1942 on glider tug duties and flying a variety of Hawker aircraft including the; Hart, Audax, and Hector at RAF Shrewton, Wiltshire and from 27 July at RAF Netheravon, Wiltshire. He said of this time: "I was flying gliders and training the army how to fly." He was desperate to fly Spitfires and in August 1942 wrote in his logbook, "There is no future in this." The Miles Master was introduced, and Tommy learned to fly that too but his frustration was always bubbling just under the surface: "Why has this happened to me?" he wrote in November 1942. Flying at this time wasn't without its hazards and on 15 November Tommy took part in a night towing exercise flying a Hector. He later wrote that he made a forced landing adding: "What a night. Saved by the grace of God." His focus was clear, and he knew what he wanted signing off his November logbook with, "Come on Spits."

At the end of 1942, someone answered Tommy's prayers. In the first week of January 1943, he wrote in his logbook: "What do you know, Ken and I are posted to Spitfires at last. So long gliders. Oh, happy day." Tommy was posted to 57 Operational Training Unit (OTC) at RAF Eshott, Northumberland. His time had finally arrived, and he was ready to fulfill his ambition. After some proving and familiarisation flights on the Miles Master on 6 February 1943 Spitfire II X OT was waiting in front of him. Tommy spoke about the day: "I can remember the instructor pointed at the Spitfire and said: 'Well, there you go. There's the aeroplane, get going.' I just started it up and away I went. That was a wonderful day." After this initial 55 minute flight, Tommy's logbook recorded his thoughts, "AT LAST. WOW." I asked Tommy about the difficulty of learning to fly the Spitfire and he said: "you had to be careful not to pitch it up on its nose. Fortunately, I managed to avoid doing that." Later that month Tommy felt triumphant as after all the training and angst from his glider days were behind him. He summed up his thoughts: "Spits are tops. I'm happy." Tommy considered himself almost ready for a front-line squadron posting. On 28 March 1943, he was starting to take on the swagger commonly associated with fighter pilots as he wrote about flying his Spitfire: "under Firth of Forth bridge." The daring stunt wasn't without its danger as he added: "Hit cold and lost the pitot tube. (No airspeed!)." With his pitot tube frozen and air unable to pass into the airspeed indicator, there was a real risk of stalling the aircraft with potentially fatal consequences.

Tommy's log showing a photo of the Firth of Forth bridge he flew under in his Spitfire

Tommy's posting to an operational squadron came through and on 11 May 1943, he arrived at RAF Redhill, Surrey where 411 Squadron, 126 Airfield was based. It was the same day that F/L Charlie Trainor, F/O Don Givens and F/O Bruce Whiteford arrived at the base. Tommy set about learning the business of flying operationally, with an intense period of local area familiarisation, formation, and air combat practice. The pilots wanted to get as many hours airborne as possible to explore the limits of the Spitfire as a fighter and to work up towards operational flying. And so, on 23 May Tommy attended his first mission briefing with Sgt R W Hogg. They would be flying a convoy patrol over the channel, seeking out any enemy raiders intent on hitting shipping targets in coastal waters. At 14.25 pm Tommy stepped up onto the wing of Spitfire Mark Vb BL897. He cranked the engine of his Spitfire and it sparked into life with a roar. His plane was soon warmed up and as he looked over Hogg nodded and Tommy pushed the throttle forward, and edge out towards the runway. The disappointment of time spent flying gliders was well and truly behind him. This was his goal and as he and Hogg lifted off into the afternoon sunshine Tommy was keyed up, but excited about the prospect of his first combat mission. The pair climbed out and as Tommy looked down the south coast soon flashed past and was gone. He was looking out across to France, bandit country. Hogg led Tommy for the next 1 hour and 25 minutes but despite their search of the clear blue skies, no enemy aircraft were sighted. They received updates from fighter control who were advised of their position by Hogg. At 16.00 pm Tommy touched down at Redhill. His first mission was complete and once they had taxied in and shut down their Spitfires, he and Hogg sat down to debrief with the wing's intelligence team. It was a great feeling to get this first mission out of the way with no issues. Tommy was now eager to get on with his next.

By the time of Tommy's next mission on 22 June he had been through an intense period of training in all aspects of combat flying, honing his skills and experience. The day had dawned bright and sunny, at 06.30 am and Tommy assembled with the squadron in the briefing tent. The rectangular tent was completely open at the front and there was a row of chairs laid out where each of the pilots randomly seated themselves. Dal Russel brought the briefing to order with a, "Good morning gentleman" a hush descended. Tommy made a few notes listing the key times and reference points. The routes in and out were identified and the bomber rendezvous point and the mission start time confirmed. Ramrod 99 would form 3 parts and the Roaring Boys would escort 12 Bostons on a diversionary bombing attack on the Dutch city of Rotterdam. Meanwhile, the main force of the Mighty Eighth, 235 B17s were to hit the chemical works and synthetic rubber plant in the Ruhr town of Huls. A separate force of 42 B17s would attack the former Ford and General Motors plants at Antwerp.

With the briefing over the pilots made for the dispersal area to pick up their parachutes and kit. For Tommy, this mission brought several "firsts." He would be flying over a long stretch of the North Sea, whilst escorting bombers and finally to increase the pre-combat nerves they would be flying over enemy territory. The line of Spitfires started their engines and was soon ready for S/L Russel to give the order for them to takeoff. The area around the lineup was dominated by the rumble of Merlin engines beating out their rhythmic tune. Tommy's apprehension about the mission reduced slightly as he now had a lot to consider with flying in formation and managing his Spitfire for the long flight to the target. As they gained altitude and formed up over Redhill, the squadron headed for the east Kent coast to link up with the bombers. Only Dal Russel's voice could be heard as he spoke in turn to sector control and the Boston bomber formation leader. In the near distance with the Kent coast in sight, Tommy saw the bombers thundering along, strung out in their neat box formation. He glanced at his instrument panel to check everything was working normally. No pilot wanted a mechanical problem once they got out over the North Sea. The flight passed by without incident and with the intensely clear visibility, Tommy could soon see the Dutch coast. He looked at the clock on his instrument panel. They were on time. His R/T came to life as S/L Russel spoke to them all: "Enemy territory ahead. Watch for fighters." The islands and estuaries southwest of Rotterdam were now passing underneath them. The silence was ended abruptly. Fighters. The R/T was alive as it was clear enemy fighters were about to attack. Tommy's eyes followed the direction of the incoming attack given over the R/T using the clock face to navigate where he was looking. In the distance, he could see several FW 190s approximately 5,000 feet above them which were now arrowing downwards to carry out a frontal attack on the bombers. They were seeking to break up the formation and split off single bombers that they could then finish off. A mass of tracer rounds flowed out from the beehive of bombers. Tommy clenched the spade grip, spinning his head around to check his tail. One FW 190 dropped away trailing smoke, but in the mayhem, the second part of the German ambush started with 8 more fighters dropping out of the sun, a classic Luftwaffe tactic. Red section of 411 broke formation to chase off the FW 190s which broke away immediately. The voices of men in combat resonated in Tommy's ears. Shortly after the attack, the bombers delivered their payloads onto the industrial port area of Rotterdam and turned out north towards the sea, changing course, westerly for the run back to Kent. Tommy's world was shaken by a loud bang somewhere on his aircraft. He checked all the vital actions and everything seemed normal. His anxiety grew, the next few moments were crucial. Thankfully, he was still in business and it was only upon landing that he could confirm and later write about what had happened: "Got a chunk knocked out of one prop blade by flak. Lots of 190s on the job." It was a lucky escape. Meanwhile, after the hit by flak, they were not out of danger as over the R/T the word was passed. They had more company. In the cockpit of his Spitfire 22-year-old, Tommy was trying to maintain his concentration. He was fearful, as all fighter pilots were in combat. It was said that this fear never went away, it lessened with experience but the knot in the pit of the stomach was always there, you just learned to deal with it and do your job. He remembered his training, the combat evasion and tail chase exercises. He had worked out what he would do if one of the FW 190s attacked. Six fighters were now shadowing them out across the sea. Tommy wanted to see and experience combat. It's why he had been trained to fly the Spitfire and what he was there for. However, a moment later the German commander had turned his formation back and the tension dissipated for everyone.

It was a welcome relief to see the Kent coast and shortly afterward the bombers streamed away northeast as the Roaring Boys lost altitude over Kent, and soon entered the circuit at Redhill. Tommy dropped his aircraft's flaps, made his way downwind and as his Spitfire's speed bled away, he dropped the undercarriage and lined up finals to land, feeling his wheels touching down at 09.20 am. He was soon chatting with his erk as he dropped off the wing and inspected his damaged propeller. He then hurried along to catch up with the other pilots. That was a hell of a second mission and experience, and he had survived it. The conversation was animated as they headed for the briefing tent, their formation tailed this time by a non-threatening menace, Joskins. Smart dog, he knew these boys had burned up a lot of nervous energy during their mission and they would be heading for a large, late breakfast. He would be in position "A" to pick up any leftovers! The ORB reported: "Five pilots of 411 Squadron fired without scoring hits but the e/a turned tail."

Tommy's Ramrod of 26 June saw him joined by Bruce. The pair became good friends during their service with 411 Squadron. This was to be an afternoon "show" and at 16.20 pm S/L Russel led the formation away to collect the 12 Boston bombers which would be attacking the airfield at Abbeville. As the beehive of bombers neared the French coast for unexplained reasons 3 were forced to turn back. With no fighter escort, they would be vulnerable to attack and easy prey for enemy fighters so yellow section, including Tommy, flying yellow 2, turned back with them to provide escort. With the shepherding job complete they returned to base. Meanwhile, Bruce and the remainder of the squadron pressed on. The ORB later detailed events: "Nine remaining Bostons made bomb hits in the SW corner of the airfield. No enemy aircraft were seen but accurate medium flak (for the height) was thrown up in defence). The mission left Tommy less than impressed and he commented, "Bostons turned for home over French coast. Yellow section escorted them back. I hate that kind of thing."

On 29 June, both Tommy and Bruce were up and away at 06.30 am for an hour-long escort mission to Hendon for a VIP. Flying in the Liberator bomber was 1st Viscount Thurso, Sir Archibald Sinclair who was then Secretary of State for the Air. During WW1 Sir Archibald was a soldier in the British Army and Winston Churchill's second in command of The Royal Scots Fusiliers. He was no doubt impressed and comforted as he gazed out of the window at his protection squadron of 12 Spitfire Mark Vbs. During June 1943, Tommy clocked up 3 hours 30 minutes flying on operations and his tour total stood at 4 hours and 45 minutes.

With the arrival of July Tommy kept up his daily routine of formation flying, cine gun camera practice, and "bouncing" fighter attack simulations. Tommy could sense his skills and proficiency were being raised which would stand him in good stead for the later operations. There was also a changing of the guard at the top when S/L Dal Russel DFC was promoted to wing commander and F/L G C Semple became 411's squadron leader. Semple had been with the Roaring Boys since October 1941, arriving as a sergeant, a rapid advancement which the squadron record described as: "well deserved. He is very popular, a splendid pilot and leader and a fine example in personal conduct." Rather tellingly the entry then goes on to say: "He neither drinks nor smokes and has a very cheerful disposition." The praise was lavished in equal measure on Wing Commander Dal Russel DFC. Amongst his achievements, the squadron diarist proclaimed: "All the dud pilots have been posted with the result that we have a squadron to be proud of. Great things can be expected of this fine bunch of pilots. We are now a fine fighting force."

On 5 July, Tommy was called to the CO who proffered his hand and passed Tommy an envelope that would see him return to his tent with an extra spring in his step. The envelope contained notification of his commission to Pilot Officer, which would be effective from 11 July. I like to think that the increase in rank and pay put Tommy firmly in the chair for a round or three of drinks at their local pub, The Hare and Hounds.

On 10 July Tommy and Charlie Trainor were briefed by S/L Semple for Ramrod 129 in which W/C Dal Russel would lead 411 and 401 Squadrons escorting 12 Venturas on a bombing mission to Saint-Omer. At 07.00 am Tommy settled down into the cockpit of Spitfire BL397, and as the Mark Vb sparked into life, the aerodrome was soon reverberating to the sound of 12 Merlin engines. He looked around at the slightly hazy conditions which were rapidly dispersing in the warmth of the summer sunshine. It was a fine day for flying he thought as he pushed the throttle forward on his Spitfire and taxied out. At 07.25 am he was airborne circling the Redhill area as the rest of the Roaring Boys formed up with their comrades from 401. They set course eastwards towards Sandwich, flying along the North Downs past Maidstone and then onwards past Canterbury and its towering cathedral. It was a pilgrimage of sorts, for these sons of Canada flying by this famous building into mortal danger, standing up for a cause they believed in just as Archbishop Thomas Becket had done in the cathedral when he was slain in 1170. It was exhilarating for Tommy to be flying the Spitfire at zero feet, the green lush fields of Kent flashing past beneath him. Either side of his aircraft, Tommy could see his comrades, their aircraft being gently buffeted in the summer breeze as they bobbed rhythmically together. The apprehension had kicked in and all the pilots were nervous. At 07.46 am, the CO's voice came over the R/T. From the northwest, Tommy could make out the 12 twin-engine Venturas heading their way towards the coast. As each squadron slotted into formation around them the bomber formation began to gain altitude and by the time, they crossed the French coast they were levelling out at 9,000 feet. The German flak batteries opened fire and Tommy concentrated hard. It was medium heavy and accurate. These units were well drilled as they targeted formations in their sector on a daily basis. The explosions, silent in Tommy's ears looked innocuous enough but the puffs of black smoke could easily destroy a Spitfire, and they often did. They flew on leaving the field of flak behind and began the bombing run on the rail marshalling yards. Tommy's eyes were intently scanning the skyline for fighters when a red flash caught his eye. A direct hit on the assembly shop sent bright orange and red flames skywards. The target area had received hits and as they turned for the north for home Tommy could see the resulting smoke clouds rising ever higher. He knew the danger was not passed and as the speeding formation reached Gravelines at 8,000 feet the barrage was extremely heavy and accurate with tracer fire also arcing around their aircraft. Tommy breathed deeply willing the coast to pass beneath his Spitfire so he could escape the flak for the sanctuary of the sea crossing. The formation closed their throttles and commenced a slow descent, reaching North Foreland on the east Kent coast at 3,000 feet. Tommy could see the airfield at RAF Manston, a welcome diversion for anyone with mechanical problems or battle damage. The two squadrons had made it through in one piece and so had the bombers which now peeled away for their base after an exchange of farewells with Dal Russel. The welcome sight of RAF Redhill was a relief as Tommy and the others touched down at 08.45 am. It was then on to the mission debrief and paperwork. The intelligence team wanted every scrap of detail they could get, even the locations of the flak positions and the intensity of their fire. Tommy and the others had their minds on different matters; mainly a hearty breakfast and a brew up of steaming hot tea.

For his mission of 26 July, Tommy would be flying a mid-afternoon Rodeo mission to Saint-Omer with 412 Squadron led by W/C Dal Russel DFC. Having taken off from base at 15.40 pm, within 10 minutes the formation crossed the English coast at Sandwich at zero feet before climbing to 13,000 feet and crossing the French coast at Hardelot. They turned left at Saint-Omer and exited via Calais. Although enemy fighters were seen they did not attack. Tommy wrote: "Fighter sweep around St Omer. I was R.2 to S/L G Semple, we didn't see a thing, only one burst of flak. Poor show."

On occasion, the Roaring Boys had to take part in nonstandard operations. On 27 July at 22.00 pm Tommy took part in an air-sea rescue mission to find 412 Squadron Leader S L Keefer who had been forced to bail out into the sea due to mechanical problems, five miles off the French coast. As Tommy and the squadron neared the search area, bad weather forced them back after only around 15 minutes. Fortunately, a Walrus air-sea rescue floatplane picked up a mightily relieved Squadron Leader later that evening. Tommy described the mission: "Went to French coast, it was too dark to see anything. First night landing in Spit."

Tommy relayed to me one of his many hair-raising experiences flying Spitfires. He was unsure of the date but said that he and one of Spitfire Elizabeth's other pilots Len Harrison were sent to fly escort to a squadron of Boston bombers returning from a bombing mission over occupied France. Tommy and Len flew low towards the coast having been vectored onto to the returning bombers over the channel. As the coast came into view the Bostons suddenly appeared from below the cliffs having flown "on the deck" across the channel. Both pilots, young and with razor-sharp reactions that were required of fighter pilots took emergency evasive action. Tommy pulled back hard on the stick and his Spitfire streaked upwards past the oncoming Bostons. Meanwhile, Len opted to stay low, very low in fact. On returning to base he was found to have shaved the tips off of his propeller blades! During July, Tommy flew 4 hours and 50 minutes on operations for a total since joining 411 of 9 hours 35 minutes.

On 6 August 1943, the Roaring Boys arrived at RAF Staplehurst, Kent where they camped under canvas as practice for their mobile wing flight operations which would start once they moved to France after the D Day invasion. There were long days of flight training, "bouncing" attacks, tail chases, formation and gun camera work all with the objective of keeping the pilots sharp.

On 31 August Charlie joined Tommy for the first part of Ramrod S.16, an attack by 36 Marauders of the USAAF's Eighth Air Force on Lille Vendeville aerodrome which is located a few miles south of the industrial city of Lille. Later on, that day, W/C Johnnie Johnson lead 127

Wing on the second part of S1.6, a bomber escort mission to Mazingarbe power station. Tommy, Charlie and the Spitfires of 411 roared into the air at 06.50 am shattering the peace of Chickenden Farm, Staplehurst. The escort proceeded to North Foreland where they picked up the Marauders, beginning the channel crossing at 12,000 feet. Only eight minutes later they crossed the French coast at Mardyck, close to Dunkirk which provided the traditional welcome for the beehive as flak sent up by the German defenders. The message swiftly went around the Spitfire escort that 6 enemy fighters had been spotted below the formation at 6,000 feet. Tommy and the other pilots' pulses quickened but they were ready to foil any attack, checking their aircraft instruments and cockpit harnesses in readiness for the high "G" twists and turns of a dog fight. The Luftwaffe, perhaps sensing the overwhelming odds declined to attack. Only 10 minutes after crossing the French coast the aerodrome at Lille was in sight and the Marauders delivered their payloads, which hit the southern dispersal area with a high level of accuracy. The defences began their barrage with seemingly every weapon they had. One of the Marauders was soon hit, beginning a steep dive that saw it crash in the centre of the airfield. On the return leg, Merville aerodrome put up a light flak barrage but to no real effect and Tommy landed his Spitfire with the others back at Staplehurst at 08.15 am. The fate of the Marauder was seared into his mind as he recalled the attack in his logbook: "one Marauder hit by flak broke in half and exploded in aerodrome. Saw two of crew bail out. Flak very accurate. No huns about. Very good bombing by USAAF." Tommy added a further 7 hours and 55 minutes of operational flying during August for a tour total of 17 hours and 30 minutes.

Tommy recalled his time in Staplehurst with a selection of amusing anecdotes. It is difficult for to imagine what it must have been like for the Roaring Boys to climb into a Spitfire, fly over to France, put their lives on the line only to return to home and head to the pub for a pint. It was how they rolled back then. Like young men everywhere the Roaring Boys were in search of a good time whilst "away from work" and the dangers associated with their "employment" must have stiffened their resolve to go in search of it at every possible opportunity. Tommy recalled that at the time many pilots struck up friendships with the locals. I remember the pause as his mind rolled back the years, "One girl was called Jill" he suddenly announced. According to Tommy, she enjoyed the company of some of his fellow pilots. His telling of the story caused much hilarity with Gail and I. Distance was no barrier to the twinkle in those eyes which were shining clear and bright. Tommy went on to recall how Jill used to give the boys free petrol coupons for their motorbikes and cars, including his old Ford Prefect. Those coupons must have been like gold dust during the wartime rationing in Britain after years of war.

On 3 September Tommy was scheduled to be back in the air for an early morning squadron takeoff, with Bob and Charlie. They walked along through the line of tents and sitting in amongst the orchard some of the trees were hanging with fruit and various items of airmen's clothing gently swaying in the breeze. The squadron would be led by F/L D R Matheson and he conducted the briefing with S/L Semple and the intelligence team. Tommy sat down on one of the chairs which were lined up haphazardly on the edge of the tent. The Mighty Eighth was hitting Luftwaffe airfields all over northern France and the Roaring Boys job was to escort 36 Marauders to Lille-Nord aerodrome. With the routes in and out mapped and discussed watches were synchronised and they assembled at dispersal ready to set forth at 07.50 am. Tommy jumped up onto the wing of his allotted Spitfire AA878 and with his harnesses done up his Merlin engine was soon warming up with a reassuring rumble. Doug Matheson led them off across Kent, the Garden of England whose landmarks like Canterbury were now quite a familiar sight to Tommy as they flew towards the rendezvous with the 36 Marauders over North Foreland. With the bombers in tow, they flew over the empty sea, the French coast growing in Tommy's windscreen rapidly. They would soon once again run the gauntlet of the flak batteries. The beehive of bombers and their "little friends" swept inland and headed southeast towards Lille. As they closed in observers in the city and at the aerodrome sounded the alarm. The visibility was rather too good thought Tommy, as he looked down and then ahead as the first bursts of flak appeared in amongst the formation. It was fairly intense and heavy, and Tommy employed some weaving, as did the others to put the spotters off their aim. Thus far, no enemy fighters or aircraft had scrambled to meet them, and the Roaring Boys looked on as the bombs made their way towards the target. From his grandstand seat, Tommy thought it looked pretty good, which the ORB later confirmed claiming, "Bombing results were excellent." With the bombing part of the mission complete, it was time for the channel dash and outgoing flak barrage. As Tommy gave his Spitfire a touch more throttle it kicked forward, the engine reaching a higher pitch. By 09.20 am they were dropping down towards the base, and as Tommy looked out of his starboard window, he could see the ancient Leeds Castle and its moat resplendent in the morning sunshine. He settled the wheels of his Spitfire back down on the runway's steel tracking at 09.20 am. With his cockpit hood back, he taxied in and was marshalled into position. He expertly kicked his port rudder, the aircraft spun around on its axis and as it came to halt it was immediately set upon by the erks looking to refuel and perform their maintenance work. Tommy shut down and saw the erk dive under his wing to insert the chocks. Tommy then stepped out of the cockpit, dropped off the wing and walked smartly towards the INT/OPS tent to debrief. His day was done.

Tommy with DB – D Little Mil II September 1943

The 9 September saw the start of Operation Starkey, a mock invasion of France designed to draw the Luftwaffe into a battle where significant damage could be inflicted on them in the air and on the ground. As the ORB reported. "This is D Day and operations are destined to make the enemy fight under conditions favourable to ourselves. Against this backdrop Tommy, Bruce and Len were expectant after the briefing. This could be their chance to get to grips with the enemy and test themselves in air combat. At 14.05 pm in great flying conditions, S/L Semple led the Roaring Boys and the rest of 126 Wing on a rendezvous with 18 Mitchells which would bomb Bryas-Sud aerodrome, located northwest of Arras.

Tommy readied himself for the flight to the coast and listened in as the R/T updated them on the progress of the Mitchells. On cue, they appeared at Beachy Head and the formation set off across the channel making landfall at the Somme estuary before turning northeast for Bryas Sud aerodrome. As the target came into view, inexplicably the box of bombers turned left before the target was even reached, leaving Tommy and the others wondering if they knew something. The Roaring Boys, as shepherds were forced to follow their flock and the R/T traffic suggested that the rest of the Mitchells dropped their bombs but missed the aerodrome completely. The presence of enemy fighters heightened expectations of an attack but the reason for the bombers turning away is not recorded. Bruce wrote: "E/A above but did not engage." This was a scenario being repeated in missions all over the north of France. The Luftwaffe wanted to protect their precious fighters against overwhelming numbers of Allied aircraft intent on destroying them. The Mitchells and 411 Squadron crossed back over the French coast at Ault and returned safely to base. Tommy and the others touched down at 15.10 pm disappointed in the whole "show" which had promised much but delivered little in the way of action. Tommy expressed his feelings in his logbook: "One hun was accounted for, let's not have too much of this sort of thing."

On 18 September 1943, Tommy was enjoying a favorite pastime of the Roaring Boys, volleyball. He had the misfortune of colliding with S/L G C Semple who dislocated his knee. Semple had survived 185 missions until that point but was crocked by a ball game! He was replaced as 411 Squadron Leader by I C Ormston. It was a freak accident but such events would not have passed without a fair amount of banter heading in Tommy's direction for knobbling the CO!

The Ramrods continued with the good weather and on occasion the Roaring Boys acted as an escort on the way in and as withdrawal cover, picking up a beehive of bombers on the return leg of their mission. One such mission was Ramrod 251 on 27 September. At 16.00 pm Tommy sat down for F/L Matheson's briefing. No. 126 Airfield was to pick up 72 Marauders over the Channel and then wait as withdrawal cover when the bombers returned from Conches aerodrome. The mission went to plan but the squadron diary reported that they: "were unable to observe bombing results. One Marauder was shot down by flak from the Fécamp area (on the French coast.)" The diary then reported that the wing, "was bounced by Spitfire Mark IXs" in a case of mistaken identity but no damage or fire was received from the "friendly" attackers. The diary went on: "At the same time, S/L Neal reported 3 or 4 FW 190s among them. When the controller reported Huns, our squadron flew well into the sun and home." The Wing returned to Staplehurst at 18.30 pm disappointed that the bounce wasn't for real and they could get stuck in. It should be remembered that Tommy, flying Spitfire BL696, and the Roaring Boys were still going into battle in the Spitfire Mark LF Vb. Unlike the Mark IX, the Vb was outclassed by the FW 190 in the hands of an experienced fighter pilot. The missions were racking up and in August Tommy flew 6 hours and 45 minutes on operations. His total flying with 411 now stood at 24 hours and 15 minutes.

In early October the weather occasionally bathed RAF Staplehurst in the warm sunshine. The dispersal area was so well camouflaged under the orchards and trees that the effects of the sun couldn't be felt too often. Small groups of pilots and ground crews moved in groups to find a sunny spot for a cup of tea and a smoke. There was no noticeable increase in practice flying. Tommy and the others were feeling highly confident as they tested their Spitfires to the limit in practice "bounces" where the dreaded "dagga dagga dagga" in the headset indicated to the pilot under attack that a fellow Roaring Boy had defeated their evasion techniques and was "on their tail."

Tommy and the Roaring Boys enjoyed their liberty runs to Maidstone and after a day's practice flying, he and the others would high tail it into my home town. I sent Tommy some photos of the Royal Star Hotel as it was back in the 1940s. He remembered going there. The hotel is now a shopping arcade but wandering around the shops today it's still possible to see the original building. Back in the 1940s, there was a balcony that stretched across the first floor with the hotel's name attached to its iron railings. This is where the dance floor was situated and the Hotel's central entrance originally allowed horse and carriages through. It's an intriguing prospect to think that my grandparents were whirling around that dance floor at the same time as Tommy and his comrades.

To us locals, the fog that can grip the Weald of Kent in the autumn is very familiar and in 1943 it was doing its worst, leaving Tommy and the squadron frequently grounded and frustrated. The squadron diary summed it up perfectly: "It hangs on with determination for the remainder of the day." Exercise came in games of volleyball which took place but also in the raiding of local woods for supplies of logs that were chopped up in a competitive atmosphere Avoiding the obvious national stereotyping one would expect the Canucks to have been rather proficient at this activity! The store of logs would soon come in useful as on 13 October 411 moved to its winter base at Biggin Hill. I discussed the airfield with Tommy. He recalled his time their fondly: "Biggin Hill was a wonderful place to fly from. Real posh." Tommy was able to look at some photos that Norm Whiteford had sent me from the time, including of himself and point out which ones he believed were from Biggin.

Tommy and the Roaring Boys finally got their hands on the Spitfire Mark IXb. On 14 October, Tommy took one of the new Mark IX's for a local 30-minute flight. It's safe to say he was impressed with the higher speed and feel writing, "Lovely, absolutely lovely! Cheers!" The following day Tommy was equally positive about the appointment of 126 Airfield's new Commander Buck McNair DSO DFC and Bar, "TERRIFIC!" He wrote.

On 22 October Tommy could take the Spitfire Mark IX into combat for the first time in Ramrod 282. This would be another escort mission to 24 Mitchells bombing the marshalling yards at Rouen. As the squadron took to the air at 14.50 pm, they had already been warned about the weather by the intelligence boys and so it proved as an hour later Tommy was back on the ground, with the formation being forced to turn back in the channel 10 miles off the French coast, "due to duff weather – cloud." Tommy landed, disappointed but impressed with the performance of his new Spitfire MH477.

Tommy returned to the briefing room at around 10.30 am on 24 October. The weather had improved and so had the location of the briefings. At least they were no longer conducted in tents. Wing Commander Buck McNair joined S/L Ormston and the intelligence team centre stage as the details of Ramrod 283 was briefed. It was a typical day of offensive operations and 126 Airfield would provide close escort to 72 Marauders from the USAAF's Ninth Air Force bombing Beauvais aerodrome. A total of 200 Marauders would also make attacks on Montdidier and Saint Andre de L'Eure airfields.

At 11.35 am Tommy pulled the flying helmet over his head and dropped down into the cockpit of MH477. The Spitfire was soon up to operating temperature and as Tommy eased the throttle forward a puff of black smoke swirled around the exhaust manifolds. The open expanse of Biggin Hill lay before him and 36 Spitfires, all ready and eager to get into the air. With the word given Tommy was lined up and soon bouncing across "the bump" feeling the surge of power from the Merlin as he gained altitude. As the formation readied itself above the skies of Biggin, S/L Ormston led the Roaring Boys south towards the coast. In their Mark IXs the Roaring Boys role was to take on any enemy fighters, the rest of the wing would stay close to the bombers in their slightly inferior Mark Vs. As they crossed the coast Tommy could just make out the formation on his port side, several boxes of bombers almost lazily making their way south. S/L Ormston warned his charges, "enemy territory boys. Watch out for fighters." They crossed just north of Dieppe and set course southeast towards Beauvais, located around 60 miles away. It was clear from the radio traffic and the cloud cover that the bombers were going to hit a satellite of the main Beauvais Tillé aerodrome. It was called Beauvais/I and was located a few miles to the northeast. Tommy could clearly see the target area in the distance and only allowed himself the occasional glance at the bombers. He was after fighters and was keyed up, expecting a bounce any second. It was difficult to keep in a state of readiness for long periods, but the seasoned pilots told them repeatedly, if you switch off, they'll get you. The visual crump of the bombs hitting the runway area and surrounding buildings told Tommy the bomber boys were spot on. Later the damage assessment indicated a cratered runway, one dispersal building and aircraft destroyed. The formation swung north and released from their payloads the bombers increased their speed and made for the coast. Tommy and the Roaring Boys left the beehive at Bexhill, Sussex soon after crossing the English coast and touched down at Biggin at 13.20 pm. The mission was a success and no enemy fighters bothered them. Tommy was impressed with the efforts describing it as: "good bombing, no flak no huns about."

The weather in early November was frequently described by 411's official diarist as "duff." Tommy did manage to take part in a Rodeo on 6 November, crossing the French coast at Dieppe. The Spitfires swept into enemy territory near Dieppe hoping to lure the Luftwaffe into a dog fight but 10/10 cloud over France hampered operations and at 17.25 pm in the darkening sky Tommy felt the reassuring bump of his wheels on the runway as he returned to Biggin following a very uneventful patrol.

In September the Germans had started construction of a major underground set of fortifications and bunkers, the Fortress of Mimoyeques. The potential for 5 V3 cannons being able to fire long-range shells on London made the repeated bombing of the secret facility a top priority. At this time, Tommy and the Roaring Boys would not have known the full significance of the target area but the fact that so many missions were now being made to facilities like this told them as much as they needed to know. On 5 November, Ramrod 291A was divided into 2 missions, with Tommy and Bob taking part in the second one of the day which left Biggin at 16.05 pm. They escorted Marauders and Mitchells. Only 24 of the Ninth Air Force's Mitchell's equipped with "GEE-H" navigational equipment for "blind bombing" made it to the target due to the dense cloud cover. The return leg was uneventful in terms of enemy aircraft and flak and so Tommy and Bob made sedate progress back to Biggin where they touched down at 17.15 pm. Tommy later said: "Everything OK, nothing seen at all. Bombers dropped a few leaflets. I flew Y.4. P/O Cam MacDougall Y.3."

With the duff weather conditions hampering flying, there was little that could be done on those days other than ground school and fitness work. On 18 November Tommy was rostered to fly in a Rodeo mission with 401 Squadron to Hardelot, just south of Boulogne-Sur-Mer and Béthune which is located around 10 miles northwest of Lens. The formation would cross the channel, and unencumbered by the slower bombers would thunder across the French countryside, their Spitfires Merlin engines going "full chat." Tommy's Spitfire was MA312. Although the mission came across no enemy forces events a few days later demonstrate the precarious nature of the job. There was a fine margin between life and death for these pilots, and not just from enemy action. Tommy was delighted with his new Spitfire. He noted her arrival: "my own kite. Little Mil I call her after Milly my fiancée woo woo." On 23 November, it was F/S Stan M Kent who was rostered to fly Spitfire MA312, Little Mil. He had flown on the same mission as Tommy on 18 November. There's a photo of him together with Tommy, Len and Sid Brooks at RAF Staplehurst. Tragically Stan Kent was killed following an engine failure. He had swopped fuel tanks causing MA312's engine to cut out and he plunged into the sea. It was a heavy blow for the group and the wider squadrons of the wing.

Despite the winter weather, Tommy racked up 9 hours and 45 minutes on operations during the month and his total now stood at 36 hours and 45 minutes.

Tommy and the squadron took a short flight to RAF Coltishall, near Norwich, Norfolk on 12 December in preparation for a busy day of Ramrod escort duties. The first of these on 13 December was Ramrod 362 which saw wheels up at 09.30 am. The wing would make a forward fighter sweep of Dutch territory ahead of hundreds of returning Eighth Air Force B17s which had been bombing Kiel, Bremen, and targets of opportunity in Hamburg. Two orbits were made successfully and some light accurate flak was thrown up to no effect. The wing landed back at Coltishall at 11.05 am. It was a quick turnaround to bring them back to a state of readiness for Ramrod 363 which was scheduled to commence at 14.00 pm.

Tommy and the Roaring Boys were led by W/C "Buck" McNair DFC and Two Bars on a close escort Ramrod mission for 72 Marauders bombing Amsterdam Schiphol aerodrome. As Tommy powered Spitfire JK795 down the runway and became airborne there was a feeling of anticipation. They were heading deep into enemy territory which didn't help defuse the tension and nerves they all felt. The enemy was one thing, the dark foreboding North Sea beneath them was unwelcoming and somewhere no one wanted to end up. With the box of Marauders safely tucked into their care, Tommy checked his instruments which were all showing normal. He felt ready and as he said to me their mission was always straight forward, destroy the enemy. The grim reality of the position may appear harsh to some but heading on these missions in a fighter plane Tommy summed up exactly what life was all about at that time for the pilots on both sides. Without the steely determination and clarity of thought, a moment's hesitation could cost you your life. Tommy's feelings about sitting in the Spitfire cockpit heading into combat with his fellow countrymen took on an almost spiritual experience: "It's like going to Heaven, I guess. It was the most marvellous aeroplane I have ever flown."

With the bombers beginning a countdown to their run on Schiphol, a call went out. Two enemy aircraft had been spotted, FW 190s. Tommy responded in an instant upon hearing the words, "Yellow section attack." He could clearly see the pair of FW 190s arrowing in and pushed his

Spitfire's throttle to maximum power. All 4 of yellow section were now engaged and a twisting corkscrew of fighters dived down from 17,000 feet to the deck. Tommy's report reads as follows:

"I was flying yellow 2 in 411 Squadron on Ramrod 363. In the target area whilst orbiting the bombers, 2 ME 109s (sic FW 190s) were reported at 11 o'clock to us at about 2,000 feet above and diving apparently to make a head-on attack on the bombers. Yellow section was ordered by the Wing Commander Flying to attack and dived down and when we were 1,000 yards away, they flicked over and dived down, we followed and Yellow 1 (F/L McFarlane) opened fire at about 600 yards. I fired one burst at 500 yards and we closed to 300 yards. One e/a broke off, followed by Yellow 1 and I followed the other on the starboard to 1,000 and opened fire at 300 yards at 20 degrees to starboard allowing one ring deflection firing for over 3 ½ seconds. I saw strikes on the starboard wing, wing root, fuselage, and tail. I broke off the attack at this point and when we last saw the e/a was weaving violently from side to side. This e/a is claimed as damaged."

It's remarkable to watch Tommy's actual gun camera footage as the action unfolds. It is exactly as he described it. Beneath the aircraft is the flat, featureless Dutch landscape of straight canals, rivers, and lakes. As Tommy fires his aim is true as strikes erupt on the FW 190, which is flying straight and level. After approximately a second there's a large puff of white smoke, and the FW 190 begins trailing thick black smoke. It looks as if the pilot is trying to gain altitude, possibly to bail out as Tommy's camera stops. For this action, Tommy was credited with 2 quarter shares of 2 FW 190s. The other two pilots who successfully attacked the enemy that day were P/O C M Steele and F/O RFM Walker.

Yellow section had to regroup and return to the formation quickly. Meanwhile, the 72 Marauders pressed home their attack at 14.45 pm. In his cockpit Tommy felt the adrenalin, the fight or flight reaction of his body begin to subside. He had to block the combat out of his mind as they were now pushing out across the North Sea on the return leg. They touched down at 15.30 pm and with their Spitfires lined up and silent in the dispersal area Yellow section was soon in an excited huddle, exchanging details of the action and getting their claims ready for the intelligence boys. They were all desperate to view the gun camera footage from their respective aircraft that would verify their claim. In an interesting postscript to the story, Tommy's Mark IX Spitfire JK795 for this mission later suffered an engine failure in the hands of Charlie, after which he was captured and interned as a POW.

Tommy was joined by Charlie, Len, and Bob for Ramrod 383 on 22 December during which the wing would be patrolling around Rouen and Amiens area. The formation swept into France near Le Touquet from where light flak was sent up. After patrolling for 40 minutes they crossed back over the French coast south of Le Touquet. On the channel crossing, Tommy was checking his fuel level as was Charlie. Both were getting twitchy about whether they would make it back to base. The ORB recorded: "Red 3, P/O Wheler, TR and Yellow 4, F/L Trainor, HC landed at Friston out of petrol. Both returned to base later." RAF Friston near Eastbourne is perched right on the coast and was frequently used as a refuelling and rearming airfield, but also by aircraft in emergency situations. It had been a busy month of flying and Tommy spent 13 hours and 30 minutes flying Spitfires. He was now just a quarter of the way towards his tour complete total of approximately 200 hours.

With the Christmas festivities behind them, the duff weather continued to allow only the occasional formation and practice flying exercises. Tommy started 1944 with a mention in the ORB: "Our pilots serviceability is low these days as P/O Wheler left for the hospital for a few days and F/O Thorpe and F/O Brooks and Steele are also down with colds." I have established the reason for Tommy's enforced absence as he wrote in his logbook, "Happy New Year 1944." This was followed by a less welcome start to the year: "Broken ear drum! Off flying. Made Adjutant." After a mission on 7 January, he noted, "Ears seem Ok?" Meanwhile, the rest of the squadron were not left to their own devices. On 2 January 1944, the wing listened to a first-hand account by F/L Smith of his experiences of being forced down in Africa and escaping from a POW camp in Italy. It was invaluable advice for everyone. Later many would come to value the advice given during these lectures. By 7 January, the weather was good enough for the Roaring Boys to go on a fighter sweep with 401 Squadron as part of Ramrod 435, Charlie, Gibby, Bruce, and Bob joined Tommy in sweeping behind Amiens and Arras. The formation observed repairs on the Amiens Gilsey aerodrome which was passed back to intelligence. No enemy aircraft or flak was encountered and the sweep was completed at 16.40 pm after 1 hour 35 minutes. S/L McFarlane returned early with engine trouble. A few days later it was Tommy's turn to have the same problem whilst on a practice rendezvous flying as Red 1. Engine trouble forced him to land at RAF Worthy Down near Winchester, Hampshire. He was back later at Biggin Hill for a session of instrument training in the Link trainer, an early version of a flight simulator that could reproduce instrument navigation and landing techniques to keep the pilots skills sharp. Trevor Matthews from the Lashenden Air Warfare Museum at Headcorn aerodrome showed me around their wartime Link trainer. An amazing piece of kit considering the time it was built.

In the early afternoon of 25 January Tommy, Charlie and Bob attended a briefing for the mid-afternoon Ramrod 482. At 15.25 pm Tommy piloted Spitfire MJ133 down Biggin's runway and into the air. They formed up and were soon storming across Kent for a sweep of the Arras area led by F/L S A Mills. They continued to climb to around 25,000 feet, where they levelled out and Tommy rolled the trim wheels to take the pressure off the stick. He could feel the intense cold around him, particularly in his hands as he gripped the spade grip and as the oxygen flowed through his mask he carried out his top of the climb checks starting with the fuel gauge. He followed this with his R/T check. Each member of the section confirmed they could receive and transmit, crucial for when they crossed the coast into enemy territory. Next, it was the engine, temperatures and pressures were normal, he aligned his direction indicator and compass and looked at his altimeter which was reading 25,000 feet. All was normal and Tommy settled back searching the bright blue sky around him. They were over France and Tommy detailed the route in his logbook, "sweeping Arras to Lille and south." At that moment a voice confirmed a sighting. "Bandits 7 o'clock angels 26." As one all heads turned and looked over the left shoulders and yes, there they were, enemy fighters flying in the opposite direction. Tommy's heart rate increased several notches as he prepared himself for a bounce by the formation above them. His mouth went dry, and the nerves kicked in as they did for everyone. To a man, they were nervous. It was a dangerous situation. The chess match began. F/L Mills called for a 90-degree turn climbing turn to port. Tommy eased his throttle forward and changed his Spitfire's angle of attack, noting the altimeter passing through 25,500 to 26,000 feet, where the Roaring Boys straightened out. Tommy's eyes looked to port and all around in case another gaggle of fighters swept in at them from another direction. They knew the tricks the Luftwaffe used in this situation. His senses were on overload and such events were seared into the memory of these young Canucks. They could assume that their move had been seen by the enemy who did not respond. In fact, they were pulling away. As the Roaring Boys headed for home intense flak opened fire over Saint-Omer. Tommy watched the deadly black candy floss bursts beneath and around their formation. The flak 88 mm gunners had their range, and at 26,000 feet the shells had enough momentum to reach the formation. They hung on, desperate to move through the barrage, each praying they wouldn't be hit. The intense cold was getting to Tommy now, but he would rather that than drop further into the hell of the flak. Soon, it was passed and F/L Mills instructed them to throttle back to begin a glide descent for home. At least the intense cold would ease and Tommy could switch off his oxygen mask once they passed below 10,000 feet. He wiped his screen with his hands as a mist formed. Through it, he could see Biggin on the bump. He knew what they would do upon landing. Head to the NAAFI for a warming brew. At 16.55 pm, they landed and taxied in. It was another significant addition to his tour time and they'd all come through an encounter with the enemy unscathed. On 28 January Tommy, Len, and Bob were led on a fighter sweep of the Arras area by W/C Buck McNair as part of Ramrod 489. The ORB reported later: "No Huns or flak were seen. F/L D C McKay of 412 Squadron had to bail out near the English coast due to engine failure. He was picked up about 10 minutes later by Air/Sea Rescue." No doubt F/L McKay was extremely thankful to be plucked from the icy channel, and he was now a fully paid up member of both the Caterpillar and Goldfish clubs.

During the month of January Tommy added a further 10 hours and 10 minutes of operational flying to his total which now stood at 60 hours and 25 minutes.

At the start of the month of February the missions to bomb No Ball sites was continuing in earnest. On 4 February Tommy and Charlie and the wing made an initial flight to Manston where their role would be to locate and escort hundreds of B17s of the Mighty Eighth returning from raids into Germany, including industrial targets around Frankfurt. Tommy and the pilots had a real challenge on their hands that would test their skill as

Spitfire pilots. There was a 50-mph wind gusting and swirling around the Manston runway. F/O Michael damaged the propeller of his Spitfire when the wind got under the tail, tipping it up. Tommy and the others knew they were in for a rough trip and so it proved as they wrestled with the controls and to stay on course at 20,000 feet in the 140 mph winds. The mission was not going to plan as the wing did not pick up the fortresses and instead reverted to a fighter sweep. Tommy noted the route as: "Ostend to St Pol. Sat at Boulogne, slight flak. No huns. 140 mph wind." Everyone was relieved to get back on the ground at 15.25 pm after 1 hour 30 minutes of extremely challenging flying.

The 22 February was a busy one for Tommy as Operation Argument, the USAAF's "Big Week" was in full swing. In the morning he was off to Manston to refuel and then to Holland to escort Marauders bombing Gilze aerodrome. After a refuel of men and machines, Tommy was joined by Bruce, Len, Gibby, and Bob as F/L R W Orr gave the briefing. The mission was to pick up a box of B17 Fortresses returning from Germany and act as withdrawal support. At 15.00 pm, 126 Airfield was airborne from Manston and heading out across the bleak North Sea. As they climbed out it was disconcerting to see the vast expanse of the ocean filling their windscreens, knowing the regular occurrences of engine failures and forced ditching. The Roaring Boys pushed on and almost with a sense of relief made landfall, despite it being enemy territory. The reassuring engine tone of the Spitfire told Tommy all was well and as he looked down, he could make out ahead the Belgium capital city, Brussels at 11 o'clock. The Roaring Boys stayed southeast of the city; in the distance Tommy could make out a large formation of bombers heading their way. He noticed several trailing smoke from their engines. It looked like they had had a mauling. The wing took up their allotted position and concentrated intently on the horizon all around them. It would be easy pickings if the Luftwaffe boys could get in amongst some of the damaged Fortresses and cause them to drop out of the formation. Nothing was seen but Tommy's R/T was alive with other disturbing radio traffic. As the ORB later described: "No enemy aircraft were encountered or flak but there was bags of engine trouble with pilots returning back to Manston. The whole show was abortive." Bruce also noted: "F/L Orr had engine trouble just as we met the first bunch of Forts. I returned with him." Unfortunately, one pilot's mission was cut short as Tommy recorded:

"small amount of flak, a chap bailed out of a Spit near the Dutch coast. Pretty cold." The Fortresses soon departed from the escort heading to their East Anglian bases. At 16.15 pm, Tommy approached the circuit at Manston and dropped his flaps and undercarriage feeling the welcome connection as his Spitfire's wheels touched down onto Manston's runway. The debrief was full of chatter, not about the mission but about the mechanical issues and these were collected together to pass to the engineers and ground crew, now swarming over the line of Spitfires as they cooled down from their exertions. It was decided that the wing would spend the night at Manston as the weather at Biggin Hill was poor. After a hearty dinner, the pilots turned in for the night. Tommy was unsure of the time as he was unceremoniously awoken from his slumber by a cacophony of firing guns, sirens and a lot of shouting. The whole building seemed to shake. All around him was chaos and commotion with pilots dashing around throwing on what clothing they could find and making a rapid exit for the air raid shelters. Tommy tore after the others through the hut door. Outside he could hear the low drone of aircraft engines. The flak noise increased in intensity as other batteries joined in the firing, the sky lit up as tracer and artillery rounds erupted from around the aerodrome. The enemy visitor was a Me 410 Hornisse, also known as a "schnellbomber." The squadron diarist described events: "An Me 410 shot across Manston at 1,000 feet but he got through even though it seemed like every gun in the place opened up on him. All the pilots thought their time had come; it sure sounded like a dive bomb attack."

At around midday on 7 March, Tommy, Charlie, and Bob assembled with the rest of the wing for a briefing. The room, buzzing with conversation was brought to order as Ramrod 634 was described. F/L Russ Orr would lead the Roaring Boys again on a close escort mission. The target for 108 Marauders was Creil marshalling yards and at 13.40 pm Tommy and the others launched their Spitfires skywards, assembling as a wing for the bomber pick up which was achieved near the south coast. The formation made its way steadily southwards and all was going to plan. The ORB later noted: "The wing was over the target at 14.15 hours and the Marauders really pranged the pot today. On crossing Creil aerodrome F/L Shepherd of 401 Squadron sighted two FW 190s on the drome itself just taking off. F/L Shepherd and F/O Kiersy shot them down and got a destroyed each. 411 and 412 Squadrons acted as cover to 401 as they fought with the Hun. It was a really good show for 401. A lot of intense, inaccurate flak was tossed up at the Marauders about halfway out but no one was worried over it. All our a/c returned to base." The Roaring Boys were envious of 401 and the action they had been in but that was the game. Tommy expressed his disappointment, "we didn't have a go." Next time it would be their turn to duke it out with the enemy.

The next day Tommy's hopes of tangling with the enemy were raised as he would be joining Charlie and 6 others on a Ranger led again by Russ Orr. It was to be a late afternoon job with two sections of 4 Spitfires heading across the French coast at Le Touquet. At 16.40 pm they set off for France, climbing up to 5,000 feet, their Spitfires swiftly moving across the French countryside. Tommy kept one eye on the lead aircraft, adjusting his throttle and making small almost imperceptible inputs to the stick and rudder to maintain his position in the formation. He was highly experienced now and he could mostly concentrate on the world outside his cockpit, looking for any sign of fighters or incoming flak. They swept inland passed Abbeville and Amiens on a near southerly course towards Paris. As they passed one aerodrome the R/T came to life as a visual reference was given on an unarmed Fieseler Storch which was on a landing approach. The pilot would have been aware of the presence of Tommy and the others as a heavy covering barrage was sent up to put them off what would have been an easy "kill." It worked, and Russ Orr decided they should press on. He could almost detect the disappointment from the others but they knew the chances of losing someone was extremely high as the Storch had ducked down under the flak umbrella. The mission was a long one, but Tommy and the others saw nothing else of note during the return leg and landed back at Biggin Hill at 18.20 pm. The absence of any action was always a source of frustration for Tommy as he wrote: "No E/A or any flak poor show." His spirits were lifted somewhat on 25 March: "GOT MY F/O. HAVE A BEER CHAPS!"

In between missions Tommy is regularly mentioned participating in some activity or another. On 12 March during a day of unserviceable weather he, F/Os Kramer and Wallace practiced their marksmanship with some skeet shooting. F/O Kramer won the keenly fought contest. For Tommy, having described conditions at RAF Biggin Hill on arrival as, "lovely, absolutely lovely" it was always going to be somewhat of a downwards step when the squadron was moved to RAF Tangmere on 15 April. Their new accommodation would be tents once again, living as they would be expected to after the invasion of France. The squadron diarist alluded to the general feeling: "Everyone seems fairly settled in their new homes even though they are a bit breezy." A few days before leaving Biggin, Tommy and several others visited P/O Jimmy Mitchell at Orpington Hospital. He had been broken his leg in a gliding accident and was expected to be out of action for many months to come. A few days before the move Tommy took possession of a new Spitfire: "Little Mil No.3 just as beautiful as her name."

The air firing and bombing practice courses continued as the pilots skills were honed further ahead of the invasion of Europe. On 23 April F/O Charlie Servos arrived with 411 to take over from Tommy as the squadron's Adjutant. He also relieved F/O P Wallace of his Assistant Adjutant duties. Tommy took part in the squadron's first dive bombing mission on the Merville viaduct which is described in Bruce's chapter. At 18.05 pm on 23 April, Tommy, Len, Bruce, and Ross were sitting in their Spitfires, each with a 500 lb bomb slung under the belly. Their target was a No Ball site, the Siracourt V1 bunker which is a few miles to the west of Saint-Pol-sur-Tenoise, and approximately 15 miles to the north west of Arras. The Siracourt site was one of two, the other being at Desvres, near Lottinghen. The underground bunkers would act as assembly points and launch sites for the V1 doodle bugs which would also be distributed to various other launch points in the Pas-de-Calais area. The Allies were determined to destroy this threat to avoid a reign of terror on London by the pilotless bombs and so a campaign of intense bombing began.

As Tommy and the Roaring Boys crossed the channel, they knew that previous raids by Mitchells and "Bomphoons" to the site would allow them to pinpoint the low rectangular bunker, which was 705 feet long and 118 feet wide with only 33 feet of the construction showing above the ground. As they approached the French coast, they crossed just south of Berck area and soon a voice on the R/T warned them they were approaching the target. Tommy could easily see the pockmarked landscape around the bunker. Divided into 3 sections of 4, Tommy's section circled at around 10,000 feet watching for fighters as the first group led by S/L Fowlow dived down. Shortly afterward, it was Tommy's turn as Yellow 4 he was the last in his section to attack. He eased back the throttle of his Spitfire banking it over and diving down towards the target below. The dust and smoke from the first sections bombs were still hanging in the air as his Spitfire sped downwards. Tommy had the bunker, which was built on a north east to south west axis, firmly in his sights. In an instant, it seemed Tommy had descended 5,000 feet as he positioned his thumb on the bomb release button easing back on the stick and a split second later pushing it to catapult the bomb downwards. As he banked the Spitfire away white vapour trails formed at the wing tips and Tommy tightened his muscles to stop the blood draining away as he performed the high "G" turn. He returned to straight and level flight, using his dive speed to put distance between himself and the target, before opening the throttle to power climb back to 10,000 feet. The Spitfire felt more like itself in Tommy's hands without 500 lb of metal and explosives attached underneath. The formation headed for home, landing at 19.20 pm. The dive bombing "pot of gold" competition winner in 411 Ross later noted: "No flak. Fairly good bombing."

During April Tommy flew for 8 hours and 40 minutes on operations and his total was 86 hours and 45 minutes.

On 3 May, S/L N Fowlow led the Roaring Boys on a Rodeo to the Cherbourg peninsula. It is one of the longest missions the Roaring Boys undertook. Tommy was joined by Len, Ross, and Dave. They would be in the air for 2 hours 35 minutes and their Spitfires were fitted with the 90-gallon auxiliary tanks to cover the estimated 600-mile flight. Tommy and the squadron took off at 17.00 pm and headed south. They must have felt a strong sense of togetherness during this operation, 12 small fighters a very long way from home over enemy-occupied France. Ross noted that they were flying at 2,500 feet as the French countryside passed beneath them and as they approached the area south of Rennes flak was sent up. Tommy later described the mission, "Bags of flak nearly wrote me off." They turned northeast for the 50-mile flight to Avranches, situated near the coast and it was here that the enemy was spotted. Tommy wrote: "Just east of Avranches F/L Johnnie Johnson Blue 1 and section chased 2 109s at 6 o'clock on the deck. Johnnie fired a burst at 800 yards. We couldn't catch them." As they flew on towards the coast, they were glad to find themselves once again over the English Channel, and back at RAF Tangmere at 19.35 pm.

A few days later on 5 May Operation Fabius took place near Littlehampton and Hayling Island. It was a practice invasion and amphibious landing which the Roaring Boys were assigned to fly over and test airfield defences, without being fired on! The 2-hour exercise left Tommy underwhelmed: "no future in this stuff. Let's get going." The fitting of the new Gyro gun sight in Little Mil did meet with his approval as he described it, "Whizzo."

The 15 May would see the Roaring Boys heading off in support of Ramrod 881, where Marauders were being sent to bomb No Ball sites including Siracourt. The operation was due to commence at 08.25 am and Ross, Charlie, and Gibby would fly with Tommy. The sweep would cover an area over Montdidier, Laon, and Charleville-Mézières. Montdidier is situated around 30 miles southeast of Amiens and upon reaching Montdidier the formation would head due east. The flight path is almost in a straight line to Laon before reaching the final destination of Charleville-Mézières, which is around 100 miles from Montdidier. The flight time would be 2 hours and 30 minutes and they were well aware that with a significant proportion of the mission time spent over enemy territory they could expect trouble.

Tommy was flying Red 3 in Spitfire MH477 and as he taxied out, he was running over the key details of the mission in his head. On the dot at 08.25 am they were away into the airspace over Tangmere. As they climbed above the airfield Tommy looked out of his starboard window and saw Chichester's cathedral towering above the city skyline. As 126 Wing formed up into its constituent squadrons and levelled out the English coast as soon disappearing into the distance. Tommy could feel the normally responsive and delicate controls of his Spitfire were replaced by more sluggish responses now that he had the 90-gallon tank fitted underneath his fuselage.

Over enemy territory, the rumble of the 36 Spitfires soon attracted the attention of the flak batteries. At Hesdin, around 40 miles northwest of Amiens, a heavy barrage was sent up which they flew through unscathed. The trouble wasn't over however and five bursts of Bofors 40mm flak were sent up at Montdidier. Tommy takes up the story: "F/L Sid Mills was shot down by flak. Lost his glycol. He bailed out OK. Cheers. Sid, what a loss!" As the formation neared one of Laon's airfields four silvery white aircraft, believed to be Me 110s were seen parked on the ground. The R/T suddenly became busy with the sound of S/L Shepherd of 401 Squadron sighting and chasing an FW 190. Tommy commented, "It got away. Very poor show." The wing continued to gather intelligence as the sweep continued with mechanized transports, "Mets" observed moving northwest on the Montidier to Compiègne road with another convoy spotted on the road between Montdidier and Amiens. By 10.55 am Tommy was back in the dispersal area at Tangmere. The pilots were in a glum mood as they headed for the debrief. There was no excited chatter or discussions of combat. No one wanted to return leaving one of their friends behind. At least, Sid Mills was able to "take to the silk" and wave to the others on the way down to indicate he was unhurt. Tommy summed up the mood in his logbook: "Here's luck to old Sid."

The pattern of long-range sweeps continued and the information gathered provided important intelligence on enemy troop movements and general activity. As an example, Tommy, Bruce, Charlie, and Dave took part in the morning sweep of 19 May which noted digging activity along the road northwest of Beauvais. The intelligence information could be followed up by other patrols, or even a reconnaissance flight in case the Germans were constructing defensive positions that ground forces might need to be aware of post-D Day. Tommy recorded: "Right around Paris. Bags of flak. No joy at all." Later that day as Tommy and the others took part in the squadron's evening dive bombing mission they were witnesses to the tragic loss of their CO. Tommy commented: "S/L Norm Fowlow blew up while diving on a target. He received a direct hit from flak. Great loss to 411." The stark realities of combat were with them every day. They all knew the dangers, but they continued to do their duty regardless of such devastating events.

On 28 May, Tommy Charlie and Ross took part in dive bombing mission 935 on a V1 No Ball installation at Le Mesnil-Allard, close to the hamlet of Saint-Léger-aux-Bois which is situated around 40 miles southeast of Dieppe. The formation took off at 08.25 am and were soon over the channel and heading for Dieppe area where they crossed the coastline at around 10,000 feet and made short work of the 40-mile flight southeast to Le Mesnil-Allard. Looking at a reconnaissance photo taken in 1945 the area is pockmarked by craters. It's possible to see the ski ramps in place, and even today little has changed in the patchwork of fields and the connecting roads. Tommy and Ross described the bombing as "very good" with Ross noting that the 500 lb bomb he dropped had a delayed detonation fuse.

With winter's icy grip a distant memory and the invasion getting ever closer Tommy saw a dramatic increase in his flying hours during May. His missions added 26 hours and 50 minutes to his total and he was over halfway towards completing his tour of duty with 113 hours and 35 minutes of operational flying undertaken since joining 411. Overall Tommy had spent 302 hours flying the Spitfire.

As June arrived Tommy and the others noted a palpable increase in tension. No 7-day leave passes were authorised and that alone told them the "big show" was imminent. On 2 June, Tommy, Charlie, Bruce, Len, and Ross took part in a squadron strength sweep between Amiens and Montdidier which recorded wheels up at 16.20 pm. F/L Russ Orr led the Roaring Boys into combat. As they patrolled the area numerous convoys and traffic were spotted. In Spitfire ML295, Tommy prepared himself for the attack on a target near Amiens. He had already watched one of the other section's dive down onto the vehicles and unleash a volley of cannon fire. When it was his turn Tommy rolled his Spitfire into a steep dive, flattening out so that he could rake his target with cannon fire. The rounds erupted from the cannons and with his aim true the car instantly disappeared in a cloud of smoke and dust. After his attack run, Tommy banked away and gave ML295 full throttle. He later wrote: "Shot up a staff car near Amiens. Damaged it." Shortly afterward, over the R/T he heard Russ Orr confirm he had been hit by flak. He was going to try to make it back to Tangmere. A telltale trail of smoke was coming from Russ Orr's engine compartment as he flew on. The others knew he had limited time as they crossed the channel. Orr throttled back as much as he dare. The others watched on helplessly as he gradually lost altitude. Over the R/T Russ said he was bailing out. His position had been fixed and notification immediately sent to the Air Sea Rescue team. They hoped they could scramble a Walrus to collect him as he tumbled from his Spitfire. The white parachute descended slowly as the Roaring Boys circled their comrade, watching on as he splashed down into the sea. Tommy recorded Russ's position as, "20 miles south of Beachy Head. Picked up ok by ASR." The squadron ORB could take a light-hearted view of the incident once it was known Orr was safe: "F/L R W Orr qualified for membership of both the Caterpillar and Goldfish clubs."

Tommy Wheler awoke on 6 June 1944 and was at a state of readiness by first light. He wrote in capital letters. "D DAY". The much-anticipated invasion was here, the culmination of years of planning and which for the Roaring Boys meant over a year of missions to "soften" up the German defences. Tommy had to wait until 13.05 pm, eagerly gathering around his fellow pilots who returned at 10.00 am from the squadron's first patrol. Tommy's patrol would be led by W/C G C Keefer and S/L G D Robertson and include Bruce, Charlie, Gibby, and Bob. The patrol itself was uneventful in stark contrast to what was happening at sea and on the beaches where men were dying in their thousands. Tommy wrote later of the big day: "Landing going OK. Reached Caen. Quite a few of our landing craft sunk by shore artillery. Let's go." The final entry perhaps summing up Tommy's character and determination. He didn't avoid danger or seek it out recklessly, but he was there to do his bit and aggressive action towards the enemy was the order of the day for him and all the Roaring Boys.

One German wag wrote about the few days after the landings and the Normandy sky being full of aircraft. "If it's green it's British if it's silver it's American and if it cannot be seen at all then it's German!" The lack of action was a source of frustration. Tommy was patrolling the beachhead twice on D Day +1. His logbook noted the success seen by 401 Squadron downing 6 Ju 88s and 412 scoring with 2 of the same aircraft. He contrasted this with his own and the Roaring Boys fortunes: "411 didn't see a bloody thing. HELL." Tommy's mood wasn't lifted on 8 June when after a sweep along the beachhead area he wrote: "SFA. All Hun aircraft painted like ours." It was truly "sweet FA" and poor hunting for the aggressive Canucks. Tommy, Bruce, Len, Ross, Dave, and Jimmy all set off in squadron strength from RAF Tangmere on 12 June at 13.05 pm with a sense of expectation that this patrol could be the one that would break their D Day duck. The Luftwaffe had been spotted the day before but after landing back at 14.55 pm with little to report, Tommy restricted his log entry: "Sweet Fanny Adams."

With the Roaring Boys move to France on 18 June, Tommy and his fellow pilots were in the thick of the action. The ALG aerodrome B4 at Bény-sur-Mer, with its location close to the main battlefront, saw huge amounts of activity in the air and on the ground as the Allied and German forces locked horns across a wide front. During one discussion with Tommy, he described landing a Spitfire, which can be tricky at times but even more so on a temporary landing ground like B4 with its steel metal plate runway and which also happened to have enemy positions close by.

It called for a rather unusual approach to B4 as he described below:

"You never ever came in straight in a Spitfire. We used to come in upside down, like a right side up. We'd put the wheels down pointing up and pull back on the stick before rolling over and dropping down onto the runway. When we were at Bény-sur-Mer the Germans were just across one river from us so if you came in high, they'd knock the hell out of you with their guns. They were very close so that's how we did it. If you had a section of 4 Spitfires the lead and number 2, you'd come in almost with your wing underneath the lead guy. The number 3 and 4 would be back behind them and follow them in. They'd get the dirty stuff, the sand and smoke, and everything. The Spitfire didn't have good brakes. They were awful. If you put too much brake on, they'd slip so you'd end up with no brakes. I never had trouble like that. I had the touch because I learned to fly a lot of different planes with the Army. They taught me to fly gliders and I had all that experience when I went on Spits. I'd flown about 15 different types of aeroplane. That was considered a lot because some got onto Spits right out of school. They'd never even been in an aeroplane before."

Although the chances of the Allied invasion of Europe failing at this stage were receding fast, mainly to the huge volume of men and equipment that was pouring into France, there was the distinct possibility that German counter-attacks could see the Allies pushed back towards the coast. Against this backdrop and with the Luftwaffe concentrating its attacks on the Americans to the West, Tommy and the Roaring Boys continued undertaking regular patrols of the beachheads as well as attacking ground targets in support of their fellow Canadian troops on the ground. The amount of artillery and anti-aircraft fire being traded by both sides was unimaginable and resulted in an almost constant "rain" of metal shards and bullets falling back from whence they came. At B4 Bény-sur-Mer, Tommy recalled his experiences of life there. He wrote in his logbook: "bags of dust. Flak all night at raiders. Ju 88 flew over drome at 500 feet." Trying to sleep with all of this going on was nigh on impossible. It got so bad that Tommy joined the others in digging a trench and covering it with drawers from a cabinet and any other solid material that would afford him some protection.

On 24 June Tommy undertook his first sortie of the day at 05.25 am climbing into the familiar surroundings of his Spitfire, MK843 "Little Mil III." The mission was an armed reconnaissance in the Falaise, Argentan,

L'Aigle and Lisieux areas which resulted in the destruction of several mechanised transports. Tommy wrote in his logbook that he had: "destroyed 1 truck and damaged 2 others South of Caen." Little Mil III had sustained flak damage in the attack and clearly, Tommy was going to have to make a perilous landing as he noted in his logbook: "no air speed. Nearly pranged on landing." Tommy also noted that eight Me 109s were caught coming into land and whilst in the circuit pattern and making their approach to their aerodrome two were "shot down by Spit patrol!" These Spitfires weren't from 126 Wing but it could have been from 133 Wing Commander SF Skalski who claimed a Me 109 and recorded that as it evaded his fire it another collided with another 109 and both crashed. Having survived the landing in his Spitfire Tommy learned that: "Little Mil III damaged by flak. She'll be u/s for 2 days. Poor show." Tommy's sons Jim and Doug told me that the family has a boat named after their mother which is called "Little Mil." Jim also told me that Tommy always carried a photo of Millie inside his officer's cap. My friend Ady Shaw who is a warbirds photographer took a photo of the cap with Millie's photo inside and we both recalled how Tommy had worn it when he came to visit Aero Legends in 2015.

A few months after Tommy's armed reconnaissance in the Falaise area during a period from 12 August to 27 August in what became known as the Battle of the "Falaise Pocket," German Army Group B with the 7th Army and the Fifth Panzer Army were encircled by the Allies. The Germans tried to escape along a narrow corridor called the "Falaise Gap" however the ensuing battle resulted in the destruction of most of Army Group B west of the River Seine. Allied forces took a heavy toll on the retreating Germans.

Spitfire NH341 Elizabeth
Tommy's flying on 24 June was not yet finished and without Little Mil III has was going to need another Spitfire to fly. At 17.45 pm he climbed into his friend Bruce's Spitfire NH341 Elizabeth for his second sortie that would last one hour and ten minutes. With the aircraft primed, Tommy's left hand rested on top of the spade grip. His other hand uncaged the two-engine switch covers. He changed hands and set the throttle and his middle finger pushed down on the boost followed by the start button. Spitfire Elizabeth spluttered and sent out smoke as the propeller slowly turned before the Merlin engine fired. Tommy taxied out across the flat

open farmland that was now at the centre of a huge sprawling airfield. He eased back the throttle and waited and with a flick of the head, he saw a lineup of Spitfires eager to get underway like horses at the Grand National. Tommy looked at the eleven familiar faces, including Len, Bob, Charlie, and Ross. The special camaraderie and bond of men forged in battle is often talked and written about. On that day, like every other day, Tommy was going to war against the mighty Luftwaffe, flying arguably one of the greatest fighters of the time. At another level, it was twelve young men, thrown together as fighter pilots, now good mates, relying on each other and not knowing what the coming hours would bring, and if any one of them might not return.

Charlie was leading the squadron and over the R/T he gave the order, unleashing the power of 12 mighty Merlins. There was little crosswind to bother Tommy as he opened the throttle, correcting the yaw with a touch of rudder as the prop wash sent clouds of dust into the air. Spitfire Elizabeth was almost instantly raised up onto her undercarriage, urging Tommy to break the earthly bond and complete the transformation to graceful flight. The clunk of the undercarriage and red cockpit indicators told Tommy his gear was stowed away. He looked down at the "T and Ps" which were all in the normal. The Roaring Boys climbed out over what was still relatively unfamiliar territory and formed up to commence the armed reconnaissance. The patrol covered a triangulated area between three towns Fleurs, Domfront and Carrouges. As other sections hammered a convoy south of Caen leaving four mechanised transports smoking, Tommy was providing top cover in Spitfire Elizabeth. He wrote: "Straf job S of Caen. Strafed trucks moving south of Caen. Didn't have a go – No joy!" Ross was similarly out of the action as he commented, "Not much doing." By 19.00 pm Tommy was in the circuit, bleeding off speed in preparation for landing. He knew every characteristic of the Spitfire by now and what inputs he needed to put into the controls which were so light and sensitive. With the flaps and undercarriage down, he gently landed Spitfire Elizabeth and wondered if Bruce was watching on to see how he was treating his lady. Tommy steered Elizabeth from the runway and at walking pace he zig-zagged the Spitfire back to the dispersal area, swinging round into a parking space. Whilst watching the erks marshalling signals he then gently pulled the brake control lever, bringing Elizabeth to a halt. With the chocks inserted Tommy ran the Merlin on low engine revs before pulling the cut out and seeing the blades of the propeller come to a stop. He shut down and unbuckled his harness, pulled out the R/T and oxygen leads and released Spitfire Elizabeth's side door. The slick extraction for a lithe 23-year-old was almost instantaneous, as Tommy stood up and with one foot on the door and a quick hop he was back on the ground. He didn't glance back at Spitfire Elizabeth as he headed off to operations to file his report, nor did he have any idea of the significance of that flight in what to him was just another Spitfire. It was a tool of the trade in which he had successfully completed a combat mission, returning unscathed. Only DJ Le Blanc had mechanical issues and returned early with a troublesome undercarriage.

Towards the end of June 1944, a fierce battle for the city of Caen continued unabated. The city sits astride the river Orne and the Carne canal at the junction of several roads and railways, which made it an important operational objective for both sides. The Allies had planned to take the city on D Day but recognizing this the Germans threw everything into the battle to thwart the advance.

On 28 June 1944, as the land forces locked horns below around Caen, the Luftwaffe began more intense operations in the sector. The operational records show that Tommy and the Roaring Boys had been carrying out their missions with very little interference from the Germans but going forward this was to change. The Roaring Boys tally of Luftwaffe aircraft for 28 June was 6 destroyed and 3 damaged, without loss to themselves. An earlier mission by 411 had come across large formations of enemy aircraft, both Me 109s and FW 190s which weren't engaged due to a lack of fuel. As Tommy, Bruce, Charlie, Len Gibby, and Bob sat in the briefing they were excited but tense at the prospect. This sighting was unlikely to be a one-off. The Luftwaffe would send up regular patrols, searching out the enemy, just as Tommy and the others were doing.

The butterflies were kicking in at 12.25 pm as F/L R K Hayward led them off. Tommy followed on his own 5 minutes later for reasons not explained. Whatever the reason for his late departure, he wasn't going to miss this show. The Roaring Boys split into sections of four. Tommy was in red section with F/L Hayward. In a short time, they identified a convoy of vehicles which they proceeded to attack. The ORB noted the damage, "Three flamers, four damaged." After the engagement was completed, they climbed up to 8,000 feet and headed east around 20 miles in from the coastline. Tommy realised he now had a partially unserviceable R/T. He signalled to his section by tapping his hand on his earpiece. He got an acknowledgment, and his problem was communicated to the others. Tommy describes what happened next in his operational report whilst flying around 20 miles south of Le Havre:

"I was flying Red 4. The squadron was SW of Caen when Huns were reported south of Le Havre by Blue 2. My R/T (radio telephone) was partially u/s. The squadron broke port and dove with wide-open throttles, leaving me far behind. I climbed alone to 8000 ft above the cloud, sighting 15 a/c at 12 o'clock below. I climbed flat out to 12,000 feet. 15 a/c turned out to be FW 190s and Me 109s. They turned toward me to port still at 6000ft. I dove out of the sun and attacked the last FW 190 on the starboard side of the formation. At 300 to 400 yds I fired 5 second burst from line astern and saw hits on cockpit and wing. The e/a caught fire flicked over, crashed into the deck and blew up. I turned to starboard and fired at another FW 190, range about 100 yds, angle off about 10°, and saw hits on the starboard wing. FW 190 broke hard towards me and disappeared into cloud. I took a cine shot of burning wreckage of first FW 190. Returned to base with four gallons of petrol. I claim 1 FW 190 destroyed and 1 FW 190 damaged."

Tommy's claim was verified by the gun camera footage and confirmed by intelligence officer Gord Panchuk. Tommy wrote: "The FW 190 went straight into the deck. I damaged a second FW 190 before losing him in cloud. This makes us even for Phil Wallace." In the same action, Charlie got a kill, shooting down one of the Me 109s for the first of his 8.5 victories.

F/L R K Hayward didn't miss out on the action when shortly before returning to base he saw Tommy break away from the squadron. He noted Tommy's intermittent transmissions but picked up that he was engaged with the enemy. They gave chase and were about to break off the engagement when another gaggle of 25 plus bandits broke down through the cloud. Hayward wrote: "I fell in behind one of the last and at 300 yards gave a burst and saw strikes on tail and elevator. I claim 1 FW 190 damaged."

It's not difficult to imagine Tommy's determination to press home his attacks and even with the passing of time, I could easily sense that in my discussions with him. It is perhaps stating the obvious to highlight

Tommy's attitude to the business of being a fighter pilot, the clues in the name after all. However, not all pilots approached air combat with the enemy in the same way. For some, it was also predominantly about self-preservation. Meanwhile, others at the opposite end of the spectrum were prone to "gung-ho" actions and paying the ultimate price with their lives. In a 2017 TV interview for Global News Canada Tommy summed up how he saw his role: "You were there to try to kill as many Germans as you can and that's what I tried to do every day." Tommy and those Canadians boys knew what their task was and in the gladiatorial sky arena above Normandy, if you didn't strike first and get your opponent, he would get you. Inevitably, June was a heavy month for flying operations. Tommy logged 37 hours and 25 minutes for a total of 151 hours. He had taken part in 98 sorties.

As the month of July arrived, the days of "fly, eat, sleep, repeat" described by the squadron ORB continued at a pace. It would take its toll. The daily combat stress mounted up and each pilot had a limit of what they could take, but their youth helped them press on. Any opportunity to "let the hair down" was grabbed eagerly. On 4 July, Tommy, Charlie, and Ross were airborne with the squadron at 08.25 am for an armed reconnaissance of the Mezidon, L'Aigle, Sées, Alençon and Argentan areas. These towns were interdiction routes along which German troops, supplies, and communications would be travelling. As the patrol unfolded, cloud conditions hampered the identification of targets on the ground. Tommy also detailed his personal tally in his logbook, "Destroyed 1 lorry south of Caen." By 09.25 am they had landed back at B4 and after filing their reports would be combat ready if needed later in the day.

On 9 July bad visibility hampered the 09.10 am armed reconnaissance mission that Tommy, Gibby, Dave, Bruce, Len, and Bob took part in which was going to Falaise, Argentan, L'Aigle, and Lisieux. The Roaring Boys got glimpses of the ground and knew that underneath the blanket of cloud the Germans would seize the opportunity to move men and equipment with a reduced threat of harassment from air attack. The ORB gave the score, "Only one met damaged." Meanwhile, Tommy who usually provided a full and detailed write up of events was reduced to the comment, "SFA." The 4 section patrols of 11 July, a day described as dull and threatening weather-wise, elicited the same one-line response from Tommy. There was very little action as 411 stood by on defensive readiness.

On 14 July, Tommy flew as "Yellow 1" and was joined by Len, F/L A M Tooley, and F/O R M Cook for a single section defensive patrol. Reports had been received from earlier patrols that the Luftwaffe were attempting to break through to the beachhead and against this backdrop, Tommy in Spitfire NH317 led Yellow section into the air at 14.00 pm. This mission is also described in Len's chapter. In a few minutes as they gained altitude they were in the vicinity of Caen. All was quiet until Yellow 3's voice spoke over the R/T. "Bandits 10 o'clock 12 of them." Tommy throttled up his Spitfire and hurtled towards the enemy formation, which immediately broke into pairs pursued by the Roaring Boys, tumbling, twisting and turning, each man trying to get onto the tail of the other. Tommy's proficiency and skill levels were now at their peek. In the dog fight, he soon latched onto an FW 190, taking up the story in his own words:

"Yellow three sighted 12 plus FW 190s at 10 o'clock in the area NW of Caen. We attacked immediately. I fired two 060 to 070 degrees two-second bursts from 400 yards with no results as my cannons had stopped. I closed in from 300 yards to 50 yards, firing from line astern on another FW 190. I saw hits on his starboard wing and then he flicked over and went straight into the deck. I fired at two more FW 190s but then my machine guns also stopped. I returned to base out of ammunition. I was using the old gun sight and had my camera switched on. I claim 1 FW 190 destroyed."

A crashed FW 190 photographed by 411 Squadron

It was Tommy's second kill and he was elated. The rueful entry in his logbook after entering the details of the chase with the other FW 190s is typical, "Oh well" he wrote. You could almost sense him shrugging his shoulders. The Luftwaffe pilot Tommy shot down was Gefreiter Eberhard Sauer of 1/Jagdgeschwader 11 flying an FW 190 A-8. He was killed when his aircraft crashed into the ground following the action. During the dog fight, both Tooley and Cook each claimed a damaged FW 190. The Roaring Boys had shown their mettle against a numerically superior force. The 4 pilots had landed back at B4 exactly one hour later to be greeted by the erks and other pilots eager to hear about their exploits. Their beaming smiles and excitement told of the success and there was much back-slapping and animated replays of the actions. They were brought down to earth by the intelligence boys who, as ever wanted a calm and detailed explanation for their operational reports and claim submissions.

During one of our chats, I was able to ask Tommy about the Spitfire: "I flew the Mark II, V, and IXb. Each mark was usually more powerful but sometimes it would only be a small change. My favourite was the Mark IXb. The Mark IXa was the top flight one used for flying high stuff, up over 30,000 feet. The IXb was usually flying down lower." With so much being written about the Spitfire it was fascinating to get first-hand impressions from a highly experienced pilot like Tommy. We went on to discuss the Spitfire's capabilities in its less familiar ground attack role. He said: "Oh, they were wonderful. I did a helluva lot of ground stuff. I shot up a hell of a pile of them. Instead of flying in the horrible British 12 plane formation the Germans went in sections of four, so we copied that. As soon as the day started, say 5.00 am we were up sitting in the cockpit. You had 2 minutes to get airborne." I commented that it generally took me 10 times longer to get airborne to which Tommy chuckled heartily. We discussed some of the high-profile fighter pilot aces amongst the Canadians including the brilliant but difficult character George "screwball" or "Buzz" Beurling DSO DFC DFM and Bar. Tommy recalled some memories of Beurling and Wing Commander Bob Wendell "Buck" McNair DSO DFC and Two Bars. He said: "McNair posted him home because he wouldn't do what he was told. We were on a sweep going across the channel. He climbed up to 25,000 feet shot a guy down and then came back down and joined up with his squadron.

The CO didn't like that. Beurling didn't give a damn what the CO said. If there was a German around he'd kill it. He was a real character and a good pilot."

Tommy was often photographed with Bruce and he confirmed that some of the photos of them together were at Biggin Hill: "Bruce was a good guy" Tommy commented. He also talked about 411 pilot Don Givens with whom he had flown regularly. Tommy said: "I saw him on TV at a golf tournament so I tracked him down but by the time I found him he had passed away. During his career, he became a full colonel." Tommy went on to say: "he was a pretty big guy and I often wondered how he ever got in a Spitfire!" I have seen film and photos of Don Givens and he did indeed look physically much bigger than the majority of the other Roaring Boys. We discussed the fact that some customers flying with Aero Legends customers have to undergo major weight loss to be within the limits to fly. Tommy, was on his usual razor-sharp form and quipped, "Do they get a haircut?"

I questioned Tommy about the Luftwaffe aircraft he was "duking it out" with and how they fared against the Spitfire: "The Me 109 could out turn you, say on a turn to the right. If you rolled right you'd be in trouble. They could get inside and that's how they killed a lot of guys. You had to watch it. They shot through the motor and propeller so as long as they could see you they could hit you. We had to work out the airspeed and know where the bullets had been set to cross (in front of the Spitfire). For pilots like Beurling, he had it set to zero. The FW 190 was also an excellent plane, it was faster than the Spitfire. It didn't have a carburetor as we did. They could dive no problem. If your Spitfire had enough height you could sometimes catch it."

From my research fighter pilots, much like racing drivers have differing skill sets in many areas setting aside the ability to fly and perform the basic requirements of a pilot. At the extreme, some may have had skills that made them brilliant at aerobatics but with poor shooting skills, whilst at the other end of spectrum others scored many a victory over the enemy due to their brilliant shooting skills. I was able to ask Tommy how he rated himself. He told me: "I was assessed as having above average flying and shooting skills. I had excellent vision and as a young boy and as an adult I was a good shot."

Tommy and the rest of the pilots and airfield crew at B4 were feeling the effects of interrupted night's sleep. As the ORB noted: "Continuous sleep is harder to get these nights with Jerry taking advantage of the moonless nights to pay visits to the area surrounding the airfield." An armed reconnaissance mission was planned for 10.10 am on 15 July. A quartet of Spitfire Elizabeth pilots including Tommy, Bob, Gibby, and Dave were amongst the 12 rostered to fly a patrol pattern encompassing the areas of Flers, Domfront, and Argentan. Tommy added to his scorecard: "Destroyed a 1500 WT truck, 9/10 cloud." With the cloud cover hampering operations only scattered enemy vehicles were seen. The total score recorded for the mission, including Tommy's personal claim, was recorded by the squadron diarist: "Two APVs damaged, 1 Met flamer and 1 Met damaged also scored." His armed reconnaissance of the evening of 17 July to Thury-Harcourt, Domfront, Alençon, and Argentan would cover the names of towns that have become familiar throughout this book, standing as they do on the main supply routes to and from Caen and the front line. The Roaring Boys would tear into anything moving along these routes and the hours of gun camera footage stand as a testament to their resolve to press home these attacks. At 20.25 pm Tommy gunned the throttle on Spitfire MK885 and thundered down the steel tracking and into the air above the flat featureless landscape that defines this area of Normandy. They circled above the aerodrome and were gradually joined by the others forming up in their sections, red blue and yellow, ready to begin the patrol. It was a relatively quiet mission for Tommy, flying Yellow 4. They had to sit out the ground attack, providing top cover against a fighter bounce as the others dived down on the unfortunate transports leaving, "one Met flamer, and four met damaged." He was less than impressed writing after landing at 21.30 pm, "Complete mess up. S.F.A!" Matters weren't helped by Givens and Cook being forced to return early with mechanical issues, escorted by 2 other Spitfires. Clearly, this was the source of Tommy's frustration! His mood may have been lifted somewhat by the arrival of his replacement Spitfire MK426. The aircraft was immediately given the name of his sweetheart which he recorded in his logbook: "Flew Little Mil IV. Very nice. My new kite is fine. Cheers!" The scarcity of action was getting to Tommy and the others as they hassled the CO and intelligence teams to get them into the fight. They didn't want the other squadrons in 126 Wing getting ahead and lose the bragging rights. An evening armed reconnaissance mission on 19 July by Tommy, Gibby, Len and Bob discovered two armoured cars near Pont L'Eveque which were not attacked and little else of note as they moved between Lisieux, Evreux, L'Aigle and Mezidon. The Allies were victims of their own success as the Germans were forced to move under the cover of darkness. After landing at 19.55 pm Tommy shut down, cutting a disconsolate figure as he and the others bemoaned the lack of action. His log summed up his mood: "S.F.A. No joy – No Huns – No transports – No flak." The next days were full of heavy rain which dampened spirits as the pilots flitted between each other's tents, writing letters, reading or catching up on sleep. The explosion in B4's ammo dump caused an unintended bit of excitement as everyone threw themselves to the ground but no one within 126 Wing was injured. By 25 July, the weather was beginning to brighten up and Tommy had hopes of going flying. These hopes were raised even further when he attended a briefing with Len, Gibby, and Bob. S/L Robertson briefed the pilots on the intelligence reports of the movement of around 30 transports in the Argentan and Falaise areas. At last, it was time to go hunting. S/L Robertson could see the desire in the eyes of his young charges. Most, like Tommy, were old hands, tested in combat and utterly reliable. Robertson stood up and looked at his watch. The pilots did the same as they synchronised their watches. Tommy mentioned this part of the briefing process to me. He said: "You know the two buttons used to start the Spitfire? Well for synchronization the CO used to say, 'We'll press tits at 17.50,' or whatever the mission time was." I laughed at the time and still do when I listen to it again. These minor details Tommy passed on about his life back then are fascinating.

After Robertson released the pilots from the briefing they went their separate ways, joining together at the line of Spitfires. Tommy pulled his parachute on and stepped onto the wing of Little Mil IV, settling down in the small cockpit. Little Mil IV started the first time and a few minutes later Tommy taxied the aircraft out, lining up ready for takeoff. At 08.30 am S/L Robertson signalled the operation was "green for go." It was a short flight to the northwest to find the southwesterly road that connects Falaise with Argentan. Hopes were high and it didn't take long for them to spot enemy movement. The Roaring Boys dived down into the attack with Tommy flying Yellow 3. He was soon tearing down towards the row of trucks, which were smoking from the initial strafing. As Tommy readied himself his sights were lined up on the first target. He pushed the gun button on the control column expecting the powerful recoil from the Hispano cannons, but nothing happened aside from the noise and recoil from his smaller machine guns. The cannons were jammed and only the machine guns plastered the target area. Tommy tried again, with the same result but by then he was forced to pull out of the dive and skim low and fast across the fields and tree line away from the light flak. He summed up the mission later, "Damaged 5 trucks. No bloody cannons." After landing in the darkening evening sky at 22.35 pm, the debrief confirmed the total damage as: "4 flamers, 5 smokers, and 2 damaged. Packing cases in woods near Falaise left smoking. Moderate light flak from Morleaux." The ORB incorrectly records the village name. It was, in fact, Morteaux-Couliboeuf which is situated around 5 miles to the east of Falaise, and which the formation flew over either on the outward leg or, more likely on the return leg back to B4.

On 31 July at 19.40 pm, Tommy, Len, and the Roaring Boys were flying area cover with 401 Squadron. The mission saw them patrol an area that was being traversed by 270 RAF heavies on their way to attack 3 separate targets. The bomber force was split into 3 formations, with 127 Lancasters bombing the rail yards at Joigny-La-Roche, which are situated around 20 miles north of the city of Auxerre. At the same time, 97 Lancasters bombed Rilly La Montage rail tunnel which is around 5 miles from the city of Reims. The smallest formation of 52 Lancasters was bombing the port area of Le Havre, and it was this formation that 411 and 401 were covering. The sector controllers kept them updated on the position of the heavies, and as Tommy and the others orbited in their Spitfires at a similar altitude of around 15,000 feet, they could be swiftly vectored onto any enemy fighters entering the sector. In addition, the Spitfire pilots were making their search of the area for bandits, looking to bounce the bomber force. The mission passed without incident, and with all three beehives clear of danger S/L Hayward DFC led Tommy and the others back to B4 where they landed at 20.40 pm. The ORB did report: "Results of the bombing were not observed but one Lancaster was seen to go down."

The briefing of 4 August informed the pilots that they would be dive bombing a ferry wharf at Berville-sur-Mer located a few miles southeast of Le Havre, on the opposite bank of the mouth of the river Seine. Tommy and Len sat together, old comrades who shared a tent together the year before at RAF Staplehurst, Back then they were flight sergeants, both were now Flying Officers. S/L Hayward continued to brief the pilots before the intelligence team took over with information about enemy land and air forces known to be active in the area, as well as potential flak hotspots to avoid on the flights in and out from the target. With the briefing complete the meeting broke up and the pilots ambled away to finalise their preparations. At exactly18.55 pm, Tommy powered up Little Mil IV and she leapt forward along the runway and into the air. Tommy circled above the airfield, as in turn, each section formed up into battle formation ready to fly 20 miles east along the coast to Berville-sur-Mer. As they approached the estuary they had thus far avoided any contact with the enemy on the ground, and in the air. The ferry dock was clearly visible jutting out into the river Seine, which is about ½ mile wide at Berville. The Roaring Boys broke into their sections and dived into the attack from the southeast, taking care to avoid the flak batteries on the opposite bank at Le Havre. When Tommy's turn came, he followed his well-rehearsed drill and banked his Spitfire over, arrowing downwards from around 10,000 feet, adjusting his aim before releasing the 500 pounder at around 4,000 feet, and then flying fast and low out to sea. Exactly one hour later Tommy settled Spitfire MK941 down onto the runway at B4. He wrote up details of the mission: "Dive bombed ferry boat dock in the mouth of the Seine. 3 hits, 3 near misses, 3 hang ups – no flak." The 3 hang up bombs that failed to release were successfully jettisoned as they presented a risk to their pilots when landing back at base.

On the 7 August, after only managing a weather-interrupted 10-minute flight the day before, Tommy and the Roaring Boys were informed that the squadron had received a movement order and would be leaving B4 for ALG B.18 Cristot, situated around 10 miles to the west of Caen. The business of war couldn't be put on hold, and the squadron attended a mid-afternoon briefing led by Bob. The armed reconnaissance mission would cover L'Aigle, Bernay and Lisieux areas. At 16.30 pm they took off and commenced their mission. Tommy was able to increase his score: "Armed recce. Destroyed 3 trucks – hit in the rad by light flak 15 miles southeast of Lisieux." He then takes up the mission story in his own report which is transcribed below (marginal notes in brackets); map references are to France, 1: 100,000, Sheets 7F and 8F:

"[7 Aug 44] I took off on 7 August on armed reconnaissance in Lisieux area, had destroyed three trucks when my radiator was hit by flak.

I climbed to 7,000 feet but my engine was running rough, so I called up to say I was going home. The engine packed up and I baled out. I landed in an orchard 467014 (Sheet 7F), hid my parachute, "Mae West" in bushes, ran up a lane where I threw my gloves down, and turned back. I ran north for two hours, crossing a river and the main road at 4605, then removed my badges, pockets etc in a barn, got out my escape kit, got my position and headed west, sleeping that night in a barn.

[8 Aug 44] I walked all next day passing north of Branville at 277059, ate raw potatoes and Horlicks in the evening, and that night walked along the railway to Houlgate, then headed south passing through some minefields on the way. At 242018 I turned west, swam two rivers at 2102 and came upon a deserted house next morning. I remained here two days cooking myself vegetables.

[10 Aug 44] On the night of 10 August I set off west through the marshes but as the water reached my waist and once up to my neck, I turned north, passed race track (2104), swam the river and crawled by the side of the main road. At the fork 2105, there were two sentries whom I got by and continued by the road going west.

[11 Aug 44] As Germans were passing along the road I turned south into the marshes and had to keep going after daybreak as there was nowhere to hide, and I was wet, cold and hungry with our shells bursting all round. I reached some woods at 182052 but walked into some guards on a radar station who took me, prisoner. They first took everything from me, including a watch, escape kit, ring, lighter, pen and ten pounds of my own money, then gave me food. I was taken by cycle to Cabourg and in the evening to Pont L'Eveque (5204 Sheet 8F). I stayed here two days without interrogation although they returned my RAF (k) 1250 and shaving kit. There were 150 various POWs here and the French Red Cross supplied many necessities.

[13 Aug 44] On the night of 13 Aug all service personnel were taken by truck towards Paris passing through Lisieux. I was in the rear and noticed it was an iron "wood burning" truck, with space for a boiler between the truck and the driver's cabin. There was small door window 1-2 feet x 2 feet in the front of the truck which kept banging. I called to the front to ask if there was glass in this opening as I meant to try to escape through it. I made my way to the front of the truck and stood with my back to the opening facing the guards at the rear. The truck was travelling fast, and there was some noise and shaking about, and it was dark. I closed the small door behind my back and then opened it slowly, keeping myself in the front of the opening so the faint light outside did not show. I eased myself out through this opening, pulled the door over it and sat on the boiler. The truck stopped at about 589813 (Sheet 8 F) because of an air raid ahead. I slipped down underneath and rolled between the wheels towards the ditch, the guards now standing at the back. An aircraft dropped a flare, so I rolled back and when it went out I got to the ditch over an edge and ran. I crossed a river bridge at approximately 586818, walked all night, crossed the road and river north of Fervaques 5476, and in the morning saw a farmer north of Livarot 4672.

[14 Aug 44] I spoke to him, and he gave me food and a bed for that day. That night he told me the English were around St. Pierre, gave me a map and leather coat, took my tunic and I started off.

[15 Aug 44] I walked all that night, stopped at another farm in the morning where I stayed all day. I continued each night and rested at a farm each day until 17 August when I ran into the front line and heard a concentrated barrage and machine gun east of St. Pierre, at 255765 (Sheet 7F).

[17 - 19 Aug 44] I lay in a cornfield by the road all day and at dusk saw some British tanks pass by, so I crawled to the road and stood up ready to hail the next ones. Two Germans came up behind me with revolvers and I was taken prisoner again. We went back to a farm where twenty Germans were ready to move off and we all started eastwards that night and walked for two nights and days, stopping only for meals and short rests, until afternoon 19 August.

[19 Aug 44] We stopped at a house where an English-speaking officer interrogated us, trying to get various information which I refused. I met F/L MacDuff here and five other POWs. On the afternoon of 20th we were moved about five miles, picked up twenty POWs and that night started off in a truck. We crawled along in circles, losing our way, and finally put up in an orchard about 2330 hours, where the guards made us stand up all night. They refused to let us put the curtains up for air. It was terribly hot, and we were very tired, and POWs were fainting all round.

[21 Aug 44] Next morning the Germans wanted to paint the top of the truck white (denoting POWs) as protection against aircraft attack, but I told them it would be suicide. I had never heard of any sign denoting POW and felt certain that any of our aircraft would spot the white and shoot it up immediately. I know of no instructions to the contrary. So, we left their truck, marched all day, sleeping in a barn that night.

[22 Aug 44.] We marched again next day into Lieurey (7495 Sheet 8F) with instructions to get to St. Martins (7801) by 2130 hours. We lost the way in some bye-woods and by dark had reached a point 778998 (Sheet 8F). We were in two files with a file of guards on each side, so I engaged a guard on my right in conversation, gradually dropped back with him, and then I quickened up ahead of him, slipping into the file of guards so the guard ahead and behind me each thought I was one of them. I slipped away to the side of the road, [and] covered my face and hands until they had passed. I set off east across a valley and river and after an hour walking I laid up in a barn north of Saint Etienne L'Allier 7898.

[23 Aug 44] Next morning a French girl came in the barn who fetched her parents for me, who gave me food. That night they took me to another farmer nearby where I remained until 26 August when the British came through who sent me through various channels to IS.9 (WEA) the same day."

The IS.9 (WEA) referred to in Tommy's report is a 55 cm X 55 cm silk escape and evasion map issued to RAF personnel after D Day. It shows the zones of France and he used this to navigate his way back to Allied lines. After returning to 411 Squadron, Tommy completed the missing entry in his logbook in his own inimitable style: "GOT THE BIG CHOPPER. HARD LUCK." It's incredible, and perhaps typical of men like Tommy, he was shot down but definitely not out. He showed great fortitude to escape twice from his captors.

The French family who risked their lives sheltering Tommy and providing him with food were Georges and Yvette Monier. He was clearly indebted and grateful to them. They corresponded after the war, and whilst flying Sabre jets with 444 squadron at Baden-Soellingen, Germany in 1961, Tommy took time out to visit them. The very act of bailing out of his stricken Spitfire qualified Tommy for membership of The Caterpillar Club. In photographs of Tommy at commemoration events, he could be seen wearing his gold silk caterpillar brooch on his lapel.

During his time "on the run" Tommy was ever resourceful and mindful of his duty to cause as much disruption to the enemy as possible. He was no longer in a Spitfire but wasn't going to let that get in the way. One night, he came upon several rail cars on the top of a small rise, which he managed to disconnect. With the carriage car brakes released, and by physically pushing the cars apart, Tommy was able to set the carriages in motion down the hill, where they eventually derailed themselves on the next curve. On another night, he was in some woods when he was startled by a brilliant flash of light and a loud roar. Tommy had stumbled across a German V1 doodle bug launching site, one of the No Balls locations he had targeted in his Spitfire. Tommy cut every wire, cable, and hose he could find at the launch site, an action which would probably have resulted in him being shot as a saboteur if he had been caught.

With his successful return to 411 Squadron, for this Roaring Boy, the war was indeed now over. According to Tommy's son Doug, the fact that the British didn't give him prisoner of war pay whilst he was in German hands rankled Tommy all his life! I discovered this fact in my conversations with him too. I agreed with Tommy's standpoint and said I would see what I could do!

Buck McNair informed Tommy that there were a significant number of new replacement pilots on the way, and therefore he was posted back to Canada. The RCAF, like the RAF, also had a policy not to allow pilots who escaped capture to return to active service for fear of interrogation if they were ever shot down and recaptured. The Germans wanted to extract details of any French Resistance or local support given during the successful escape attempt, a death sentence for those French people involved.

Tommy was posted to an auxiliary unit in St Hubert, Quebec. On 7 May 1945, he saw a French lady run onto the street shouting, "La Guerre est fini!" The War is over. Right there and then Tommy packed his stuff and began hitchhiking back to Toronto where a large party and celebration with family and friends was awaiting him.

After the war, Tommy went to work at his father in law's Company Supreme Aluminum Industries. Eventually, the desire to fly again was too much and he reenlisted in the RCAF where he went on to fly fast jets including; Avro Canada CF100, F-86 Sabre, Lockheed T-33 and Canadair CT-114 Tutor. Tommy retired from the air force in 1968 with the rank of Lieutenant Colonel. At the age of 74 he flew an F18 and according to his son Jim was, "like a kid in a candy store" after climbing out of the cockpit!

Many years later Tommy caught up with his old 411 Squadron comrade Bob Hyndman and commissioned him to do a portrait. Tommy takes up the story of the subterfuge that followed. It involved a bogus trip he took to his and Mil's lakeside holiday cottage as cover for the fact that he was heading for Bob's art studio in Ottawa:

"Bob took some pics of me. It was a surprise for Mil. I went to the cottage and then went to Ottawa. He didn't have enough time so I had to stay over. The family sent the police out to look for me. I told them we got hung up on the rocks fishing, right out in the country. Sensing trouble and seeing through the tale one family member said: 'Well that's your story Tom, stick with it.' I did. Lied right through my teeth. I couldn't blow the whole thing. It was a surprise because I didn't know that they had been looking all over for me!" He later told Mil the whole story when the portrait was unveiled. You can see a copy of Bob Hyndman's portrait of Tommy in this book.

At the time this book was started on 8 April 2018, Tommy was the last surviving Spitfire Elizabeth pilot and over the previous year, up to and beyond the start of this project I was able to see and talk to him at his home in Toronto, Canada via Facetime calls organised by his daughter Gail. These discussions were a complete joy and privilege. Gail, Doug, and Jim who are Tommy's children, also sent photos and videos along the way, including from Tommy's 97th birthday party. It was very touching to be allowed to share in these private family celebrations.

A few years earlier, in July 2015 I was lucky to meet Tommy during his visit to Aero Legends. He was visiting as a VIP guest at our inaugural Battle of Britain Air Show at Headcorn Aerodrome, Kent. Tommy and his son Doug Wheler also planned to visit the Imperial War Museum at Duxford to see Spitfire Elizabeth's restoration project. To have a surviving pilot, one of Elizabeth's "nine" with us was very special indeed.

On the morning of the air show a chauffeur-driven limousine arrived outside Aero Legends HQ and Tommy, helped by Doug was soon in his chair and raring to go. To those of us who have spent so much time in and around Spitfires reading and researching them, it was a great moment and there was an extra frisson of excitement amongst the crew. The use of the word "raring" to describe Tommy's demeanour is deliberate. As I was to learn during the day and afterward, despite his years Tommy was going to make the very most of this visit with boundless energy that would be admirable in someone half his age. Pinned proudly to his chest was the Legion d'Honneur, France's highest award for military and civilian merit established in 1802 by Napoleon Bonaparte, its red ribbon and ornate five-armed Maltese asterisk resplendent against his white wool cardigan. He was also wearing an RAF No1 service dress cap, a sensible move in the scorching summer sunshine.

A BBC TV South East News crew duly appeared to interview Tommy. Watching and listening to the interview, it was clear to me that Tommy held the Spitfire in great affection as a fighting machine. He described it as: "better than anything else. To fly a Spitfire was a top job, everyone wanted to fly them. They were the thing to fly as they could hold their own against the Germans." And, it was also my first introduction to Tommy's razor-sharp wit as he gently ribbed the interviewer, chuckling as he said: "I really like the British people because they have more guts than brains!"

In the time before Spitfire Elizabeth's restoration was completed, Aero Legends used Spitfire PV202 for customer flights. The airshow pilot for that day was John Dodd. "Doddy," as he is universally known in the warbird community was also interviewed and said of Tommy with a big grin: "He's travelled all the way from Canada, arrived here this morning and he's wanting to climb into a Spitfire!" It was evident Tommy was a man of considerable determination.

During the day I saw Tommy at various times around the aerodrome watching proceedings with great interest. He was centre stage for the "tail chase" finale involving two Spitfires and one Hurricane pursuing two German Messerschmitt Me 109s in a mock battle. It was epic stuff with explosions and gunfire adding to the spectacle. With the battle over, all of the aircraft landed, including the 'enemy.' As one of the German Me 109's taxied past on the way to refuel Tommy availed himself of one last opportunity to tangle with his old foe, flicking a "V" sign from his chair! This was completely understandable after what he went through during the war. It also gave Doug, me and the other Aero Legends crew members in the vicinity a damn good laugh. It was classic Tommy. He was irrepressible.

With the day wrapping up I saw my opportunity to meet the great man and shake his hand. With all the research and writing of this book that has followed, the short time I spent with Tommy, one of the Roaring

Boys, was a precious and treasured memory. I asked Tommy if he would like a drink and he said, "apple juice please." Perhaps, I thought, he was recalling his days at RAF Staplehurst all those years before drinking the Munn family's potent scrumpy cider. The brew was one of Kent's lesser-known contributions to the war effort which was the downfall of many unwary Canadian airmen. After a few more minutes chatting about his day, it was time to get ready for the evening.

At the evening black-tie dinner in Headcorn's main hangar, my wife and I were seated with legendary SAS veteran Rusty Firmin and his wife Torky. With my interest in all things military, my day was just getting better and better. As the event was about to begin, I was quite surprised to see Tommy in attendance, accompanied by Doug and other family and friends. Even after a long day under the scorching sun, he was still going strong. Never underestimate this man I thought to myself. After an excellent dinner surrounded by Spitfire gate guardians, Tommy was invited to the stage. He talked about the war, flying Spitfires and his experiences of being shot down and captured in Normandy in August 1944. Tommy told the story of being put in the back of a German lorry after he was captured during which he struck up a conversation with his guard. They agreed to teach each other some words from their native tongues, a sensible move as Tommy was facing a lengthy spell in a prisoner of war camp. Tommy took his turn as a teacher and asked the guard to repeat after him as he spelled every letter, "I am a S.H.I.T!" This story brought the house down, or more accurately the hangar. I like to think that the German guard went on to impress many a comrade and English-speaking prisoners with his newly acquired command of the language. At this point, Tommy was really warming to his theme. Inevitably, the time came to move proceedings on, and he was approached on stage in a carefully choreographed pincer movement by his son Doug and Aero Legends owner, Keith Perkins. Tommy, now in full flow had other ideas. Keith and Doug were sent into an immediate and full retreat with a polite, but firm response, a shake of the head and wave of his hand, "No!" he said. Tommy wasn't going anywhere just yet as the audience laughed uproariously!

During his wartime service with 411 Squadron, he embodied the spirit, bravery, and determination of the Roaring Boys. In August 1944, his last month of operational flying in Spitfires, he flew 8 hours and 10 minutes in combat before being shot down. His tour total of operational flying was 199 hours and 25 minutes, spread over 140 sorties. Tommy had spent 390 hours and 25 minutes in the cockpit of the mighty Spitfire, his "Little Millie's."

Sadly, Tommy passed away on 12 October 2018. To Canada, the RCAF and the free world, he was a hero. To his family, Tommy was a husband to his Millie, a father, papa, uncle, and friend to many. To me, Keith and all our colleagues, Tommy was our "aero legend" and we will never forget him.

CHAPTER SIX

DAVE EVANS

David Henry Evans hailed from Renfrew, Ontario. He joined the RCAF in 1941 and was posted to Course 22 which ran from March 5 to May 16, 1941, at No 6 Service Flying Training School (SFTS), based at RCAF Dunnville, Ontario. After graduating from his initial flight training, Dave was posted to England where he was enrolled onto a course at 53 Operational Training Unit based at RAF Heston, situated to the west of London. It was on this course that Dave took his first flight in the Supermarine Spitfire. After successfully completing the course he was posted to 411 Squadron on 23 August 1941, with the rank of Pilot Officer. At the time he joined the Roaring Boys, he would be serving with notable, and legendary 411 pilots Tex Ash and Buck McNair. In those early days of the squadron, Dave and the Roaring Boys were mainly flying in convoy patrols and Rodeo missions.

The official records indicate that Dave made an inauspicious start to his career as a fighter pilot. The 411 ORB entry for 4 February 1942 noted: "Five pilots posted to other units at the request of Squadron Commander in order to improve the flying standard in squadron…P/O Evans posted to 222 squadron." During his time with 222 squadron, Dave continued to fly the Spitfire Mark Vb. In March 1943, 222 squadron became an early member of 2nd TAF. For Dave, a return to 411 Squadron was on the cards when he was stationed at the No 3 Personnel Reception Centre, Bournemouth. One of the original pilots from his time with the squadron at RAF Digby was now 411's commanding officer, S/L J D McFarlane. The 411 ORB entry for 9 March 1944 read: "F/L D H Evans arrived to join the squadron today. He was with 411 2 years ago and is an old acquaintance of the boss, J D McFarlane." The circumstances of Dave's transfer are not known but his timing was fortuitous as in the following month on 10 April Joe McFarlane was posted to HQ at the Air Defence of

Great Britain pending a transfer to the USAAF. For Dave, rejoining with his old squadron, and fellow Canadians in the RCAF was much more preferable. The rest of the entry for that day perhaps explains the timing of Dave's arrival: "P/O J C Mitchell and F/O C F Armstrong crashed in a glider just east of Biggin; P/O Mitchell was taken to Orpington Hospital with a broken leg and F/O Armstrong was shaken up a bit but was not seriously injured. We've got 5 chaps in hospital now. The squadron strength is certainly diminishing…it is hoped that improvements are shown very shortly, or we'll require more pilots to fly on operations."

With limited opportunities to adjust to life in his new surroundings of Biggin Hill, Dave managed to secure flying time, mainly focussing on local familiarisation, formations, and drills for the upcoming Ramrods which were the squadron's main activity at this stage of the war. On 12 April, Dave awoke early and after washing and dressing, he went to the mess for breakfast. Later that morning, he was sitting in the intelligence operations briefing as the new boss, S/L N R Fowlow addressed the squadron on the details of Ramrod 725. Alongside Dave were some faces he would get to know well, as close comrades in combat and unbeknown to any of them at this point, their common connection to Spitfire Elizabeth; Tommy, Bruce, Len, and Bob. Norm Fowlow outlined the plan, the insertion and extraction routes, and the bomber strength. They would be supporting a formation of Marauders bombing No Ball targets.

At around 14.00 pm Dave walked along to dispersal and climbed up onto the wing of Spitfire MH850. The combat nerves were jangling and he knew that they would lessen once the operation got underway and he was concentrating on his job. Dave was also keen to show his mettle to his new comrades and prove his worth, especially having been transferred out previously to improve his flying skills. At this point, he was an unknown quantity to them. With his Sutton straps fixed and tightened, and his flying helmet securely fastened he plugged in his headset and oxygen. Shortly afterward, R/T tests confirmed his transmission and receiver functions were all normal. The row of Roll Royce Merlins was turning as the squadron taxied out and launched forth. As Dave climbed into the sky above Biggin Hill he closed into formation with the others. S/L Fowlow turned south, where after a short flight over Kent, they rendezvoused with the Marauders from USAAF's Ninth Air Force. The Roaring Boys moved past the formation to take the lead across the channel. Their part in the mission was to patrol a thirty-mile line running east and west, just to the south of

Dunkirk. Should the enemy decide to strike the bombers, the fighters were in position and should be able to intercept them. As the mission unfolded, Dave was feeling more confident, no flak was being targeted at them and so far, no fighters were in the area to impede the bombers as they sought out their targets. Dave's R/T sparked into life as S/L Fowlow passed on the message that the mission was complete and that it was time to return to base. In the distance, Dave could see the Marauders serenely heading back across the channel. With their work done they signed off, and the bombers soon were specks in the distance as they flew towards their East Anglian bases. The rolling hills of Kent were passing by and soon Dave could see London and, in the foreground, Biggin Hill where he touched down at 16.15 pm. His first mission back with the Roaring Boys was completed and he was soon walking purposely towards the intelligence section to debrief and complete his report and logbook. Tommy Wheler summed up the mission in his logbook, "S.F.A. No flak or Huns."

The spring weather unsurprisingly hampered operations, but Dave was settling in well and was as eager as the others to get back into combat. On 24 April, a bomber mission was planned to attack shipping in Dieppe harbour. At 17.50 pm the squadron strength formation took off and headed for the south coast. It was a cloudy day and on the way over everyone stared down and wondered whether there would be any break to allow them to see and dive bomb the target area. As they approached across the sea at around 10,000 feet S/L Fowlow briefed his men, who included Bruce, Tommy, and Gibby. They would perform an orbit for a time as it looked as if a break would soon appear through which the Spitfires could dive. Dave searched the surrounding sky, as there was a risk that their prolonged presence in the area would allow German defences time to organise a response and send fighters up to bounce them. Just as they began to contemplate abandoning the mission, the anticipated break appeared in the mist and gloom. They could make out the outline of Dieppe harbour, and the area where a few years before so many Canadians had lost their lives during the disastrous amphibious assault. The mission to bomb the minesweepers was on and Dave prepared himself for action. When his time came, he pointed his Spitfire downwards into a shallow dive. With others having already unleashed their bombs, smoke was now marking the target area as the thin wisps of vapour trails arced away from the wings of the Spitfire in front, the pilot pulling up hard from his dive. Dave followed suit and nearing the end of his dive pulled back on the column. The 500-pounder speared earthwards. Flak was his biggest concern, and almost instantly he tore back into the gloom of the cloud. It would disguise his escape route from the flak as he made for the relative safety of the sea. The formation had completed their mission and pushed hard on the throttles for home, with wheels down at Biggin recorded at 19.15 pm. These longer missions were an ideal opportunity to build tour time and experience. Tommy Wheler commented on the mission: "Yellow 3 dive bombing minesweepers in Dieppe harbour. 9 to 10/10th light 3 thousand. Target obscured, bombs fell in town and harbour. Very abortive."

On 30 April, the schedule determined that this would be a day of No Ball missions with two operations scheduled for the day preceded by some earlier practice. Dave checked the roster and saw he was listed along with Bruce, dive bombing specialist Ross, and Len. The mission was scheduled to be airborne at 16.25 pm with F/L S A Mills leading the Roaring Boys into battle. The ORB confirmed the target as: "a rocket gun installation south of Abbeville." All was going well until at the scheduled time they reached the target area. By now the bombing attacks and attention being afforded to these installations meant that the enemy was increasing their efforts to camouflage them. The flak protection in the surrounding areas had also been stepped up. They had extreme difficulty in finding the target and therefore the bombing was not effective. It was clear to the pilots that they were in the right place as three puffs of flak were sent up. Ross used some nonmilitary language to express his opinion of the bombing performance: "Couldn't find target. Piss poor bombing." Bruce Whiteford meanwhile restricted his assessment to, "poor bombing." With no further excitement manifesting itself, the formation turned and flew back to base, landing back at 17.50 pm. The subsequent debrief would have made for an interesting exchange of views, particularly as the earlier part of the day had been spent practicing the art of dive bombing.

The 9 May dawned as a perfect flying day as Dave, Bruce, Tommy, and Ross readied themselves to dive bomb a No Ball target south of Abbeville as part of Ramrod 857. With such conditions, the squadron was determined to press home an attack with a high level of accuracy. They set out at for France at 17.55 pm crossing the channel into enemy territory. Things were going well, and no flak was sent up to bother them. The location of the target was quickly found, and Dave was satisfied with his efforts. Ross later wrote, "Very good bombing" whilst Tommy's description of their efforts was simple and to the point, "Lovely." There was a different atmosphere after the pilots landed back at Biggin at 18.45 pm. Gone were the gloomy faces as their smiles matched the sunny conditions as the pilots walked along to the debrief comparing notes as they went. Steadily as the mission count grew the Roaring Boys were improving their accuracy and competence with this new form of offensive operations.

For Ramrod 908 on 22 May the squadron left for an evening mission to bomb a No Ball target at Bois Coquerel, in the Pas de Calais. This site had previously been bombed on 20 April by the USAAF's 401st Heavy Bombardment Group. The mission would be led by new boss S/L G D Robertson, who replaced Norm Fowlow, tragically killed a few days before in a dive bombing attack. Dave was joined on this operation by Bob. At 18.55 pm, with the squadron at a state of readiness Robertson gave the order to takeoff and soon they were on their way for the short flight to France. The Roaring Boys soon encountered what others such as the USAAF bombers had previously found when attacking this target, the flak was heavy, albeit inaccurate. The diving Spitfires presented a more difficult target than the extended formation of slow-moving bombers with their high-speed dive bombing runs. Dave and the others continued to dive at the target area. In total, eight 500 pounders were dropped including one 18-hour delay fuse bomb. One of the Spitfires experienced a hang up, with the bomb failing to release from its rack. The flak did score a hit on F/L Hayward's Spitfire, but he was able to make it safely back to base where the squadron landed at 20.05 pm. All then assembled around Hayward's Spitfire to inspect the damage. The ORB summarised the pilots assessment of their night's work: "Three or four hits only were observed but it is believed several others registered in the same spot."

With the arrival of D Day on 6 June, Dave was by now well established within the pilots roster and on the momentous day of the invasion, he was first in action at 13.05 pm, with a further beachhead patrol at 18.10 pm. The next day the weather conditions were still unfavourable but patrols had to be put up to protect the developing lodgement. For the British, amongst the forces opposing them in front of their lines near Caen was the fearsome 21st Panzer division who were putting up almost fanatical resistance to the British offensive. The Roaring Boys were assigned to patrol above the eastern sector and at 08.15 am Dave was soon flying a squadron strength patrol, before returning to RAF Tangmere. He was prepared and ready to lift off again at 18.10 pm with Ross and Tommy for a patrol along the same eastern sector. Many of the patrols were uneventful but, on this occasion, the Luftwaffe was out in force and the potential for air combat was high. S/L Robertson led the formation up from Tangmere. Dave allowed himself a momentary glance down at the stream of ships below. Surely, with this amount of firepower, the landing must be a success he must have thought. He was also vigilant for enemy aircraft which might have infiltrated the air space in amongst the massed ranks of Allied bombers, transport aircraft and fighters. The briefing was crystal clear and this sharpened everyone's senses. The formation arrived at the beachhead patrol areas and all was going well. Then, the warning "enemy sighted" came over Dave's R/T and jolted him into an elevated state of concentration. A formation of FW 190s and Me 109s was heading straight for them. Dave peeled away following close behind Tommy as aircraft scattered across the sky. Aircraft flew in all directions, a glimpse of an elliptical wing, then a wing with black cross hurtled past him, a Spitfire close on his tail. There were shouts, swearing, warnings barked out, "He's on your tail Yellow 2." In amongst the mayhem came a voice of almost serene calmness, "Take that you bastard." Dave stuck close to Tommy and no sooner had the dog fight started than it was over and all was quiet. Suddenly Dave's engine cut. He immediately trimmed the Spitfire into a glide to maintain his airspeed and avoid stalling. Desperately he tried to restart the engine. Tommy could see what was happening and later told the story: "Dave Evans kite packed up over beachhead. He got all set to bail out, but his kite picked up again at 200 feet." They could see no other Spitfires and Tommy radioed across to Dave. With fuel getting low it was time to make for the safety of Tangmere. Tommy and Dave touched down safely at 19.30 pm, a full half an hour before the others. He had come within a whisker of bailing out, and at times he wondered if he would make it. Both men talked through the engine failure and tried to fathom out what caused it. They moved on to talk about the enemy attack and both thought that the boss had made a kill. At 20.00 pm, the remainder of the squadron came into Tangmere's circuit and as they taxied in Dave and Tommy were relieved to see all had made it back safe and sound. There was a sea of smiles, it looked like it had been good hunting. At the debrief,

S/L Robertson talked through his kill, a butcher bird FW 190, whilst F/L G W Johnson was ecstatic as he had bagged a Me 109. The ORB noted: "The two enemy aircraft were attacking a Thunderbolt when first seen." The combat took place a little north of Caen at 19.15 pm. It had been a successful day for 2nd TAF with 19 Me 109s, 9 Ju 88s, 5 FW 190s, and a Ju 52/3m scored. The day had not been without its costs as 18 Spitfires and Seafires were destroyed, 6 damaged, 12 Typhoons destroyed and 2 damaged, 6 Mustangs destroyed and 3 damaged. The Allies could absorb these losses, but for the Third Reich this rate of attrition was unsustainable, and the die was cast for their gradual descent into defeat and destruction.

For Dave's missions of 10 June, there was the new experience of refuelling and rearming in France at B3 St Croix-sur-Mer. The Roaring Boys had landed at 18.30 pm and were fully prepared by 20.20 pm for a return sweep along a patrol area that took in the towns of Evreux, Chartres, and Argentan. The squadron strength formation split up for reasons that are not known but may have been due to a technical issue as Dave, Don Givens, and Art Tooley were recorded as landing at 21.05 pm, 55 minutes before the rest of the squadron. Their early departure meant they missed a combat action that involved 401 and 411 Squadrons. A solitary FW 190 was spotted and attacked by both F/Ls A A Williams of 401 and H J Nixon of 411 who shared a half kill of the downed fighter. The continuing bad weather meant that on 13 June operations could only begin again later in the day. For Dave, Tommy, Bob, and Charlie the call to a briefing eventually came with the plan to undertake a solitary late evening operation over the Omaha sector of the beachhead. The plan was for the Roaring Boys to spend the night at a refuelling and rearming strip, but late on these plans were cancelled after the patrol commenced at 20.40 pm. S/L Robertson advised the pilots that they would be returning to Tangmere after all, although F/L Russ Orr had already returned early with technical issues before the rest of the squadron saw wheels down at 22.35 pm.

The ORB entry for 23 June pronounced: "The unit is on some state of readiness during practically all daylight hours these days and while this is tiring the pilots are extremely keen to get into action against the Hun aircraft." At 16.55 pm on 23 June Dave, Gibby, Bruce, Tommy, Len, and F/O H W Kramer were led on a scramble alert by S/L Robertson. Within a few minutes, the formation of Spitfires tore down B4's runway and were airborne. It proved to be a false alarm and the elusive bandits could not be located. S/L Robertson confirmed over the R/T that they would instead commence a sweep of the Caen area. This proved productive as a light van and 3-ton truck were raked with cannon fire on the L'Aigle to Argentan road, a happy hunting ground for the Roaring Boys. Two staff cars were also attacked north of Falaise before F/L G W Johnson was hit by flak, on the starboard side of his engine, crash landing just south of the base. He managed to avoid injury. Robertson returned with his wingman Hal Kramer around 20 minutes later than the others, the dual action of the bandit chase and ground strafing had separated them from the rest of the formation. Ross wrote up details of the mission in his logbook: "CO got 2 MT vehicles. Red 3 and 4 chased 3 FW 190s." Tommy wrote: "Swept behind Caen at 1,000 feet. Shot up trucks. F/L Johnnie Johnson hit by flak – crash landed ¼ mile from airfield. OK. Good show!"

Spitfire NH341 Elizabeth

The 26 June was a full day for Dave and several of the other pilots, commencing with a patrol at 6.05 am, followed by a midday operation before he could take a further break. As Tommy later wrote it was also an important day in the ground offensive, "The Big Push for Caen has started. Cheers!" After a quick bite to eat at around 18.00 pm, Dave made his way to the operations tent where Charlie, Gibby, and 5 others had assembled for a tea time briefing from the intelligence, army liaison, and operations teams. The earlier missions had been largely uneventful, but sector control had reported several enemy aircraft in the area which the Roaring Boys had been unable to locate. Every pilot in the mission knew their designated section colour code, yellow, green, red or blue and their 1-4 number within the section. In whatever position they occupied they knew exactly what their role was and what was expected of them. The meeting broke up and with a final few words to each other they made for the dispersal area. Dave quickly located DB – E, Spitfire NH341 Elizabeth. His allocated steed was a new aircraft to him, and he asked the erk about any little foibles she might have. How were her brakes? Did she need an extra squirt of fuel to prime the engine for starting?. Better for Dave to know anything unusual now. It's possible Bruce himself offered some advice as pilots always do. In such a small roster of pilots, he was her unofficial "owner" and would have readily known how she handled. At 19.10 pm, Dave made his way out to the runway. He quickly dabbed Elizabeth's brakes to check they were working normally and then alternating pressure on each of the rudder pedals he moved forward, weaving and checking the way ahead by poking his head out of the cockpit into the hot draft of Merlin exhaust gases. He lined up and made a quick final check of the aircraft's vital actions, checking his mirror so that he could see the elevator and rudder movements before looking out over the Spitfire's elliptical wing to check his ailerons. He waited, Spitfire Elizabeth was purring, and the engine temperature was building up quickly. Dave power checked the engine for takeoff and then its slow running, flicking the magnetos off and on, in turn, to check they were operating normally. A short while later, he opened the throttle and the blades of grass and weeds poking up through the mesh planking instantly laid flat as Elizabeth's Merlin engine roared and launched the aircraft forward. With wheels up, the formation orbited B4 assembling into the finger-four patrol formation and heading for the beachhead. Over the next 1 hour and 30 minutes, they flew their patrol pattern several times, waiting for the moment sector control would call up with some trade for them. The R/T remained silent, perhaps the Luftwaffe like the Roaring Boys had looked out at the grey, sullen skies and considered they would not put in a major appearance. On this day, 2nd TAF only claimed 4 destroyed and 1 damaged enemy aircraft. With the patrol complete, Dave dropped Spitfire Elizabeth into the circuit pattern for B4. The conditions for landing were "sporting" and he compensated for the strong variable, gusting winds, positioning his aircraft into the wind slightly as the height dropped away. He didn't want to prang the aircraft. As Dave reached the flare position, he kicked the rudder pedal straight and the Spitfire snapped into line, executing a perfect touch down, with the reassuring rattle and hum of the wheels over the mesh planking. The speed fell away, and he moved quickly off the runway to enable the next section to land. The pilots assembled in the briefing area however there was not much to discuss, or even tell the intelligence and ops boys about the patrol and so, shortly afterward, the Roaring Boys made their way back to their "funk holes."

On 28 June Dave was once again rostered to fly Spitfire Elizabeth on a morning armed reconnaissance mission. He checked the list, seeing that the show would be led by S/L Robertson with Tommy, Len, Charlie, and Ross joining 7 others in squadron strength. The area for the recce would be south of Caen. They were told the area was "hot" in terms of enemy activity and

Dave and the others knew they could expect to come across trouble. However, the boys were eager to get on with the job. The slight improvement in the weather, along with the ground offensive to outflank and seize Caen, Operation Epsom, had them eagerly anticipating getting to grips with some enemy fighters. At 08.30 am the formation took to the sky, each man flying with the nerves that only combat could stir. The Roaring Boys were seasoned fighter pilots who could depend on each other, and that trust and skill would at some time be tested once again. The patrol seemed to have only just got underway when S/L Robertson's voice drifted calmly into Dave's headset. The vehicles below were going to be attacked. Dave stayed in the group providing top cover for the attackers, who lead by Robertson, took it in turns to dive down on the transports below. Dave only allowed his attention to switch for a few seconds to the drama below. Like the faintest scent of blood in the ocean could draw in sharks from far and wide, the covering section knew the enemy on the ground was almost certainly radioing for help, and any enemy fighters stooging around the area would soon be vectored in to attack them. The pilots' volley of bullets speared down and acrid black smoke billowed up from the road below. With the attack over the formation reassembled and the reconnaissance mission entered its final stages as they made a final pass of the south of Caen. S/L Robertson turned the formation onto a new course to the northwest, in the direction of Bayeux. Without warning, a voice hurried and breathless called out "bandits." The sight of around 50 plus Me 109s and FW 190s upped Dave's heart rate. His mind was locked fully into the drills and preparation for combat. All Spitfire Elizabeth's pressure and temperature gauges were normal, but he looked at his dwindling fuel supply. They might have to engage the Huns if they came onto them, but it would be suicidal to attempt to chase them all over the sky whilst running low on fuel. Robertson gave the order they knew was coming but didn't want to hear, "Return to base." At 09.50 am, Dave brought Spitfire Elizabeth into land, past the maintenance area where aircraft of all shapes and sizes were awaiting repair. Elizabeth touched down and with the Merlin engine finally silent a disappointed Dave stepped onto the aircraft's wing and slid gently to the ground. It would be last time he would fly her. He caught up with Tommy, Charlie, and Ross. All of them were up for a fight and cursing that bad luck and that timing was against them. They hoped for better fortune later that day, which it certainly delivered. Ross later wrote about the operation: "Ran into 50+. We were all too short of fuel to chase them. F/L Stayner and F/L Halcrow of

401 each destroyed an FW 190. F/O Banks 412 got a 190. F/L Foxx damaged one. Got some M.T vehicles. Huns coming up now – cheers." Tommy provided his own version of the mission: "Shot up transport south of Caen. Ran into 40+ Huns FW 190s and Me 109s west of Caen. I chased 30 of them for 5 minutes and fired a long burst at a Me 109 from 1,000 yards. No claim. No gas. Landed at B4 with 5 gals."

The month of July kicked off with a high patrol activity. On 3 July, Dave awoke early and in the dawn light headed over to the briefing area where the increasingly battered line of fold-up chairs was already filling up with pilots, some yawning and stretching, looking far from combat ready, whilst the "morning people" were already alert and at their best. Sitting around him were Bob, Bruce, Tommy, Len, and 8 others. The mission plan was presented, and the best-known position of the ever-changing front line was pinned with a ribbon to the map of the Normandy area. Tommy later described the conditions for the patrol, "Duff weather. Very very duff!" At 06.00 am F/L Hayward led the formation towards the runway, a blur of whirling propeller blades, heat haze, and noise. The pilots had their "game faces" on as the gentle vibration and heartbeat of the Spitfire MK462 came up through Dave's feet and hands. He was ready, just a quick check of the control column, which he moved back and forwards and side to side in a rhythmic motion, checking how each moveable part behaved. He had full and free movement. The audible increase in engine revs around him told him they were off and on the stroke of 06.00 am they were airborne, quickly climbing out to a patrol height of 5,000 feet where they systematically divided the sky into segments that were carefully checked for enemy aircraft. All they needed was a sign, the glint of sun off a canopy or the silent puff of black smoke as a flak shell sent its deadly shards towards them. Nothing much was moving on the ground, or in the air. A small single truck was spotted, and Hayward allocated one section to break away from the rest of the squadron to attack it. Dave gazed down as the truck was repeatedly shot up. The ORB later noted, "One Met flamer scored." It was to prove the only action of the patrol and exactly one hour later the formation landed at B4, in time for a debrief. As they taxied in the sight of steam emanating from the mess area encouraged Dave and the others to rapidly shut down their noble steeds and begin an unseemly scramble to the queue for breakfast.

On 5 July the Roaring Boys were on defensive readiness all day. Dave, Tommy, Gibby, and C D Cross were required to stay close to the dispersal area in case of a scramble alarm. They knew a shout could come at any time. Just as it seemed the Luftwaffe was shutting down for the evening the alarm was raised. Dave rushed for MK462 and in a flash he was up on the wing and with the practice honed over many missions he completed his entry into the cockpit, his hands a blur as buttons and switches were pulled and pushed. With his strap buckles fixed the erk made a spectacular jump from the wing whilst Dave flicked his clenched fists sideways, his thumbs pointing outwards to signal the erk to remove the chocks. He was rolling, and in a short distance, and with a check of the sky approaching the runway he pushed the throttle forward, lifting off before forming up on the others. Sector control gave them the course to fly and "angels" rating to mark the last known altitude of the incoming enemy. Dave could feel he was hot and breathing rather more heavily. They pushed on and orbited the area but there was nothing. Sector control had no trade for them so Dave and the others decided to see what other action they could find. There was plenty. Perhaps, the land forces felt it was less risky to move with nightfall approaching. This was a small, but still potent force and with determined fighters like Tommy and Gibby armed and ready above them, the convoy they happened upon was about to regret its evening journey. As Dave turned his Spitfire into a dive, he lined up a truck and unleashed a long volley of 20 mm cannon and machine gun fire, which, despite the muffling effect of his flying helmet, instantly filled his ears with a cacophony of noise and vibration. The impact of the rounds lifted the truck off the ground, the fuel tank erupting in flames. By the time they had finished smoke billowed up from several vehicles and with a quick final look at the destruction they had meted out below, Dave pointed his Spitfire towards B4 for the short return flight, noting later that he touched down at 21.35 pm. For Tommy the short return to base was vital. He wrote: "No huns. Hit by flak in oil rad. Me 109s in circuit." For Tommy, an ailing aircraft and the enemy in the circuit was literally double trouble, but fortunately, he landed without being attacked.

The 11 July was a test of stamina for the Roaring Boys. The pace of operations was unrelenting, and the top brass was keen to keep up the pressure on the retreating Germans. The Roaring Boys themselves were hungry for missions and continually badgered the intelligence team for targets. Dave knew he was rostered to fly four patrols on this day, starting at 07.00 am and ending at 21.55 pm when he took NH462 on a patrol with Gibby, Bruce and C D Cross. They turfed around their patrol area for 40 minutes in the fading light, the serene summer evening's flying punctuated by the occasional flash of guns and tracer fire all along the front line as the two armies continued to exchange unpleasantries.

Squadron strength armed reconnaissance missions were the order of the day on 15 July, and Dave was scheduled to fly an evening mission with Tommy, Gibby, Len and Bob which would see "tits pressed" at 20.45 pm. The briefing detailed the area for the reconnaissance as the road network around Vire, Domfront, and Flers, one of the main interdiction bombing targets. Essentially, this area represented the resupply route for enemy forces from the southwest to Caen. At 20.45 pm Dave's left hand pushed forward the throttle and MK462 responded immediately and was soon rumbling down the metal sheet runway, with him making further right rudder adjustments to keep her straight. As they formed up over the aerodrome, they all felt this was going to be a busy patrol with the near certainty of finding evening traffic on the main supply route. Dave looked across at the others and like him, they were peering down out of their cockpits knowing that pinpointing the road network in the reconnaissance area was going to be difficult due to the excessive cloud. It was later reported that the attack on the transports was carried out further to the east. The Roaring Boys were now flying lower to see the ground, and as the weather cleared they could not believe their eyes. This was an almost reckless level of transport movement, risked because of the desperation by the Germans to halt the Allies advance. It should be remembered that despite the landings being a month before, Hitler and his senior commanders still believed that the Normandy landings were a feint to disguise the main invasion in the Pas de Calais area. The code name for the Allies deception plan was the highly sophisticated Operation Fortitude. The strategy of deception involved military and intelligence services, double agents like the famous agent Garbo who transmitted false information to the Germans, as well reports of phantom armies (including dummy inflatable tanks and aircraft) and communications, plus air raids on targets in the Calais area. The Germans swallowed the deception plan completely with the Pas de Calais landings never taking place.

In the cockpit of their Spitfires, Dave and the others readied themselves for the attack and one by one they swooped down on the convoy. Dave's Spitfire almost seemed to fly on its own where he wanted it, reflecting the frequently reported comments from pilots that you only need to breathe on the Spitfire's controls and the aircraft will respond. He opened fire and saw a good number of cannon shells slamming into the vehicles below. Flak was coming his way too; the Germans wouldn't move this amount of transportation without some flak batteries being in support. As he pulled up through a cloud of smoke several low thuds reverberated around the fuselage and up through the control column and rudder pedals to his hands and feet. "Damn, they've hit me" he muttered under his breath. He transmitted the flak strike to the other pilots. For a few moments, his Spitfire climbed away normally and gained altitude, but telltale signs of trouble were now visible to him, a thick trail of white vapour pouring out from the Merlin engine. It was glycol, and his engine was doomed. It would soon overheat and could catch fire. He wrestled the throttle back to extract as much life as possible from the engine as he dare and to gain height without receiving the shuddering sensation through the controls that told him his Spitfire was about to stall and go into an unrecoverable dive. His engine was soon devoid of most of its coolant and was rapidly overheating. Another Spitfire appeared alongside, he was too busy to speak but the company was welcome, they were protecting the wounded aircraft from any marauding enemy fighters who could spot the white vapour trail against the sullen grey sky from miles away. His last words were "bailing out" and in an instant, his helmet leads were unplugged, and his Sutton harness was undone. Dave jettisoned the canopy as with an awful grinding sound the Rolls Royce Merlin engine seized, the giant propeller fixed, no longer turning. It was time to leave dear old MK462. She had given him height and distance from the ravaged convoy who would certainly have meted out revenge on him had he landed nearby. He crouched on the seat threw stick forward and leapt out as the aircraft passed just below him. He felt for the ripcord, found it and pulled it feeling the snap of the straps as the canopy deployed. He looked around as a Spitfire circled him, to prevent any enemy aircraft who might be tempted to fire on him as he floated down helplessly. He waved to his fellow 411 pilot to signal he was OK and received waggling wings in return before the sound of the Spitfire engine faded away to disguise his exact position to any enemy ground forces. Dave made a good landing northeast of Caen and was in one piece, but his luck was out because as he neared the ground he saw a reception committee sprinting towards him, unmistakable in their grey Wehrmacht uniforms, and brandishing their Schmeisser MP40 machine pistols. No point trying to run and virtually as soon as he reached the ground he was captured.

The rest of the Roaring Boys landed back at B4 at 22.05 pm. F/L Hayward landed five minutes earlier and could have been the aircraft who stayed with Dave. The squadron ORB summarised the mission: "Considerable transport movement observed. Score 1 tank and trailer damaged, 2 APV damaged, 6 Met Flamers, 3 Smokers, 3 Damaged. One of the damaged held 20-30 troops. Intense accurate heavy flak from woods and open space near rail line U-2226. A/C flown by F/L D H Evans developed glycol leak, probably caused by flak. He bailed out N.E. of Caen, but no further word has been received." Tommy Wheler noted in his logbook: "Destroyed 3 trucks. Bags of flak. Too close! F/L Dave Evans hit by flak, Bailed out near Caen," Dave did not stay long in captivity, he knew from his training and the experiences of other pilots who had been shot down that the longer the time went on so the chances of escaping would diminish. They would be processed by the Germans and gathered into larger groups with guard units dedicated to stopping any escape attempts. How Dave managed to escape his captors is not known but he got away and was on the run for the rest of July and into August. It's almost certain he was helped by local French people, possibly by the Resistance too. No word of him was heard until 23 August when the ORB announced: "F/L D H Evans returned following his baling out on July 15th. He was taken prisoner but escaped soon after and kept under cover until our troops advanced." No 126 Wing's Senior Intelligence Officer Monty Berger also noted Dave's return on this date. He interviewed him and wrote about his: "getting back after many exciting experiences." With the debrief complete, Dave Evans was removed from operational flying duties. Replacements were already in place and his name was now known to the Germans. If he was captured on another occasion, he could be subjected to interrogation by the Gestapo to reveal the details of his successful evasion. Dave's war was over, and he was posted back home to Canada.

What became of his life after the war is not currently known. I hope I can find out more about his story one day. He will be forever linked with 411 Squadron and the Roaring Boys. He flew his Spitfires with courage and bravery throughout his service, and that commands our utmost respect.

CHAPTER SEVEN

GIBBY GIBSON

The first reference I can find to J/3743 W R 'Ronald' Gibson, or Gibby as he was called is in photographs from the time of his enrolment in the RCAF's Course 13, No 2 Service Flying Service Training School, Uplands, Ontario which ran from November 18, 1940 - January 24, 1941. He was learning to fly under the harshest conditions of a Canadian winter. At his graduation ceremony, Gibby and the other pilots were presented with their wings by Group Captain Frank McGill. He told the young men gathered before him not to show off over towns or girls houses! He went on to say: "You will be fighting against unscrupulous opponents, devoid of any idea of fair play or sense of sportsmanship. Shoot the dirty dogs down." With that final message ringing in their ears, the graduating pilots were posted on to their units.

Gibby was posted into 411 Squadron on 7 October 1943 from 430 squadron RCAF, which had been established in England on 1 January 1943 as a reconnaissance unit flying the P-40 Kittyhawk fighter. Just before he was posted to the Roaring Boys, 430 squadron converted onto the P51 Mustang, continuing its reconnaissance role. Gibby arrived at what was by now the well-established ALG at RAF Staplehurst, albeit within a week the squadron would move to Biggin Hill. Quite what he made of the tented encampment we can only speculate. As Gibby was already experienced, having served with 430 squadron he had an easier time during the settling in process. There was still plenty of work ups to be done to understand 411 squadron's procedures in wing formation flying, mock air combat, gun camera practice, and navigation exercises. With lives at stake, no one wanted a new pilot causing a problem for themselves, let alone anyone else. As the winter weather set in, Gibby would have to wait a short while to experience his first taste of combat as a new Roaring Boy. On 10 November he attended his first mission briefing. He would join Tommy on a squadron strength Ramrod 307, to Lille Vendeville airfield which would be led by S/L Ian Ormston. Gibby had some time to think about his mission. He was experienced enough to know already what it meant to be waiting to go into combat with a new squadron, and he was determined not to "cock it up." Once airborne, he hoped the nerves would dissipate as his training, and concentration on flying the Spitfire kicked in.

After settling into the cockpit of his Mark IX Spitfire EN633, Gibby was ready to go as the 12 Spitfires taxied out for a 12.45 pm takeoff. Once airborne, the formation of Spitfires took shape for the short flight to the coast, where they picked up the 72 Marauders, and the beehive flew on. Gibby was conscious of flying escort to such a large formation, and the relative closeness of so many fighters and bombers made him doubly aware of the need to concentrate. As they crossed the French coast and moved in on the target area the 411 ORB takes up the story: "The bombers became lost, however, and so they bombed gun positions at Calais as an alternative target." For Gibby, the spectacle of 72 Marauders delivering their payload was something he never tired of seeing. Each bomb was a step closer to the war's end. With the bombs gone, Gibby the pace picked up in response to the bombers which were now going full tilt for England. The Roaring Boys saw their charges safely away before as Tommy wrote later, they: "stooged around France for a time, didn't see anything." They crossed back over the channel, passing over the English coastline the tension eased. Gibby ran through his pre-landing checks and procedures before feeling the welcome terra firma of "Biggin on the bump." As he taxied in and shut down he must have felt a sense of pride and relief that his first mission was over, it was a good feeling to successfully achieve this. In the following days, when the weather allowed, there were practice sessions of formation flying, cine gun camera practice, and occasional night flying exercises for Gibby, all without the additional ingredient of enemy intervention. Any experience and advice that could be gleaned from the "wise heads" amongst the squadron was eagerly taken in by the new pilots.

The winter weather prevented regular flying over the following weeks and there was a pause before Gibby could get back into action. On 5 December, he was joined by Ross and Len for a two-stage mission. The initial phase required the Roaring Boys to take a 1-hour flight from Biggin Hill to RAF Exeter in the early morning. Once there, the Spitfires and their pilots refuelled ready for Ramrod 354. As Gibby strapped himself into Spitfire MH477 he knew this would be a new experience and on a giant scale. The ORB recorded that No 126 Wing would: "provide withdrawal cover to 240 Flying Fortresses." All the formation flying practice he had undertaken thus far would be needed as the 36 Spitfires covered the huge beehives of B-17s. With wheels up at 12.05 pm the wing quickly formed up into it battle formation, with 411 being led by S/L Ian Ormston. Gibby settled into his section and as one the formation swung south. His eyes flicked down to his instruments. All systems were normal as the directional indicator span around to point 180 degrees due south, whilst the altimeter worked overtime to register the increase in altitude as the Spitfires powered their way through the dense grey cloud. The grey murky blanket disappeared as they broke through into bright sunshine and soon after transmissions were relayed into his R/T, pinpointing the location of the Fortresses and the wing was vectored onto them. Gibby and the others were now flying high above the channel and scoured the blue sky ahead for the planned rendezvous with the USAAF's Mighty Eighth. The bombers had set out to hit several airfields in the Paris area, but the thick cloud prevented any target identification being confirmed and they had turned back for England with their payloads intact. The ORB commented, "The Forts were met at Brest." Ross provided further details of the mission in his logbook: "Yellow 4. 45 gal tanks. Picked up Libs over 10/10 cloud. Whole trip over water. Almost missed England. Landed Port Reith." It is interesting to note that the ORB described the mission as involving B17 Flying Fortresses whilst Ross refers to "Libs" meaning B24 Liberators. On balance, both versions could be correct as there were mixed formations of bombers but the scale and other reporting suggest that this was a B17 mission. The wing landed at RAF Portreath, which is located on the north Cornwall coast around 95 miles to the west of RAF Exeter, from where they had set off 2 hours earlier. Clearly, the cloud cover had contributed to the dramatic navigation error. The relief was palpable that they hadn't inadvertently pushed on across the sea towards Wales, or even Ireland where running out of fuel might have resulted in a catastrophic mass ditching. It was a sobering lesson for everyone and all involved redoubled their efforts with their navigation skills. Once the Spitfires had their 45-gallon tanks replenished the wing took off to fly the return leg to Biggin Hill.

Gibby and the Canadians were, of course, used to harsh Canadian winters and perhaps the fresh snow covering that blanketed Biggin Hill in the middle of December reminded them of their homeland. Flying was undertaken whenever the weather allowed. The hazards of flying under these conditions were numerous with mechanical failure always a concern, particularly on takeoff or landing. This fact was brought home to Gibby and Ross on their outing of 21 December. Ramrod 381 was an escort job to bombers attacking various targets behind Dieppe and Neufchatel. It was a cold, windy morning as Gibby climbed up onto the wing on Spitfire MJ133. He put one foot on the cockpit door and stood on the seat and gripping the top of the windscreen and in one movement he slid down, shuffling around until he was comfortable on his parachute which acted as a cushion. The erk passed him his Sutton harnesses and shortly afterward he fired up his Spitfire, before taxiing out to join the rest of 411s aircraft who were moving from dispersal to the holding point ready for takeoff. He looked over to see 412 Squadron zigzagging their way out, forming up behind them. Soon Biggin was filled with the sound of Merlin engines as Gibby and the others became airborne. At that moment, he saw one of the leading Spitfires drop away from the formation. It was clear someone was in trouble. The ORB later recorded the event: "Just after takeoff for this operation S/Ldr Ormston's engine failed. He was unable to land back on the runway as 412 Squadron was just taking off and so he was forced to land on the east side of the drome. His aircraft crashed and was completely wrecked and S/Ldr I C Ormston was rushed away to Orpington War Hospital where the degree of his injury was determined. Unconfirmed injuries suffered by the CO were a traumatic shock, a fractured spine and multiple bruises and abrasions." It was a bad start, but the Roaring Boys had to go on with the mission and forget about their leader for the time being. As the formation neared the south coast, they picked up the formation of Marauders. Shortly after, Gibby looked on as the bombers unloaded their bombs through the cloud cover onto the targets below. There was no way of knowing what the effect was as the cascade of black bombs trickled out from the underneath each aircraft. With their job done and extra power applied Gibby could relax just a little, but he turned his head round routinely to check in case of a bounce by the enemy. Gibby and P/O R W Hogg went ahead of the returning formation and landed at 10.30 am, around 15 minutes ahead of the others. The notable loss of S/L Ormston was also included by Ross in his mission write up: "Blue 4. Patrolled over Dieppe. Boss crashed after takeoff."

Gibby was to experience a new type of mission on 23 December when along with Len, Tommy, Charlie and Ross the squadron would join the other two squadrons of 126 Wing, and 127 Wing from Kenley for a massed fighter sweep. The areas covered would be wide-ranging and included Nieuwpoort, Belgium, Lille and Béthune, France. The Roaring Boys were airborne at 13.30 pm and for Gibby, the sight of around 70 Spitfires climbing up through the cloud cover into the bright winter sunshine was impressive to any observer. As they gained altitude, to traverse the channel, Gibby switched on his oxygen supply. The Roaring Boys would be acting as top cover, flying at 23,000 feet. The formation made landfall at Nieuwpoort and headed southeast towards Courtrai, before changing course to a southwesterly track, passing Lille and heading for Douai. From there, they turned west for Béthune, where the ORB later summed up the mission: "the flak was very accurate from Béthune airfield but not one of our a/c was hit. No enemy aircraft were sighted, and the operation went to plan and was uneventful." Ross helpfully detailed the direction of the sweep in his logbook, "Out at Somme." Effectively, from Béthune the formation of Spitfires headed southwest for to the estuary of the river Somme on the French cost for their return leg across the channel to England. For Gibby, this experience of heavy accurate flak was always sobering, and a warning of the dangers that he had to face almost every day. It was with some relief that the welcome sight of Biggin Hill came into view, and at 15.15 pm he touched down before taxiing in and heading off to the mission debrief. It had been a long trip, some 1 hour and 45 minutes in duration in freezing temperatures.

With 1944 only 4 days old, and having brought in the new year with a series of formation, cine gun camera, and cannon firing exercises, Gibby attended a briefing by S/L McFarlane for his next operation, Ramrod 419. Alongside him would be Charlie and Len. The ORB detailed the mission, which was to escort Marauders bombing No Ball targets, and which would commence with wheels up at 15.05 pm: "The Wing took off on a sweep around Saint Valery sur Somme – Rouen area at 18,000 feet." As Gibby and the formation moved towards Rouen, 12 FW 190s at 24,000 feet, and 8 Me 109s at 12,000 feet were sighted. The ORB added: "A general mix up started and 411 engaged the 109s." Gibby was engaged in the combat and stayed close to his section leader as protection, whilst constantly checking behind his own aircraft. The adrenalin surged around his body. The sky was full of aircraft, a jumbled mess, flying it seemed in all directions around him. The ORB described the dog fight: "F/L R W Orr damaged one of them. Blue section of 411 was jumped by 190s and F/L N J Nixon while shooting at one of them was shot up by an enemy aircraft; his aircraft was hit in several spots by machine gun fire, but he returned safely to base. The wing was all split up and returned to base in sections; four aircraft landed at Ford and our CO and two other pilots landed at Tangmere. All our aircraft returned safely." With his mind still racing from the dog fight, Gibby landed with the damaged Nixon and Russ Orr who had damaged one of the enemy fighters. The pilots gathered to debrief with the intelligence boys, to establish even the tiniest details about the Luftwaffe's approach to the combat action. What moves did they try? Did they work together as a leader and wingman, or with others who joined the melee later? What aerobatic manoeuvres did their pilots use to evade?

On 24 January No Ball sites were once again the focus for offensive operations as Gibby, Bruce, Charlie, and 9 other Roaring Boys were briefed for Ramrod 475 which would bomb targets north east of Amiens. At 9.20 am led by F/L S A "Sid" Mills, the mass formation of Spitfires, propellers whirling, manoeuvred themselves from the dispersal area towards the runway and launched forth for France. Close to the south coast of England, the Spitfires climbed steadily and were vectored by the sector control onto the formation of 54 Marauders packed together and visible in the distance, warily inching their way out into the channel. The routes in and out to the targets in Amiens aren't documented but the insertion and extraction routes were always different for tactical reasons, confusing enemy observers who might be tracking their course and trying to alert and organise both flak and air defences. As the bombers closed in on Amiens, the flak opened up, 88 mm heavy artillery which sent shells hurtling up towards them, the black candy floss appearing in an instant and lingering in the air as the hot metal shards zinged in all directions seeking out an aircraft. The accompaniment to this deadly orchestra was the rapid firing but smaller 37 mm rounds from the Flakzwilling 43. Gibby sat in his Spitfire like everyone else, flying through the maelstrom with everything crossed that a bullet or shell would not have his name on it. He glanced over just as the 54 bombers dropped their bombs, and immediately swung north at a gathering pace, newly unburdened by their 2,000 lb bomb loads. The escape across the channel was on, and as the flak petered out the formation was soon high above the sea and heading for home. With the bombers safe to continue over the north Kent coast the Roaring Boys changed course towards London and their base, landing at exactly 11.00 am. The ORB provided the official account of the trip: "No enemy aircraft were encountered but the bombers received quite a bit of heavy flak (also light flak) over target area; however, all our a/c returned safely to base. F/L J Sheppard of 401 Squadron had to bail out in the channel due to engine failure. He was picked up by the Air/Sea Rescue in forty minutes. Good show!"

With February came an ever-increasing flood of Ramrods for Gibby to fly in. Although the Luftwaffe was withdrawing more units into Germany in preparation for the defence of their homeland, they were still a threat. Along with this danger were the flak defences which had been enhanced by the arrival of thousands of Flakvierling 38s, firing their 20 mm calibre rounds. These weapons were deadly against low flying aircraft, particularly when positioned around aerodromes and No Ball sites. Gibby, Charlie, Bruce, and Bob listened intently as first thing in the morning S/L McFarlane and the intelligence team briefed them on the upcoming mission and reports of a step up in flak batteries. A ripple of mumbling voices circulated around the briefing room. Along with 401 and 412 Squadrons, they would be providing close escort to 56 Marauders on a mission to bomb No Ball sites as part of Ramrod 526. At the same time, B17 Flying Fortresses would separately "blind" bomb the railway marshalling yards and other targets of opportunity around Frankfurt. The use of "blind" bombing meant that a combination of radar and pathfinder aircraft were used to pinpoint the target area, the pathfinders illuminating the target for the main bomber force which followed shortly behind them. By using radar, the bombers could also release their bombs in poor light or if the target was obscured by cloud.

With their watches synchronised, the briefing broke up and the pilots filed out to gather their parachute, life jacket, and escape kit. The area around dispersal was a hive of activity as the erks and pilots completed their final checks before the noise of growling Merlins filled the air around Biggin Hill. At 9.05 am, Gibby pulled back the control column as his Spitfire, bouncing along the grass runway reached its takeoff speed, and he was into the air. The Roaring Boys and the other 2 squadrons assembled over the airfield, ready to set course for the south coast where they would meet the 56 Marauders, flying at 12,000 feet over Hastings. Gibby settled in for the channel crossing. The ORB describes how the protection of the Marauders was organised as the formation approached the targets, which were located just east of Amiens: "Nos 401 and 412 Squadrons acted as guards on the flanks of the bombers while we orbited above the whole at 14,000 feet. The flak did not bother us neither did the Hun." Gibby and the Roaring Boys were certainly happy to escape the attention of the flak batteries as they eyed with trepidation the silent burst of explosive flak shells all around, and in amongst the formation. With the target attacked and no sign of the enemy, Gibby followed his comrades on the return leg back to England, landing at 10.35 am.

On 11 February, Gibby flew a fighter sweep, the first stage of which necessitated a short 30-minute flight to RAF Manston where the Roaring Boys were joined by 401 Squadron to refuel. Slung underneath the belly of each Spitfire was the 45-gallon auxiliary fuel tank, known as a "jet" tank. A few days before the tanks were causing a major headache as pilots were struggling to jettison them, due to the ingestion of grit thrown up by the propeller during start up and taxi. It was vital this could be achieved easily if they encountered the enemy. No pilot wanted to be in a dog fight with their graceful thoroughbred of an aircraft devoid of its key advantage, out turning the enemy, along with the even greater danger of up to 45 gallons of aviation fuel. The day before the mission Bruce noted: "Led yellow section for drop tank test." Clearly, it was felt necessary to do a shake down test to satisfy themselves that the tanks were operating normally.

At 12.25 pm the two squadrons left from Manston to begin Ramrod 543, which was a fighter sweep in support of 223 Flying Fortresses of the Mighty Eighth, returning from another mission to bomb the rail marshalling yards at Frankfurt. The ORB recorded what happened next: "Things went badly from the start of the operation; the W/C's tank fell off (45 gal. jet tank) while taxying out and S/L McFarlane who took over the wing lost his tank on takeoff and had to return. F/L Orr then took over the squadron while S/L Cameron took over the wing. F/O's Tooley and Wallace had to return with engine failures." For Gibby and the others, the sight of this unfolding disaster didn't help their confidence and heightened their own concerns around any unusual noise or mechanical issue, as well as what might happen if they lost or were unable to jettison the problematic jet tanks. Bruce commented: "Only 8 Spits got away. Led yellow section for a while then became part of red."

With the channel crossing behind them and enemy territory ahead the sweep began, and soon contact was made with the huge formation of B-17 Fortresses. According to the ORB: "the weather over France was 8/10 cloud. We met with P.47s who were on the same job as we were." Bruce also wrote about the USAAF fighters and the discomfort of flying at high altitude in the depths of winter, "Bounced by T-Bolts. Bloody cold." Rather matter of factly, the ORB describes the coming together of the two friendly forces: "they bounced us but shots were not exchanged." This was no doubt a relief to both sides.

As the heavies slowly disappeared towards their East Anglian bases, the Roaring Boys put down at Manston at 14.20 pm. Some welcome tea was provided by the erks, along with fuel for the short hop back to Biggin Hill. It had been a far from routine operation which everyone was glad to complete without further incident.

Tommy and Bob joined Gibby on 15 February for a mid-afternoon sweep behind Cayeux and over Saint Valery sur Somme, protecting boxes of Marauders. At 17.10 pm they returned; their mission completed without incident. Tommy wrote up a brief summary in his logbook, "No E/A or flak."

On 22 February the target choice changed to airfields as part of Operation Argument, the USAAF's

"Big Week," which was also supported with nighttime raids by RAF Bomber Command. For the Ramrod mission Gibby, Bruce, Tommy, Len, and Bob would depart from Manston. Having arrived from Biggin Hill and refueled, the Roaring Boys took off for Holland at 09.45 am. They would need the extra fuel they had on board in their jet tanks as the ORB described: "The Marauders were quite a bit late for rendez vous as we stayed around a bit waiting for them to show up; it was finally carried out about ten miles off the Dutch coast. One of 403 squadron pilots baled out of a Spit just off the Dutch coast of Holland." Bruce took to his logbook to express his frustration, "Marauders buggering about." With the beehive of 66 Marauders from the USAAF 9th Airforce located, the formation set course for Grilze-Rijen airfield which sits between the Dutch cities of

Breda and Tilburg, around 50 miles northwest of Eindhoven. The results of the bombing were good, with 3 Do 217s destroyed or damaged and the runway and surrounding taxi ways rendered unserviceable. It seems likely that the waiting around for the Marauders had created a potential fuel problem for the Roaring Boys in their Spitfires as Bruce wrote, "Had to leave them." Although they accompanied them to the target and part of the return leg, they had to push on for Manston or risk fuel issues. The reception for Gibby and the Roaring Boys was uncomfortable, in and around the aerodrome as Bruce drily observed after returning from the 2 hours 10-minute mission: "Flak right up my Jackson. Two bombers lost." Tommy seemed less concerned: "No Huns and only a small amount of flak. A chap bailed out of a Spit near the Dutch coast. Pretty cold."

At some point in March, Gibby was admitted to hospital. The nature of his complaint is not recorded but he may have succumbed to flu that was present amongst the wing at the time. He returned to operational flying on 18 March. His mission on that day was Ramrod 665, led by Charlie and which also included Bruce, Ross, and Bob. The mission was briefed to the pilots. They would be on station as a protective fighter umbrella to Marauders attacking No Ball targets, once again in the Amiens area. Despite Ross highlighting the "hazy cloud" conditions, the bombers were able to get a good sight of the targets, which were duly plastered to great effect. Bruce recorded: "Bags of T-bolts. Bags of vectors but no dice." The Roaring Boys were sent in several directions to intercept potential threats from enemy aircraft but without success, and at 14.00 pm after 1 hour 50 minutes, the wing landed back at Biggin Hill without incident.

On 12 April Gibby, Bob, and Ross were briefed for Ramrod 728 in which they would be escorting 12 Bostons bombing the engine sheds at Monceau-sur Sambre, near Brussels. Ross filled the gaps in the ORB about the outcome of the mission which landed back at Biggin Hill after 1 hour and 55 minutes. He observed, "Evening show. No go." The Bostons clearly had been unable to find the target area and had aborted their mission.

On 16 April, a day after relocating to their new base at RAF Tangmere Gibby and the Roaring Boys were due to fly to RAF Fairwood Common, Wales for air firing and bombing practice. For Gibby, this was going to be a day of days. The ORB takes up the story: "Although three pilots and two of the groundcrew left by rail at 10.00 hours the Air party didn't get airborne until after dinner and since the weather still was unfit for flying, they had to return. F/L W R Gibson crashed on the takeoff; his engine didn't have sufficient power to get him airborne, so he retracted the undercarriage to avoid piling up into the Airfield boundary. F/L Gibson wasn't hurt, and the A/C can be repaired in a week or two. It's the first accident 411 have had in a while and it certainly wasn't the pilot's fault. The weather continued to grow worse, so the boys left in the afternoon and went into Chichester for a while. Everyone seems fairly settled in their new homes even though they are a bit breezy." One could imagine that Gibby would have headed for a local pub in Chichester for a couple of "liveners" and to reflect on what was a narrow escape. His split-second decision to retract the undercarriage probably saved him from a catastrophic accident. From research undertaken for this book, it's apparent the Spitfire was very robust in its construction and able to withstand quite heavy forced landings, thereby increasing the pilot's chances of surviving the impact.

With engine failures and pranging aircraft a regular occurrence, Gibby wouldn't have dwelled too long on his engine failure. In fact, it would have been far worse if it had been over enemy territory or perhaps worse ditching into the freezing channel where survival times at that time of year were measured in minutes.

For Gibby and the others, the daily routine of Ramrods was now interspersed with dive bombing, following a period of instruction and training at Fairwood Common. On 25 April, Gibby, Len, Tommy, Ross, and Bob were part of a squadron strength Ramrod 791. They would be providing an umbrella of cover for a mixed formation of Bostons, Mitchells, and Marauders. The good weather enabled the takeoff to go ahead at 09.35 am, and almost on autopilot Gibby followed the routine of easing his Spitfire into formation before the short flight along the coast where the beehive of bombers attached themselves to their fighter escorts. As S/L Fowlow's voice calmly delivered his instructions, Gibby's left hand pushed the throttle forward, whilst simultaneously easing back the control column, and Spitfire MH498 responded eagerly before Gibby levelled off at the patrol altitude, which Ross noted was "18,000 feet." The patrol was soon underway and going well. No enemy activity was reported, and the dreaded flak batteries weren't in play. After reaching Amiens, S/L Fowlow changed course and the Spitfires of 411 headed for the town of Grandvilliers, which is around 15 miles to the southwest of Amiens, where the bomber force was closing in on their targets. With confirmation that the mission was completed, Gibby and the formation rolled their Spitfires north for the run to the channel. Ross later commented in his logbook, "No nothing," referring to flak and enemy aircraft, which for the Roaring Boys was a great feeling, although they all knew with the "big show" around the corner, not every day would be such a milk run.

For the operation of 27 April, Gibby, Bruce, and Dave were scheduled to dive bomb a bridge to the southeast of Coutances, which is located around 30 miles to the west of Saint Lô. From their base in Tangmere, the thrust of the Roaring Boys attacks had been shifted to the western end of Normandy. The objective was to destroy and damage transport and communications in areas where post-D Day, the Germans would be seeking to quickly reinforce their defensive forces. For Gibby and the others, their techniques and proficiency at dive bombing were still being perfected. At 12.20 pm he checked over MJ229, now complete with a 500 lb bomb. He strapped in, and after starting the Merlin engine, waited as the oil temperature rose, all the while feeling the cooling backdraft from his propeller. As the order was given to form up the 12 bombed up Spitfires made their way from the dispersal area, each just a little more conscious of obstructions, heads popping in and out of the sides of the cockpits. As Gibby increased the power MJ229 crept forward, feeling a little more sluggish than normal due to the extra weight. Soon, the formation was gaining altitude, the sea instantly visible to the south through a light mist. Everyone was away from Tangmere with no issues. Gibby and the others crossed the channel and made landfall on the Normandy coast. They were flying at around 10,000 feet. Checking his map and location from visual reference points he thought Coutances would soon be in sight amongst the lush green patchwork of Normandy fields. His headphones crackled as last-minute instructions came in. After checking his instruments, he ran through the bombing procedure, reminding himself of key things he must not forget. It would be curtains if the bomb smashed through the propeller. Watching his section commence their bombing run he fixed the bridge in his sights, throttled back and commenced his dive. The altimeter spun around as hundreds, then thousands of feet evaporated. His thumb gently rested on the bomb release button on the throttle. He pulled back and pushed hard on the button, feeling the instant change in the Spitfire as the bomb sped off downwards. To avoid flak, he peeled off eastwards towards the sea before levelling off in excess of 350 miles per hour. Any flak batteries would have a job bracketing him as he flashed across the sky and out towards the sea. He gave MJ229 some right rudder and moved the stick to the right. He was climbing again to join the formation of Spitfires above him. As soon as the final stick of bombs were delivered, they would head back home. The official account of the mission says: "unknown results. Pilots reported that four trains were observed at one end the viaduct which was the target of our first bombing show on April 23rd. This gives ample indication that the job was successful." Looking today at photographs of the stone-built rail viaduct, its columns rise high above the road and valley with each arch created from brickwork. The damage caused by the bombing could not reasonably be repaired before D Day, which was less than six weeks away, depriving the Germans of one less route to the north. As Gibby peered down he could see the Isle of Wight to port and as his height decreased, he knew he would make landfall if his engine gave out. He was now flying over Sussex and to the port side was the landmark of Chichester cathedral as the formation dropped into Tangmere's circuit ready to land. With a welcome touchdown of wheels at 13.55 pm, the taxiing Spitfire left the runway and headed back to the dispersal area. It was job done for another day.

With the arrival of May, just over five weeks remained until D Day. The pressure to smash the French railway system intensified with the good weather seeing the Roaring Boys on repeat ramrod and bombing operations, almost unimpeded by the Luftwaffe. For 1 May, Gibby would be in action twice, the second of these a No Ball mission leaving Tangmere at 17.00 pm with Bruce and Bob. The ORB summarised the operation, which lasted for 2 hours and 25 minutes: "The squadron acted as close support to 36 Mitchell bombers to targets in France. The show was carried out without incident."

It was an early start for the Roaring Boys on 7 May on a day that would be packed with operations and incident. S/L Fowlow and the intelligence team ran through the mission in great details and the pilots listened intently, some taking notes as the routes to and from the target area near Laon were plotted out on the map board. With watches synchronised and a departure time of 07.20 am, there was little time for

Gibby and the others to loiter as one by one the pilots found their assigned Spitfires. In Gibby's case, he was flying Spitfire MJ237, and in turn along the line of aircraft, pilots stood almost in gladiatorial poses on their chariots, as they moved as one into their cockpits. They were confident, this band of brothers and for Gibby with a good number of missions into his tour total, he now felt able to handle whatever the Luftwaffe could throw at him. At 07.20 am the Roaring Boys and the rest of 126 Wing took off and headed south to pick up the formation of B-17 Flying Fortresses and B-24 Mitchells. They would be bombing targets in the Laon area, situated about 30 miles northwest of Reims which included rail marshalling yards. All was going well as Gibby's eyes flicked between the formation of heavies and his fellow Roaring Boys. It was anticipated that the sight of such a large formation would draw a response from the nearby Laon-Athies aerodrome, and so it proved. As the Roaring Boys patrolled nearby to the aerodrome two FW 190s from 3/JG 26 were scrambled to meet the incoming bomber threat. It was at that moment that the Roaring Boys sprung their trap having positioned themselves in anticipation. F/L R W Orr and his wingman were in place and ready as the FW 190s left the ground and retracted their undercarriage. With little opportunity to gather any speed or altitude they were sitting ducks. As Gibby and the others watched they saw smoke streak out from Orr's Spitfire. The cannon shells ripped into each aircraft, and in turn, they rolled over onto their backs and slammed into the ground resulting in a flash and mushroom cloud of dense smoke and flames. The pilots, Oberfahnrich Erich Scheya and Obergefreiter Thomas Schwertl were both killed. The loss of an *experten* like Schwertl was significant. He was an ace with 20 kills to his namem a score he had accumulated in the 188 missions he had flown since August 1941. He was posthumously awarded the German Cross in gold. Ross, although not on the mission, commented on the action: "F/L Orr destroyed 2 FW 190s in 5 seconds. Wizzard." The ORB was triumphant: "It brought his score up to 3 dest. And one dam. And the squadron's up to sixteen. It was the first kill since January and naturally the boys were all happy." With the threat over the Germans were reluctant to sacrifice any more precious fighters and pilots, and the formation returned to base, splitting off from the bombers over the channel and landing back at Tangmere at 10.00 am. F/L Orr was swamped with praise by the other mission pilots and wider 126 Wing comrades. You could be pretty sure there was rather a large celebration that evening in Chichester's many pubs.

On 10 May, Gibby, Bruce, Dave, and Bob were up early and briefed and ready for a 07.10 am fighter sweep which would range far and deep into enemy territory. After crossing the French coast, the formation would: "sweep over Lille, Chietres, Leculet, Florennes, Laon, and Montdidier." Although some of these place names written in the ORB are incorrect (a common occurrence) there are enough that are correct to plot the route of the sweep as it patrolled southeast from the northern French city of Lille, before crossing the border into Belgium and progressing to towns in the area south of Brussels. As the formation took off and formed up for the long flight, Gibby and the others contemplated the trip. Although the Luftwaffe were less active, the risk of mechanical issues or flak was a danger along the planned route. As they reached their patrol altitude, which was likely to have been around 5-7,000 feet, the formation flew over the French coastline and encountered their first enemy opposition. As they approached Saint-Omer a trickle of flak wound its way skywards towards them before the full complement of guns began their deadly barrage. Gibby knew that as the formation comprised Spitfires only, there would be less time for the gunners to find their mark. And, as they weaved and slightly altered course this would further limit the potential for a hit. With Saint-Omer disappearing behind them, the flak died away and the remainder of the patrol was uneventful. Later in the day, there was some action for 401 Squadron against Me 109s near Saint-Omer. F/L H K Hamilton fired and saw strikes on one of the enemy before the flak caught him and he hurriedly bailed out, only to be taken prisoner. The ORB recorded later: "Column of Met reported on the Béthune road. One Me 109 seen taxying into dispersal of Monchy- Breton. Weather hazy." Monchy-Breton is located around 10 miles to the west of Lens, and was originally used by the RAF in the early years of the war. Pilots from 412 Squadron claimed one Me 109 destroyed on the ground at Monchy-Breton. They also shot down two FW 190s for the loss of two of their own Spitfires with one pilot killed and the other captured. With the sweep complete the Roaring Boys flew back over the channel, landing back at Tangmere at 09.45 am.

The 24 May was a special day for the wing as they were visited by 2nd TAF's commanding officer Air Marshal Sir Arthur "Mary" Coningham, an Australian who served in WW1 in the Royal Flying Corps. He was raised in New Zealand, hence the corruption of the nickname "Maori" to Mary! Most of the pilots met the Air Marshal who gave them a pep talk ahead of the "big show" before they returned to the business in hand. For Gibby and Dave, there was a briefing to attend for Ramrod 917 in which the Roaring Boys would join 401 Squadron in escorting a bomber force attacking Lille-Vendeville aerodrome. The ORB later commented on the mission: "Flak was meagre, light inaccurate from (unreadable). Slight haze with no cloud. All A/C returned without incident."

With the arrival of D Day, like all the Roaring Boys, Gibby was in action. His first mission on that day was at 13.05 pm, a high patrol of the whole assault area at around 3,000 to 6,000 feet due to the low cloud base. The patrol lasted 1 hour and 55 minutes and passed without incident. On D Day + 1 at 13.05 pm, Gibby and Bruce took part in another low patrol of the Eastern Assault Area which passed without incident. The Luftwaffe did appear, although for the German defenders the skies were clearly dominated by Allied aircraft sporting their black and white invasion stripes.

The weather on 10 June dawned bright and clear in Normandy as advanced units of 126 wing continued preparations for the first landing for fuel and rearming on French soil. It was an inauspicious start, a flak-damaged RAF Typhoon being the first aircraft to land on the newly completed B3 St Croix-sur-Mer before the strip was officially ready for its first customers. At 16.55 pm, Gibby, Dave, and Len taxied out from dispersal for a wing strength sweep. This was something new, they had a certain amount of apprehension about landing on French soil for the first time but were reassured by the intelligence officers that the bridgehead was secure and expanding. None of the pilots was keen to land anywhere near the front-line fighting, preferring to be a few thousand feet above the action. As the wing gathered into formation over Tangmere, Gibby felt sure the Luftwaffe would not stay quiet for long. The enemy digested the news of the landings and could begin to plan how they would counter the unfolding Allied offensive. The fighter sweep would cover the area of Evreux, Chartres, and Argentan. The now familiar triangular pattern of the sweep had Chartres as its southernmost point, with the objective of attacking enemy forces on the ground, or in the air. Both Evreux and Argentan were at the southern end of two interdiction routes and would certainly present a target-rich environment. Both routes led to the frequently mentioned strategic city of Caen. As the formation moved across France, Gibby gazed down from on high in his Spitfire and let his imagination consider for a few moments what was unfolding beneath him in the maelstrom of the land battle. As the patrol moved onwards a convoy of trucks was spotted and the Roaring Boys moved into attack. Gibby took his turn as the convoy was halted and strafed. Shortly afterward, a barge was spotted and given the same treatment with large columns of water shooting upwards as the cannon shells impacted. With the initial part of the patrol completed, Gibby lowered his Spitfires flaps, and eased back on the throttle, touching down at 18.30 pm on the mesh steel plating of B3 for his first landing on French soil. The erks marshalled the Spitfires into the hastily constructed refuel and rearmament area where, after a quick enquiry to each pilot about any technical issues, they set about topping up the fuel and reloading the guns. After a respite for the pilots to refuel themselves, and to be briefed about the upcoming mission, Gibby was soon ready to climb onboard MH498 for the evening patrol which was scheduled to leave at 20.20 pm.

On 12 June the Roaring Boys spent a whole day patrolling the beachhead. For Gibby, his day started with the first patrol at 08.05 am and continued at 18.15 pm when he, Charlie, Bob, and 9 others covered the beachhead for 1 hour and 45 minutes without incident. Despite the lack of Luftwaffe interference in the sector, there was still plenty to provide a momentary distraction as the endless snake of ships stretched out into the channel, whilst inland the blink and flash of artillery and explosions reminded the pilots of the proximity of the front line.

With life at B4 Bény sur Mer settling into some sort of routine, Gibby was desperate for the weather to improve so that they could get at the enemy and have a break from Flanders Field and its glutinous mud, a greater evil than the swirling dust bowl. On 23 June, the Roaring Boys were on action stations all day as enemy aircraft incursions were plotted heading towards the beachhead. This was not the only danger as earlier the ORB reported the dawn patrol was: "shelled by Allied A.A. from north east and south west of Bayeux." Enemy flak was one thing, but nervous Allied flak gunners fired up by the prospect of sighting the enemy was quite another and the Roaring Boys were briefed not to stray into their zone or take any chances.

Following an earlier scramble, during which no enemy was sighted, a rather unique and unusual situation happened which would have passed by without notice back in 1944 but which is of interest today in respect of

Spitfire NH341 Elizabeth and this book. The six pilots rostered, and on duty for the next operation all flew Elizabeth and it is the only occasion they all flew together with no other 411 pilots. Gibby, Bruce, Tommy, Len, Ross, and Dave were waiting nervously for the alarm to be raised. A couple of them chatted, the others snoozed, or sat quietly. It was a scene straight out of the summer days of the Battle of Britain in 1940. A phone rang. They all sat up, "Scramble!" In an instant, the pilots were running at full speed for their aircraft. The erks were already outside the cockpits, ready to pass over the straps of the Sutton harness. The Roaring Boys were proficient by now and didn't wait to complete the preflight process until they were taxiing out. Their eyes alternated between their instruments, checking temperatures and pressures were normal and the zig-zagging taxi from the dispersal area. They also didn't forget to check the sky around B4. The dread was seeing small distant pinpricks that would herald the unwelcome arrival of a formation of bandits, ready to pounce. They all knew that a few weeks before Russ Orr had shot down two FW 190s in 5 seconds shortly after they left the runway, and both pilots had no time to escape and were killed. The six lined up in two lines of three and with throttles opened their Merlins roared their approval, launching the Spitfires, along the runway and into the air. They checked the sky around them, particularly their "6." They set their throttles to climb power to gain altitude, whilst allowing the second trio to catch up. Shortly, they were in battle formation and confirming their position, they were vectored by sector control onto the last known position of the enemy fighters. The official records commented: "Another scramble without incident." Tommy wrote: "Saw some Huns - nipped into cloud. Got away." Ross noted, "Quiet. Nothing doing." Bruce later gave his version: "Vectored onto Huns. Did not make contact." After the sighting, the formation patrolled and waited in case they were called up and vectored onto the enemy. It was clear that the bandits had moved away and after 45 minutes they returned and touched down at B4.

Spitfire NH341 Elizabeth
With the start of the British offensive on Caen, Operation Epsom on 25 June, the 2nd TAF was severely limited in the support they could offer due to the poor weather. On 27 June the weather improved enough by lunchtime to allow patrols to begin again in earnest. Gibby, Charlie, and Bob would be part of the squadron strength armed reconnaissance mission which was

scheduled to takeoff at 12.55 pm. As the pilots sat in the briefing S/L Robertson and the intelligence team talked through the route and patrol area which would be south of Caen, pointing out key visual reference points as well as the latest positions of the front lines. With the battle around Caen raging, the Roaring Boys knew they would be certain to come across the enemy, both in the air and on the ground. As S/L Robertson synchronised watches there no further questions from the assembled pilots, so the meeting broke up and the pilots began to ready themselves. Gibby walked down the line of Spitfires for his allocated charge, DB – E Spitfire NH341. He saw the familiar name "Elizabeth" painted on the cowling. An erk was busying himself around the aircraft, making final checks before, seemingly without any effort skipping straight up onto the wing. Gibby followed suit and as he did so the asked the erk how she was running, "All fine sir" came the reply as he stepped into the cockpit and with his hands either side of the windscreen slid down until he felt the bump of his parachute. He reached down for the two Sutton harnesses under his seat before bringing them together with the two being held by the erk and locking them together with an immediate tug to check the connection. The erk stepped down and Gibby methodically checked through his instruments and controls, moving the control column in all directions to see that the elevator and ailerons all moved as they should. He followed this by pushing on the rudder pedals looking in his mirror to see the rudder responded. He was ready. He looked along the line of Spitfires. His time with the Roaring Boys was short but he was now classed as a proficient, combat-tested pilot, and like him, the others were eager to get going, find the enemy and attack them. He clipped on his mask and saw S/L Robertson's Spitfire let out a puff of black smoke. With a small lick of flame, its engine fired into life, followed shortly after by eleven others. Spitfire Elizabeth started first time and Gibby felt the vibration of that mighty engine throughout the cockpit and airframe. He signalled for the chocks to be removed and watched as the erk darted under his wing. He returned the thumbs up signal and with a wave settled in behind another Spitfire to taxi out to the holding point. Everything was where it should be as the first section thundered down the runway of B4 and lifted off. Gibby moved forward and began his takeoff roll. In an instant, the rear wheel was up off the ground and at 12.55 pm he was airborne. The formation was no sooner airborne than F/S D J Le Blanc radioed in that he had a mechanical malfunction and was landing back at B4.

The formation flew towards Caen at around 5,000 feet, a rumbling formation of menace and intent. The area was hot, with signs of battle on the ground and the occasional trail of bright tracer travelling towards them. Gibby could see ground traffic moving below. It would be up to the boss where they attacked. His headphones were now full of Robertson's voice as he gave the order. In turn, each section of Spitfires gently rolled into a dive. In Spitfire Elizabeth, Gibby watched the aircraft in front head downwards. He followed suit, flicking his guns and camera button to fire, subconsciously he adjusted and positioned the aircraft on the road below. No need to search for the target area, the smoke and flames were already dancing and swirling around from several vehicles. At around 1,000 feet he opened fire and the shells ripped into the vehicles below. Flames shot up as Gibby executed a sharp, high G turn to avoid the incoming fire which was increasing in severity. He was exploiting every ounce of turning potential from the aircraft. Spitfire Elizabeth climbed effortlessly away Gibby searching and scanning for incoming flak or enemy aircraft. He formed back up with his section. The attack was a success, and one section remained to circle the area as a cover for the attackers.

The Roaring Boys regrouped and moved back onto the planned track of their reconnaissance patrol. Gibby took a few deep breaths. For the Roaring Boys, the day's excitement was not done. They had company. A voice called out, "bandits" followed by their position. They'd been bounced, but the training kicked in as the unmistakable shape of butcher birds came flashing down towards them. As pairs of Spitfires peeled away the sky was turned into a melee of aircraft, all flying and fighting to survive. Although not recorded it's likely that Gibby would have got onto the tail of one of the attackers, and maybe he had one on his tail too. Loud Canadian voices occasionally filled Gibby's ears with warnings and curses, "Red 1 behind you." Gibby attention was caught by a FW 190 which fell into a steep dive, the only trace of its presence being a trail of thickening, white smoky glycol. The German pilot was finished, and no pilot could ever recover from that steep a dive. Another FW 190 trailed smoke and dived away with a Spitfire glued to its tail. In a moment it was over, Gibby gathered himself, and conscious of any remaining danger heard himself breathing hard, with sweat gently running from under his flying helmet. S/L Robertson's radio calls to F/O P Wallace were met with silence, confirming that one of their number was now missing. No training flights could ever prepare the pilots for a proper dog fight. Their senses were at their maximum during the action, but in the aftermath, Gibby was left feeling drained of energy as the adrenalin dissipated. In a short while the formation let down into B4's circuit, and to Gibby the previous 1 hour and 15 minutes seemed like another, almost surreal world. One minute he had been fighting for his life in the heat and hell of combat, and the next he was dropping the flaps, and undercarriage on Spitfire Elizabeth as if returning from a pleasurable Sunday afternoon bimble around the countryside. He guided Elizabeth in and lined up finals preparing for the welcome reception from B4's noisy steel track runway. The Roaring Boys taxied in and were soon gathered for the debriefing. The ORB reported on what had been a successful mission: "Ten Met attacked resulting in six Flamers, 1 Smoker and 2 Damaged. One tank was left burning and another left smoking. Later encountered 15 plus FW 190s. S/L Robertson destroyed one; F/L Johnson damaged two and W/O Kerr damaged another one. F/O P Wallace disappeared into clouds and has not been seen or heard from since." It later transpired that Wallace had been shot down and bailed out, returning safely to B4 on the same day with his membership of the Caterpillar Club assured.

By early July, the wing was operating its rotation of continuous patrols comprising four Spitfires. On 2 July Gibby was flying number 2 to Charlie with Dave and F/O R W Hogg making up the quartet. They were scheduled to leave B4 at 15.45 pm with the ORB recording a patrol of, "William and Easy areas." The William sector proved uneventful but Easy sector control picked up the presence of "15 plus FW 190s five miles east of Caen. They were engaged but no claims were made." The extent of the engagement is not recorded but any combat was not prolonged otherwise official claims from both sides would have probably followed. The odds were also not in the Roaring Boys favour on this occasion, so it was likely that they withdrew for the fight.

The next day at 4.45 am Gibby was awoken by one of the duty officers. He had drawn the early shift and as he peered out at the murkiness, he wondered how the patrol would go with a thick layer of fog hugging the Normandy countryside. He got up, washed, shaved and dressed, tucking his silk scarf in around his neck before walking over to the briefing. The erks were already busying themselves around the squadron's Spitfires, with one being fed a final belt of machine gun bullets. He sat down and was joined in the intelligence briefing by Dave, Bruce, Tommy, Len, Bob, and a further six pilots. The intelligence boys and S/L Robertson briefed them as to the latest state of the front lines and the disposition of enemy forces on the ground and in the air. The spectre of coming across the elusive Luftwaffe ace Hauptmann Walter Matoni of 5/JG 26 grabbed everyone's attention. As mentioned on several occasions in this book, he was a well-known and sought-after adversary. Matoni was a deadly foe, and he had struck again only three days before claiming his 24th kill, a Spitfire. As the pilots looked out through the fog, it was 05.45 am as their wheels left the planking of B4. Shortly after they burst through the murkiness into the bright sunshine and the extent of the carpet of fog became apparent. As they peered down, they quickly recognised the position of the front as flashes of momentary intense light broke through. The hot summer sun was making short work of the fog and mist and as if on cue as they moved between Villers Bocage and Aunay sur Odon, around 20 miles to the south west of Caen the flak batteries began their day's work sending up intense, accurate tracer fire. The formation changed course repeatedly, and with a certain amount of weaving were able to prevent the guns from bracketing their formation, or any individual. At 07.00 am, with no further incidents or contacts the patrol landed back at B4, to debrief and take some time out before their next mission of the day.

By this stage of the invasion, the 2nd TAF was operating with maximum efficiency which was morale-sapping for the Luftwaffe. On 7 July, the Roaring Boys were kept on defensive readiness, as the enemy made their presence felt again. At 11.45 am, the call to scramble was made and alarms sounded all over B4. Soon the air was filled with Merlins as Gibby, Tommy, Bruce, Len, Dave, and F/L C D Cross taxied quickly across B4 and lifted off. They were vectored by control onto to the last known position of the fighters. The ORB later recorded they tried: "to locate and engage Huns that 401 Squadron left." The action by 401 Squadron had destroyed 2 Me 109s and an FW 190. Bruce commented in his logbook: "chased Huns but could not close." Tommy noted the action too: "Turfed after 10+ 190s and 109s in Caen area. Saw 2 109s heading for Paris flat out for Der Fuhrer. No catch. No Joy!" With no further excitement, it appeared that after suffering a mauling from the 401 boys the Luftwaffe had retreated, and so the formation turned back for base and landed at 12.15 pm.

The 14 July was a day of heavy flight activity with the Roaring Boys putting up 14 defensive patrols of the Low Eastern Sector, the majority of which were largely uneventful for Gibby, but not for Tommy and Len as described in their chapters. Gibby was in action for hour-long patrols three times during the day; at 14.35 pm with Dave and C D Cross before taking his favoured Spitfire NH196 up again at 17.00 pm. Finally, at 19.40 pm, he flew in a 3-ship patrol led by S/L Robertson. NH196 would later down a Me 109 on 12 August in the hands of F/L H A Crawford.

On 18 July, the battle for Caen took another decisive step with the launch of Operation Goodwood by British and Canadian forces, the attempted encirclement of the city. This operation followed the raid by 1,000 RAF Lancasters on the city, which, sadly amongst the devastation, saw accidental casualties amongst Canadian forces. In the air, their Canadian brothers were planning another day of defensive patrols over the battle area. It was essential that an instant response was available to counter any incursion by the enemy that could wreak havoc on the congested land forces below. Gibby's patrol took to the skies at 17.25 pm and was led by S/L Robertson and A Flight Commander Bob. The other 8 Spitfires included Tommy and Len. The relative calm of the patrol in the air belied the carnage for the soldiers engaged in battle on the ground as the patrol returned to B4 after an uneventful 1 hour and 15 minutes.

The 27 July turned out to be a busy day for 126 Wing. Gibby was briefed and ready for his 09.15 am armed reconnaissance mission which would be led by S/L Robertson. The plan was to patrol Yvetot, which is located around 20 miles northwest of Rouen, as well as the Rouen area itself. Tommy and Len joined Gibby and 9 others. At precisely 09.15 am the first sections of the Roaring Boys powered their Spitfires across the flat expansive runway of B4 and into the sky, forming up shortly after. Gibby throttled up Spitfire NH196 and gained altitude, checking around as he did so for any potential bounce by the enemy. At around 5,000 feet the patrol was ready to move off towards Rouen. Everything in NH196 was green for go and Gibby settled down. Shortly, the authoritative voice of S/L Robertson spoke to the formation: "Yellow and red sections. Prepare to attack." Gibby checked his harnesses and tightened them a fraction more, his gun button was on and all the Spitfire's systems were operating normally. He followed S/L Robertson into a dive and watched the CO's Spitfire as it sent spears of cannon fire down onto the vehicles below, followed by thin trails of white vapour from the wings as Robertson pulled the Spitfire up hard and broke to port. Gibby lined up and selected his targets and pressed home his attack and in a split second the convoy was raked again with devastating fire. He broke to starboard and flew at treetop height, weaving and then powering upwards and away from the incoming light flak. A few 500 lb bombs were dropped and Gibby caught sight of the developing bloom of a giant fireball and black mushroom cloud pushing upwards. The transports had taken a real pounding and with most of the formation, aside from the covering section who were acting as top cover, low on ammunition, S/L Robertson called a return to base, where Gibby settled NH196's wheels back at B4 at 10.30 am. After the scores were added up and a debrief held, the ORB reported the damage done: "Two APV flamers. 6 Met flamers, 3 smokers and 5 damaged scored. Light flak east of Rouen."

The pattern of armed reconnaissance missions continued unabated for the remaining days of July. On the 30th day of that month, F/L R K Hayward led the squadron. He would be replacing the popular S/L G D Robertson who had just completed his second tour of operations. He briefed the pilots early and gave them a start time of 09.25 am. They had time for a quick breakfast and to contemplate the upcoming mission. The 411 boys would fly in squadron strength behind their new leader. Gibby was joined by seasoned pilots including Bob and Ross. The ORB describes the patrol area as: "Pont L'Eveque, Lisieux, Bernay, L'Aigle, and Falaise." With such an expanse of territory to patrol the Roaring Boys would be looking for targets and fully expected to find them to keep up their impressive scoring record. Shortly after leaving B4 the formation began to execute the pattern of its reconnaissance mission, happening upon several vehicles of which the ORB recorded, "Two flamers, 3 smokers scored." There was a cost to attacking at such low altitudes and on this mission F/O H W Kramer's luck ran out. Gibby and the others heard him report in that he was hit. Ross noted, "Lost F/L Kramer." The ORB reported some additional information: "F/O H W Kramer reported after attacking transport at 400 feet that his engine had packed up. Nothing further has been heard from him." Kramer managed to successfully crash land Spitfire MK676 near Fauguernon, around 5 miles northeast of Lisieux, and avoid being captured. It was still a bad feeling to lose a comrade and landing back at B4 at 10.40 am the pilots talked through the unfolding drama, hoping Kramer had got his aircraft down and survived the impact.

All around the Caen area Allied armour and infantry were on the move and against this backdrop, Gibby's bombing and armed reconnaissance mission of 31 July can be put into context. In a few days, time on 8 August Operation Totalize would begin. The plan was for II Canadian Corps to break through the German defences south of Caen, on the eastern flank of the Allied positions and drive south. In advance of this mission, the Roaring Boys would play their part by bombing a forest near Bretteville-sur-Laize, which was on high ground and therefore of strategic importance i.e. both sides wanted to occupy it. Intelligence sources had identified an ammunition dump, and this was to be the main target. If it could be destroyed, then it would deprive the enemy of vital munitions with which to defend against the Canadians armoured thrust.

At 16.25 pm led by S/L R K Hayward, now shown in official documents with his DFC, Gibby, Bob, and 9 other Roaring Boys departed B4, for the short flight to Bretteville. It's not known which of the 4 Spitfires carried the bombs, but the ORB later reported a successful mission: "Two hits in the target area and two near misses. Two flamers and four damaged Met also scored." With their ammunition nearly expended the Roaring Boys returned to base landing after 50 minutes flying.

In the August heat, Gibby added to his tally of operational flying and progress towards completion of his tour time. On 3 August he joined Len and Tommy for a squadron strength armed reconnaissance which would cover Rennes, Châteaubriant, La Flèche, and Alençon. At the furthest point south, La Flèche, the Roaring Boys would be over 120 miles south of Caen, and therefore well behind enemy lines. The prospect of this and the fact that they would be carrying drop tanks of fuel did little to settle their nerves. Ditching here would mean no quick hop back to find Allied lines. The mission objective was to assess the enemy's dispositions south of Le Mans and disrupt their general traffic ahead of the General Patton's 3rd Army move south towards Le Mans. The destruction of Wehrmacht machinery and equipment was also an important part of the operation.

At 12.45 pm S/L Hayward led the formation out and soon after the Spitfires were thundering down the runway, arranging themselves into their battle formation and heading south. Enemy transports were less fearful of air attack the further south they travelled. Thus, it didn't take long for the Roaring Boys to pinpoint a target rich area which was duly raked with cannon and machine gun fire. The ORB provided the official score for the attack: "6 Met flamers, (four of which held troops) and 1 damaged." Tommy added to his own scorecard during the mission. He wrote that he: "destroyed 1 truck and 1 bus." It was a positive and successful attack and despite some light return fire, none of the attackers were hit. After 1 hour 50 minutes the welcome sight of B4 came into view. Gibby breathed a sigh of relief, they had made it and the stress of combat began to ebb away. As he approached the circuit the vast expanse of B4 was laid out before him, the ammunition storage area alone was vast, with living quarters, an engineering area as well the operational support near the runways, B4 resembled a small town. The gentle kiss of his wheels touching down kicked up the usual swirling clouds of dust and was followed by a short taxi into dispersal. There he found the welcome committee of erks, some resplendent in anti-dust goggles, ready to get to work on his aircraft

As August progressed the weather maintained its intent of summer heat interspersed with days of heavy rain which played havoc with the flying schedules. On some days flying was completely abandoned and 411 pilots and crews mooched around not quite knowing what to do with themselves. When the weather allowed, Gibby and the Roaring Boys kept up their defensive and offensive patrolling. From 6 August, the pilots were sent in turn on a week's "R&R," which is short for "rest and relaxation." They had all earned the downtime, and although the understanding of mental health in the military was less developed than in modern times, lessons on the effects of prolonged exposure to combat stress had been learned from WW1.

The ORB shows us Gibby's last day of operational flying was on 9 August, from B18 Cristot where they had moved to the day before. He would have known from his logbook that he was nearly 'tour complete' and a few extra nerves kicked in. A quiet day's patrolling without too much enemy activity would be just the ticket. He was highly experienced and knew that each pilot could have another man's life in his hands if the enemy were engaged, so concentration was key along with a high state of readiness to meet any threat that should materialise.

At 07.45 am, he joined up with Bob for a 6-ship patrol which would cover an area of the front line from Vire to Falaise. Vire is located around 30 miles to the south west of Caen. In the first mission, 2 of the 6 Spitfires returned early with engine malfunctions and by 08.55 am Gibby, Bob, and the others were back in the dispersal area, and then straight into intelligence to debrief. The latest, weather and information about the front and known friendly and enemy forces in the area was shared in preparation for his later patrols. He, Bob and 2 others were airborne again at 10.45 am, landing back at B18 at midday. At 18.40 pm, Gibby walked over to Spitfire MK721 accompanied by Bob who would lead the patrol. They were joined by P/O J T Olsen and F/O B Eskow. Bob wished him good luck and stepped away towards his own Spitfire. For Gibby, this represented a situation of mixed emotions. Many of the guys from October 1943 at Biggin Hill were now posted out of the squadron. There were lots of fresh young faces around the airfield. He was the old guard and now his time was just about up. He pulled on his flying helmet for the last time, plugged in the leads and reached down for the black leather gloves in his lap. They were worn in and showed the wear and tear of the missions he had flown. With a small puff of smoke, MK721 fired up and was soon running ready. He looked over at Bob who nodded, and they moved off, soon filling the air with the guttural roar of their Merlin engines. As they reached the patrol area below their fellow Canadians and British divisions were pushing south as part of Operation Totalize. It was important to cover the front to search for incursions by enemy aircraft, but also to observe and gather any useful intelligence, particularly on large scale troop or armoured vehicle movements. The patrol was uneventful and shortly before 20.00 pm, Gibby dropped the flaps on his Spitfire and listened for the mechanical whirr of the undercarriage coming down and locking in place. He checked his green lights were on, his undercarriage was down and secure, and made a curved approach to the runway, lining up and touching down on B18's mesh tracking, the rhythmic and welcome hum of a "greased on" landing. As he completed the shutdown of his Spitfire, he allowed himself a momentary glance around the cockpit. He hopped out of the cockpit and down from the wing, shook hands with his erk and made for the debrief with his old comrade Bob.

The ORB recorded on 23 August: "F/L WR Gibson was posted on completion of his operational tour. J.3743 W R Gibson posted "R" depot wef 1.9.44." Gibby's war was finished, and he had survived. What became of Gibby Gibson's post-war life is not currently known, but like the other Roaring Boys, he fully deserves our respect and admiration for the part he played in this momentous period of the war.

CHAPTER EIGHT

LEN HARRISON

Norman Leonard Harrison, hereafter known as Len, was also frequently referred to in photos as Len "Fat" Harrison. His slim build means the origin of his nickname "Fat" will remain a mystery as despite an extensive search I have been unable to find any of his family or friends. Len's origins were in Toronto and in 1941 he enrolled into the RCAF. His initial training took place at No 9 SFTS, RCAF Summerside, Prince Edward Island on course 39 which ran from 25 September 1941 to 19 December 1941. Len Harrison, service number J/18963, completed his flight training and in 1942 he was posted to England. The 411 Squadron ORB records his arrival at RAF Redhill, Surrey as one of several pilots: "reporting in for flying duties on 5 May 1943 Sgt. N L Harrison of Toronto." Charlie and Bruce were already stationed at Redhill with 411 Squadron. On 11 May another native of Toronto, Tommy Wheler would report into 411 and he and Len would have an immediate common connection.

After an intense period of advanced flight training and work ups, involving formation flying, mock combat, and local area familiarisation, Len was ready for his first combat mission. It was time for a calm head, which was easier said than done as he was on standby to scramble in case of any incursion by enemy aircraft. He may have been praying that the phone wouldn't ring, but it did. The alarm was sounded, and pilots and crew shot in all directions. Len raced to his allocated Spitfire. Soon all 6 Spitfires were turning and burning, taxiing out and into the air. Len formed up with the others and listened intently as sector control gave them the course to steer and last known altitude and direction of the incoming enemy. He watched as the direction indicator span round to the course heading. He composed himself and studied all the instruments carefully. Everything was in the green and looked normal, as he set his mind to the job of scanning the sky for any Luftwaffe aircraft. Len knew he was inexperienced, but he had been well trained and drilled and knew what his priority was, stick close to the more experienced pilots. The squadron ORB noted: "Red, yellow and white sections ordered to scramble and then ordered to do a patrol. Sections on their return reported no enemy encountered." At 22.20 am, Len approached the circuit of RAF Redhill and looked down at the wide-open green aerodrome which stood out against the surrounding patchwork of small fields with their mixed hedge borders. After executing a good landing, he taxied in with his first mission completed. After a debrief with the wing intelligence boys he ran through each aspect of the flight with this section commander, noting any areas to improve. He was now a Spitfire fighter pilot and Roaring Boy. The next mission would be that bit easier, albeit he hadn't come under fire or seen the "whites of the enemy's eyes."

On the 26 May, Tommy joined Len to take their Spitfire Mark VBs on an evening flight patrol over the Horsham area of Sussex. They were off at 20.55 pm and back an hour later with nothing to report, but with valuable experience for the fights to come and an opportunity to test their Spitfires handling, knowing that with this practice they would be better placed when they in combat with the enemy. The early days of June 1943 were spent on an air to air firing exercise at RAF Martlesham Heath. Marksmanship on the towing drones was vital and the Roaring Boys eagerly developed their deflection shooting technique. The famous fighter pilot F/L George "Buzz" Beurling, of 412 Squadron was known to be a crack shot and thought by many to be one of the war's greatest exponents of deflection shooting, a skill he developed by using a combination of obsessional levels of practice and "one in a million" eyesight.

On 13 June, Len was once again engaged in formation flying and cine gun camera exercises and over the coming days, there was no letup in the practice. At 10.15 am he took part in a 4 Spitfire coastal patrol. The area covered was Eastbourne to Hastings and the objective was the tricky task of intercepting small sections of enemy fighters, the tip and run raiders intent on attacking south coast towns with bombs and machine guns before hightailing it back to France. After 1 hour 30 minutes, they returned to base having reported nothing of interest. Some light relief came in the evening on this day as it was the second anniversary of the squadron's formation and all personnel attended a celebratory party and dinner in the Airmen's Mess Hall.

Len was looking forward to his first ramrod mission which duly arrived on 24 June, when he and Charlie were part of a squadron escort to 12 Lockheed Ventura bombers. Ramrod 102 was scheduled to bomb Yainville power station which was situated on the river Seine, around 10 miles to the west of Rouen. At 16.45 pm Len throttled up his Spitfire and was soon airborne with his section. They gained altitude over the Surrey countryside, and as Len looked north he could see the London skyline. After a short flight to the south coast, he listened as sector control confirmed the position of the Venturas at "Angels 15." The boxes of bombers were in tow and the Roaring Boys guided their charges over the channel. As they approached the French coast and enemy territory the fear and nerves increased dramatically. Yainville was close to the city of Rouen and they expected the Luftwaffe air defences to detect their presence. Through his R/T, the word was spread that a Ventura had mechanical trouble. He looked across as it slowly dropped away from the formation and headed back across the sea to England. In the cockpit of his Spitfire, Len noted his position. If trouble started and he became separated he had already mapped out in his mind the return leg to the safety of England. Meanwhile, a reminder to watch for fighters drifted into his headset. The opening of bomb doors signalled that the target was close and soon with some minor weaving and course adjustments the bombs began to tumble out from each Ventura, followed shortly by impacts and shock waves as they exploded thousands of feet below. The ORB later gave an assessment of the bombing: "11 made bomb hits on or very close to powerhouse in the river and adjoining field. No enemy aircraft were observed."

The return leg, although at a faster pace, left his Spitfire, a thoroughbred straining at the leash. The formation crossed the English coast and the Roaring Boys released the Venturas back to their base. At 18.15 pm, Len touched down at Redhill. What he and the others weren't to know was that they passed over the territory of Jagdfliegerführer 3 and 1/JG 2. In fact, JG 26 had been scrambled to intercept them but was held in reserve and did not contact 411, or their bombers.

For his mission of 15 July, Len would be part of Ramrod 142 with Tommy and Charlie. They set out in the warm afternoon sunshine at 15.55 pm where on the south coast they made the rendezvous with 12 Boston bombers from 107 squadron over Rye at 11,000 feet. The other squadrons in 126 Airfield, 401 and 412 Squadrons, along with 6 other squadrons joined up with the whole formation being led by S/L "Jeep"

Neal as they flew across the channel to bomb Poix aerodrome. The landfall point was Bayeux, but halfway across the channel the call went out, "Bandits!" The Luftwaffe was intent on breaking up this raid and II/JG 26 tore into the escorting fighters. As drilled Len held formation, his eyes darted all over the sky as he told himself to stay calm and take a methodical approach. He watched the boss, S/L Semple and the more experienced pilots across the three squadrons launch into the attackers. His R/T was active with the sounds of men fighting for their lives as aircraft dived and climbed all around the sky. It was difficult to tell friend from foe. Another RAF squadron 602, lost 4 Spitfires in the skirmish but the boss, S/L Semple later claimed a damaged FW 190. Amongst the Luftwaffe claimants was Leutnant Walter Matoni of 5/JG 26, a constant figure throughout this book and a well-known thorn in the side of Allied pilots in the lead up to D Day and beyond. Things quietened down and Len put out of his mind the men who had just been lost. He had seen several aircraft, including a Boston roll over into a vertical dive, before smashing into the sea. The ORB later reported the attack: "The escorts were bounced by 20 to 25 FW 190s the enemy getting strikes on three aircraft of 401 Squadron. In addition to S/L Semple F/L N A Keene DFC, F/O A M Barber and F/O D R Matheson fired bursts but have not claimed any strikes on enemy aircraft." The reality of air combat was brutal and visceral. Like all men who experienced combat, the mixture of terror and exhilaration would stay with him for the rest of his life. As he flew onwards in his Spitfire, he focussed on his job. The mission was still on despite the attack and they were getting close to the target at Poix aerodrome, which was located around 15 miles west-southwest of Amiens. Yellow section of the Roaring Boys left the formation to escort a damaged bomber back to Rye. It made a wheels-up landing at Eastchurch. Len was now about to get his first taste of flak. A mix of heavy and light flak headed up towards them, the silent black balls of cotton wool developing all around the extended formation looked innocuous enough as did the tracer fire. The Spitfires zigzagged around the sky, as the visibility for the flak gunners was unlimited. The return journey saw more flak come their way but as they made the coast Len was relieved to see it abate, and the rest of the flight was uneventful. The Roaring Boys touched down at Redhill at 17.30 pm where there was much to discuss. It had been an action-packed sortie and this time the enemy had left their mark. Tommy later wrote his own account: "Bostons pranged aerodrome. FW

190s gave us a go, two of them got in shots hitting near Boston. S/Ldr Semple F/O Barber & F/O Matheson had a go at them. Yellow section escorted lame duck home."

Len was keen to get in as much flying practice as possible. He knew hours in the air at the controls of a Spitfire would help him greatly when the crunch came, as it surely would someday. At 20.10 pm, on the day of the Poix aerodrome raid, he accompanied P/O J C McDougall on a coastal patrol off Beachy Head, returning at 21.25 pm with no enemy aircraft seen. It is poignant to read about patrols like this knowing that during my own flights along the same route I have gazed down on scenery that has changed little since Roaring Boys like Len passed that way.

The month of August and the endless round of formation, tail chases and cine gun camera practice continued. There was also a move for Len and 411 on 6 August to RAF Staplehurst where he and Tommy shared accommodation in the Sergeants mess tent line which was part of No 126 Airfield. They would soon be receiving welcomed supplies from the local farmers with fresh eggs high on the list of their favourite foods, and much preferred over the powdered egg in their rations.

On 30 August Len was rostered with Bruce and Charlie to fly on a wing strength Ramrod, S-14 which would see 33 fighter squadrons support Mitchells, Venturas, Marauders and Bostons on a bombing mission to what was listed as an ammunition dump in La forêt d'Eperlecques, near Saint-Omer. In fact, it was the raid was targeting the secret Blockhaus d'Eperlecques V weapons complex. The operation was scheduled to commence at 18.35 pm and the Roaring Boys would be led by S/L Semple. As Len throttled up Spitfire BL347 she responded, climbing up through the dense cloud into bright blue sky until they levelled off at 12,000 feet over Herne Bay, where the 36 Marauders from the USAAF's Mighty Eighth quickly came into view. All was on track, and in his cockpit, Len busied himself with instrument checks and some map reading. With such a huge formation and layers of fighters acting as a protective screen around the boxes of bombers, Len was confident that they had the firepower to see off any enemy threat that materialised.

S/L Semple's spoke to the squadron and alerted the Roaring Boys that they were now over enemy territory, as they crossed the coast between Calais and Gravelines. The flak batteries opened fire and Len moved his Spitfire from side to side and hoped he wouldn't be hit as the intensity increased. It was very heavy and accurate with 14 of the Marauders receiving some damage. Len looked on as the bomb doors of the Marauders opened and a minute later at 18.55 pm, the bombs were disgorged from the aircraft. They dropped away in straight lines towards the forest below followed by shock waves and smoke which was soon blanketing target area, on top of the already hazy conditions. From Len's vantage point the bombing looked accurate, later confirmed by the Mighty Eighth who reported that 33 of the Marauders hit the target. Len was alerted by the sudden announcement that 20 bandits had been spotted circling the area. He was ready, with his gun button flicked to fire, tugging his harness to be sure he was welded to his seat and was at one with his Spitfire. The bandits kept their distance as the odds for a hit and run attack looked unfavourable with 33 fighter squadrons sweeping the area. Len and the others were on the home run as they crossed the French coast again at 19.05 pm, landing back at Staplehurst at 19.25 pm. Everyone in the wing returned safely and with the debrief complete the boys set off for The Hare and Hounds pub for a well-earned pint of local Kent beer.

The weather in the early days of September continued to be excellent for flying and ideal for endless games of volleyball, amongst the orchards of the "Garden of England." The conditions meant missions could be scheduled in by the planners to maintain the pressure on the Germans. As part of Operation Crossbow, the campaign against the V1 and V2 sites, Len was scheduled to fly on Ramrod S.27. The Roaring Boys would be part of a wing strength operation escorting 24 Mitchells who were returning to the V weapons complex at La forêt d'Eperlecques. As Len taxied out across the flat grass of RAF Staplehurst, surrounded by its trees and orchards he gently worked his rudder pedals and throttle to weave Spitfire BL780 into takeoff position. S/L Semple led the 411 boys who lined up 3 abreast, releasing their steeds along the runway at 12.50 pm. As they circled the base Len could look over and see 127 Airfield nearby RAF Lashenden, where Spitfire Elizabeth now spends her summer days.

The rendezvous with the Mitchells occurred at Angels 12 at 13.05 pm over North Foreland. Within 15 minutes they were crossing into occupied France near Gravelines. Len looked at the cloud base which was later recorded as "8/10 cloud condition." By 13.23 pm the Mitchells were unloading their deadly cargo which streaked through the thick cloud cover. The incoming drone of so many aircraft alerted the flak crews who sent up a heavy protective barrage. Once through this, the return leg saw a small amount of flak emanating from the Calais area. The Luftwaffe was present but chose to keep their distance, giving the formation a relatively comfortable return to base, with everyone reported as landing safely at 13.45 pm.

After a period of heavy rain that saw the pilots confined to their tents, Staplehurst was flooded and unserviceable for flying. The sun finally broke through and was still of sufficient strength to dry up the standing water. This allowed Len to take part in a Rodeo operation to France, with 401 and 412 Squadrons. The wing was scheduled to leave the base at 17.50 pm. The formation was in position and climbed to 11,000 feet before making the short flight across the channel. They reached landfall at Le Touquet before then settling out at 15,000 feet for the patrol. From here, the sweep moved around 40 miles southeast to Doullens where flak was intense and accurate, before completing the final leg in a westerly direction for the flight to Abbeville. Once again, the German flak defences also put up quite a showing. Len hunkered down in his cockpit as he heard over the R/T the unwelcome notification from W/C Dal Russel and P/O Barber that they both received hits from flak despite the overcast conditions. Len was now dry in the mouth as the flak explosions continued all around them. He was praying they would all get through and that lady luck was on his side. As the wing made for the return leg across the channel the flak petered out. The patchwork of Kent's farmland was soon in view, and they throttled back for the steady descent into RAF Staplehurst which was reached at 19.00 pm. Both Russel and Barber were able to fly on and nurse their flak-damaged aircraft back to base.

The 15 September is now commemorated as Battle of Britain day when in 1940 the Luftwaffe launched their pivotal offensive, in which they believed they would destroy the RAF. In fact, this day was an overwhelming defeat for the Luftwaffe. On this day Len and Tommy's ramrod mission accompanying 72 Marauders to Lille-Nord aerodrome was aborted at North Foreland. No specific reason was noted but the weather in the target area may have been a factor and Len and the Roaring Boys returned to base after 40 minutes flying.

The target for Len and Bruce at 17.20 pm on 18 September was once again the marshalling yards at Rouen. The attackers for Ramrod 240 would be in the form of 18 Marauders. At 17.20 pm the squadron was airborne and soon communicating with the Marauders. They formed up over Hastings at 12,000 feet moving quickly across the channel. The ORB described how the formation was forced to turn back over France due to the inclement weather. By 18.20 pm Len let down the undercarriage on Spitfire BL727 for what the ORB described as, "an abortive do."

On 19 September, Len was ready mid-morning for Ramrod 232 where he and Bruce would head once again for Lille-Nord aerodrome with 72 Marauders from the Mighty Eighth. Len listened intently as Doug Matheson, who would lead the Roaring Boys described the operational plan, the insertion and extraction routes. No 126 wing would be joined by 306 squadron. At 10.45 am, Len turned onto the runway and commenced his takeoff roll in Spitfire RL726. He retracted the undercarriage, listening and watching for any signs of mechanical failure. It was so far so good as he climbed high into the sky above Kent. The wing orbited above Ashford, waiting for the bombers, in the distance Len picked up the glint off one of the Marauders glass screens. They moved off towards Deal and flew over the channel in unpromising weather conditions. As they moved inland it was soon clear around 5 miles from the target that the mission would have to be aborted. W/C Russel ordered Fatland leader (F/L Doug Matheson) to turn the bombers around. The first boxes in the formation containing 36 Marauders turned to starboard, then the formation split into two and 18 bombers continued to the target, as they were likely to be using radar controlled blind bombing technology which did not require sight of the target. It is interesting to note the ORB's use of the term "Fatland" leader, which described 411 Squadron. In photos from the time Len is often referred to as "Fat" Harrison. Len was flying Red 2 to Doug Matheson as Fatland leader, Red 1, which could be connected, but this is pure speculation. As the second group made up of 36 bombers turned for home the enemy seized their opportunity to attack. Blue and yellow sections of the Roaring Boys were engaged as they accompanied the first boxes containing 18 bombers. The attacking force comprised 6 FW 190s, and in the ensuing dog fight, F/O Vic Haw was shot down near Brugge by Unteroffizier Wiegand of 8/JG 26, who claimed the Spitfire after a long chase. Upon landing Vic Haw became a prisoner of war. Meanwhile, Len was glued to the side and rear of Matheson as their bombers hit the target with unknown results. Their R/T informed them this time the enemy was sticking around to fight. A substantial force of fighters had been scrambled to deal with them. As the 18 bombers turned to starboard heavy and intense flak peppered the formation. Len could see hits going in the area around the bombers. As they headed out Red section knew the fighters could be waiting. Multiple dots on the horizon gave them an uneasy feeling, and sure enough, with destructive intent enemy fighters dived towards the bombers. Doug Matheson called out "Red section Tally ho." Matheson and Len broke into the attack. Matheson fired a burst; Len saw the rounds arc towards the enemy aircraft which flick rolled down and away. He asked his Spitfire for maximum power as they duked it out with the force of fighters, some of which flew head-on, diverting away at the very last second. He kept tight to Red 1 and saw Matheson's head turn around to check to see he was there on his wing. The enemy had passed through the screen of Spitfires to the boxes of bombers, some of which were taking punishment. As they continued north, and regrouped Red section were intact and had seen off the attackers who were now heading back to their bases around Lille. Len and Doug Matheson knew their job was to stay and protect the bombers, so they gave up any thoughts of chasing down the attackers. As Len settled himself, the excitement wasn't over as the parting gift from the enemy stationed near Dunkirk was to send up a barrage of highly accurate flak. He was incredibly hot in the cockpit and sweating due to the fear and adrenalin. He had never known real fear like this as he engaged in first real scrap with the Luftwaffe. His breathing eased. He was ready to get back to the safety of their base. As he processed what had happened in his mind it was tinged with disappointment that he didn't get to fire on the enemy. Len also thought about Vic Haw. It was a sharp introduction to the perils of his role as a Spitfire pilot. He knew Vic had caught it and was lost, hopefully, he managed to bail out or crash land. Meanwhile, around 10 bombers had sustained damage and their crews were nursing the aircraft back. Frantic measures were underway on some to keep single engines running whilst others put out fires on board. Finally, over southern England, the bombers departed for their bases and Len brought his Spitfire into land, the welcome relief of 3 wheels touching down on terra firma once more. As he taxied in and shut down, he rested his head against the seat and closed his eyes. He had survived and was only alone with his thoughts for only a few seconds before an eager erk appeared next to his cockpit, ready to get to work on his plane. After a quick conversation, he hopped onto the open door and down off the wing, pulling his black flying gloves off. He felt the cool air on his hands as he ruffled them through his hair. He stopped by Doug Matheson's aircraft and they talked over the action, the hand movements and whirling arms told any observer these pilots had seen battle. The Roaring Boys assembled, and inquiries were made about Vic Haw's fate as the intelligence boys started the debrief. No claim was made by Doug Matheson on the enemy fighter he shot at.

The start of October saw Len and the others take part in the escape and evasion exercises, lessons learned that were vital in the event of landing in enemy territory. On 3 October, Len took part in Ramrod 258 which would see squadrons of Bostons bombing power stations, including Orleans which was to be attacked by 12 Bostons from 107 squadron, RAF. At 13.00 pm the wing assembled to be briefed, lifting off at 13.45 pm for a point 10 miles north of Beauvais, which is around 60 miles north of Paris, where they were due to link up with the Bostons from 107 squadron. As the Roaring Boys pushed south towards the rendezvous point S/L Ormston spoke over the R/T. There was no sign of the bombers at the set time of 14.27 pm so they would orbit the area. Len scanned the horizon, hopeful that they would soon appear. No one was keen to stay orbiting the area for too long as the risks of a bounce by the enemy increased immeasurably. The plan was not working out, and much to everyone's relief Ormston gave the order to turn back. The boys from 412 Falcon squadron did engage the enemy on the return leg and destroyed 2 FW 190s. At 15.10 pm Len touched down safely at Staplehurst where an investigation was held as to the whereabouts of the missing Bostons.

The weather was now turning, and cloud would hamper several of the planned operations that Len took part in, including Ramrod 264 where he and the Roaring Boys accompanied 72 Marauders to Lille-Vendeville aerodrome, but after crossing the French coast at Hardelot the mission was abandoned due to haze and thick cloud. On 19 October the ORB noted that Len was sent on a 4-day Rolls Royce Merlin engine handling course at their factory in Derby. It was also the first time he was mentioned with his new rank of warrant officer.

On 10 November Len was ready for Ramrod 308 (IV). He found the surroundings of Biggin Hill much preferable to the tents at RAF Staplehurst. At around 14.30 pm, S/L Ormston and the 126 Wing intelligence team provided the briefing for the mission. At 15.35 pm Len was strapped into Spitfire MH477 and speeding down the runway at Biggin Hill. The battle formation of 36 Spitfires headed south to rendezvous with 24 Mitchells that would be attacking gun emplacements located in the Calais area. Without warning, F/S S M Kent broke away with engine trouble as they climbed, and he was back on the ground 10 minutes after liftoff. The bomber pick up was completed without incident and as they made the short hop across the channel Len knew that a major port like Calais had an extensive network of flak defences, and as the port came into view true to form the guns began their barrage. They Spitfire pilots weaved and rocked their aircraft, as S/L Ormston adjusted their course to confuse the enemy observers. The sticks of bombs were duly unloaded, and the Mitchells turned away sharply for the English coast. As no enemy fighters were in the vicinity, the second phase of the operation could commence as Len turned his Spitfire eastwards for a sweep of the coast to Gravelines before turning southeast for Hazebrouck, which is around 20 miles northwest of Lille. The Roaring Boys were hoping to tease out a scrambled fighter response from the air bases in the Lille area. None was forthcoming as S/L Ormston turned the formation westwards where they left enemy territory at Hardelot-Plage, a few miles south of Boulogne-sur-Mer. Flak shells exploded and tracers whistled around the aircraft as they approached the coast. The danger was ever present. They were achieving their aim of provoking plenty of attention from the enemy which Len anxiously observed from his Spitfire, a seemingly insignificant and vulnerable machine in the barrage. They headed out across the sea and the flak died away as he settled in for the flight back to Biggin Hill, where he touched down at 17.05 pm.

The missions were now ranging into Belgian territory, and with the use of auxiliary drop tanks, the Spitfires of 411 could extend their flying range, accompanying the bombers right to the target area, flying with them for the return leg. Ramrod 339 would see 126 Airfield link up with 72 Marauders of USAAF Ninth Air Force to bomb Chievres aerodrome in Belgium. Other units would bomb the aerodromes at Cambrai and Epinoy. With such a large bomber force Johnnie Johnson's Kenley Spitfires would also be on hand as top cover. At 09.00 am they lifted off and having formed up, headed out across the channel where they crossed the Belgian coast at Nieuwpoort. F/O S A Mills was soon out of the mission with mechanical problems when his engine cut out repeatedly after swopping fuel tanks. The bombers commenced their run into the target and Len watched on expectantly as a one by one the bombs dropped away from the Marauders. Suddenly, there was a terrific explosion and a giant ball of flame rose into the sky, developing with thick black smoke into a large cloud. It turned out that a direct hit had been made on the aerodrome ammunition dump. From where he was sitting Len gave a nod of approval, the Yanks dropped their bombs right in the pickle barrel. As the formation turned to starboard and began the return leg Len looked out across the horizon. He could see Doug Matheson around 200 yards away, to the front. A call went out, "Bandits! High coming down." With the call, in an instant, as the enemy aircraft zipped past, Matheson dropped the nose of his Spitfire and dived down, chasing after an FW 190. Len did his job as wingman weaving behind Matheson and looking out for any enemy aircraft trying to get line astern for an attack. He saw the barrels of Matheson's Spitfire smoking as he closed in on the 190, and as the ORB reported: "could fire into his fuselage and cause parts of the aircraft to break off. The aircraft immediately crashed for a 411 Victory." Matheson and Len rejoined the formation and crossed back over the channel, landing at Biggin at 10.45 am. Doug Matheson was soon surrounded by an excited group of pilots as they made their way to the debrief and for Doug to make his claim report for the downed FW 190.

The December weather patterns enabled the Roaring Boys to continue training and practice flying as and when the weather was conducive. Operationally, it was a different matter as conditions in France or Belgium often prevented target identification. On 20 December Len and Tommy were together for Ramrod 376, which would see the Roaring Boys take to the air at 13.15 pm to provide top cover at 20,000 feet to a formation of bombers. Only 7 of the squadron, including Len and Tommy, made it to France, the others all either failed to get into the air or turned back due to unserviceability or engine trouble. The ORB later described the mission: "Huns were reported in our vicinity at 25,000 feet heading north. We sighted them at 12 o'clock high above. They dove in behind us but turned out to be Spitfires. We crossed out of France at Hardelot." This was a favourite exit point on return legs back to England. Both Len and Tommy returned to Biggin Hill at 14.45 pm, no doubt with mixed emotions that the "bounce" by other fighters had turned out to friendlies. Tommy later offered his thoughts: "No Huns about or anything of interest,"

As the new year arrived, on 7 January 1944 the newly promoted Pilot Officer Len Harrison was rostered to fly on Ramrod 431, where 72

Marauders were targeting No Ball targets in the Cherbourg area. The Roaring Boys were led by S/L J D McFarlane and took off from Biggin Hill at 10.45 am. The ORB later recorded: "Heavy inaccurate flak was encountered over the target. No e/a were seen and all our pilots returned safely to base." Len's mission on 8 January was to act as cover for RAF Typhoons flying a sweep north of Paris. The rendezvous was scheduled to take place at Chartres, but with the Typhoons scattered they made their own way out and 126 Wing returned, encountering only some minor flak after 1 hour 15 minutes, at 15.05 pm.

On 11 January the squadron ORB noted: "S/L I Ormston left for RCAF "R" Depot, Warrington this morning and will soon be riding the waves back to Canada. P/O Harrison accompanied him to Warrington and then went onto Blackpool to see his fiancée." It's not known if Len's partner was a local girl or a Canadian serving overseas in the UK. Hopefully, one day the story of this wartime romance will be told.

For Len's mission of 25 January, Ramrod 479, he was joined by Bruce and Bob. The plan was to sweep the Abbeville area whilst bombers attacked No Ball targets. As the formation entered France, they noticed condensation trails high above them, enemy fighters. As they climbed to meet the enemy threat, which the ORB reported was: "up sun to 30,000 feet," they were hoping to get above the formation which was heading inland and dive down to attack. Bruce described the action in his logbook: "20+ Huns over St Omer. Climbed to intercept. Oil temperature 105 degrees+ 10 miles inland." Bruce was in trouble and he immediately throttled back and turned for England. Len Harrison dropped away with Bruce to cover him as he flew his aircraft back across the channel. They hoped his engine wouldn't give out over the sea. At least he had high altitude on his side and could glide a significant distance. By throttling back, the temperature on Bruce's Merlin engine began to fall, he reached a point over the sea when he knew even with a complete engine failure, he could make landfall and safely bail out if necessary. Bruce and Len landed back at Biggin Hill at 10.40 am.

Once again on 26 January, the weather caused a mission to be aborted, this time Len and Tommy were frustrated when escorting 54 Marauders attacking No Ball targets north of Rouen. They climbed through 10/10 cloud and stayed in the bright sunshine for the whole operation. With the bombers turning back, unable to locate their targets and the flak batteries quiet the only action was provided by F/L D C

McKay of 412 Squadron who was forced to bail out into the sea near the English coast. He was fortunate to be picked up quickly by the ASR boys.

The February weather did little to cheer up Len and his comrades. It was miserable and cold but "off the field" activities including numerous dances, trips to the cinema and social events kept spirits up. On 20 February Len was rostered to fly with Charlie and Tommy on Ramrod 568, which was a diversionary mission to cover the Eighth Air Force's Liberators and Fortresses returning from an attack on Leipzig. It was the start of the "Big Week" in which German aircraft plants and airfields were attacked. The initial part of the operation saw 126 Airfield fly to RAF Bradwell Bay, east of Maldon where they refueled before lifting off at 09.55 am for the Dutch coast. As Len and Tommy passed over the sea at around 15,000 feet, they heard a voice on their R/T. It was F/O Armstrong flying as Yellow 2, reporting trouble just after crossing the coast. As he dropped out of the formation he kept in touch, and at several thousand feet below the formation he managed to get his engine running again, mightily relieved that he could join back up with everyone. The formation of Marauders came into view just inside the Dutch coast having bombed Eindhoven, and in short order, the Spitfires positioned themselves around the bombers for the return leg. The Roaring Boys were back in Biggin Hill at 11.35 am, cold but pleased with their morning's work and in the case of F/O Armstrong mightily relieved that he had made it back in one piece.

Inevitably, parts of the month of March were subject to poor weather, but the 23rd day began bright and warm as Len and Ross attended a briefing for a mission to Creil marshalling yards, located to the northeast of Paris. No 126 Airfield would act as close support to a force of 226 Marauders from the Ninth Air Force which would also be targeting Beaumont-le-Roger and Beauvais Tillé aerodromes. At 11.00 am Len lit the fires on Spitfire MJ239 and was soon climbing out into the bright sunshine around Biggin Hill. With the formation in position, they set off to meet up with the bomber force heading for Creil. Ross later described it as: "a lovely ride. Close escort to 72 Marauders. Saw Paris." From this note and other records, it is safe to assume that the huge formation flew across the French countryside with little interference from the flak batteries or enemy aircraft. To further improve the mood of those involved, the ORB described the bombing results as "perfect." Ross, who had previously been scathing about the performance of the Marauders bombing proficiency described their efforts as, "S.H. Bombing." I'll stick my neck out and suggest that is a nonmilitary description of "Shit hot" bombing! The only action came with 412 Squadron when F/L Don Laubman and F/L W B Needham shot down a Ju 88, forcing it to crash land. Exactly 2 hours after taking off the Roaring Boys were back at Biggin Hill.

April lived up to its moniker of "April showers," operations and flying were cancelled on several days. There was also a period spent at RAF station, Fairwood Common, Wales for air firing and dive bombing practice. In addition, ahead of D Day 126 Airfield moved to RAF Tangmere. It was business as usual for Len on 30 April when he, Bruce, Ross, and Bob were briefed for a bombing mission on No Ball targets south of Abbeville. Earlier, they had all been up for 2 work up sessions of dive bombing practice before the mission. At exactly 14.00 pm, having led the Roaring Boys out from the dispersal area, S/L Fowlow gave the order and the squadron lifted off. They formed up over the airfield and headed south, soon crossing the English coastline for France. It's probable that they would have flown one leg of the mission via the estuary at Saint Valery sur Somme, following the Canal Maritime d'Abbeville à Saint-Valery southeast directly to Abbeville. As they approached the target area Len checked his aircraft's instruments and controls once again. As all pilots know you it's important to study the dials and not be fooled into making only a cursory check and think that the aircraft is functioning as it should. The moment you don't check would be the time suddenly you have problems, at which point it would potentially be too late. Throughout this period, as this book attests, Spitfires suffering mechanical failures was a routine occurrence. Dive bombing itself was a hazardous business and a nasty surprise with mechanical issues in a high-speed vertical dive was to be avoided at all costs. As Len watched expectantly, the first section of 4 aircraft dived down. He readied himself, and using the rising smoke and dust as a marker, squinted through the windscreen waiting for the precise moment to pull up at around 3-4,000 feet, whilst pushing the bomb release button. He didn't look at the trajectory or the impact of his 500 lb bomb, preferring to jink, weave, and keep flat out and low, to make his escape. Len knew one thing, with this level of barrage protecting the No Ball sites they must be of high importance to the Germans. The barrage of heavy tracer rounds seemed to be coming from multiple points as he dodged through them hoping to avoid the dreaded dull thud as a cannon shell connected with his fuselage. Len hit full power in an attempt to climb away, seeing the green fields get smaller in his peripheral vision. He soon reached 10,000 feet, where he rejoined the formation. With the job done they headed back across the channel. Len soon felt the welcome clunk of his undercarriage locking in place and the bump of his wheels touching down at Tangmere. It was 15.15 pm, time for a post-mission debrief and a cup of tea. The ORB recorded the score as "two or three direct hits." For their part, Bruce and Ross respectively wrote: "Good hits in target area" and, "Fairly good bombing."

On 7 May Len, Tommy, and Dave were all rostered to fly a close escort mission to Mosquitoes which would be dropping their ordnance from 20,000 feet through the cloud. No information can be sourced about the intended target, but at this point in the lead up to D Day pressure was increasing on the Luftwaffe's air bases, and this could well have been the intended target. The ORB provided details of the operation: "The Mossies were 45 minutes late so the squadron aircraft were recalled." After 1 hour 25 minutes in the air, at 13.50 pm Len and the others touched down, rather disappointed with the way the show had turned out.

With the fairer weather conditions, the Roaring Boys were able to increase the level of operations, knowing that all the damage and havoc they could create on the Germans would contribute to the potential success of D Day. On 11 May in the late afternoon Len, Tommy, and Dave sat down with the Falcons from 412 Squadron to listen to the briefing for their mission, which was scheduled for wheels up at 18.25 pm. The location of the No Ball is not specified but the mission was deemed successful in the ORB record: "Jet black smoke was reported and the target was covered with smoke. Medium-light flak and three bursts of heavy flak were experienced in the target area. One of our A/C (F/O P Wallace) returned before reaching the target due to engine trouble. No enemy A/C encountered, and all our A/C returned safely to base." By 19.35 pm Len, Tommy, Dave, and the others were back, and no doubt post briefing thinking about a mid-week liberty run to Chichester to chase down a few pints, and maybe some of the local ladies. Such was their life, living every day as it came, carefree in one sense, but in another shouldering great responsibility. Tommy later had time to write up the mission: "Dive bombing No Ball. South of Abbeville. Bags of sweet Fanny Adams. No joy."

On 16 May the whole squadron was given 48-hour passes whilst the new Gyro gun sights were fitted to their Mark IX Spitfires. For Len the leave was doubly welcome as he was given a 7-day pass, perhaps making one last trip to Blackpool to see his fiancée before the "big show." With his leave over, and very much a distant memory on 27 May Len, Dave, Charlie, Gibby, Bob and 6 others, including S/L Robertson were ready for a sweep as part of Ramrod 930. There were literally thousands of aircraft from the RAF, RCAF and the USAAF's Eighth and Ninth Air Forces in the air on this day, hitting targets all over France, Belgium, and Germany. The USAAF strength alone on this day was over 2,400 bombers and fighters.

As Len sat in the cockpit of Spitfire MJ313, there was a palpable sense of tension in the air over the mission. They were scheduled to fly a long distance across France, and up into Belgium. The mission was expected to take over 2 hours, and in terms of the period covered by this book, it is one of the longest missions flown. Len gingerly eased the throttle forward on MJ313. With his drop tank on board, the aircraft was extremely heavy on takeoff, and any sort of crash landing could spell disaster. The Roaring Boys always carried out their pre-flight checks carefully. It brings to mind the exploits of British Naval Fleet Air Arm and test pilot Captain Eric "Winkle" Brown CBE DSC AFC RN who flew 487 types of aircraft, more than anyone in history, including 14 marks of Spitfire, and virtually every type of Luftwaffe aircraft. He survived 11 aircraft crashes, which he put down partly to his short stature and naval service (hence his nickname "periwinkle" which was shortened to "winkle"). He extolled the virtues of proper preflight procedures and checks and was aghast at his more cavalier colleagues who seemed to approach the whole business of flying with the attitude of: "kick the tyres, light the fires and last one up's a sissy." At 19.00 pm Len was airborne, and with all systems functioning normally the formation settled down behind S/L Robertson who led them south across the channel. With the estuary at Saint Valery sur Somme in view from their vantage point 5,000 feet above, they began heading southeast following the Canal Maritime d'Abbeville towards Abbeville. On the eastern side of the city, F/L Nixon was sent down to attack a solitary truck, which was stopped in its tracks.

He rejoined, and the formation headed southeast towards Amiens and then onto the southernmost part of the sweep at the town of Montdidier. They turned northeast to complete the next leg towards Cambrai, some 60 miles to the northeast before setting course for the city of Lille. The mission was going according to plan and was routine, and thus far no bandits had been sent up to intercept them. On the last leg of the sweep to Lille, they did observe and note the position of 50 stationary barges on the River Scheldt, around 6 miles south of Tournai, Belgium. It wasn't long before the welcome sight of the channel meant that they would soon leave enemy territory, all unscathed. Len felt it was an almost serene flight across the channel and just occasionally it was possible to imagine they were not at war. Eventually, they landed at between 21.10 pm and 21.20 pm. As he slung back the cockpit hood and the cool air and Merlin fumes hit his face Len dropped the flaps on MJ313 ready for landing. The Roaring Boys shut down their aircraft and headed for the debrief.

Len was to finish the month of May with a very early morning shipping reconnaissance patrol. He was joined by Ross, F/L Russ Orr and F/O Gord Lapp with the patrol leaving at 04.50 am. They would be patrolling an area from Cap de La Hague which is the cape at the tip of the Normandy peninsula, moving eastwards along the coast past the D Day beaches to Le Havre. They then flew in an easterly direction along the coast towards Dieppe. It was here that they spotted one ship about 3 miles out, heading south towards the port. Upon their return to Tangmere at 06.00 am Ross described the conditions in his logbook, "Weather very bad." With D Day less than a week away, it was postponed for 24 hours from the scheduled date of 5 June, the significance of patrols like this cannot be underestimated, the intelligence team wanted every scrap of information from the pilots. A significant presence of German naval vessels, especially the fast and maneuverable E boats with their torpedoes could create havoc amongst the invasion force, just as they had done the month before during Operation Tiger, the practice invasion exercise at Slapton Sands.

When D Day arrived, the Roaring Boys had less than 2 hours sleep overnight following the late-night briefing and readiness at first light. Len and Charlie were rostered to be on the first patrol along the D Day beaches at 08.10 am. Although disappointing in terms of the anticipated action against the Luftwaffe Len felt immense pride that he was there to take part, but like the others in the squadron they knew their countrymen, and those of all the Allied nations were sacrificing their lives in their thousands on the beaches below. When they returned at 10.00 am, full of stories, it felt like an anti-climax as the official squadron diary described it: "All four sweeps uneventful. No Hun A/C in evidence any place. This was very disappointing." Len watched the other patrol go off at 13.05 pm, and eagerly waited in dispersal for their return, before himself taking off again at 18.10 pm for an evening patrol of the beachhead.

The 7 June was a contrast to D Day as the Luftwaffe started to counter the invasion and send units onto the offensive. Having flown the late-night patrol on D Day itself Len was rostered to fly in the evening patrol, along with Charlie, Gibby, and Bob. As they were briefed for the mission, S/L Robertson who, earlier in the day along with F/L G W Johnson had bagged an FW 190 and Me 109 respectively, gave the latest assessment of the landings, the front line and last known movements of enemy forces. Len was hopeful. Across the front, units were tangling with the enemy, and he wanted a piece of the action. They took off at 21.30 pm, with S/L Robertson turning back almost immediately with a faulty engine. Charlie took over and led the formation on a patrol that whilst action packed in terms of what was happening on the ground was without incident in the air. On D Day +1, No 126 Wing alone had claimed 12 enemy aircraft shot down for the loss of 18 Spitfires and Seafires, 12 Typhoons and 6 Mustang IIIs. The Luftwaffe had decided to stay in their bases and regroup, and at 23.35 pm a sullen group of Roaring Boys touched down at Tangmere after an uneventful patrol.

The 11 June was a black day for 411 Squadron when on only his third mission, F/S T W Tuttle was killed in action. The Roaring Boys quickly set the loss aside. It was a timely reminder if any was needed of the ever-present danger. Len was joined by Gibby, Dave, and Bob as they set off for a lunchtime patrol of the eastern end of the beachhead, which recorded wheels down at 15.00 pm. after 1 hour 50 minutes of uninterrupted patrolling. The weather had restricted operations across the front and most of the Allied losses were pre-dawn to night fighters, or to flak batteries and technical malfunctions.

The 17 June dawned for another day packed with patrols of the beachhead. For Len, Tommy, Ross, Bob, and 2 others, there was a slightly different mission when starting at 16.30 pm, Tommy took off with Hal Kramer to provide air cover and escort for barges. A pair of Spitfires took off each hour, and the last of the 3 pairs was Len and Ross who ventured out at 18.30 pm, touching down again at 20.15 pm. Ross's description of the operation speaks volumes: "Very boring escorting landing barges off the Needles. 412 lost F/S Love." In fact, WO L W Love was shot down and killed in air combat north of Troarn. Following the wing's move to France, Len was settling into life at B4 Bény-sur-Mer, and like the others finding the extremes in the weather difficult to contend with. B4 was either covered in thick, glutinous mud hence it being called Flanders Field which was followed by the sun drying out the ground and replacing the mud with choking dust.

Len had made an early start on 29 June with a dawn armed reconnaissance patrol. It is incredible to be able to watch the gun camera footage of Len attacking a ground target at around 06.30 am. The footage is dark, but the smoke rising from the area of the attack is clearly visible and after a few seconds as the ground rushes up at an alarming rate, he pulls Spitfire MJ313 upwards and away. This mission was followed by another early morning operation taking off at 08.25 am. He had the rest of the day off before settling down in his chair at around 20.00 pm with the familiar faces of Tommy, Bruce, Bob, and a newer face around the squadron, Jimmy Jeffrey. They listened to a briefing for the patrol, which was scheduled for 21.00pm. S/L Robertson outlined the patrol area, his pointer marking out the eastern and western sectors of the beachhead which they would patrol. The intelligence boys then added in the vital background about the latest disposition of the opposing forces on the ground and in the air, along with the weather reports, which didn't make for good reading.

Spitfire NH341 Elizabeth
At around 20.40 pm Len and the others headed for the dispersal area. He looked along the line of Spitfires before taking a momentary glance at the dull grey skies. There was another front coming in and the sky was looking ominously dark. As he made his way along the line, Tommy, Bruce, Bob, and Jimmy moved towards their respective steeds. Len could see the letters DB – E over the wing of the aircraft. After a brief chat with the erk, he settled down into Spitfire Elizabeth's cockpit. He gave Spitfire Elizabeth a superstitious pat on the side as he shut the door. He said

quietly to himself: "Don't let me down old girl and bring me back safely." Len pulled on his flying helmet and black gloves, and with all his pre-flight checks complete, he fired up Elizabeth's Merlin engine which roared instantly, sending out a solitary smoke ring, which punched its way through the wispy smoke trails. All along the line aircraft were idling and warming up, the heat haze forming above them as thousands of horsepower was readied for flight. As his aircraft came up to temperature, everything was normal. He heard S/L Robertson's voice over the R/T and he moved off, pinching Elizabeth's brakes to check they were sharp and true.

As Robertson led the way, Len was soon speeding down the runway, kicking in a healthy boot of right rudder to counteract the torque. Like all Spitfires, Elizabeth was eager to be free of the ground and as the wheels came up Len powered upwards to the patrol height of around 5,000 feet. He marvelled at the design and engineering of the Spitfire, with its sensitive controls which he felt he only had to breathe on to send the aircraft where he wanted her to go. It was soon clear that they would have to lose altitude as on the horizon the cloud base dropped away before their eyes. After a few minutes, they were at the western end of their patrol area over Gold beach, before S/L Robertson turned the formation to the east. The weather was deteriorating fast, and the cloud base seemed to fall away even further. Len saw raindrops hit his screen and thought that continuing in these conditions was pointless. If he thought that he was sure the other Roaring Boys would too. The R/T came to life shortly as S/L Robertson said in a calm, steady voice: "Return to base." As they entered the circuit at B4, the wind had strengthened and in these sporting conditions, Len brought Spitfire Elizabeth into land. The rain hammered down on the hood and Len thought that they had made for base just at the right time. He shut down Spitfire Elizabeth as an erk, ran over, his face screwed up, looking in every sense like was he was going through a world of pain in the downpour. Len unplugged his headset, undid the Sutton harness and jumped down, taking care not to slip off the wing which had rivulets of water gently flowing off it. He broke into a sprint and saw Tommy, Bruce, Jimmy, and Bob doing the same, At least the debrief of the uneventful mission would be swift and they could make a rapid exit to the mess tent to attend to the important business of supper.

On 1 July, Len looked out from his funk hole at the gloomy, grey sky. The Normandy weather was looking as bad as the famed English weather he had seen throughout 1943. Always unpredictable and rarely settled, but he had a day of armed reconnaissance and patrols to undertake. At 10.00am he was out of his Spitfire and into a briefing for the next mission which was a patrol of the William and Easy sectors of the bridgehead. After 1 hour 10 minutes the patrol was again uneventful with no enemy activity to bother them, and so they returned to base. The 4 July was livelier for Len. His patrol of the frontline at 13.20 pm with Bruce, Dave, Gibby, and Bob was uneventful, but he was involved in a melee later in the day when several enemy aircraft were engaged; Charlie and F/L Hayward made kills, Bruce and Bob each damaged Me 109s. The action is described in Charlie's chapter.

The Roaring Boys had a busy schedule of missions planned for 11 July. The flight planners had planned 18 single section patrols of the beachhead sector, each made up of 4 Spitfires. Len's 4 patrols included Tommy and were evenly spread out throughout the day. All 18 patrols passed without incident, with Bruce and Ross unusually making no additional comments about the day's activities.

The 14 July was the day 2nd TAF was reorganized, and No 442 Caribou squadron joined 126 Wing. In another change, Wing Commander Keith Hodson was replaced by Group Captain G E McGregor DFC, one of the first Canadians to receive the DFC during the Battle of Britain by achieving "ace" status. At 13.00 pm Len, Tommy and F/Os AM Tooley and R M Cook sat down with for their intelligence briefing. Thus far, it had been a quiet day for the Roaring Boys. At 14.00 pm precisely, the hourly takeoff pattern for the day continued as the 4 Spitfires roared into the air above B4, levelling out at 3,000 feet from where they began their patrol. All was quiet but as they reached an area northwest of Caen, Len's radio sparked into life as 12 FW 190s had been spotted by Yellow 3 at their 10 o'clock. Without hesitation, they broke to port and zeroed in on the formation. Len firmly increased the power on MJ468, and the Merlin engine sent his Spitfire hurtling into the formation of butcher birds who were in pairs and had already made sharp turns towards their attackers. It was a free for all with aircraft scattering in all directions. Len latched onto one FW 190, which weaved violently to shake him off, before feigning a break to port and rolling downwards, pursued by Len. He sucked in the great lungfuls of air his body demanded as he flicked his head over each shoulder to check he didn't have company on his own tail. This enemy pilot was no rookie and knew how to evade Len's attack. All the months of tail chases and mock combat were coming together for these climatic few seconds that would decide Len's fate, and that of the FW 190 pilot. As they lost altitude Len saw his chance and unleashed a volley of Hispano cannon shells which streamed towards his quarry. There was a bright instant flash from the engine compartment and a glycol stream poured from the BMW 800 series engine. The aircraft was finished, and as Len watched, expecting the stricken fighter to impact the ground at any second, the pilot catapulted out of the cockpit. Len flashed past and looked back as the butcher bird's impact was followed in an instant by an erupting fireball. He thought he caught a glimpse of a parachute, but the pilot exited at such a low height, surely he must have been killed. That wasn't Len's concern. The Luftwaffe pilot would have done the same to him given the opportunity. Len's first thought was his for 3 comrades who were still engaged in combat with 11 FW 190s. He gained altitude at full power looking around the sky. He called out for any Yellow section call signs. In turn, they replied, the Huns had broken off the engagement. All 4 Spitfires were intact. He heard Tommy confirm his kill, and Tooley and Cook confirm hits on a further 2 FW 190s. Despite the Roaring Boys being a much smaller force, this may not have been known to the enemy who had seen or heard 4 of their number being shot down or hit. Post-combat analysis now tells us an additional possible explanation for their withdrawal. When Yellow section had engaged, Len had shot down Hauptmann Werner Langemann who, on 24 June 1944 had taken over command of 1/JG 2. He was a North African and Malta campaigns veteran with 8 kills to his name. Langemann had a lucky escape. Len's attack and the ensuing dog fight had taken place on the deck and, wounded in the elbow Langemann had bailed out at only 50 metres above the ground, receiving additional injuries from his impact with a haystack that had almost certainly saved his life. His parachute had deployed for a vital few seconds, long enough to reduce his speed. Langemann landed near an anti-aircraft battery where he was captured. He spent the rest of the war as a POW. In August of that year, the command of 1/JG 2 would pass to the legendary figure of Luftwaffe ace Walter Matoni. Meanwhile, at 15.00 pm Yellow section swept into B4. Len was excited as he shut down MJ468 and looked across at the satisfied faces of Tommy and the others. They were going to celebrate this debrief like never before. All of them had got onto the scorecard. Today was their day.

The start of Operation Goodwood on 18 July, the attempted encirclement of Caen by British and Canadian forces, signalled a day of patrols of the front line by the Roaring Boys. Len was joined by Tommy, Gibby, and Bob for the squadron strength lunchtime patrol of the battlefront. They would be sweeping low over the front, engaging any ground targets they could find. During the day they chalked up an, "APV flamer and 1 Met damaged" which was eagerly added to the squadron's expanding scorecard of enemy transports. After 1 hour and 15 minutes, at 14.45 pm, the squadron touched down and prepared themselves for the coming late afternoon patrol. On 20 July, the same quartet of Spitfire Elizabeth's pilots was once again on the attack in the Mezidon and Falaise areas scoring: "one large truck, one low APV flamer, 1 van damaged and two DRs shot up." There are only infrequent mentions of attacks on "DR" which are dispatch riders. They were an essential battlefield communication resource for both sides and a legitimate target. If they could be stopped from delivering communications, then this could cause delay and confusion across the enemy command and control structure.

The harassment of German ground forces continued unabated, albeit hampered by the unpredictable and appalling weather. On 1 August, Tommy led Len and Bob on a squadron strength armed reconnaissance in the L'Aigle and Alençon areas during which the ORB noted: "Four flamers, 4 smokers, and 1 damaged Met scored as well as military observations made." Tommy wrote that he personally damaged: "2 trucks. No cannons!" Len's mission a few days later on 5 August was led by A Flight Commander Bob and took him, Tommy and Gibby on an evening armed reconnaissance of the river Seine, from the estuary to Vernon. It was a happy hunting ground that resulted in: "two Met flamers, 1 smoker and 1 Met with two trailers flamers."

On 11 August, at around 14.00 pm Len made his way to Spitfire MJ468 where he would join an armed reconnaissance patrol in the Argentan, L'Aigle, and Dreux areas, led by Bob. The Roaring Boys were hunting ground transports and managed to destroy two during the operation. At 15.40 pm after 1 hour and 10 minutes, Len entered the circuit at B4 for the final time. His operational flying hours had reached the maximum and he was tour complete. With conflicted feelings, he shut down his Spitfire and made his way to the debrief. He would, of course, have thought about his squadron companion, Tommy who had been shot down by flak a few days before and was either on the run or already in captivity. Perhaps, his thoughts about leaving active service with 411 were that he did not want to push his luck, which must run out for everyone at some point. He may also have been thinking about getting back to his fiancée who was mentioned previously as residing in Blackpool. The last entry in the 411 ORB for Len Harrison and his comrade Gibby was on 23 August: "F/L W R Gibson and F/O N L Harrison were posted on completion of their operational tours." Len had been a successful fighter pilot who had taken the fight to the enemy in the tradition of 411 Squadron and came through the high stakes game unscathed.

Len Harrison died peacefully at his home on Sunday 26 March 2006, aged 85. He survived his wife June Haigh with whom he had three daughters, Judith, the late Carole, and Janet. He was also the grandfather of Rebecca, Anthea, Derek, and great-grandson Isaiah.

CHAPTER NINE

BOB HYNDMAN

Robert Stewart Hyndman was born 28 June 1915, the son of the Honourable J D and Mrs. Hyndman. The law featured on both sides of Bob Hyndman's family, his father was a judge sitting on the Alberta Supreme Court, and his mother was the daughter of politician and Chief Justice of the Supreme Court of Canada Sir Louis Davis. When he was growing up in Edmonton, like many children of the time flying was still a wondrous new activity which caught the imagination of the young Bob. He was particularly fascinated by the World War I aircraft and used his artistic talent to sketch pictures of the planes, accompanying them with descriptions of the ensuing air battles. Amongst the legendary aviators who inspired Bob was the splendidly named Clennell Haggerston "Punch" Dickins OC OBE DFC, a Canadian WWI pilot who joined The Royal Flying Corps, the forerunner of the RAF. He had the distinction of being one of the few bomber pilots to become an "Ace" by shooting down 7 German aircraft. Another pilot who inspired Bob was the equally wonderfully named Wilfrid Reid "Wop" May OBE DFC, so called because his young cousin couldn't pronounce Wilfrid and called him "Woppie" instead. May was also an air "Ace" and it was these legendary war figures that would inspire a new generation of budding aviators in Canada and around the world. On 21 April 1918, May had the distinction of being the last Allied pilot to be pursued in air combat by the legendary German "Ace" Baron Manfred von Richthofen, the "Red Baron," who flew a distinctive bright red Fokker DR1 Triplane. Upon seeing May attacking his young cousin, Wolfram, von Richthofen pursued "Wop" May, descending from 12,000 feet to hedgerow height where von Richthofen was shot and fatally wounded by ground fire. May put his survival down to the fact that he didn't know what he was doing, and therefore neither did the "Red Baron." He said. "If I had known it was him I would probably have passed out!"

Bob Hyndman was educated at Shawinigan Lake School, British Columbia and Ashbury College, Rockcliffe. The legal profession was clearly not for him as he studied commercial art at the Central Technical School, Toronto between 1931-34. Amongst his teachers were Charles Goldhamer, and Carl Schaeffer who both became RCAF officers and Canadian Government war artists during WW2.

After completing his studies, Bob went to London and during his time there he worked as an artist providing sketches for children's books. When World War II commenced in September 1939, the young Hyndman was back in Canada and joined the RCAF on 5 June 1940. He said he didn't know why but that, "it was the thing to do," driven like so many at that time by patriotic duty. He entered service as a 2nd Aircraftsman and was posted to No1 Manning Depot, Toronto for pilot selection to assess his suitability as a pilot. Having passed selection, service number J/3492 - R/53938 Hyndman was posted to No 1 Initial Training School, where he stayed from 24 June to 19 July 1940. A promotion followed to Leading Aircraftsman and a posting to No 2 Elementary Flying School, Fort William, Ontario. On 21 July 1940, he began his training on a course run by a civilian company called Thunder Bay Air Training School Limited.

Initially, the BCATP only had a few training aircraft available, but with de Havilland having an assembly plant near Toronto, many flying clubs had adopted the DH 82C Tiger Moth as a standard trainer. It followed that the RCAF ordered 1,384, modified versions for pilot training. The aircraft was different from the standard open British cockpit version. Due to the colder climate, the Canadian Tiger Moth had cockpit heating, a sliding canopy, and padding around the instruments in case of accidents, of which there were to be many. During the long Canadian winter, they were also fitted with skis.

Bob Hyndman began his flying training on the Tiger Moth, and on 6 August 1940, he soloed after around twenty hours of dual instruction. In mid-September of that year, he was posted to No 4 Service Flying Training School, Saskatoon, Saskatchewan and found the base to be unfinished, with student pilots being forced to stay in the local YMCA. This was followed shortly after by the harsh prairie winter. Attempts to resume flying by rolling the compacted snow on the runway only succeeded in flattening most of the runway lights! The trainee pilots were flying Harvards and

Ansons, both monoplanes and rather more challenging than the Tiger Moth due to their size, speed, and retractable undercarriage.

Towards the end of 1940, Bob Hyndman was painted in flying gear by renowned artist Frederick Steiger, a painting named "Challenge." The painting was featured in the Canadian press in 1941 as an example of young Canadians rising to answer their countries call of duty. Bob completed his initial training on 17 November 1940 and was presented with his "wings" by Air Vice Marshal G.M. Croil, Inspector General of the RCAF. Bob Hyndman was now Pilot Officer Hyndman. At this point, the RCAF needed these newly qualified pilots to train as instructors to then be able to teach the increasing numbers of new intakes who were joining up. Bob was posted to Camp Borden, Trenton and upon completion of his instructor training, he was posted to No 2 Service Flying Training school, Uplands, Ottawa.

Whilst engaged in training pilots on the Harvard, Bob Hyndman and his colleagues did enjoy some interesting distractions at Trenton. Warner Brothers studios filmed Hyndman and his colleagues flying their Harvards for the movie *Captains of the Clouds* starring Hollywood tough guy James "Jimmy" Cagney, he of the famously misquoted movie line from the 1932 film *Taxi*, "you dirty rat!" Many of the flight school pilots were reported as going all "Hollywood" during the filming. After the filming was completed it was back to flying training for Bob and the daily routine of unpredictable landings and "ground loops."

Bob Hyndman was progressing well as an instructor and was promoted to Flying Officer on 5 January 1942 and later in the December of that year to Flight Lieutenant. On 29 January 1943 Bob's time as an instructor was over, and he was posted to No 1 Operational Training Unit, Bagotville to train as a fighter pilot. The aircraft used for advanced training here included the Hawker Hurricane and Harvard. The course curriculum was centred around teaching air combat tactics. For Bob, the flying in Course No 8 was focused upon fighter pilot training and during this course, he progressed from the Harvard to his first fighter, the Hurricane. The trainee pilots learned the important operational requirements of flying in formation, mock combat dogfights with instructors and gunnery skills. The weather made for challenging flying conditions with freezing temperatures and blizzards interrupting the training schedule.

On 14 March Bob Hyndman and the other trainees attended a meeting with a Canadian national hero and legend, George "Buzz" Beurling DSO DFC DFM and bar (also known as "screwball"), one of the Allies and Canada's top "aces." He had 30 combat air victories to his name from both German Luftwaffe and Italian air forces over France, but mostly in the air battles over Malta. Hence, he became known as the "Falcon of Malta." Beurling was a complex character, somewhat of a loner, brilliant but controversial. His eyesight was legendary, and he always spotted enemy aircraft long before any of his fellow pilots. Bob's daughter Brydie recalled her father telling her a story about George Beurling. She said he was driving along in a car with Beurling when he suddenly said: "do you see that plane up there Hyndman?" Bob told Brydie that he couldn't see a thing!

It was common practice to sharpen the pilots skills by skeet shooting with shotguns. In another example of Beurling taking this practice to the extreme, Herb Strutt, who was Spitfire Elizabeth's ground crew in 411 Squadron, recalled to his son Roger how Beurling would take to the skies in the squadron Tiger Moth armed with a shotgun, and shoot rabbits whilst flying. Beurling used the bolting rabbits to practice his deflection shooting technique whilst flying, with the unfortunate rabbit representing a jinking Luftwaffe fighter. It brought a whole new meaning to the saying "riding shotgun!" Although it was probably an effective method of sharpening shooting skills, it was unlikely to have found its way into any RAF procedures manual. Herb also recalled how Beurling was very particular about setting his Spitfire's 20 mm Hispano cannons and machine guns, using tin cans to zero them to his exact specifications. Bob went on to paint George Beurling, a painting that depicts a ground view of him in Malta. Thereafter, they became friends. The 126 Wing Commander, Bob Wendell "Buck" McNair DSO DFC and Two Bars was another formidable Malta "ace" who mistrusted Beurling's unorthodox ways. He flew stunts in the No 412 Squadron's Tiger Moth at zero feet and raced a lorry around the aerodrome against orders. As their relationship deteriorated, McNair had Beurling sent back to Canada in April 1944. In 1948, Beurling was recruited to fly P51 Mustangs for the Israeli air force. En route to Israel, his Noorduyn Norseman aircraft crashed whilst landing at Rome airport and he was killed.

Bob completed his course at No 1 OTU on 24 March 1943 and was posted to the north of England to No 57 OTU, Eshott, Northumberland.

Here he was trained to fly the Spitfire in June and July, having flown a total of 1,798 hours on all aircraft. Bob's next posting was to 411 Squadron. He joined the Roaring Boys at RAF Redhill, Surrey on 27 July 1943. Like many trainee pilots, following his posting Bob had a fellow trainee from Bagotville with him, F/O George W Johnson. They arrived at 411, a fully operational squadron with a sense of apprehension. There were Malta combat veterans and aces like Wing Commander "Buck" McNair who they were very much in awe of. This was a very different atmosphere to that which they experienced in Canada. In addition, their host country was on the front line and had been at war for over three years. Like all new intakes, Bob was welcomed in and assimilated into the ways of the Roaring Boys.

On 8 August 1943, Bob was transferred along with 411 Squadron to RAF Staplehurst and recalled his own experience of the "Ringo" escape and evasion exercises that took place during those days.

He wrote: "I remember one that I hated - a terrible thing. We were taken down, somewhere, out of uniform, just in civilian clothes, and a fellow (one of the lads I painted) and I - he was bolder than I was - we got into a little town and there was a big British convoy. I didn't want to have anything to do with the thing. But, he said, 'Bob, let's take a jeep, and I said, Christ, we'll get killed.' The British didn't know at the time this was going on. So, I said 'you take that Goddam thing, but I'm not going to drive it.' It belonged to some Colonel who was in a pub, and all those tough British soldiers were lurking around. Well, then we got in the jeep and they started to chase us. Finally, we were up a road and a car came right- up beside us and they had a gun pointing at us and they yelled: 'Stop that thing or we'll blow your head off.' Jesus, did we stop in a hurry. Then they took us in, locked us in a room, and interrogated us. Boy, were they mad; I was embarrassed, the Colonel was in a rage – we had mucked up the whole convoy. I just wanted to forget it. I don't like playing games like that unless they're the real McCoy. I felt about the size of a little cockroach, in spiritual agony."

Bob flew his first operational mission on 17 August 1943, Ramrod No 206, with Tommy, Len, Charlie and the rest of the squadron. W/C B D Russel DFC led the Roaring Boys, 401 and 412 Squadrons of 126 Airfield. These Ramrods were made up of several missions which all took place at the same time with Marauders bombing Bruyas-Sud aerodrome, Mitchell bombers to Calais, and bomb-carrying Typhoons the

"Bombphoons" to Poix, Lille, and Woensdrecht. Bob was content to stay close to the seasoned combat pilots as the squadron escorted 6 B-25 Mitchell bombers on a mission to attack the railway marshalling yards at Dunkirk. As mentioned earlier, missions like these were all part of the wider Allied deception plan to convince the Germans that the main invasion force would land in the Pas de Calais area, the shortest route across the English Channel, rather than in Normandy. Of course, they would also disrupt and degrade the warfighting capability of the enemy. At 11.35 am the 3 squadrons took off for France for the initial phase of the operation which was a rendezvous with the Mitchells over North Foreland. Bob had successfully negotiated this initial phase and was feeling as comfortable as he could do under the circumstances, when inexplicably the Mitchells turned back mid-channel, before recrossing the English coast and returning to base. Bob landed back at Staplehurst, slightly disappointed after exactly one hour's flying, but the link up with the bombers was a good work up and added to his experience. The ORB reported on the mission: "Visibility was good at 7,000 feet with a slight sea haze. No shipping was sighted. A small amount of local low flying was executed during the day." The 411 Flight Commander for Bob's first mission was F/L Douglas R Matheson, who was later shot down over France in December 1943. He confirmed in Bob's logbook that he was now: "capable of flying at 0 feet where necessary."

There followed over the coming weeks a mixture of armed reconnaissance and ramrods. On 4 September Ramrod S.31 was launched at 17.15 pm and Bob, Len, and the Roaring Boys escorted 36 Marauders flying at 12,000 feet to the marshalling yards around the city of Lille. The ORB gave the operational details for the mission: "The formation crossed the French coast at Blankenburg (author's note Blankenberge, Belgium) where medium flak was experienced. The bombers reached the target at 17.55 pm. Very heavy flak over the target area was encountered; bombing results, however, were very good." Although the ORBs identified Luftwaffe fighters as being seen, the force was not attacked by them, or pursued by any of 411's Spitfires. This "cat and mouse" game continued in the following months with the enemy looking only to pick off easy targets, rather than engage in a mass air combat. Both sides knew there was a "big show" coming down the track. Bob was anxious, tucked in his cockpit as the flak bombardment found the formation's range. It was a dramatic introduction to combat, and with much relief, he guided his Spitfire back across the coast at Nieuwpoort, Belgium at 18.05 pm. He could then see in the distance the welcoming green fields of Staplehurst, where he landed at 18.45 pm.

Bob continued to build up experience and took part in Ramrod S.42 on 8 September to the coastal defence batteries at Boulogne. S/L G C Semple briefed the pilots who along with Bob included Len, Charlie and 8 others from 411 pilot roster. Bob listened intently and took some notes of the key points from the operation. At around 17.00 pm with the briefing concluded, he headed out to pick up his parachute, helmet, and equipment. He wanted a little extra time to check over Spitfire AB946 before they set off. S/L Semple gave the signal to move off, and at 17.40 pm 126 Airfield sent their 36 Spitfires upwards into the sky. The formation flew towards Dungeness, where the Marauders duly appeared on time, and they prepared for the short flight to Boulogne. Bob knew what was waiting, hell and fire from the heavily defended Boulogne area. And, that's exactly what happened as the Germans poured everything they had onto the formation. Every firing position and field of fire had been carefully mapped. To Bob's alarm, the shells exploded with a frightening degree of accuracy around, and in amongst the formation. The ORB later reported: "Bombing results were very good. A number of enemy aircraft were seen but made no contact. Two warships, presumably destroyers seen in Boulogne harbour. Visibility was good with 5/10 cloud at 7,000 feet." The stress of flying over the target was condensed into a relatively short period, due to its coastal location, and much to everyone's relief the English Channel offered immediate refuge from the barrage. Survival was all they cared about. For Bob, it was an almost surreal experience flying his Spitfire into the maelstrom with no chance to deploy its legendary fighting capabilities. He felt like a duck at a fairground shooting gallery, sitting in his cockpit, flying in formation whilst the gun batteries tried their best to knock him out of the sky. At 18.35 pm, Bob guided Spitfire AB946 down onto Staplehurst's runway.

Ramrod 235, at 08.55 am on 21 September involved escorting 18 Mitchell bombers to Lens, the target being the coke ovens. The briefing was all wrapped up by 07.30 am, and by 09.00 am the Mitchells had been met at Dungeness at 12,000 feet, by 126 Airfield. The French coast was crossed at Berck sur Mer a few miles south of Le Touquet. On this occasion, the

Luftwaffe was present in numbers and the bombers weaved all over the sky to put them off. The second group of bombers dropped their bombs, and at this moment 11 enemy fighters took the opportunity to attack the formation, resulting in only the second group of bombers being able to find the target. The first group had been concentrating on evading the attacking fighters. One of the Mitchells was shot down, and another damaged for the loss of one German fighter which 403 squadron bagged. Bob and the Roaring Boys were itching to get stuck into the attacking fighters, but the practicalities of air combat when in close escort to bombers is described in the ORB. The Roaring Boys were on the wrong side of the formation to repel the attack, and the escorting fighters were too far back as the bombers were weaving around the sky to avoid the attacking Germans. Overall, the ORB reported that this was the first bomber loss from a total of 1,850 the squadron had escorted. The ORB noted: "A little further on another attack was made on the same side by six huns. No 401 Squadron was able to account for one hun during the engagement which followed. The formation recrossed the French coast south of Boulogne. The damaged bomber crash-landed in the sea and the crew was picked up by the rescue launch." By 10.20 am Bob and 126 Airfield were back at RAF Staplehurst.

On a similar mission, Ramrod 243 on 24 September, Bob, Charlie, and Bruce once again escorted 12 Mitchell bombers, this time to Saint-Omer aerodrome where the results were described as poor. Although no fighters were seen, moderately intense flak was experienced over the French coast. Meanwhile, the other part of ramrod which was targeting Beauvais bore the brunt of the Luftwaffe's attacks, with 12 of the attackers being shot down for the loss of 2 escorting Spitfires. The cumulative effect of the daily exposure to danger, whether from ground fire or air combat took its toll on the pilots. For Bob, his art was all important, and he spent much of his spare time drawing and painting scenes from the squadron, in particular, his fellow pilots who were often sketched or painted formally.

The month of October saw a slow up of operations as the squadron was upgraded from Spitfire Mark V to the faster Mark IX. On 2 October Bob joined his biggest ramrod to date, Ramrod 236 when the Roaring Boys formed up with 72 Marauders at 12,000 feet over Dungeness before heading to raid the Luftwaffe aerodrome at Saint-Omer. As could often happen in the autumn operations, fog and cloud obscured the aerodrome target and the formation was forced to abandon the attack and return to base.

On 13 October 1943, 411 Squadron left Staplehurst for Biggin Hill and were soon busy improving their surroundings. Having Bob Hyndman in the squadron was a bonus, as he was tasked by the commanding officer with painting some "interesting" frescoes on the dispersal hut walls. His family told me he recalled to them his days at Biggin Hill: "Everyone else played cards but I didn't. I did hundreds of drawings and ended up being asked to decorate the walls with scantily clad young ladies." He duly produced three ladies which as you can imagine the squadron viewed with keen interest. It was observed that Bob: "shared with Michelangelo a sound knowledge of "significant form." The reports of Bob's artistic talents were recorded in the official 411 Squadron's ORBs on 2 December 1943. Of all the things to read in the documenting of air combat and operations, I was somewhat surprised to read the following: "F/L R S Hyndman, the artist of the squadron painted a life-like picture of a beautiful but bare woman in a high position on one of the walls. Two more pictures of a similar nature were painted by him, one on either side of the large fireplace. Above the fireplace is a row of pencil drawings of the present members of the squadron. These efforts were all accomplished by our Artist." Having been provided with a copy of one of the frescoes by the Hyndman family I was inclined to agree with the assessment of his eye for "significant form!" The Senior Intelligence Officer for 126 Wing, Monty Berger described Bob's sketches as featuring: "two graceful lovelies which always hung over the wing's bar no matter where it travelled!" Bob also painted a map of Canada to which he pinned drawings of his fellow Roaring Boys showing their hometowns.

The month of November started with Bob taking part in a Ramrod 289 on 3 November, escorting 72 Marauders on a bombing mission to the Luftwaffe aerodrome at Tricqueville. Although, the Marauders of the US Ninth Air Force's 386th Bomb Group did not make the rendezvous they did successfully bomb the aerodrome. Meanwhile, Bob and the Roaring Boys were able to form up with their comrades from 127 Airfield offering close support to another 72 Marauders bombing the aerodrome at St Andre de L'Eure. The bombing attack was successfully carried out and buildings were set on fire. Bruce was also on this mission but returned at 10.30 am after only 20 minutes. He wrote: "Turned back. Drop tank failed." As expected, the weather was now starting to restrict flying operations. Ramrod 297 to Montdidier that Bob took part in was cancelled. The aerodrome was the home of the Luftwaffe's 1.KG 66 (Kampfgeschwader 66), flying the Junkers Ju 88 and Ju 188 medium bombers.

On 23 November Bob flew with Len and his fellow Roaring Boys on two operations. The first was Ramrod 326 to Lille Vendeville aerodrome where I./JG 3 was stationed. The mission commenced at 11.50 am and the 72 Marauders were picked up and the channel crossing began. Suddenly over the R/T, F/S S M Kent, flying as Blue 2, alerted the squadron that his engine had failed as he switched fuel supply from the auxiliary tank to the main tank. He turned around and was escorted by P/O H W Kramer, Blue 4. Approximately halfway across the channel from an altitude of 2,000 feet, Kent's Spitfire was seen to roll over on its side and drop into the channel. P/O Kramer, who saw the aircraft plunge in circled the area for 15 minutes hoping for a sign that Kent had got out. Nothing was seen and he had to return to base. The Roaring Boys had lost a popular pilot, everyone was sullen and quiet during the debrief. It was difficult for them all to reconcile themselves to this life.

The second sortie of 23 November was Bob's first Rodeo, a fighter sweep over enemy territory, starting on the French coast at Calais in which he would also be flying with Len and Bruce. No German aircraft were spotted. On 25 November in Ramrod 333 Bob, Bruce, and Len joined the rest of 126 Airfield to take part in a roaming escort to a bomber force attacking No Ball sites at Audinghem. Bob and his comrades returned without incident but No 122 Squadron of the RAF was in the unusual position of witnessing two Me 109s join up with their formation over Béthune. The German pilots, realising their error, broke away rapidly with No 412's Spitfire IXs in hot pursuit and a hail of cannon and machine-gun fire ringing in their ears! One Me 109 was later claimed as damaged.

On 29 November, whilst flying on a Rodeo to Abbeville and Amiens, Bob had to undertake a slightly unusual diversion. Enemy aircraft were reported, and the Spitfires dropped their auxiliary tanks in anticipation of air combat. The combat never materialised but F/L Dick Stayner's Spitfire had an engine failure at 17,000 feet. Bob was detailed to escort Stayner as he glided down to 10,000 feet. He could see that he had removed his flying helmet and was preparing to bail out. Bob's role was to pinpoint his location in case he ended up in the sea and required rescue. Fortunately, his engine restarted, and he and Bob were able to return to base.

When December arrived, the winter did what it does and restricted Bob's flying severely. On Christmas Eve, Bob, Tommy, and Gibby took part in Ramrod 390 a mission in which the Spitfires were providing close support to 72 Marauders bombing military targets around Dieppe. The briefing was led by S/L Keefer, who requested that watches be synchronised for takeoff at 11.45 am. Bob fired up Spitfire EN579. He taxied out, content that the aircraft was mechanically sound and that all the control surfaces were operating normally. At 11.45 am F/L J D McFarlane led the squadron off. The bombers were picked up at 16,000 feet over Hastings as planned, and McFarlane positioned the Roaring Boys on the starboard side of the formation. As soon as they crossed the French coast they received reports of 30 bogeys a few miles northeast of Rouen at 18,000 feet. The news grabbed Bob's attention. If that was the enemy and they attacked, it could develop into a major dogfight. He made his preparations, mentally and with the aircraft, leaving nothing to chance. Nervously they waited for an update from their air controllers. With several Allied raids running in parallel on most days these bogeys could well have been bombers on their return leg heading back to England. The ORB gave an account of the rest of the mission: "We were not bothered, although on the way out smoke trails were seen above us at 7 o'clock. The bombers returned to England without loss." The mission was a success and Bob and his eleven fellow Spitfire pilots returned safely, although they were diverted to RAF Manston from Biggin Hill due to the inclement weather. For Tommy, his participation ended after just 20 minutes. He wrote in his notes later: "The weather was duff and so was my R/T. I landed at Dunsfold." He awoke on Christmas day 1943 and made a snap 20-minute flight back to RAF Biggin Hill in time for the festivities. Flying on this mission to Dieppe would have been poignant for the Canadian pilots. In 1942, 411 Squadron and the Canadian Army took part in Operation Jubilee, the amphibious landing at Dieppe. Although badly mauled during the operation the lessons learned from 1942 were invaluable for the D Day operation in 1944.

Bob was able to kick back and relax with squadron comrades during the Christmas day celebrations and dinner at the Biggin Hill mess. Later that evening the squadron attended a party which the ORB reported: "went over in rare style." In the afternoon of the next day Bob, F/O Hogg and F/L S A Mills decided to take themselves off to London to a dance at the Stanmore Hall, the operations centre for Fighter Command. On New Year's

Eve, Bob ended the year in the air as part of Ramrod 403 during which the Roaring Boys made a fighter sweep of the Brussels area. The plan was to cover enemy airfields and hit any fighters that were scrambled in response to the bombers. As they crossed the coastline, the Roaring Boys flew a straight course for Brussels. In Spitfire EN579 Bob was enjoying the freedom that the sweep offered, to fly at a higher speed across enemy territory, unencumbered by the slow-moving bombers that were nicknamed 'flak bait.' The ORB later gave the official account: "Neither flak nor E/A were encountered on the way in. F/S Kerr J A was forced to return after his engine cut for a few thousand feet shortly after the French coast. On reaching Brussels area the wing turned starboard 180 degrees and maintained a steady course for home. Nearing the coast 401 Squadron flying at 10,000 feet experienced some light flak and climbed to 14,000 feet. The wing landed back at Biggin Hill after an uneventful trip." As had happened on previous missions, Bob was given the responsibility of escorting Kerr in his ailing Spitfire in case of attack or ditching in the channel. Kerr returned at 15.35 pm a full half hour later than the rest of 411 Squadron. Having seen Kerr return, Bob orbited Biggin in case Kerr made an emergency landing, touching down 10 minutes afterward.

Bob, Len, Charlie, and the Roaring Boys were straight back into action on New Year's Day 1944. They took part in a fighter sweep near Abbeville, acting as cover for De Havilland Mosquito fighter bombers which concentrated on bombing targets near the coast. The "Mossie" was nicknamed the "wooden wonder" because its main structure was made of wood with a stressed skin of thin, laminated plywood over a balsa core. The lightweight construction, and twin Rolls Royce Merlin engines, the same as was used in the Spitfire, made the Mosquito a light, fast and effective bomber. The attacking aircraft could well have come from 2nd TAF which had 138 Airfield, Lasham, and 140 Airfield, Sculthorpe, flying the Mosquito VI, each with a payload of up to 4,000 lb of bombs, typically configured as four 500 pounders.

At 14.17 pm W/C Buck McNair led 411 Squadron and the rest of 126 Airfield into the air. They formed up at 1,000 feet before heading for the coast at under 500 feet. It was exhilarating flying as Bob trimmed Spitfire EN579 to take the pressure off the control column and she flew herself with minimal input to the controls. He needed to concentrate on his position in the formation as they sped over the Weald of Kent. The formation, with their beautiful elliptical wings, brushed away the stiff wind that buffeted them with impudence, returning the aircraft to their steady, almost serene progress. Bob made an occasional glance to the side, and over his shoulder. How magnificent they looked; the 36 Spitfires spread out across the sky. What a terrifying sight for the Luftwaffe too, aware that the Spitfire was an iron fist in a silk glove, flown by the highly trained and aggressive Canucks. They would seek out this enemy in their graceful machines and destroy him wherever, and whenever they could. Bob knew that most of the enemy pilots had fewer flying hours and were less well trained. The enemy's aircraft were good, but as a fighter pilot, you had to know every corner and ounce of power and performance your aircraft could give you when your life depended on it. That thought gave him, and his comrades their swagger and confidence.

By now they were nearing the English coastline, and on cue the Mosquitoes appeared, to Bob, their side profile screamed speed and power. They were galloping along at full tilt. At around mid-channel 411, which was in the centre of the 3 Spitfire squadrons began to climb through 10/10 cloud. With no visual reference points, Bob was flying on his instruments, flicking his eyes outside the cockpit to make sure no other aircraft was drifting into his path. They broke out into the clear sky before immediately entering another thick layer of cloud, levelling out at 15,000 feet. Bob's ears popped as he switched on his oxygen supply and breathed slowly. Buck McNair spoke to the formation. Enemy aircraft had been spotted. The ORB noted: "Vectors were given but no e/a were sighted." The Mossies headed for the target area whilst Bob and the others, "turfed around" waiting for notification of an enemy attack. By 15.20 pm, the 3 squadrons were back in the circuit at Biggin and lining up to land. Much to his annoyance and embarrassment, but to the behind the scenes amusement of some of his pilots the ORB reported: "W/C W R McNair damaged his wingtip slightly on landing."

On 6 January Bob, Bruce, Charlie, and Gibby were flying together at 11.45 am on a mission where they caught sight of the enemy at relatively close range. Four FW 190s bounced the squadron whilst they were taking part in Ramrod 428 to Rouen. S/L McFarlane led the Roaring Boys, along with the Rams of 401 Squadron on an area sweep as cover for Mitchells and Mosquitoes from 2 Group, which were simultaneously bombing No Ball sites. As Bob and the others crossed the coast and began their high patrol at 20,000 feet, one of 411's sections was bounced by four FW 190s. The ORB later told the action as it unfolded: "F/L Orr, Yellow one, called a break to port for Yellow section. The 190s closed into about 600 yards and then flick rolled for the deck with Yellow section in hot pursuit. F/L Orr, Yellow 1 closed to about 150 yards and opened fire. The FW 190 smoked and lost height, finally crashing into the deck." Bruce was flying Yellow 3 and, in his chapter, he describes his part in the action. Bob was an observer as the drama unfolded, everyone was hoping they might get a dink at the enemy fighters. By 13.30 pm the formation was back and had touched down at Biggin Hill with several stories to tell at the debrief.

On several occasions Bob and the squadron found themselves taking off on fighter sweeps to France, only to turn back at the English coastline as the weather forced the operation to be aborted. On 14 January, for Ramrod 452 Bob, Tommy, Ross, and Bruce were accompanying 72 Marauders and providing "umbrella" cover as they bombed No Ball targets. The Roaring Boys were joined by 401 Squadron, the Rams, as well as Polish Spitfire squadrons. The formation traversed the channel and made landfall on the French coast at Hardelot, joining up with the Marauders before sweeping around Amiens and Doullen areas. The ORB reported that the Spitfires, "stooged around at 17 and 18,000 feet." Tommy noted in his logbook, "Jumped a couple of Spit sqns." The ORB gave further details of a combat incident: "Squadron Leader L M Cameron DFC leading 401 got into 3 FW 190s and fired head on but was unable to close in on the others. Quite a few of the big boys were pranging different targets." Bob and the others had an uneasy sense the Luftwaffe were about to bounce them and crash the party as very unwelcome guests. Although enemy aircraft were seen at high altitude, they did not attack the beehives. The ORB further recorded, "the Wing returned and landed at base safe and sound." The language used to describe these missions in the ORBs is somewhat surprising and was of course from a bygone era. It belies the inherent dangers of flying over enemy territory.

On 6 February, Bob was asleep when the invasion alarm sounded and rudely awoke him with a start. A mock invasion exercise was underway which deployed an attacking force that would try to capture Biggin Hill airfield. All the pilots rushed to their Spitfires, which were set up ready to launch at a moment's notice. A dense smoke screen enveloped the airfield, under cover of which the attackers advanced from the south and east. The defensive forces at Biggin held firm and repelled the attackers. It was a useful reminder of what might occur once the Roaring Boys were on the ground in France, close to the front lines. Capturing 3 squadrons of Spitfires as well as other 2nd TAF aircraft would be a propaganda coup for the Germans. With the exercise complete, most of the pilots decided that any return to their slumbers was now pointless and they might as well continue their preparations for the day's flying.

Bob, Ross, and Bruce would be taking off at 13.10 pm for Ramrod 523, flying their Spitfires in escort to 400+ Fortresses and Liberators on bombing missions to several airfields, including Rosière Airfield, which is in northeast France, located east southeast of Amiens. At the time FW 190s were operating from this base. All 3 squadrons were once again led by W/C Buck McNair and were providing top cover for the trip to Rosière. The Fortresses were met at Hastings at 18,000 feet. The ORB described the action: "We stayed at 3,000 feet above the Forts which levelled off at 20,000 feet. The field was well bombed." The Roaring Boys were kept on their toes during the mission as P47 Thunderbolts which were providing top cover, "kept diving down as if to attack." The ORB went on: "They kept diving down and caused a little panic at times." Bob and the others were muttering some choice words as the Thunderbolts were sent scurrying away to shouts over the R/T of "Friendly forces." To go down in combat under fire from one's own side would be the worst fate of all. Both Ross and Bruce wrote about the mission saying respectively: "9/10 cloud. Damn cold. Nothing doing," and, "Quiet and cold." All were pleased to land back unscathed at 15.05 pm.

Bob, Bruce, Len, and Tommy took off from Biggin Hill for Ramrod 567 on 20 February, which marked the start of the Eighth Air Force's "Big Week." They provided support and cover to Flying Fortresses and Liberators returning from bombing airfields and aviation industry targets around several German cities including, Leipzig. German air defences became increasingly sophisticated as the war went on, including radar control to direct their fire. As a result, they could exact a heavy toll on any attacking force. The bombers were picked up near Brussels, and with reports of up to 20 German fighters active in the area, everyone was on their guard. The strength in depth of the fighter protection made the odds almost suicidal for any attack, and the Luftwaffe did not engage the formations. The Roaring Boys landed back at their base at 16.10 pm.

On 14 March, Bob and the others were unceremoniously raised from their beds and summoned to intelligence with an urgent potential "show" which was subsequently cancelled before it got airborne. The squadron ORB goes on to mention Bob on the same day settling down to the business of painting one of his fellow pilots, F/O Dusty Thorpe. For both artist and sitter, it was a relaxing experience, diametrically opposed to the daily business of risking your life as a fighter pilot. Clearly impressed, the squadron diarist described it as: "absolutely perfect looking. Bob certainly is a wizard with his brush."

Bob's late afternoon mission on 27 April, from RAF Tangmere, was to be his first dive bombing operation with the squadron. Bruce, Ross, and Len were also flying on the mission. The target was a road bridge west of Carentan, and two direct hits were witnessed. The Germans retaliated with accurate flak, some of which hit F/O C D Cross's Spitfire forcing him to dash back to England. Unfortunately, he had to bail out into the sea near Selsey Bill, at about 200 feet altitude. Bob and the squadron watched on helplessly as he tumbled downwards with his parachute only streaming and failing to fully deploy. The ORB later gave details of Cross's fate: "F/O Cross's position was marked and he was picked up by a Corvette before being moved to Wroughton RAF hospital with serious injuries." On the next day, Bob and 411's medical officer visited Cross at St Richard's Hospital, Chichester where he was found to have a broken shoulder, collarbone, sprained ankles and blindness in one eye. After the war in a TV interview, Bob reflected on these missions and the whole business of flying with the Roaring Squadron. He said:

"It was a tremendously different way of being alive. You'd get up in the morning, have breakfast then go over to France try and get into trouble, or cause trouble and then come back for lunch. I just said to myself I hate this war. I was just filled with disgust. Something awful. It was a terrible feeling."

Bob's feelings could well have been triggered by witnessing many terrible scenes, the death of squadron colleagues, and those in the wider 126 Wing. The events of 19 May 1944 made a lasting impression on Bob and many of the others. He, Tommy, Gibby, Ross, and Charlie were taking part in a bombing mission to Hazebrouk when 411's Commanding Officer Squadron Leader N R "Norm" Fowlow DFC, was killed instantly after his Spitfire was hit by flak, resulting in the detonation of his aircraft's 500-pound bomb. Bob took part in this mission and described how on these dive bombing sorties, they would head straight down before releasing their bomb and "getting the hell out of there." He witnessed at close quarters Fowlow's demise and described how his Spitfire disintegrated, "into a million pieces." He added: "it's funny. We went back to the squadron and everyone was deathly silent, you know nobody said a word and then one fellow made a joke." It had the desired effect of lightening everyone's mood. The use of "dark" humour around tragic events to break the cycle of sorrow and tension is a well-known coping mechanism for the military and enables everyone to move on and remain focused on doing their job. Squadron Leader Fowlow would have wanted his Roaring Boys to carry on the fight despite his death. He is buried in Longuenesse Souvenir Cemetery, near Saint-Omer.

A 411 ground crew with the much feared German 88 mm anti-aircraft gun

Bob continued daily missions throughout the month of May with a mixture of dive bombing, fighter sweeps, and patrols. On 30 May he, Tommy, Ross, and Gibby took part in a fighter sweep to Eindhoven to provide an escort for the withdrawal of heavy bombers. During the mission, F/L Hayward spotted a train which he strafed, and which was reported as being literally stopped in its tracks. In contrast to the posts of a few months before, flying in a small enclosed cockpit in spring and summer saw sent temperatures soaring. Ross even wrote, "Very hot" in his logbook account of the operation. For Tommy, the added heat under his collar was caused by his approach to landing at Manston from Eindhoven after the mission, where they planned to refuel before taking off back to RAF Tangmere. He later gave details: "Bags of low flying. Too damn hot. No joy at all. Engine cut out over Manston. Did a glide approach. No prang thank goodness. Cheers."

As D Day loomed large and speculation reached fever pitch amongst the squadron, Bob readied himself for what would be a momentous day. At 13.05 pm on D Day 6 June, Bob, Tommy, Dave, Gibby, and Bruce took off with their squadron colleagues for a patrol over the Juno, Gold and Sword beach sectors. The patrol was uneventful, but the sights below were incredible for Bob to witness. His second patrol of the day with Bruce and Gibby over the same sector left Tangmere at 21.35 pm, with a return to base at 23.25 pm. No doubt exhausted, the mess room was still buzzing as the pilots exchanged accounts of what they had seen. Bob and his colleagues continued these beachhead patrols for the following days, and in Bob's missions, although no enemy aircraft were seen in their sector, several German Army transport vehicles were shot up.

Like several other of Spitfire Elizabeth's pilots, Bob's mission of 16 June was to act as air cover to a destroyer and escort cruisers carrying King George VI who was visiting the Normandy beachhead. At this time most of Bob's missions were flown in Spitfire MJ985, generally strafing ground transports with the Luftwaffe conspicuous by their absence. He painted a picture of his favourite Spitfire, including a depiction of "Sad Sack" on the cowling. "Sad Sack" was an American comic strip and comic book character created by Sgt George Baker during World War II. The character was part of the United States Army and was depicted as an unnamed, army private experiencing some of the absurdities and humiliations of military life. The name was derived from the shortening of the military slang "sad sack of shit," which was in common use during the war. No doubt the addition of "Sad Sack" to his Spitfire also reflected Bob's sense of humour and his take on the circumstances he found himself in.

On 23 June enemy fighters were detected in the sector and the alarm raised. Bob, Jimmy Jeffrey and four of the Roaring Boys were scrambled urgently to meet the incoming threat. Although it proved to be a false alarm, it may have been on this occasion that Bob's drawing of Bruce was cut short, the sitter left literally where he sat as the artist high tailed it to his waiting Spitfire. The drawing, which is included within this book hangs on the wall of Norm Whiteford's home, and it was he who pointed out that due to a squadron scramble the picture was missing key elements of his father's service uniform. In an interesting twist, artist and sitter may have reconvened at around 12.30 pm, after Bob returned. Once again, the alarm sounded and at 13.20 pm, this time it was Bruce who was scrambled! The result was that the sketch was never finished.

At around this time in June the reappearance of the Luftwaffe threat in 126 Wing's sector led to the possibility of air combat in Bob's missions, with an enemy force flying either FW 190s or Me 109s.

Spitfire NH341 Elizabeth

On 30 June Bob put his boot on the wing of Spitfire NH341 Elizabeth and climbed up, moving forward he dropped down into the cockpit and strapped in. Bruce was taller than Bob, and after some adjustments to the seat position, Bob was settled and ready. Lined up in 3 of the other Spitfires were Tommy, Gibby, and Len. The erks had prepared and armed all eleven aircraft loading a 500 lb bomb under the belly, and two 250 lb bombs, under the wings. Their mission was one of over 650 flown by the RAF in support of Operation Epsom, part of the plan to capture the strategically important city of Caen. The objective was to dive bomb the crossroads at Bretteville-sur-Laize. The town is to the south of Caen, and the high ground and was of strategic importance. It covers the approaches to the city and was located on the Allies eastern flank. Both sides threw everything into the battle on the ground, and in the air. On the Anglo Canadian side was VIII Corps, consisting of over 60,000 men which led the offensive. Facing them was II Schutzstaffel (abbreviated to "SS") Panzer Corps containing the fanatical and elite fighting troops of several SS divisions.

At 16.15 pm the Roaring Boys took to the air, Bob climbing out in Spitfire Elizabeth, settling into an orbit above B4 as they gained altitude up to 8,000 feet, ready for the 15-mile flight southeast to the target. In his cockpit Bob was running through his top of the climb checks, his oil pressure and temperature were all showing in the green, he was ready. The formation moved off in their sections. A few minutes passed, then over the R/T one of the Roaring Boys alerted the others to 4 unidentified aircraft above and behind them, flying on the same track. Just then, a shout went out, "Enemy attacking" as 4 FW 190s streaked down towards them. In unison, Bob and the others ditched their bombs, feeling the instantaneous return of the Spitfire's nimble controls as the bombs smashed down onto the road approaching Bretteville. The Roaring Boys turned towards their attackers. Bob pushed the throttle forward, and Spitfire Elizabeth responded. Within seconds, FW 190s flashed past and banked around joining several Spitfires in a circling mass of aircraft. Bob checked his "6" and saw his wingman in position behind him. He threw Elizabeth into a tight turn to port, climbing through the cloud in search of the enemy. As he burst through into the sunshine there was just an empty blue sky, devoid of aircraft. In his ears the sounds of combat, shouts, and warnings. It sounded like the CO was in business. Bob and his wingman dived back down through the clouds. Meanwhile, in his Spitfire Tommy was chasing down a 190: "I chased 1 and fired from 500 yards. He disappeared into cloud – HELL. Climbed above the cloud and fired at another 190 from 800 yards. He got into cloud, HELL AGAIN!" Meanwhile, S/L G D Robertson had latched onto an FW 190 and with a burst of deadly cannon shells sent it crashing to earth in flames. The Roaring Boys regrouped, but one section was unaccounted for but confirmed they were returning to base. Bob was breathing hard, and like the rest was now hot from the exertions of combat and throwing Spitfire Elizabeth around the sky. Robertson called a return to base, and as they proceeded northwest they spotted a lone truck. A section of 4 dropped down and duly strafed it, causing it to burst into flames. B4 was ahead as they lost altitude and entered the circuit. There was a welcome cooling breeze rushing into Bob's cockpit as he slid back the hood and prepared to land. With the flaps down, there came the sound of a mechanical whirl from the undercarriage followed by green lights to say both legs were locked. He throttled back and smoothly brought Spitfire Elizabeth into land, touching down on terra firma at 17.20 pm. He vacated the runway and followed Tommy and the others back into the dispersal area where the first section of 4 had already parked up and gone into intelligence to debrief. Robert parked Spitfire Elizabeth, put the brakes on and shut the aircraft down. A swarm of erks got to work immediately as Bob unbuckled his straps and pulled out his R/T leads before stepping out and down. There was certainly plenty to discuss, and a 'kill' for the boss to be celebrated.

It was 4 July when Bob next took off for a frontline patrol. He was joined by 5 other Spitfire Elizabeth pilots; Bruce, Charlie, Gibby, Len, and Dave on what would turn into one of the busiest missions the Roaring Boys had experienced. The actions of Bruce and Charlie are covered in their respective chapters. Whilst flying to the south-east of Caen, the Roaring Boys engaged a force of Me 109s at between six and nine thousand feet. During the ensuing dogfight, the Me 109 Bob attacked was seen to disappear in the clouds with glycol streaming from the engine. I have been able to see the actual footage from Bob's gun camera. The Spitfire's gun camera footage was often reviewed by the pilots for training purposes, and to corroborate their tally of personal "kills" and damage against the enemy, both in the air and on the ground. It was also a vital source of intelligence at a squadron, wing, and higher allied air force level. However, as might be expected there was always a fair amount of good-natured banter and rivalry between the pilots. Bob and his fellow pilots were reviewing the footage of his action with the 109. His daughter Brydie takes up the story: "I remember dad told me the story about coming back from a sortie and being ribbed by all the guys when they were watching his gun camera footage. They were yelling 'oh come on Bob get him, get him!' And teasing him when he missed the target!" After the war, Bob was filmed in his studio retelling the story of his air battle with the Me 109. He said:

"The most extraordinary thing happened during the war. I was flying Spitfires over France. I was pursuing a Me 109 and did get quite right close behind him and it was all this kind of thing, weaving to and fro. At one point, he threw his flaps down at about 300 miles per hour and I just went right over the top of him and looked right down into his eyes. And I said, 'Jesus, what am I going to do?' I had one second to make the decision, so I did a loop right in front of him and managed to get him after."

In the action Bob described, with the Luftwaffe pilot's 109 rapidly losing glycol and the engine certain to overheat quickly, it would seem highly probable his aircraft crash-landed, with the pilot possibly bailing out of his stricken fighter before the impact. The Roaring Boys ribbing of Bob was clearly misplaced. However, with the rules as they were, and no third-party corroboration of the kill, Bob was credited with damaging the Me 109.

As the July days passed Bob continued his daily patrol routine, many of which were uneventful, albeit there lurked the ever-present danger of being hit by flak or bounced by fighters and this was at the forefront of all the pilots minds. On 15 July Bob, Dave, Len, Gibby, and Tommy's mission took off from B4 Bény-sur-Mer at 20.45 pm. Whether the Germans thought this was a better time of day to move, or a major troop movement was underway is not known but the Roaring Boys came across a significant number of transports in a patrol between the towns of Vire, Domfront, and Flers. The ORB recorded: "excessive cloud prevented pinpointing an area so operation carried out somewhat east. Considerable transport movement observed. Score of 1 tank and trailer damaged, 2 armoured fighting vehicles (AFVs) damaged, 6 Met flamers, 3 smokers and 3 damaged. One of the damaged held 20-30 troops. Intense accurate heavy flak from woods and open space near rail line."

As with the air combat footage I have watched several gun camera attacks by Bob and the other Roaring Boys. I felt it was important to try to see the action through a pilot's eyes. Some quick searching on YouTube also produced a clip of a ground firing 20 mm Hispano cannon. I could then imagine the power and noise of these guns blasting out from a diving Spitfire. As my grandfather described to me in the desert war when he was bombed and strafed by Stuka dive bombers, it was every man for himself as he recalled that the SAS jeeps and soldiers scattered in all directions. He told me it was truly terrifying to be on the receiving end of such an air attack. In some of the actual gun camera footage, the Roaring Boys were flying incredibly low and close to these targets. They were highly skilled and courageous. Not that the Roaring Boys had it all their own way. In the ground attack mission described above, Dave was hit, and the story is taken up in his chapter.

On a similar armed reconnaissance mission in the Trouville, L'Aigle and Chartres areas at 16.05 pm on 24 July, Bob and his five fellow pilots watched on as F/L Hayward attacked a radar station, from which they observed "strikes and flashes" as the 20 mm Hispano cannon shells found their target. In addition, two Mets were recorded as flamers, and one despatch rider was shot up. They also observed a stream of refugees on the road south from Cabourg, a reflection of the price the local French population was paying for its liberation.

For the remainder of July, Bob and the Roaring Boys continued their patrols, including high flying groups of 4 Spitfires south of the front line to act as a deterrent against Luftwaffe activity. With the departure of Charlie to No 401 Squadron after his promotion to squadron leader, Bob's experience and leadership was recognised, on 27 July he was made "A" Flight Commander. On the last day of July, Bob, Gibby and the squadron located some enemy transport in a reconnaissance of the Domfront and Argentan areas and dived in for the attack. The attack was successful and 1 "flamer", 1 "smoker" and 3 damaged Mets were scored.

The month of August started pretty much as July had ended for Bob, with missions at all times of the day and evening consisting of armed reconnaissance, and dive bombing of specific targets. His dive bombing mission with Ross on 4 August was to the area of the river Seine where the squadron looked for targets of opportunity. A bridge, lock, and dam were selected. Ross recorded the results in his logbook: "Bombed bridge. Good bombing. Landed at B6." The ALG B6 is near Coulombs, to the southeast of Bayeux and was the base for the RAF's 137 squadron flying Typhoons. There was no recorded reason for the landing, although one pilot, P/O P O Thomas had engine trouble and Ross may have escorted him there for an emergency landing. The squadron's intelligence team had clearly targeted this area with good reason because as well as the infrastructure on the river, significant numbers of German military vehicles were attacked and good scores of "flamers" and "smokers" were added to the growing tally of destruction.

For much of the rest of August Bob did not fly on any operations. On 14 August the ORB listed him as heading to the UK on leave. Bob was back in the air on 24 August with his new responsibility as A flight commander. He led his section of 4 for a high patrol of the areas between Falaise and Orbec, taking off at 18.35 pm and landing back at B4 with nothing to report at 20.00 pm.

At 08.00am the next morning Bob and his section of 4 pilots assembled in the intelligence area to hear the briefing for their next armed reconnaissance mission which would take off at 09.00 am. A few days before, the Luftwaffe had employed a defensive screen of fighters in an effort to protect their retreating armies so Bob briefed his pilots that they could and should expect trouble. As he strapped into Spitfire MK423 he looked over at the newer faces, thinking that he was now the 'old hand.' To his side were new, 'green' replacement pilots like P/O A Ustenov and F/O J J Boyle who were posted in during the month. Bob led his charges out across B4 where on schedule they recorded wheels up at 09.00 am. As they flew due east and approached the river Seine Bob soon identified a convoy of vehicles and radioing his section he noted the position and prepared to attack. His gun button was switched to fire, and line astern the other Spitfires followed his steep dive. The convoy grew larger and began to fill Bob's windscreen as he unleashed a volley of devastating fire, raking the vehicles below. The narrow road prevented easy movement as panic set in amongst the troops. When all the aircraft had completed the attack, a trickle of flak flickering past them, Bob assessed the damage and reformed the section. He looked across to check all was well with his new charges, spaced out in the loose finger-four formation, around 200 yards apart from each other. He knew what, and how they would be feeling at that moment. As they circled above the Seine Bob pinpointed a series of barges, rafts and a tug. These new boys were going to experience attacking a range of targets today. He quickly briefed the section over the R/T and then dived down again, feeling the power of his cannons as the shells ripped into the craft, and surrounding river. There was no flak to distract them on this occasion. No sooner had the mission started than Bob called in the return to base. He warned them, "watch out for fighters." Bob led the boys back in, landing at 10.10 am. After shutting down it was time to meet the ever-present intelligence team to make his report. The ORB gives an official account of the damage: "Score 3 Met damaged, 8 barges, 25 small rafts and 1 tug strafed."

On 27 August Squadron Leader R K Hayward DFC departed on leave and Bob was asked to assume temporary command of 411 Squadron. In preparation, he had spent time shadowing Hayward to understand the role and what was expected of him during his time in command. One of the challenges of even temporary command would have become immediately apparent to Bob. The squadron was scheduled to move to St Andre de L'Eure, at Evreux two days after Hayward had departed on leave. He must have rolled his eyes at the prospect of the headache Hayward had left him with! Unfortunately, as the landing strip there was unserviceable the transfer was delayed. The ORB noted that they were, "all packed up and no place to go." The decision was taken for the squadron to visit Caen for the evening. The city had finally fallen to the Allies on 6 August after a long drawn out battle and a heavy pounding by the RAF and the Americans. The pictures from the time show a city of rubble, so a scenic tour was unlikely to have been on the menu, but what is certain is that the Roaring Boys would have located plenty to entertain themselves. By 31 August Bob's leadership was being severely tested as the frustration of not moving to St Andre was growing with the squadron diarist joining in with the discontent: "what a fine way to earn a living and to get cheesed off."

The squadron was continuously on the move in September, as the Germans retreated towards their homeland under pressure from the Allied advance. This was also to be the final month of Bob's tour of duty. On 4 September with 411 Squadron based at ALG B44 at Poix, he led a forward patrol with Ross and 4 others in the Brussels and Antwerp areas which were recorded as uneventful.

With the squadron on the move again to B56 Evere near Brussels, Bob's combined fighter sweep and armed reconnaissance patrol with 412 Squadron to Aachen on 8 September received a hot reception from German flak batteries, but all aircraft returned unharmed. The daily operations of the squadron were interrupted by the high number of C47 Dakotas arriving at B56, with fuel for the armoured divisions that would take part in Operation Market Garden, and the relentless drive east towards Germany.

With his tour drawing to a close Bob was counting down the days and hoping not to fly on difficult missions. The familiar faces of Spitfire Elizabeth's nine pilots were no longer with him on these final operations. Only Ross remained, and his tour was also nearly completed.

Bob's mission of 10 September was an armed reconnaissance in the Venlo, Geldern and Nijmegen area. It was to be his final mission of the war, having flown 155 sorties and logging 219 hours 40 minutes of operational flying time. At 10.30 am Bob "lit the fires" and went through his pre-flight check, all to the accompaniment of the low rumble of his Spitfire, MJ849. Armed and ready, he and the other 11 Spitfires took off.

The mission was far from uneventful. Two motor barges were attacked with one left smoking and the other beached. The ever-present danger from ground attack missions was demonstrated once again as P/O Mercer attacked a locomotive with the resulting explosion from the boiler sending debris 400 feet into the air. He was unable to manoeuvre his Spitfire away from the flying debris and was lucky to get away with damage to just his spinner, and rear-view mirror. Bob and the rest of the squadron went on to attack 3 more locomotives before wheels down at 11.45 am.

Bob was posted to the Base Planning Committee for 411 Squadron, a non-operational role. On 15 September he was appointed as an Official War Artist by the Canadian Government and was posted to RCAF headquarters in London. He shared a studio with another Canadian War Artist, Eric Aldwinkle. During his time as a war artist, Bob created 68 works, and painted most of the RCAF's senior officers and flying "aces," many of whom visited his London studio for the three to four sittings each portrait took to complete. He also drew fellow Spitfire Elizabeth pilots Bruce and Tommy, as well as visiting Yorkshire to paint No. 6 Group. After the war, Bob's works were put on display in the Canadian War Museum Ottawa where they remain today, whilst other works can be seen in the Beaverbrook War Art Collection's touring Canvas of War exhibit. His talent as a portrait artist shines out from these paintings, capturing what he described as, "the magic of the human face."

In April 1945, Bob returned home on leave to Canada and in June was posted to Air Force Headquarters in Ottawa, where he was able to apply the finishing touches to many of his earlier works. He also travelled around the various headquarters of the RCAF, painting senior officers. His portraits weren't restricted to military figures, he was commissioned by the Canadian Liberal party to paint former Liberal Prime Minister Sir Wilfrid Laurier on the 100th anniversary of his election, a work he presented to the Canadian Prime Minister Jean Chrétien.

After the war, Bob lived in Old Chelsea, Quebec and continued to paint professionally and successfully sell his art. He explained that one of his inspirations had been the famous Welsh painter Augustus John. Whilst walking in London Bob had seen a painting by John in the window of a Bond Street art gallery. The gallery manager gave Bob his address in Fordingbridge, and he went by train to meet him. He said: "I couldn't believe it. It was like meeting Leonardo da Vinci!" In World War I

Augustus John had been a war artist attached to the Canadian forces and as an artist, he and King George V were the only army officers allowed to wear beards. A large-scale mural produced by John was unveiled by the Duke and Duchess of Cambridge during a visit to the war museum in Ottawa in 2011. In the 1920's John was one of Britain's leading portrait painters and his studies included many famous figures such as; Colonel TE Lawrence (Lawrence of Arabia), Thomas Hardy, WB Yeats, and George Bernard Shaw.

In 1959 Bob received a commission from Canada's Chatelaine magazine to paint HM Queen Elizabeth II. He attended an investiture to observe the Queen at close hand, but he was not allowed to sketch or take photos. Bob's art career saw him take a succession of teaching roles, initially at Banff School of Fine Arts for eight summers (1964-72). He also taught at Elmwood School (Ottawa) (1966-71) and then at Ottawa School of Art (1971-2007) at the end of which he was in his nineties. His students talked of him as a real gentleman who clearly loved what he did. Bob's daughter Brydie spoke of her father when in his nineties, "he has more dates than I do!" Bob was certainly blessed with the kind of looks and charm, which combined with his background as a dashing fighter pilot, made him attractive to women throughout his life. Both of Bob's daughters said their father painted and sketched right up to the end of his life, and with his talent and enthousiasm, he enriched many lives. In a 2002 interview, he was asked about retirement and he said, laughing: "I can't retire or the bailiff will be at the door. I just keep on going until I disappear."

One person whose life was changed by Bob was artist Patrick Mason. Bob Hyndman was his friend and mentor for over forty years. He told me that he first met Bob when he was doodling on the Sparks Street Mall in downtown Ottawa on a spring morning. Bob leaned over Patrick's shoulder and enquired if he had taken art lessons. Patrick said no, and after affecting introductions he suggested that he enroll in Ottawa School of Art life drawing courses. Patrick was eventually able to thank Bob after becoming a high school teacher by inviting him as a guest of honour to a Remembrance Day service at West Carleton Secondary School, for which the Ottawa Museum lent some of Bob's wartime works. It was by all accounts a moving occasion for all. As Patrick, who now sells his art online, said of his first chance meeting with Bob, "one brief encounter can make a difference." It is, without doubt, safe to conclude that those who encountered Bob as an artist were forever left with art and experiences that made a difference both to them and to others who continue to view and appreciate his talent.

During my meeting with Vic Baker's daughter Julie, we discussed her father's role running the 126 Commemorative Society. We were reviewing his records and correspondence when I spotted two handwritten letters Bob had sent to Vic. The letters are reproduced below;

28 May 1990
Dear Vic Baker,
　　Your kind letter of February 1990 I have just found again and hope this late reply will be forgiven. It was interesting indeed to hear of Staplehurst and our old tents there and the 126 Wing HQ now at the "Eagle." If there is any hope of being in England September 14-16 I shall certainly come down and join you (all).
　　In the meantime, If I can find any photo of those days long ago, I'll send them to you. All good luck with everything and I hope we'll meet again. You sound like a fine fellow!
　　Sincerely,
　　Bob Hyndman 411 Squadron May "43 and September "44 126 Wing.
　　Cheers and all the best

19 June 1990
Dear Vic Baker
　　Your fine letter and card re The Shant Hotel has just reached me. Merci!!
　　Re your request for photos wartime and present I enclose these two; ghastly are they not!!
　　However, there we are. Great to hear of your new HQ and mess at The Shant. I do hope I can get over. Will really try.
　　Yes indeed, I still paint every day one way or another, and teach also at the Ottawa School of Art, just three times a week.
　　Old Chelsea where I live is 10 miles northwest of Ottawa in the Gatineau Hills. Have my studio there as well. Thanks, Vic and all the best.
　　(Bob had drawn a pint of beer). Let's down one or two!
　　Bob Hyndman

During the war, Bob did his duty as a Spitfire pilot with bravery, and later in his tour with great leadership when taking the additional responsibility of leading men into combat. He displayed the utmost courage as one of 411 Squadron's Roaring Boys. The realities of those 155 combat missions and what he had witnessed stayed with Bob throughout his life, as it did for so many veterans. In 2002, he was interviewed for Legion Magazine, the magazine of the Canadian military and said: "I was terrified each of the 150 missions I flew over the English Channel. I was 25. I did not really understand why I was there. I didn't want to die. I wanted to live to get back to my painting." In another interview in 2005 with The Gatineau Valley Historical Society, Bob revealed more about completing his operational tour: "I saw my squadron leader blown to pieces in front of me. My nerves were shot. I was not a born fighter."

Bob Hyndman passed away on 29 November 2009. He is survived by his daughters Margot and Brydie.

CHAPTER TEN

JIMMY JEFFREY

Jimmy in Ontario, 1943

James Stanley "Jimmy" Jeffrey was born on August 23, 1922, at 32 Warren Crescent, Toronto, Canada. Jimmy's son Lawrie Jeffrey and granddaughter Denise take up the story of his early life: "Jimmy was raised in a small two-bedroom house built by his father in the West end of Toronto in the Humber River Valley. He was the youngest of a family of 3 girls and 4 boys, with one of the girls sadly passing away in her first year. The kids were born over a span of approximately 25 years. Jimmy's oldest brother, William and oldest sister, Ada, had moved out of the house and were married when Jimmy was born. Jim's father was Harold Henry Jeffrey. I believe he fought in the 2nd Boer War, and was also a medic in Egypt, France, and Belgium in World War 1, serving in the British Army. He was married to Jemima Jane Booker; both were from the east end of London and as cockney as they come. The family history is kind of interesting in that one son was born in England before they emigrated to

Montreal, Canada where 2 kids were born. Then, they went back to England. At that point I believe Harold Henry was turned down by the Canadian Army, so he packed up the family and sailed back to England to join the Brits. The neat part of the story is on the voyage back to England, Jemima gave birth to a girl. I believe the ship was the liner Oceanic and the girl was named Oceanna."

The ship was RMS Oceanic, part of the White Star Line and, in an ominous portent of events to come she nearly collided with another ship which broke loose when Oceanic's White Star Line sister ship Titanic sailed from Southampton creating a large bow wave. The fate of Titanic is universally well known, but Oceanic was commissioned into the British Royal Navy as an armed merchantman. At the outbreak of the First World War in 1914, she was the first Allied ship lost when she ran aground off the Orkney Isles.

Lawrie provided details of his father's early years: "Jimmy attended Lambton Mills and Warren Park Public Schools and went on to attend Runnymede Collegiate in Toronto. When he was 7, he severely broke his right leg falling off a rope swing and was in a cast for 9 months, missing a year of school. Fully recovered he played hockey, lacrosse, softball, and football in high school. Again, like a lot of kids back then, he did not finish high school and dropped out to go to work. In 1936, his dad purchased a piece of property north of Toronto, near Lake Simcoe and built a summer cottage. It was about 50 miles out of the city as that was about all the gas you could afford during the '30s. The Jeffrey's survived the "dirty thirties" as Jimmy's Dad and his elder brothers Bill and Charles all worked for the post office. Jimmy's older brother, Harold Henry was around 12 years older than him. When Harold was first married to his wife, Bea, as they had no kids at that time, they would take Jimmy away on summer vacation fishing trips. As the cottages had no running water, Harold would send Jimmy down to the dock to get a bucket of water, specifically "bottom water." He would return with a bucketful and Harold would look at it, declare it to be "surface water," dump it out and send Jimmy back down to the dock. I don't know how long this went on, but it sets the stage and gives you an idea of the sibling relationship!"

After enlisting in the RCAF in 1942, Jimmy was posted to No 6 Service Flying Training School (SFTS), based at RCAF Dunnville, Ontario where he enrolled on Course 66. Jimmy's logbook charts his progress at 6 SFTS, and there are entries showing a first 1-hour solo in the Harvard on 25 October 1942. A few days later, Jimmy was receiving instruction on the North American NA-64 Yale, which he soloed in on 4 November. On 5 February 1943, Jimmy Jeffrey was presented with his pilot wings by Air Commodore Frank McGill, a Canadian who knew first-hand the rigours of being a fighter pilot, having flown in combat with the Royal Flying Corps in World War 1.

Jimmy was posted to England and sailed across the Atlantic in the liner Queen Elizabeth in March 1943 to begin his advanced fighter pilot training. He was stationed at 53 OTU based at RAF Kirton in Lindsey, Lincolnshire. It was here that Jimmy took his first flight in the legendary Spitfire. Lawrie Jeffrey takes up the story of his father's time in England: "During a period of leave, Jimmy was able to meet up with his brother Harold who was serving with The Irish Regiment of Canada. He must have been well into his 30s, so I assume he had some kind of administrative role. They managed to get together on leave before Harold's regiment departed for Italy in November 1943. Along with Harold on this escapade was his good friend George Pate, who was the regiment's Pipe Major and who was known as "Pudge." The story goes that Harold and George took Jimmy to a pub in the Aldershot area. Jimmy was receiving a lot of pats on the back and a good number of free pints of beer. As people were buying him a beer, he felt obligated to drink them and he probably drank way more than usual. The next day Harold and Pudge came clean. They had been working their way around the pub, pointing out the young lad in blue serge uniform and telling the locals that he had shot down 2 German aircraft and damaged a third. He was awarded the DFC, but he was too proud to wear it. Jimmy felt real bad about drinking all the free beer and had to nurse a god-awful hangover. I'm sure he got even somehow!" It seemed for Jimmy whenever his brother Harold was around, he was on the receiving end of some form of a liquid-based prank, whether collecting buckets of lake water or drinking bucket loads of beer.

Lawrie recalled another of Jimmy's wartime adventures: "I have one more story that Jimmy told me. This one we won't find in any logbook. While Jimmy was working his way up through the various levels of training OTUs in England, he became friends with a fun-loving character by the name of Percy Gomm. Jimmy told me that Percy had an older brother, Wing Commander Cosme Lockwood Gomm DSO DFC of 467 squadron, and that he had once met him with Percy." (Author's note. Cosme Gomm was killed in a bombing raid on Milan 15/16 August 1943. His Lancaster bomber Serial no. ED998 was shot down by a night fighter near Chartres, France on the return leg with the loss of all crew). "The Gomm brothers were born in Brazil to British parents. Well, I guess Percy and Jimmy were going on leave, and Percy felt that he was a little underfunded to conduct the skirt-chasing and boozing he had planned. Jimmy said that you could only take so much money out of the bank during the war unless you had a really good excuse. Percy and Jimmy went to see the bank manager. They told him a story that Percy was getting married, Jimmy was his best man and they required extra funds to pay for the wedding. The boys got the extra coin, Percy gave some to Jimmy and then jumped on the train to London. Jimmy took the train to visit relatives in Sidcup, Kent. He later recalled that on one occasion during their flight training Percy landed a Spitfire dragging telegraph wires from the undercarriage!" (Author's note. Percy Gomm later became a fighter pilot flying Spitfires with the RCAF's 443 squadron, part of 144 Wing. On one occasion, after unsuccessfully chasing Me 262 jets his propeller split, and he was forced into a dead stick landing near Asch, Belgium. He had to hitchhike back to the base at Evere. On another occasion, in the final few days of the war, an official account for 443 squadron noted: "the flak gunners gave an impressive display of their shooting ability when P/O Gomm was recorded as returning to base with his Spitfire covered in bullet holes!" Jimmy lost contact with Percy during the war and the pair were never reunited).

During Jimmy's time at 53 OTU, he became good friends with several pilots, some of whom like Bob Dieble he was with during his initial flight training on course 66 at No 6 SFTS. He also met up with Bob Davidson, Bob Wallace, and Ross Kelly. Lawrie Jeffrey and I discussed these friends. Lawrie said: "They met on the ship on the way over, became fast friends and were together before being posted to squadrons. They called themselves the four horsemen."

Many years later Jimmy himself told the story of his friends: "We met in March 1943, aboard the ocean liner Queen Elizabeth. Dave (Bob Davidson), Wally (Bob Wallace) and I were 20-year-olds who received our pilot wings the month before and were now on our way overseas.

Dave was from Hamilton and Wally from Tilbury, near Windsor (Ontario). In the following months, we trained as fighter pilots and we became great friends. We flew together, played softball for the same team, went on leave together, shared our parcels from home, went to dances and played practical jokes on each other. We wound up in different squadrons, but a couple of weeks after D Day we were posted to Normandy."

With his fighter pilot training finished at 53 OTU, Jimmy was posted to RAF Bognor Regis with 83 GSU where he, Bob Davidson and Bob Wallace awaited their squadron postings. In January of 1944, Jimmy was posted to No.2 Tactical Exercise Unit at RAF Grangemouth, Scotland. Here, he would receive further fighter pilot training including in ground attack tactics, which had been added into the syllabus. Lawrie was able to provide details of an incident that was recorded in Jimmy's logbook from his time at RAF Grangemouth: "He received a Red Citation for "GROSS CARLESSNESS (which for added effect is written in red ink and double underlined). 'Collided with obstruction on perimeter track.' As I recall Jimmy said they had had a very heavy snowfall and the snowbanks along the taxiways were quite high and the sunlight with the white made visibility difficult. On taxiing, his wing tip touched the snow bank which revealed a cement mixer. I'm assuming there was not a lot of damage (more to his pride) but he was up on the carpet trying to explain this to a crusty old Group Captain by the name of L F Forbes M.C." (Author's note. Group Captain LF Forbes M.C. originally joined the Army in 1914 before transferring to the Royal Flying Corps in 1915). "Jimmy's argument was that the cement mixer did not belong there. Apparently, the discussion was short and very one-sided, hence this citation. As my daughters can testify, this was probably a very early act of Jimmy pulling "a grandad."

Aside from the arrival of D Day, 6 June 1944 the 411 Squadron ORB announced: "W/O II J S Jeffrey, pilot, reported in on posting from No.83 GSU." Jimmy, like every other pilot, was ready for action and awaiting the start of the "big show." There was little time for him to adapt himself to life with a front-line squadron. He was rostered to fly on D Day +1, and at around 07.00 am sat in the briefing with Dave, Charlie, Ross, Tommy, Len and 6 other pilots, including S/L Robertson who led the briefing. The situation reports by the intelligence team told of the British facing stiff resistance from 21st Panzer division positioned to the north of Caen but of progress being made to the east and west. From an air force point of view, they were informed that units were already ashore, and engineers had started work on the ALGs. The pilots were warned to expect a backlash from the Luftwaffe. Jimmy was nervous to be flying his first combat mission under these circumstances, but he knew and understood now the calibre and confidence of the men around him and what he was required to do. Stick close to his no.1, and don't get separated was his primary role. Lawrie Jeffrey sheds some further light on his father's character: "Jimmy was very superstitious. He read his horoscope every day." It was very common for fighter pilots to be like this and carry good luck charms. They would also personalise their aircraft with the name of their favourite lady, as we have seen elsewhere in this book. It was, after all, an extremely hazardous activity, and anything that could provide an element of comfort was worth adopting. At 08.00 am, Jimmy made his way down the line of Spitfires and found Spitfire DB–S, MJ985. He had his parachute over his shoulder, and quickly he put it on and fastened the straps. He pulled on his leather flying helmet and was soon up on the wing and sliding down into his seat. He was ready. Spitfire MJ985 started first time, belching black smoke out across the airfield where it mingled with the smoke from the other 11 Spitfires, which were all now warming up under the grey blanket of cloud. At 08.15 am, Jimmy Jeffrey became a combat fighter pilot with 411 and an honorary member of the Roaring Boys. He quickly settled into the formation as they gained height with the rest of 126 Wing and headed out across the channel to view the quite extraordinary sight of the flotilla of ships. The industrial and military might of the free world engaged fully in its monumental struggle with the tyrannical regime of Nazi Germany. The blustery conditions meant Jimmy was concentrating hard on maintaining his place in the formation, as he had been taught, and practiced so often. As they reached the patrol area over the beachhead, Jimmy managed to get a good look at the action on Omaha beach. He relayed to his wife, and granddaughter Denise during a trip to Normandy in 1998 that he as he gazed down, he was surprised to see how close to the beaches the Americans still were on D Day +1.

After an hour of the patrol, they received word that a formation of Ju 88s was attempting to attack the landing beaches. Both 401 and 412 engaged the formation at around 09.10 am with 8 Ju 88s shot down, including by 126's commander W/C G C Keefer. As the attack broke up, and the remaining Ju 88s made for their bases 411 moved in to attack. Jimmy later recorded in his logbook. "Chased some Ju 88s – couldn't catch them." On this occasion, the reason for 411's unsuccessful chase was that the Ju 88 was designed as a "schnellbomber" (fast bomber) and the head start meant the Roaring Boys engage them. After the Ju 88s introduction into the post-D Day air war it had little effect, and when caught it was mauled by Allied fighters as this engagement illustrates. S/L Robertson called off 411's chase and turned the formation back across the channel where Jimmy once again eyed the fleet of ships. At 10.30 am he touched down at Tangmere and taxied to the dispersal area. He shut down, exchanged a few words with the erk about the aircraft's performance and made his way to the debrief. He had seen combat, and unlike the previous day's missions, the Luftwaffe had made their presence felt. Meanwhile, Ross was having his own challenges during the patrol. He wrote in his logbook: "Weather bad. Engine cutting very badly. Bags of twitch."

On 8 June, Jimmy once again took part in a beachhead patrol, which took off at 18.10 pm and lasted for 1 hour and 45 minutes. He described it as, "very quiet." Jimmy's patrol of the eastern beachhead on 11 June is described in Bruce's chapter but was the beginning a difficult month for Jimmy. The realities of war, death, and destruction were all around on a daily basis. For Jimmy, the rest of June was a time when events became very personal for him. From all we have seen so far, the Canadian boys were tough fighters and knew the job in hand. And, we can definitely place Jimmy in that category. He had proven he had what it took to be a competent fighter pilot. In previous years the squadron had posted out pilots they didn't consider up to the job.

On 11 June, as Jimmy swept along the runway and into the air there was a familiar face from 83 GSU flying who had been posted in a day after him, F/S Thomas Weldon Tuttle. Lawrie Jeffrey believes that Jimmy and Thomas knew each other from playing hockey in Toronto. During the mission, Tuttle's Spitfire was hit by flak, whereupon it crashed, erupted in flames and he was killed. One can only imagine Jimmy's reaction. It's likely he would have known it was his friend at that moment, as the R/T traffic confirmed it. Jimmy still had a job to do, trying to complete the immense task of seeing the mission through, whilst still being an inexperienced combat pilot. It must have taken incredible fortitude and strength of character to carry on. The realities of war had planted their flag centre stage for Jimmy. Knowing the connection with Tuttle, and his position as a "green" combat pilot, the CO and other pilots would have talked with each other and to Jimmy about the loss of Tuttle. Jimmy was also keen to get back to the action, doubtlessly. Perhaps, he now had an even greater incentive to take the fight to the enemy. We'll never know exactly what he was thinking at this time, but the ORB shows us that the very next day, 12 June at 13.05 pm Jimmy was "back in the saddle," and ready to go into combat once again, a patrol he described as, "quiet."

Jimmy sat down in the tented briefing and intelligence area. Dotted around him in various conversations were Tommy, Charlie, Dave, and 8 other Roaring Boys. S/L Robertson strode down to the front of the seating area with Panchuk and Berger of 126 Wing's Intelligence section. The Army Liaison Coordinator was also present as the pilots conversations died away. The mission details were relayed to the assembled group along with an update from the front, and the expected weather conditions for the patrol which was planned to be away at 08.15 am. Jimmy had his note pad and jotted down 15 June, 07.00 am along with salient points he would tuck into the top pocket of his tunic, of course containing no information that could be of use to the enemy if he was captured, or worse. As watches were synchronised, Jimmy checked the roster, his allocated Spitfire DB – V, NH243, and his section colour and number. He would be a wingman to the experienced F/L R K Hayward. With the briefing concluded, the pilots dispersed to make their final preparations and to ready themselves. At 08.15 am the formation lifted off from Tangmere and headed south. Jimmy settled back, after levelling out, checking his instruments and winding his trim wheel round to keep his Spitfire trimmed in straight and level flight. All his instruments were in the green and normal. He couldn't see any noticeable reduction in cross channel traffic in the air or on the sea. In fact, with more men and equipment pouring in daily, if anything the area was even more alive with fevered activity. As they reached the beachhead area and swept along the coast, they were flying at around 8,000 -10,000 feet. Soon his R/T sprung into life as Hayward let them know they had crossed the front line and were now over enemy territory. In the distance, they could see Le Havre as the eastern end of Sword beach passed beneath them. As they approached Le Havre, someone had zeroed in on a 2-ton truck that was moving briskly along a road. F/L Hayward told the formation he was attacking and called in his wingman to follow him down. It was Jimmy's time to put into practice everything he had been trained and told. His job was to attack the truck after Hayward, but also to keep an eye on his leader's tail, as well as his own.

They didn't want to be bounced whilst distracted and away from the main formation. Jimmy's training took over as he readied NH243, following Hayward's lead by throttling back, and banking over and down. With Hayward a few hundred metres ahead Jimmy's gun and camera button were ready as he peered down through his gun sight, the trucks clearly in view, and getting ever larger by the second. As Hayward's guns fired Jimmy concentrated on his own flight path, arrowing ever downwards. He saw Hayward pull up and peel away at well under 1,000 feet. Jimmy pushed the gun button; the cannons instantly roared and sent a volley of rounds down towards the truck which disappeared in a billowing curtain of smoke and dust. He was conscious of not going in and pulled back on the control column moving it to port and kicking his rudders, skimming at treetop height away across the fields towards the sea. As he throttled up to climb power, the speed and ascent even now left him with a sense of wonder. He tore up behind F/L Hayward who led them back to the others. With the remainder of the patrol passing without incident, the Roaring Boys headed for base. Jimmy drew a few deep breaths. It felt as if during the attack his heart would jump out of his chest. Now he was calm and needed to stay switched on. He tried but failed not to replay the attack in his mind as France disappeared behind them. With RAF Tangmere approaching, Jimmy followed Hayward into the circuit, dropping his undercarriage and feeling the gentle bump of the grass strip at 10.10 am. Jimmy's taxi in was different this time. He had successfully taken the fight to the enemy as he was trained to do and at least gave meted out some punishment for the loss of Thomas Tuttle. After the debrief session, Jimmy reported his version of events to the intelligence team and noted in his logbook: "Attacked German truck with F/L Hayward on road near Le Havre." Ross offered a similar version of events whilst adding, "Le Havre still burning."

The 16 June presented Jimmy and the Roaring Boys with the opportunity to record a significant event in their logbooks. Jimmy was one of the 12 pilots from 411 chosen to take part in an escort to cruisers and destroyers heading for France. The mission was top secret, the VIP didn't get much more important. As Jimmy wrote later: "The King went to France visiting the front-line troops." It would be something to pass on to future generations. Jimmy's patrol of 17 June was described by him as, "quiet - some flak though." In terms of firsts, this was the first reference Jimmy made to being exposed to incoming enemy fire. A sobering experience. The day also saw the ORB document: "The appearance of the Huns pilotless planes last night was the main topic of discussion today, but no one was lucky enough to see them."

The 18 June was an eventful one as Jimmy scurried around packing up his kit. The Roaring Boys were on the move. It was the much-anticipated relocation to their base in Normandy and put the wheels in motion for the wing to kick off its mobile tactical air force role. With his kit stashed away, Jimmy had a chance to catch up with his friends, Bob Davidson and Bob Wallace who were moving to France too, Davidson with 401 Squadron and Wallace with 427 squadron, 127 Wing. They could set up camp again at B4 when they arrived. At the scheduled time, Jimmy and 411 Squadron departed on a fleet of Dakotas for France. They wondered what fate awaited them and were both excited and apprehensive in equal measure about the future.

Jimmy's initial impressions of Bény-sur-Mer were shaped by the swirling dust, and the immediate desire to dig underground to protect oneself against any incoming fire. And, on this basis, it was a task which the Roaring Boys undertook with gusto. The weather then conspired to soften the ground by providing a liberal dose of rain, which promptly turned the whole airfield into a mud bath. On 22 June, the weather cleared, allowing a full day of operations to be undertaken. Jimmy was selected to fly as S/L Robertson's No.2. He was proving himself in combat as a wingman and was gaining experience rapidly. At 16.55 pm Jimmy, Bob, Charlie, Gibby, and Tommy took off from B4 for an armed reconnaissance of the Caen to Flers road. As they reached the patrolling height, around 3-5,000 feet, Jimmy noticed a Spitfire drop away from the formation. It was Bob, who was returning to B4 with an R/T failure. As they passed Villers Bocage, to the southwest of Caen, the flak batteries opened up. Jimmy was weaving and moving his Spitfire as he deployed energetic inputs to his controls in an effort to avoid the growing fire that was bursting around them. These flak boys were on the money Jimmy thought as the intensity of the barrage increased. As soon as they passed over Villers, the flak died away and S/L Roberston briefed the formation. He had "eyes on" to a target. Jimmy later wrote, "strafing German motor convoy." He was to follow S/L Robertson in a dive and unleash his own deadly fire and destruction on the hapless convoy. As he pulled away

Jimmy saw good hits on two trucks which, with a split-second confirmatory flick of his head he saw were now burning fiercely. There was no time to admire his handiwork as he asked his Spitfire's Merlin engine for every ounce of power to fly him safely away from the attack zone. Jimmy noted his success later: "Attacked several German vehicles. Destroyed two trucks with S/L Roberston." Tommy Wheler gave his version of events: "Shot up a truck. Turned out to be a hay cart." At 18.10 pm the Roaring Boys landed back at base. They had recorded information and observations of the enemy's movements which were disseminated to the intelligence team. A tired, but happy Jimmy made his way back to his funk hole to talk about his day and compare notes with his friends. That evening, Tommy wrote about some unexpected visitors to B4, "Crew bailed out of Fort over base." As they descended to the ground by parachute the crew of the B17 Flying Fortress was welcomed to 126 Wing with some traditional Canadian hospitality.

Jimmy's pal W/O Bob Wallace was posted to 421 squadron, 127 Wing and maintained his friendship with Jimmy whilst they were both located at RAF Tangmere. With both wings based at B4 Bény-Sur-Mer, they were together again and flew regular missions with their respective wings from the base. On 23 June, 421 squadron was on a late evening patrol east of Argentan when they were attacked by 15+ FW 190s and 8+ Me 109s. F/L P Johnson shot down an FW 190 and saw a Spitfire trying to crash land northeast of the town of Le Merlerault. It was Bob Wallace, and tragically he was killed in the crash. Like Jimmy, he was posted to 421 squadron around D Day and had flown several patrols before surviving a combat engagement on 15 June. Bob Wallace is buried at St Gauberge St Couloumbe Cemetery. Jimmy Jeffrey wrote about the death of his friend: "On June 23rd we heard that Wally was shot down, but no one could tell me what happened to him." It was a devastating blow for Jimmy, and the news was tough for him to process. He lay on his bunk stunned. First Thomas Tuttle, and now Wally. On both sides, men were losing friends and comrades in arms. The cause was just but the sacrifice and reality were plainly awful.

Having already learned from Lawrie Jeffrey that his father was superstitious, one can only imagine what the stars were telling him, the rituals he would follow, and the good luck charms he took with him to keep him safe. On 24 June, the Roaring Boys were feeling the pace.

Perhaps, some would welcome back the bad weather so that they could have a break from the relentless patrolling. The conditions were bright and clear for Jimmy and Gibby's midday armed reconnaissance. He was once again flying No.2 to S/L Robertson. Jimmy was about to have his own brush with danger. As he dived down on the target behind Roberston, flak was pouring up at him. He had been trained to ignore it and concentrate on bracketing the target with cannon and machine gun fire. As he was about to pull up, he felt a thump on the front of aircraft. It was distinct. He had been hit. His priority was to gain altitude and get away from the fire. Jimmy called in that he had been hit by flak. He could see Spitfire MK843's temperature gauge rising as he throttled back. He was leaking coolant and could see it streaking away from his aircraft. Jimmy processed the options. He confirmed to S/L Robertson that he thought he could make B4. He had other ALG landing options he could take if necessary. Jimmy was cleared by flight control to make a straight in approach as a priority. With a puff of his cheeks, he was mightily relieved when the welcome embrace of B4's runway met his wheels. He later wrote, "Radiator leaked badly. Got home OK." He shut down as soon as he could and in what seemed like an instant the erks were removing cowling panels to cool the engine and check out the extent of the damage. Jimmy stepped out of the aircraft, jumped off the wing and peered into the engine compartment. The erk showed him the trajectory of the cannon shell and the neat hole in his radiator. We can only wonder what his thoughts were. He knew he had been lucky as had many others in the squadron who had their own close shaves and stories to tell.

With his previous day's Spitfire away for repair to the flak damage, the 25 June was to be another dramatic day for Jimmy. The exact circumstances of the events that unfolded on that day are not certain, and the only official 411 Squadron reference we have is from Jimmy himself in his logbook. He wrote: "Fighter sweep. Crashed on takeoff – "Nuff said." Whatever the circumstances were, Lawrie Jeffrey recalled his father telling him about the accident in which the Spitfire MK532 overturned, leaving Jimmy trapped and hanging upside down in his harness: "I know he was in a hurry. It could very well be that he was supposed to fly another aircraft, couldn't get it started, or it had problems and switched aircraft and he was rushing to catch up to the others. He said the fellows on the ground who watched the incident told him they thought he was dead for sure. He hit his forehead on the gunsight and jammed his knee against the control panel. When he came to a stop, he said he heard a cockney voice telling him he'd be okay, they'd get him out and it was not a "flamer." I know they bandaged his head and Squadron Leader Robertson let him go into Bény-sur-Mer with the others that evening."

A liberty run trip to Bény-sur-Mer that evening would not have had the same entertainment potential as the trips the Roaring Boys managed on nights out in Maidstone, or even Biggin Hill, with its closeness to the bright lights of London. After a google trip around Bény-sur-Mer as it is today, it's clear that not much entertainment would have been on offer back then in such a small village. With a large aerodrome appearing on the doorstep, it is reasonable to conclude that local entrepreneurs would have quickly filled the void, offering all kinds of entertainment that might interest young fighter pilots, with cash in their pockets and who were looking for a good time! Throughout the research for this book, it's clear that "pranging" Spitfires for one reason or another was an occupational hazard, and Spitfire Elizabeth's 9 pilots did their share. After some initial concern about Jimmy's bandaged head, there was likely to have been a fair amount of good-natured joshing bandied around from his squadron mates.

Lawrie Jeffrey and I have speculated as to the circumstances of the crash, and after some research, I found a clue in the official history of Spitfire MK531, which bore the 411 Squadron code DB-W. Jimmy's logbook shows he previously flew the same Spitfire on 16 June, and the history of MK531 confirms that it was assigned to 411 on 26 May 1944. The entry reads: "Hit mound of earth beside runway on takeoff and overturned. Bény-sur-Mer 25-6-44. Cat E." The aircraft was beyond repair and Jimmy was extremely fortunate he wasn't too. As mentioned earlier, Jimmy was superstitious and with the events that had befallen him in the previous few days, the omens weren't looking good. Lawrie gave a further insight that Jimmy had told him: "Being the young fighter pilot and wanting very much to look the part, upon reaching 411 Squadron, Jimmy decided to grow a moustache. After the Spitfire crash, he immediately shaved off that moustache."

Jimmy's other friend F/S Bob "Dave" Davidson was posted to 411's sister squadron, 401, also part of 126 Wing, and so he could also spend time with Jimmy and Wally; they even shared a tent. On 28 June, Dave took off for a late evening armed reconnaissance patrol. During the mission,

401 Squadron was bounced by 12 FW 190s near Couterne, south of Caen and in the ensuing combat, Dave became separated from his leader and was shot down and killed. He was 21 years of age and is buried in the grounds of the chapel of Our Lady at Lignou, in the community of Couterne. Jimmy reflected on the respect shown to his friend by the local villagers: "The villagers buried Dave in the church graveyard. His grave has become a shrine and the villagers place flowers on it every day. In 1991 I visited Dave's grave. It has a military tombstone and where his plane crashed the French have dedicated a beautiful memorial to him." Pierre Vauloup, then a seven-year-old living in the area believes F/S Bob Davidson is a hero and that he and his family's lives were saved by him. As they were watching the combat unfold overhead Bob Davidson's Spitfire, trailing smoke, was flying a direct course for their house, but was steered away by him in the last seconds before it crashed and exploded a few metres away. Bob Davidson was posthumously promoted to the rank of Pilot Officer. For Jimmy, this was another dreadful blow. It's clear from Ross's logbook entry of 28 June mentioning the event that Bob Davidson's loss was quickly known throughout the wing. The Spitfire pilot community of a mobile fighter wing was a small, tight-knit group. What we can't be sure of is when Jimmy actually found out Dave had been killed, but it was enough to know his friend was missing. His loss followed so soon after Thomas Tuttle and Wally were both killed. It was a time of huge stress for a young man like Jimmy at the age of just 21. All around Normandy young men were having to grow up very quickly in the most extreme circumstances, just as they had in conflicts in the past. Jimmy had to continue to do his duty and go on despite the losses. His friends would have expected him to do exactly that.

Jimmy reviewed the pilot roster. He had recovered enough from his accident to declare himself fit for service, and the squadron's medical officer had drawn the same conclusion. Jimmy was next in action on 29 June. He was raised from his bed in the early dawn and was quickly washed and dressed. He made his way to the briefing with Gibby, Bruce, Tommy, and Bob. The planned mission was an armed reconnaissance of the road which runs northeast between Sées, located around 45 miles southeast of Caen, and L'Aigle. With all the activity at the front, the Roaring Boys knew their search for trouble had a high probability of success. At around 05.00 am Jimmy walked over to Spitfire NH240 and checked her over. The panels were cold to the touch as he moved around the aircraft, his hand checking the movement of the elevator, rudder, and ailerons. Sitting in the dawn light the Spitfire 'looked right' as pilots often say, and on the wing, an erk was proudly wiping down the canopy and removing the last of the squashed insects from the windscreen. He swung his head inside the cockpit and peered through the gun sight and windscreen, removing the last smears and smudges with his cloth. The line-up of Spitfires was a hive of activity as pilots and ground crews busily prepared themselves. Jimmy wasn't showing any outward sign of nerves; he was determined to make sure that he flew and fought to the very best of his ability. He put the events of the last few days behind him. His sole focus was the coming mission which is described in more detail in Bruce's chapter. When the squadron landed back at B4 at 06.55 am, Jimmy completed his log entry for the mission with a sense of satisfaction, tinged with relief for a well-executed mission. He wrote. "Found large convoy of German vehicles. Squadron got 10 flamers and at least 15 damaged – what a field day." He had meted out some punishment to the Germans for the loss of his friends. Tommy added to his personal score: "Destroyed 3 trucks. Damaged 1 staff car in the area south of Caen." At 21.00 pm that day Jimmy was back in the air for a squadron strength patrol of the eastern and western beachhead. He described the 10-minute flight: "No joy. Weather u/s so turned back."

Following an eventful day before Jimmy had a day to rest up while he waited for his evening patrol which was briefed in at around 19.30 pm by the boss S/L Robertson. Amongst the 12 pilots who would be flying on the mission were Charlie, rapidly making a name for himself with his growing number of kills, Ross and Dave. The plan was to fly a patrol of the front line around Caen, hoping to catch enemy fighters searching for Allied ground forces to attack. At 20.30 pm, the squadron was led into the air by S/L Robertson, climbing rapidly to the patrol height. The approach of dusk gave Jimmy a different perspective on the fighting below as he peered out of his cockpit. In concentrated areas, tracer rounds glowed brightly as they appeared to drift across the countryside, seemingly in all directions. There was intense fighting going on down there Jimmy thought, perhaps grateful for now that all was quiet at 7,000 feet. He scanned the horizon as suddenly an unidentified voice said: "Bandits ahead. Tally ho Yellow section." Jimmy could see the enemy fighters around a thousand feet above and crossing their path. He knew yellow section was led by Charlie in Spitfire Elizabeth, on a hot streak of downing Germans and he and three other Spitfires were instantly streaking after the enemy FW 190s. The combat action that followed is described in Charlie's chapter but for Jimmy his eyes scanned the horizon leaving no part of it unchecked, listening intently to the R/T traffic in case a warning came his way. With the dogfight over, yellow section rejoined the formation and they touched down at B4 at 21.40 pm. After landing, Jimmy offered his congratulations to Charlie as he and the other pilots and erks gathered round eager to hear details of the combat action. Jimmy was clearly impressed with Trainor's record: "Charlie shot down a Me 109 – This is his fourth in three days." For new pilots like Jimmy, Charlie was a pilot, and leader they could really look up to.

Spitfire NH341 Elizabeth
The morning of 2 July dawned with a grey, sullen sky, momentarily brightened as the sun did its best to break through. At around 05.00 am Jimmy, Charlie, Ross, and 4 others settled down for the briefing for their early morning patrol of the Easy and Eastern sectors of the bridgehead. Jimmy would be flying wingman to F/O E G Lapp in yellow section, with Charlie as leader and Ross as his No 2. As the pilots listened intently, S/L Robertson who would lead the other section spoke quickly and concisely mapping out the patrol area, the operational procedures, along with the expected weather pattern. He then handed over to the intelligence and army liaison officers who provided further background on known enemy Luftwaffe forces operating in the sector, and the relative dispositions of the opposing ground forces.

At 05.30 am Jimmy was ready, parachute on, pistol holstered, and escape kit tucked away. He wiggled his flying helmet down onto his head, squeezed the R/T leads between his fingers and jumped up onto the wing of Spitfire NH341. He was feeling warm in the chill morning air as for extra insulation and good luck he was wearing Thomas Tuttle's hockey jersey under his jacket. As he did so he saw the white joined up writing with the name "Elizabeth" glowing brightly on the cowling against the dull green camouflage paint. He settled down and hoped Elizabeth would keep him safe just as she had Bruce and all the others. His superstitious side was also positive about the two kills painted near the cockpit, marking the two enemy aircraft Charlie had shot down in NH341. She must be a lucky aircraft. Shortly, the fires were lit as the seven Spitfires Merlins reluctantly coughed and spluttered into life in the cold air, delivering a further layer of greyness to complement the overcast morning sky. Inside the cockpit of Spitfire Elizabeth, Jimmy was going through the post start-up procedures. Everything was looking good. He ran his hand over his mouth and chin and felt the new growth of his moustache. He buttoned his face mask on and pushed the fingers on each of his flying gloves down until each of his fingertips was at the end of his gloves. He heard Charlie's voice call Yellow section forward moving his hands in a cross-motion signalled for the erk to remove the chocks, which he did with a thumbs up as Jimmy then eased Elizabeth out of the dispersal area. At 05.50 am Jimmy throttled up, released the brakes and launched Spitfire Elizabeth along the runway and into the air, flicking his eyes onto the instruments to check all was within limits. He selected the undercarriage up lever and felt the low rumble as the landing gear was stowed with a short clunk into the wing. With the successful completion of several missions, Jimmy knew exactly what Gord Lapp needed him to do as his wingman. Lapp looked over and saw Jimmy moving into position on his starboard side. The formation was now approaching 7,000 feet, where they levelled off to begin their patrol of the bridgehead area. The ORB described the initial phase of the mission, "Easy section was uneventful." As the Roaring Boys pressed on heading east past Caen Jimmy heard Yellow 3, Gord Lapp's voice over the R/T: "Bandits, 2 o'clock low heading this way. Yellow Leader. Going down. Yellow 4 cover me." Trainor replied. "Roger Yellow 3." Jimmy banked Spitfire Elizabeth over and followed Lapp downwards, their Spitfires rapidly increasing in speed. Jimmy felt the adrenalin kick in, and his heart rate soared. His eyes were fixed on the enemy ahead of them. Butcher Birds, the distinct and unmistakable black crosses on their wings were growing in size and clarity with every second. His gun button was already switched to "fire." The memory of drills practiced endlessly over many months were now being performed subconsciously. In Gord Lapp's official account he wrote: "The FW 190s dropped their tanks but I closed in quickly and gave the nearest one a short burst from approximately 150 yards." Jimmy saw Lapp's guns pumping out rounds. Lapp continued: "He broke upwards into light cloud. I followed him through and gave him another burst at 100 yards, saw pieces come off his cockpit, he caught on fire then he rolled over, hit the ground and burst into flames." Gord Lapp's victim was Unteroffizier Gerhard Kraft of 6 Staffel Jagdgeschwader 26, who was flying an FW 190A-8 as Blue 5. Meanwhile, it's possible that Jimmy was able to squeeze off a few seconds of fire on the leading FW190, which was some distance away, the pilot seeing the fate of his wingman took immediate evasive action. The remaining pair of FW 190s had also broken away and after completing their climbing turn reentered the fray and tore after Lapp and Jimmy in a desperate attempt to save their comrades. They latched onto Jimmy's 6 o'clock. He was in trouble. He looked around and fear gripped him. He made the call, "Yellow 4. Two on my tail." He pushed Spitfire Elizabeth's throttle "through the gate" to get the maximum power, available only for a short time, but the FW 190s had dropped down onto him and had the greater momentum. Jimmy threw every feint, twist and turn he could before pulling the Spitfire into a tight turn. As he turned, he knew before stalling Spitfire Elizabeth would judder, and so holding the tightest turn with this judder, right on the limit he might just shake them off. Sweat was now running down Jimmy's forehead, the high G-forces he was experiencing he could handle, but he knew on no account must he blackout. Time seemed to stand still. Jimmy flicked his head round again. They were still there. One FW 190 had turned inside him. Silver streaks whistled past the cockpit. Nothing. Then again. The cockpit echoed to the sound of shearing metal and loud bangs as cannon shells ripped into his engine compartment. Jimmy instinctively ducked his head down behind his armoured headrest. Smoke poured out, and boiling oil splattered onto the windscreen. His engine cut and Jimmy had to make a split-second decision to get out, fast. He had lost all forward vision as the oil-streaked over his screen. His harness was undone in an instant, the oxygen hose pulled out and R/T leads unplugged. He pulled down and forward on the rubber knob at the top of the cockpit hood, dropping his head down as he flung his elbows at the bottom of the hood which sprang away instantly. His side door was thrown down as the sound of rushing air filled the cockpit. Jimmy crouched on his seat and with one hand on his parachute ripcord he used the other to throw the control column forward. He was lifted out into the air at around 3,500 feet, tumbling clear of Spitfire Elizabeth which was entering a shallow dive to the ground, smoke pouring out. He waited for what seemed an eternity but was actually only a few seconds as he was trained to do. His body would fall more slowly now than when he first exited the aircraft. Jimmy pulled the ripcord and felt the strong jolt on his harnesses and with some relief a full white canopy billowing above him. All was well. He was not out of danger as he anxiously looked around. The butcher birds were circling. No other Spitfires to be seen. Jimmy Jeffrey himself takes up the story: "One FW 190 followed me right down to the deck taking pictures of me, I think to confirm the kill." Jimmy must have had his heart in his mouth. German pilots had been known to fire at Allied airmen as they floated down. Surely, he would not meet his end like this, hanging helplessly from a silk parachute? Fortunately, the enemy aircraft flew away. The FW 190 pilot who shot Jimmy down was Fähnrich Waldemar Büsch of 6 Staffel Jagdgeschwader 26, flying FW 190A-8, Blue 1. He had already shot down a B17 and 2 B24 Liberator bombers, the last of which he accidentally rammed, losing his propeller and crash landing. On this day when he went into combat with Jimmy, Büsch led a schwarm of 4 FW 190s on a weather reconnaissance patrol, taking off at 06.20 am from Guyancourt aerodrome, located a few miles southwest of Versailles, Paris. As well as Gerhard Kraft and Büsch, the patrol included the hugely experienced Lt Peter Crump, a JG 26 ace and *experten* who held the Deutsches Kreuz Gold. The German Cross was instituted in 1941 by Adolf Hitler for repeated acts of bravery, or achievement in combat. Crump was shot down and wounded twice but survived the war with 24 confirmed (up to 31 including unconfirmed kills) to his name. Gord Lapp and Jimmy had joined battle with a fearsome opponent that day. Crump's tally from 1942 until the war's end included shooting down 17 Spitfires accumulated in over 202 combat missions. This may explain why Lapp and Jimmy were only able to attack Crump's wingman, Gerhard Kraft. Crump was able to take evasive action and knew exactly what the Spitfire's capabilities were in a dog fight. For Waldemar Busch, his euphoria at shooting down Spitfire Elizabeth, his first fighter aircraft was short-lived. Two days later, on 4 July he was engaged in combat with a "Free French" Spitfire from 340 squadron between Bayeux and Caen, an action in which he was shot down and killed. He was posthumously promoted to Leutnant. Jimmy's loss was felt by his 411 colleagues: Tommy wrote, "W/O Jimmy Jeffrey's shot down by two FW 190s" whilst Ross added in his logbook, "W/O Jeffries shot up and bailed out." Bruce made no comment in his log book about Jimmy's loss, or that of Spitfire Elizabeth but his concern was the same as the others. They didn't want to lose any of their fellow pilots. Spitfire Elizabeth's combat service with the Roaring Boys was at an end. The aircraft had flown 27 combat operations and had been in the thick of the action in the hands of the 9 courageous Canadians.

With the FW 190 threat passed, Jimmy beginning to contemplate his landing. He had not seen but had heard the dull crump as Spitfire Elizabeth crashed landed some distance away. He drifted downwards in the silence of a grey early morning; bird song filled the air. It was the polar opposite of the noise and hell he had experienced only a few minutes before. With the ground rushing up to meet him, Jimmy clamped his knees together for the impact. He collapsed his knees and rolled over, finishing up in a textbook side on position. Jimmy wrote: "I made a really smooth landing in an orchard, and immediately put my parachute and Mae West under a hedge." He felt fine and had no discernible injuries, so he moved quickly in case a German patrol had seen his descent or were alerted by the smouldering wreckage of Spitfire Elizabeth. The Germans would send patrols out to the wreckage and immediately see that he had escaped. They would be looking for him, with alerts going out across the sector.

Lawrie tells what happened next: "He came down in a farmer's orchard northwest of Orbec, a small town situated around 45 miles southeast of Caen, and around 12 miles south of Lisieux. After my father had stashed his parachute in a rocky hedgerow he ran to a farmhouse about 1/4 mile away. At the farmhouse, he saw a farmer standing outside the door of his house." Jimmy then approached the farmer and Lawrie gave details of what his father said: "I asked him for a change of clothing, which he fetched without hesitation. I told him to burn my battledress and all my equipment. I learned later he had dyed my uniform so he could wear it himself." Lawrie said his father recalled the scene in the house: "Sitting on the stairs inside the house watching the exchange was a young lad of about 6 or 8 years of age. This was M. Charles Haelewyn, the nephew of the farmer. M. Haelewyn currently lives and operates a bed and breakfast and dairy farm in Port en Bassin. From there, my father started to run down a road and was met by a fellow of about 15, and his sister. This fellow was M. Albert Soetaert, who I believe is still alive and lives in Orbec. He led my father through a stand of hardwood trees to the edge of the valley of the L'Orbiquet River. I believe they were travelling west or southwest toward the D519, a road which runs northwest from Orbec to Lisieux. Albert hid my father in a chicken coop and then he went off to contact the resistance. He brought a man who told my father that he knew someone who could help him. In the meantime, they brought him to the

Soetaert family house which is on the D519. At the time Albert's sister was living in the house with her husband, and they operated a dairy farm on the left side of D519 as the road heads northwest. When we visited in 2002, Albert took me down to a stone bridge over the L'Orbiquet river and showed me brown trout in the river. He said he leased a kilometre of the stream to a local trout fishing club. Albert's mother cooked my father a steak and frites, and Jimmy said he drank champagne, although we now think it might have been cider. Albert's mother also gave him a 'scapulaire' (A Roman Catholic item of religious belief) to keep him safe. After breakfast, Jimmy was returned to the chicken coop until 2 men came and took him into Orbec. He went to the Hotel de Ville with the escape photos he carried with him." Jimmy was impressed with the efficiency of the French, and he told Lawrie: "In less than half an hour my identity card was stamped, and my photograph affixed." This all happened apparently before about 9:30 am in the morning.

Lawrie continued: "From there I believe he walked, rode in a horse-drawn wagon and may have ridden a bicycle. He was passed off between different guides 3 times on his way to the Lecor farm north of Livarot, arriving after dark. He said he woke up in the morning, and the Lecor children were lined up around the bed looking at him. My father had learned basic Canadian high school French and he made the effort to communicate which was very much appreciated by the Lecors. My father got along very well with Paul Lecor. I know that he took my father into Livarot for a haircut and also to buy some cheese. It was at this time that my father had his first bad experience with Calvados liqueur which the family thought was hilarious." Clearly, the Canadians hadn't learned the lessons after their experiences the year before with the Munn family's scrumpy cider at RAF Staplehurst. Calvados is apple brandy and is extremely potent.

Lawrie returned to the subject of his father's superstitious nature: "After his earlier attempt to grow a moustache when joining 411, which he shaved off after his previous crash, Jimmy had decided to grow it back. After he was shot down on 2 July, and upon reaching the Lecor family farm, he shaved it off again so it would match up with his I.D. card photo. Mme Lecor thought he looked better clean shaven. He never attempted to grow a moustache again. When I got into my 20s, I decided to grow a moustache as was the style of the '70s. Whenever anything went wrong in my life, such as breaking a fishing rod, scratching the car or doing poorly in an exam, it was followed by my father saying: 'now will you shave off that goddamn moustache!' In his mind, they were seen as bringing continuous bad luck on the Jeffrey family!"

In the area of Orbec, like most areas of France, there were active Resistance cells in operation. These groups were involved in a range of activities designed to damage the Nazi occupiers. At risk of death, the Resistance carried out sabotage missions and assisted in returning Allied military personnel back to their lines. Jimmy was staying with the leader of one such network, Paul Lecor. His resistance fighters were joined by a number of Allied airmen and soldiers who helped continue the fight whilst awaiting their opportunity to get back to their units. As we have seen, any local French people who hid or assisted airmen like Jimmy risked capture and interrogation by the feared Gestapo, who were desperate to infiltrate and destroy the Resistance networks. If caught by the Germans, members faced almost certain death, either by immediate execution or sometime later after transportation to a concentration camp.

One Allied airman who was active in Jimmy's area was Major Donald W McLeod, a USAAF P47D pilot with 83rd Fighter Squadron, 78th Fighter Group who was shot down north of Argentan on 10 June. He spent a number of weeks helping the resistance to blow up bridges, and lay mines on local roads around Lisieux. He was joined by Lt Bob McIntosh of the USAAF, a P38 Lightning pilot from 485th Fighter Group. Two other pilots were also part of the group, 2nd Lt George Tripp who was also shot down and was sharing a house with an Australian Typhoon pilot from 609 squadron, WO George KE Martin DFC. Martin was shot down on D Day. He had been lucky to survive having bailed out at 200 feet after 609's Typhoons had attacked and hammered an SS unit from the air. The SS soldiers had found his parachute and raked the hedgerow in which he was hiding with gunfire, shattering his ankle.

On the morning of 14 July McLeod, McIntosh and George Martin were moved to Paul Lecor's house where Jimmy was staying. McLeod wrote in his official escape and evasion report about the Lecors: "They were harbouring a Canadian Spitfire pilot WO James Jeffrey RCAF 126 Wing stationed at Bény-sur-Mer. For the next 3 weeks, we all laid low. Some German soldiers moved into the adjoining barn, but they took no notice of us. M. Lecor and his wife continued to look after us and behaved splendidly." Lawrie commented: "I can clearly recall my father telling me when Major Mcleod and Lt. McIntosh came to the farm. He referred to them as 'big Mac and little Mac.' He also mentioned the Australian pilot. My father did not speak to them for 3 days. Paul Lecor told him to listen to them and then question them to see if they were legitimate pilots, or should be shot as spies. They were quite surprised to hear him speak English. Jimmy met Lt McIntosh again in 1998 when they were attending a memorial for some executed resistance folks. I don't think my father and the major got along very well. He continuously ordered McIntosh around and he tried to do the same with my father. My father told him he was in the RCAF and was not under the major's command. On one occasion when the Lecor house was surrounded by German soldiers the major wanted to get the guns out of the hiding place and prepare to fight. My father told him to let Paul handle it and Paul told the Germans there were no flyers there and they went away. My father was ready to leave on his own until Paul talked him into staying and the major was gone the next day."

"Paul Lecor and the resistance group were regularly listening in to BBC radio during which codes were broadcast advising of supply drops by the RAF. On 26 and 27 July, Jimmy accompanied 'big Mac and little Mac,' Paul Lecor and other members of the Resistance on a successful supply drop collection." You can imagine Jimmy and the others moving out of the Lecor farm in the dead of night. Each person was checked for 'shape, shake and shine.' This is military shorthand to check that there was no obvious light coloured clothing showing, perhaps twigs etc were added to break up their silhouette. Each man would have jumped up and down in case there was any jangling keys, or loose equipment, etc. Finally, there was a check that nothing shiny was showing. It's likely they would have blackened their faces too. Soon it was to time lock and load their weapons, safety catches on. Paul led the formation out across the fields in strict silence, hand signals only were allowed. He knew all the backways and pathways in the area like the back of his hand. At the prescribed hour, a number of small beacons were lit by Paul and his men. In the distant sky, the sound of droning engines signalled to Jimmy and the others that the

British supply aircraft would soon arrive. A morse code signal was flashed from the ground, which received an immediate reply. The aircraft circled and began its run in. Jimmy and the others laid in the hedgerow, as in the night sky several small white parachutes appeared, gently swinging rhythmically from side to side. Suspended underneath each was a container full of weapons, ammunition, explosives, and general supplies. Upon impact, several of the Resistance fighters sprinted out to flatten the billowing white chutes. They quickly returned, so far so good. For Jimmy and the two Macs, the danger inherent in this exercise was massive. They could be ambushed, or caught by the Germans. Despite being downed airmen, it was a flip of the coin as to whether they survived or not. Jimmy was mightily relieved as the small group made its way back to the farm. Lawrie said: "Jimmy was not big on going out to receive the equipment drops. He was scared most of the time and afraid of getting his ass shot off! He came home with post-traumatic stress disorder and he would wake up in the night claiming the Germans were chasing him."

Around 28 July, Jimmy and the others were joined by 2 paratroopers who had become separated from their units after D Day. They were Private William Osborne and Private Colin Lewis of the British and Canadian Parachute Battalions respectively. Lawrie recalled his father telling him about them: "My father did mention that they moved off the farm and were living in a cave up a hill from the Lecor farm. I think the Canadian trooper now lives in Buffalo, New York.

"My father also told me about a German Army Officer who moved into the house. He took the grandparent's room and bed. Jim said that the German used to listen to the BBC on short-wave radio, and they would be upstairs listening too." Major McIntyre also mentioned the German in his official account. He said that the German spoke several languages and that he, Jimmy and McIntosh pretended to be deaf mutes and sat and ate several meals with him. They even went hunting rabbits and behaved naturally. The thought of three young men in their early 20's, who all happen to be of fighting age and were deaf-mutes, does lead to the natural conclusion that the German Army officer probably had his suspicions about them. Perhaps, after listening in to the BBC, he realised that Germany would probably lose the war and that if he appeared suspicious then Jimmy and the others might execute him, or even report him for listening to the BBC, which could have resulted in a court-martial. It was well known in the Resistance that German patrols would regularly test the claimed deafness of those they came across. On one such occasion, the Australian RAF pilot George Martin was stopped by 2 sinister looking Gestapo men in black coats. Without warning one of them fired his pistol behind Martin who fortunately didn't flinch, and they let him go on his way.

The remaining part of Jimmy's escape story back to Allied lines is not known. Lawrie commented: "That's pretty well all I can recall my father telling me about his time behind the lines. I can recall that he was back in Bayeux by his birthday, 23 August and that he flew back to England in a C-47 Dakota wearing a British Army private's uniform. Ross also noted in his logbook: "Wheler, Tew, Evans, Jeffrey, Trainor. All escaped back." The son of Herb Strutt, Spitfire Elizabeth's ground crew also told a story that his father was waiting at a bus stop in Bayeux when the bus arrived and as the doors opened, he was amazed to see Jimmy get off!

Lawrie gave further details about the end of the war: "I know that after war Jimmy was not really anxious to go back to France as he felt it was just a part of his life and he had lost many friends. Henriette Lecor (Paul's daughter) moved to Windsor, Ontario after the war with her husband and made contact with my father. When Henriette's husband died, she moved back to Normandy and as far as I know still lives in Livarot. She was the main reason Jimmy went back to Normandy in 1998, and to go to the memorial dedication. Jimmy had spent approximately 3 months in Bournemouth with a ton of pilots waiting to get posted to a squadron. He really liked it there and during the 1998 visit, he made a trip there with Jean and Denise. My father also recalled meeting George Tripp on that visit.

Jimmy Jeffrey wrote about his Spitfire pilot friends:
"In the year 2000, I learned that Wally is buried in the village of St Coulombe. So, I returned to Normandy and found that he too was buried in a civilian cemetery and his grave is marked with a beautiful marble tombstone. I spoke with some villagers and learned that when he crashed, they arranged for a local priest to conduct the funeral. The three surrounding villages purchased the tombstone that marks his grave. As in

Dave's case, the villagers place the flowers on his grave every day." Jimmy Jeffrey recalled his discussions with Wally and Dave's families: "When I came home after the war, I drove to Tilbury to visit Wally's parents and Dave's mother and father came to my home in Toronto. These parents were seeking answers that I couldn't give, but I tried to explain my friendship with their two sons and how deeply I felt their loss."

Jimmy visited France in 1999 where he was reunited with Charles Ellewyn, Albert Soetaert, and Paul Lecor's widow Henriette and her son Louis. Lawrie Jeffrey said: "The whole of the Jeffrey family went back to Normandy in 2002 and retraced my father's steps through France. My daughter Denise also met Henriette Lecor during a visit to Normandy in 2011. We are especially grateful to our French friends and the families of Normandy who risked their lives to save our airmen. For that, we will always be in their debt.

"Jimmy survived the war and returned to Toronto, Ontario where he married his teen sweetheart, Jean Glazier. He worked for Canada Customs for 35 years, the last 20 as an investigator. Most of the guys he worked with were bomber crew, mostly RCAF Lancasters. I was born in 1953, the only child of Jimmy and Jean. I have 2 wonderful daughters with my wife Jocelyne, Denise in Ottawa and Julie in Victoria. Jimmy loved them very much and the girls loved to be in his company. He loved to play golf and watch sports especially baseball and football. He also loved to go to the track and bet on the harness racing. His other interests included coaching and umpiring baseball, hockey, and basketball.

"Jimmy and Jean moved to Lefroy, Ontario in 1988, to live in their renovated family cottage on Lake Simcoe. They made friends quickly through the United Church and these were the best years of their retirement. My father passed away in October 2005. Jean lived in the house until she passed away aged 94." Lawrie reflected on his father's life. "He was kind of a private character. He was not a big Canadian Legion supporter and kept a lot of his feelings bottled up and to himself. He didn't think that the war was any reason to sit down and drink beer. Although I know he would certainly appreciate the re-build of Spitfire Elizabeth, he would downplay his part and point at the other guys, especially Charlie Trainor and Tommy Wheler. He lost 3 friends who were shot down before him, and I think he felt some guilt that he came home, and they didn't. I guess those who were fortunate to come home each had their own memories and way of dealing with the trauma."

Jimmy had more than played his part during the war and as is so typical with the veterans, past, and present they were modest about what they did. Throughout the relatively short period, he was flying on operations before being shot down in Spitfire Elizabeth, Jimmy had taken the fight to the Luftwaffe and the Germans. He continued to disrupt the enemy on the ground too after he was shot down, in the traditions of the courageous Canadian pilots and servicemen who fought in the war.

"In France, my friends are remembered every day. I remember them every day."

James Stanley Jeffrey Spitfire pilot 411 Squadron.

CHAPTER ELEVEN

A PHOENIX RISES

The return of Spitfire NH341 Elizabeth to grace the skies above southern England once again opened a Pandora's Box of history and hidden stories that one could have never imagined all those years before. The inspiration behind the aircraft's return to flight and that of Aero Legends is Keith Perkins. He gave me an insight into the project, his wider thinking about Aero Legends and his role as a custodian of unique pieces of aviation history:

"Well, it has been quite a journey since that team building event in Hong Kong in 2010 where I announced my ambition to own a Spitfire. The seed of this deep-rooted admiration for such an iconic aircraft had been sowed when as a young boy the role it had played in saving our country during the darkest period of modern history was subtly everywhere. As with many boyhood dreams, the realities of life mean they are pushed to the back of your mind and dismissed as unachievable. For me, I had arrived at a point in my life where having had a successful career and enjoyed some exciting hobbies including a successful period racing superbikes, I was already looking for the next exciting challenge. The team event that I mentioned at the beginning of this chapter helped me to clarify what was truly aspirational. One of my team had a private pilot's license and a friend who flew Spitfires which made the road to owning one a little easier. I had seen that following a full restoration, Spitfire SM520 G-ILDA had been sold in 2009 and I assumed that a less pristine example could be bought for a figure within my budget. This proved to be a wildly optimistic assumption as there were no classic Spitfires for sale regardless of the funds available. However, there were some restoration projects available but rather worryingly the prices were on the rise. Following an introduction to Peter Monk at Biggin Hill, I made the bold move to purchase Spitfire IX TD314 as a turnkey restoration project. The Spitfire ownership journey had truly begun, and I looked forward to several years of funding the project at a monthly rate equivalent to the value of a new Aston Martin! At this time, I had not learned to fly but the ambition was always to be able to fly a Spitfire, so I thought that having my own two-seat trainer version was the way to go. At this time there were a number of restoration projects available and I selected NH341 knowing nothing of its history. The rebuild commenced and about that time I launched a flight experience business called Aero Legends based on the Second World War pilot training programme from the time; Tiger Moth, Harvard, and Spitfire. The plan was to restore and operate NH341 in this business for passenger rides and research into the history of this Spitfire became much more important. And what a history this machine has. This book tells the personal stories of the pilots who flew her on her 27 combat missions during 1944 and being shot down on the 2nd of July.

"This is a special Spitfire with a wonderful history and through the endeavors of the author, a friend since school Elizabeth's story has been told. I was proud to have met Tommy Wheler in 2015 when we invited him over to witness the rebuild of "his" Spitfire and was so privileged to have heard his recollections of his wartime experiences from the man himself. To know that he was stationed with 411 Squadron at RAF Staplehurst, a mere stone's throw from where Elizabeth operates on any summer's day is a poignant reminder. The joy of owning a piece of history such as NH341 is balanced by the responsibility that accompanies it. Whilst any Spitfire is admired and often revered, we should never allow the romantic images that such a beautiful machine conjures up to be confused with the reality that this Spitfire was a front-line fighter designed to shoot down enemy aircraft and strafe ground targets. Brave young men went into combat flying Spitfires and many never returned. Nine such stories are told in this book together with the importance that the RCAF's 2nd TAF and 126 Wing played in helping win the war.

(Author's note. Several years before Aero Legends started as a business my family had taken a holiday to Normandy and inevitably because of my passion for all things military we visited the Juno Beach Centre Museum which contained a diorama of a crashed Spitfire. I later found out during Spitfire Elizabeth's rebuild that this display was put together from the wreckage of NH341 and another Spitfire, ML295 flown by 411 Squadron pilot Hal Kramer. In fact, both Spitfires NH341 and ML295 had been flown by Tommy Wheler. Kramer was shot down by flak in Spitfire ML295 on 30 June 1944, after which he escaped from the Germans and returned home to Canada).

Martin Overall: Historic Flying Limited
Having closely followed the Spitfire Elizabeth's rebuild I was keen to meet with Martin Overall who led Historic Flying's project team. "Mo" as he is known, kindly agreed to my request for an interview and this was arranged at Duxford where, the Company, part of The Aircraft Restoration Company, known as ARCo is based. It's a hugely impressive facility they have there. Looking down on the hangar from the meeting area it was a hive of activity and for a plane buff like me, it was a wonderland! I began the meeting by discussing Mo's background:

"I had always been into aeroplanes, mainly models, but also all mechanical things like tractors and boats, etc. I did an aerospace engineering degree at Farnborough worked for the airline for a little while at Stansted. Then the opportunity came to work with Historic Flying Ltd which at the time was based at Audley End, Saffron Walden. So, I started there as a systems engineer which was absolutely fantastic. We didn't get involved in the flying side too much. In 2000, John Romain became chief engineer and a year later the company moved here to Duxford where a lot more flying went on which interested me. I gradually worked my way up to become hanger manager on the restoration side and primarily on the Spitfire projects.

Historic Flying had historically carried out the "deep" Spitfire restoration and we still do. The Aircraft Restoration Company deals with all sorts of different aeroplanes both restoration and maintenance wise. Traditionally, Historic Flying build the aeroplane and restore it and then once it has finished test flying it gets handed over then ARCo will operate it. Both operations are managed by John Romain."

Having seen the diorama in the Juno War Museum in 2002 I was keen to find out where Mo's team started the rebuild of Spitfire NH341 Elizabeth. Mo said: "It had already started with the fuselage at Airframe Assemblies. They had probably got 50% of the skeleton done and that's when we collected the aeroplane to complete the build as we had the capacity to complete the project. This was the first complete rebuild of a two-seat Spitfire by Historic Flying. Previously, we had completed the rebuild of Spitfire PV202. There was substantially more of this aircraft available than there was of NH341 as it was previously a two-seat Spitfire."

Mo and I discussed the original panel from NH341 that Aero Legends still have on display and which Tommy Wheler was photographed with during his visit to ARCo in 2015. Mo commented further on the aircraft: "There are lots of original Spitfire parts in NH341 Elizabeth from a variety of other aircraft. These include the dials in the instrument panel. Instruments are not too much of an issue as they fit every aircraft and so are freely available. Equipment like airspeed indicators are challenging. Getting the right 480 miles per hour airspeed indicator is difficult so we have to manufacture a face for the dial and then fit it to the appropriate indicator gauge to give it the correct appearance." I mentioned to Mo that I couldn't think of many Spitfires which carry the signature of one of the original pilots, which in Spitfire Elizabeth's case is Tommy Wheler's. He signed the panel during his visit to Historic Flying.

I asked Mo what the particular challenges are with building a two-seat Spitfire. He said: "canopies are quite difficult. Spitfire Elizabeth has the high rear bubble canopy with the internal winding mechanism and the front screen for that is very time consuming, You also have double the number of rudder pedals and control columns and interconnections than with a single seat because the aircraft is fully dual control. With the T9 Spitfires, there are complications with the drawings and the methods they employed to do the conversion. The process was based on starting with a single seat Spitfire. You can see exactly what they were thinking and how they have gone about it. It's not ideal in some ways. You look at it and think why would they have done that? Of course, they already had a perfect single seat Spitfire, to begin with. If they were building a T9 two-seat Spitfire from scratch it would be completely different. Pretty much all of the drawings are available. The originals are at Hendon and you can get copies of those."

I questioned Mo further about the difference between the rear bubble canopy and what is called the "Grace canopy," and whether this was a subject of debate for Spitfire Elizabeth. Mo said: "Keith was clear he wanted a bubble canopy as he was a fan of the Vickers conversion and so that's the way it was." We discussed the relative merits of each type of rear canopy and Mo added: "For some people, the Grace version presents a sleeker profile." Mo has flown in both styles and said: "in the Grace version there's a Perspex tunnel between the front and rear cockpits to see through and out at that level. It's different, but not necessarily better or worse. As a training tool though it's not as good as the instructor is in the back and needs to sit as high as possible to see over the nose of the aircraft." I recalled watching when Mo was training to fly the Spitfire with retired Air Vice Marshall Cliff Spink, with whom I worked on Spitfire ground crew duties many times. They used to fly back from Headcorn to Duxford, Cliff in the front and Mo in the rear. Then one day I noticed they had switched. Mo said, "that was a big day!"

Mo and I went on to talk some more about other changes to the T9 Spitfire's structure and he said: "the external dimensions of the aeroplane are exactly the same to the single seat. The T9 has the larger rudder with a pointier fin just to make it a bit easier for landing and also to counteract any effect that the rear bubble canopy might have on rudder authority."

Mo and I then moved on to discuss the engine that was installed in Spitfire Elizabeth. He said: "Keith Perkins decided that the Packard Merlin 266 would be fitted. They are a little bit more tolerant to the way we operate with a different supercharger arrangement and they are a slightly smoother engine as well. A lot of the "high engine time" users opt for the 266 over the Rolls Royce Merlin 66 which would have been fitted in the original aircraft. They are serviced throughout the flying season, for example at 25 and 50 hours where oil changes and more detailed checks take place." This trend to use the Merlin 266 has followed the expansion of the passenger flight business in the UK where a Spitfire can fly hundreds of hours in a year, and so the Packard 266 is preferable. The importance of the Merlin engine to the war effort meant that production was also undertaken by the Packard Motor Company in the United States. The various marks of the Merlin engine were not only fitted in the Spitfire. They were also fitted in the Hurricane, Mosquito, Lancaster Bomber, aircraft that were all critical to Britain's RAF during the war. The Packard Merlin was also famously built into the North American P51 Mustang as a replacement for the original Allison V-1710 engine, transforming the aircraft's performance and allowing it to join the Spitfire in a small elite group of incredibly successful Allied fighters.

I asked Mo about the availability of the Packard Merlin engines. He said: "it was simply a case of order one and a year later it arrives. The engine was supplied by Retro Track & Air (U.K.) Ltd. They are getting more difficult to find now and a lot more expensive as the companies producing them have had to get many more parts made. There are no longer components available, or the recovery process is more elaborate to keep them going. There will come a time when more significant components will need to manufactured to supply aircraft owners worldwide." I had previously visited Retro Track & Air with Keith Perkins during the project to build Aero Legends single seat Mark IX Spitfire, TD314. It was a fascinating insight into this most famous engine, a power plant that helped shape Britain's future and which made a significant contribution to winning the Battle of Britain, and the war.

The Spitfire's famous elliptical wings were manufactured by Mo's team at Historic Flying, and if you've ever looked at the wing tips you can see how amazingly thin they are. He went to describe the process: "the challenge of the wings is that there are a just so many bits and there is very little commonality as every rib is a different shape. Each jig is different just because of the shape of the wing. There's a taper in thickness and a curve to it, the whole thing is individual. It's very time consuming to make all those bits. We have some excellent jigs here and all the layup boards so that we can make wings from nothing." Mo explained that Historic Flying has their own team who are dedicated to wing manufacture: "All the skills are general to make the bits, to shrink and form things. It's having the experience of putting the wings together that is the difference in terms of time and quality of the finished and the final product."

With regards to the weight of Spitfire Elizabeth compared with her wartime version Mo commented: "She would be lighter now than she would have been during the war as we are not carrying any of the armour plating, guns, and ammunition, so she is well below service weight even with two people, and full of fuel." Of course, as we have seen earlier in the book Spitfire Elizabeth was also set up to carry 1 x 500 lb bomb and 2 X 250 lb bombs.

Mo and I then talked about him flying Spitfire Elizabeth which was a special moment. He displayed the aircraft during the Aero Legends Air Show, and also at Flying Legends in 2017. He thought he probably had a total of about 20 hours flying time in her at the time of writing. I asked Mo what he and the engineers were thinking and feeling during the first test flight Spitfire Elizabeth made with John Romain at the controls. I stood there on a misty morning at the Imperial War Museum, Duxford on 11 March 2017. He said: "I would say that the engineers were more nervous than the pilot in the aeroplane at that stage. You know you've had it tied down, it runs as it should, it meets the numbers, everyone has been through it and of course, it's why you have highly experienced test pilots like John Romain." I for one look forward to seeing Mo at the controls of

Spitfire Elizabeth for many years to come. He and the team at Historic Flying certainly built Keith a magnificent Spitfire, which is bringing joy to so many people. And, as one of the former Roaring Boys said about Aero Legends customers who fly in Spitfire Elizabeth today:

"It's just amazing that you can understand what we got to go through by flying the same aeroplane that I flew." Honorary Lieutenant Colonel T R "Tommy" Wheler MBE DFC CD Legion d'Honneur, 411 Squadron.

Doug Wheler pointing at the panel in Spitfire Elizabeth
which is signed by Tommy

The current pilots who have followed in the footsteps of the Roaring Boys to take the controls of Spitfire Elizabeth are cognisant of her history and the broader legacy of the Spitfire itself. I caught up with F/L Antony "Parky" Parkinson MBE, F/L Charles "Charlie" Brown and Squadron Leader Andrew "Milli" Millikin to seek their views. It's always a pleasure to watch them taking customers for flights or displaying the aircraft. In aviation terms, I can't imagine it gets much better for them as pilots, or for flyers in Elizabeth. Parky, Charlie, and Milli are three masters of their craft. Parky said of the Spitfire:

"So much has been written and said about the Spitfire. Its place in history is unquestioned. The sight and sound of this beautiful aircraft symbolise the sacrifice of a generation and the freedom they gave to us. The Spitfire is the very definition of an icon and it was as a fighting machine that she earned this status – even amongst her foes.

Aviation technology has always moved at a lightning pace – no more so than in the first half of the last century - with the advent of better aerodynamics, avionics, and ever more powerful engines. In early 1936, the Spitfire made the new 200mph biplanes arriving on front line RAF Squadrons obsolete overnight. Her performance and firepower were staggering, and these were to be continually improved throughout her service life. An aircraft perfect for constant development as technologies advanced.

The Spitfire does everything so well. It's fast. It's powerful. It's agile. Happy flying fast or flying slow. Happy flying down low "in the weeds" or in the thin air of the troposphere. But it is the ease that it does it - the lightness and sensitivity of the controls that are so well harmonised and provide instant feedback to the pilot inside. Flying a Spitfire is the ultimate aviation delight – the controls are so precise and delicate that it is hard to believe it is an 80-year-old design. The stall (deliberately flying too slowly so the wings will not produce enough lift) in a Spitfire is a perfect example. As the speed washes off, the controls remain light with a gentle buffet from the wings fed through the stick to your hands. Buffet increases until finally she can fly no more and a wing (usually the right) gently drops. Recovery is immediate - just slight forward pressure on the stick and she's flying again. And these handling qualities is what endeared the Spitfire to all who flew her. Fighting for your life against a deadly enemy – she could be flown to her limits and literally thrown around the skies in the lethal arena of aerial combat. The Spitfire conveys to you that it has your back.

And so, it was upon this hallowed backdrop that I watched NH341 slowly take shape in the Duxford hangar throughout 2015 and 2016. From a partially complete fuselage, she slowly transformed into a beautiful 2-seater Spitfire resplendent in her 411 Squadron codes. I recall vividly my first flight in her – an absolute delight and joy to fly. Seeing her reunited with one of her pilots, Tommy Wheler was simply wonderful. His affection, like that of the country, remained undiminished. That is a Spitfire. Legendary. And in my opinion, the greatest aircraft ever built."

Milli shared his thoughts on the Spitfire and like the other pilots his passion and affection shine through:

"She's a *femme fatale*. She's the girl you first fell in love with at school. She makes your heart beat faster. She makes your stomach flip and the world a woozy place in her presence. She's the reason you wanted to fly. She's both aloof and alluring; her long proud nose inviting admiration, yet proffering disdain. She's all this and more. She is the Supermarine Spitfire.

She invites cliché and hyperbole. Finest, best, greatest. And there is a good reason for this adulation. That reason is simple; she is deserving of all these accolades. A more accomplished fighter with a prouder and more successful combat history you will not find. None of the current generations of fighter aircraft, or those that will come in the future, will match her.

But why? The brutal beauty and potency of the Su35 Flanker. The F-22 Raptor's world-beating performance and sensors. The new F-35 Lightning II with its stealth and vertical landing ability. None can hold a candle to her. Because none of these new pretenders to the throne will get the chance to prove themselves in the way the Spitfire did. Across Europe, North Africa, the Far East and even Australia; the Spitfire saw action and victory wherever she flew. In hundreds of thousands of skirmishes, dogfights, and strikes around the globe, the Spitfire shot and bombed its way into the history of aerial combat.

Having had the privilege of flying both the Spitfire and also the Typhoon I am in some way qualified to compare the two types. Both are exceptional fighters; boasting Rolls Royce engines generating thrilling amounts of thrust. Both are agile and capable of out-turning and out-climbing almost every adversary of their day. Both are incredibly receptive to the pilot's inputs - eager to prove their agility with the lightest touch on the control column.

When I'm asked which I prefer to fly, there is no question about the answer. It's the *femme fatale* for me. Every time."

Spitfire Elizabeth is now in the next chapter of her life and she carries in and around her those echoes from the past, the 9 Canadian pilots, the Roaring Boys of 411 Squadron. Their memory lives on in those who sit and fly in Elizabeth today, and who will hopefully spare a thought and remember those men and what they did all those years ago.

Bruce, Charlie, Ross, Tommy, Dave, Gibby, Len, Bob, and Jimmy. I have learned so much about your incredible lives, and your unbounded courage and determination. You are in my eyes the embodiment of what is often called the greatest generation. Fly high.

High Flight

Oh! I have slipped the surly bonds of earth,
And danced the skies on laughter-silvered wings;
Sunward I've climbed, and joined the tumbling mirth
Of sun-split clouds, -and done a hundred things
You have not dreamed of -Wheeled and soared and swung
High in the sunlit silence. Hov'ring there
I've chased the shouting wind along, and flung
My eager craft through footless halls of air...
Up, up the long, delirious, burning blue
I've topped the wind-swept heights with easy grace
Where never lark or even eagle flew -
And, while with silent lifting mind I've trod
The high untrespassed sanctity of space,
Put out my hand, and touched the face of God

Pilot Officer John Gillespie Magee Jr, 412 squadron

APPENDIX

SPITFIRE NH341 ELIZABETH: MISSION AND PILOT SUMMARY

14/6/44: Ramrod 1000: Time: 22:10 to 23:00: Pilot: F/O A B Whiteford
One of 12 Spitfires providing fighter high escort (25,000 feet) to Lancaster bombers on a mission to bomb the docks at Le Havre. The ORB says: "intense flak was encountered initially but petered out. Pilots reported a good job done to wipe out the E-boat menace to channel transportation."

15/6/44: Beachhead Patrol: Time 18:10 to 19:55. F/O A B Whiteford
One of 13 Spitfires on beachhead patrols during which 3 staff cars and 1 armoured vehicle were destroyed.

16/6/44: Beachhead Patrol: Time 15:15 to 17:15. F/O A B Whiteford
One of 12 Spitfires on beachhead patrols which were described as, "uneventful".

17/6/44: Beachhead Patrol: Time 06:10 to 08:00. F/O A B Whiteford
One of 12 Spitfires on beachhead patrols which were described as, "uneventful".

17/6/44: Beachhead Patrol: Time 13:35 to 15:30. F/L H C Trainor
One of 12 Spitfires on beachhead patrols which were described as, "uneventful".

17/6/44: Beachhead Patrol: Time 21:00 to 22:55. F/L H C Trainor
One of 12 Spitfires on beachhead patrols which were described as, "uneventful".

18/6/44: Beachhead Patrol: Time 06:00 to 08:15. F/O S R Linquist
One of 11 Spitfires on beachhead patrols which were described as, "uneventful".

18/6/44: Beachhead Patrol: Time 14:55 to 17:00. F/L H C Trainor
One of 12 Spitfires on beachhead patrols, "carried out uneventfully."

22/6/44: Dive bombing: Time 15:10 to 15:35. F/O A B Whiteford
One of 12 Spitfires on a dive bombing mission over 2 bridge targets: "Buildings were hit on the east and west side of the river. Light flak was encountered east of Caen".

22/6/44: Fighter sweep: Time 21:00 to 21:45. F/O A B Whiteford
One of 13 Spitfires on: "a fighter sweep Caen, Lisieux, Largle, Argentan area. Two trucks, one bus destroyed. No enemy aircraft or flak encountered. Mechanised transport was observed travelling west. Convoy travelling North East."

24/6/44: Armed reconnaissance: Time 17:55 to 19:05. F/O T R Wheler
One of 12 Spitfires on: "an armed recce in the Fleurs, Carrogues, Domfront area. Four mechanised transports were attacked – all left smoking. One aircraft returned early with undercarriage trouble."

25/6/44: Armed reconnaissance: Time 04:40 to 05:10. F/O A B Whiteford
One of 10 Spitfires on: "an armed recce. One truck damaged"

26/6/44: Beachhead Patrol: Time 06:05 to 07:35. F/O A B Whiteford
One of 12 Spitfires on beachhead patrols which were described as, "uneventful".

26/6/44: Beachhead Patrol: Time 19:15 to 20:40. F/L D H Evans
One of 8 Spitfires on beachhead patrols which were described as, "uneventful".

27/6/44: Armed reconnaissance: Time 12:55 to 14:10. F/L W R Gibson
One of 11 Spitfires on: "an armed recce south of Caen. Ten mechanised transports attacked resulting in 6 flamers, 2 smokers and 1 damaged. One

tank was left burning and another left smoking. Later encountered 15 plus FW 190s. S/L Robertson destroyed one; F/L Johnson damaged two and W/O Kerr damaged another one. F/O Wallace disappeared into clouds and has not been seen or heard from since."

27/6/44: Front line Patrol: Time 16:45 to 17:40. F/L A B Whiteford
One of 11 Spitfires on front line patrols: "Five FW 190s momentarily engaged the squadron south of Bayeux but escaped into clouds. Enemy flak hit F/L Nixon's aircraft and he was forced to bail out south of Bayeux. He sustained no injuries."

28/6/44: Armed reconnaissance: Time 08:30 to 09:50. F/L D H Evans
One of 12 Spitfires on: "an armed recce south of Caen. Results were two mechanised transports damaged. Between 40-50 FW 190 and Me 109s were seen but not engaged due to shortage of fuel."

28/6/44: Armed reconnaissance: Time 12:25 to 13:55. F/L A B Whiteford
One of 12 Spitfires on: "an armed recce south of Caen. Results were three flamers, four damaged. More than fifteen ME 109s and FW 190s were engaged south of Le Havre. F/O Wheler destroyed and damaged FW 190s (one each); F/L Trainor destroyed an ME 109 and F/L Hayward damaged an FW 190."

29/6/44: Armed reconnaissance: Time 05:30 to 06:55. F/L A B Whiteford
One of 11 Spitfires on: "an armed recce in the Sées L'Aigle area. Results of the operation were 13 flamers, 5 smokers and 10 damaged. One armoured vehicle damaged, and one ammo truck was seen to explode. Accurate light flak was encountered in the Flers area."

29/6/44: Armed reconnaissance: Time 08:25 to 09:40. F/L A B Whiteford
One of 7 Spitfires on: "an armed recce in the Vire, Aunoy sur Oden area. Four flamers and six damaged mechanised transports were scored. Heavy accurate intense flak was encountered at Villers."

29/6/44: Front line patrol: Time 15:30 to 16:45. F/L H C Trainor
One of 8 Spitfires on a front-line patrol: "Two mechanised transports were damaged and 15 Me 109s were engaged east of Caen. One was destroyed by F/L Trainor. Our pilots broke off the engagement due to our ammunition being expended."

29/6/44: Beachhead Patrol: Time 21:00 to 21:10. F/O N L Harrison
One of 9 Spitfires on beachhead patrols: "Eastern and western beach patrol. Recalled due to weather. Uneventful."

30/6/44: Dive bombing: Time 16:15 to 17:20. F/L R S Hyndman
One of 11 Spitfires on a dive bombing mission: "Dive bombing crossroads in Bretteville. Six FW 190s from Caen followed and engaged our aircraft. Bombs were jettisoned on road to target to enable us to engage the Hun. S/L Robertson chased a 190 in and out of the cloud and finally shot it down in flames. One mechanised transport flamer was also scored."

30/6/44: Front line patrol: Time 20:30 to 21:40. F/L H C Trainor
One of 12 Spitfires on a front-line patrol: "F/L Trainor saw an Me 109 and after chasing it scored many strikes causing it to crash after the pilot bailed out. Otherwise, patrol was uneventful."

1/7/44: Armed reconnaissance: Time 07:50 to 08:30. F/L A B Whiteford
One of 11 Spitfires on: "an armed recce in the Falaise, Flers, Condi sur Noireau, Thury Harcourt area. Uneventful."

1/7/44: Bridgehead patrol: Time 09:10 to 09:50. F/L A B Whiteford
One of 8 Spitfires on a: "patrol of the William and Easy sectors of the bridgehead. Uneventful. The weather was bad – rain."

2/7/44: Bridgehead patrol: Time 05:50 to Missing. W/O J S Jeffrey
One of 7 Spitfires on a: "patrol of the William and Easy sectors of the bridgehead. Easy section was uneventful. Four aircraft on Eastern sector became engaged with four FW 190s southwest of Caen F/O Lapp E G destroying one. WO II J S Jeffrey was apparently shot down southeast of

Caen as he reported on his R/T he was being chased by two enemy aircraft and later that he was going to bale out. No word has been heard of or from him since."

Spitfire Elizabeth made a total of 27 operational combat missions over the Normandy battlefront before being shot down on 2 July. The summary of these missions is as follows;

- 1 escort to Lancaster bombers on a mission to attack E-boats at Le Havre
- 10 patrols over the Normandy Beachhead
- 8 armed reconnaissance patrols
- 2 bridgehead patrols
- 1 fighter sweep
- 2 dive bombing missions
- 3 front line patrols
- 2 Messerschmitt Me 109s shot down

GLOSSARY

10/10	a definition of cloud density with 10/10 as the thickest and 1/10 as light scattered clouds.
AA	anti-aircraft guns.
Ace	a pilot who has shot down 5 or more enemy aircraft.
A/C	short for aircraft.
Adjutant	an officer who assists the squadron's commanding officer with administration duties.
AFV	Armoured fighting vehicle.
Angle of attack	the angle between the oncoming air and a reference line on the wing of an aircraft.
Angels	an RAF term used to describe altitude e.g. enemy fighters at Angels 25, meaning 25,000 feet.
ASR	Air Sea Rescue.
Base leg	a descending flight path a landing aircraft makes prior to lining up and pointing directly at the runway to begin its final approach to landing.
Battery cart	an external power source used to turn over an aircraft engine.
BCATP	British and Commonwealth Air Training Plan.
Bandits	hostile enemy aircraft that have been identified.
Beehive	a small formation of bombers (hive) with escorting fighters (bees).
Blue on blue	a friendly fire incident from your own side.
Bogeys	unidentified aircraft which could be friendly or enemy forces.
Bombphoon	a bomb carrying Typhoon.
Box of bombers	a section of bombers flying in formation.
Cat E	RAF description for damage inflicted on an aircraft which for Cat E means it is unrepairable.
Caterpillar Club	a club for pilots whose lives had been saved by a parachute after bailing out of an aircraft.

Circus	RAF term where bombers heavily escorted by fighters were sent to enemy territory in order to draw Luftwaffe fighters into combat.
Circuit	The standard approach path flown by aircraft taking off or landing at an airfield whilst keeping visual contact with the airfield. The direction of the circuit can change with the prevailing wind direction.
CO	Commanding officer.
Deutsches Kreuz Gold	The German Cross. Instituted by Adolf Hitler in 1941 for repeated acts of bravery.
Dead stick landing	A forced landing when an aircraft has lost power and effectively glides into land.
Deflection	firing an aircraft's guns at an angle ahead of the aircraft being attacked so the bullets intersect.
DFC	Distinguished Flying Cross a military decoration awarded for exemplary gallantry during active operations against the enemy in the air. Further awards for gallantry merit the addition of a Bar to the award.
Drang nach osten	an 19th Century German term to describe the expansion eastwards from Germany into Slavic lands.
DSO	Distinguished Service Order a military decoration Distinguished services during active operations against the enemy. Those awarded the decoration can add a Bar for further examples of bravery.
E/A	an abbreviation of enemy aircraft.
Erk	ground crew in a squadron.
Experten	elite German Luftwaffe pilots many of whom had been killed, wounded or captured by 1944.
Fahnrich	Luftwaffe officer cadet.
Finals	or final approach is where an aircraft begins its final descent to landing on the airfield runway.
Goldfish Club	a club for pilots who had have escaped an aircraft by parachuting into water.
Ground loop	miscontrolling an aircraft on the ground causing it to spin round.
Glycol	ethylene glycol was used as a coolant for aircraft engines in both RAF and Luftwaffe fighters.

F/O	Flying Officer.
GEE-H	radio navigation system developed in Britain during world war 2 which could direct up to aircraft at a time onto a target up to 200 miles away from England. Targets could then be bombed "blind" from above any cloud cover.
Hypoxia	oxygen deprivation which at high altitude could result in blackouts and ultimately death.
INT/OPS	Intelligence and Operations briefing area, where the pilots were given mission briefings and post-mission debriefs.
Jagdgeschwader	Luftwaffe fighter wing.
Jet tanks	short for jettisoning auxiliary fuel tanks used to extend the Spitfire's flying range. They came in various sizes e.g. 45 and 90 gallon sizes.
Ju 88, Ju 188	Luftwaffe medium bomber.
Kampfgeschwader	Luftwaffe bomber unit.
Kriegsmarine	the German Navy.
Les Rosbifs	literally "the Roast beefs." An inoffensive 18th-century term used by the French to describe the English developed from our style of cooking.
Lodgement area	an enclave taken by and defended by force of arms against determined opposition made by increasing the size of the beachhead into a substantial defended area, at least the rear parts of which are out of the direct line of fire.
Mae West	a life jacket nicknamed after the Hollywood actress of the same name.
MBE	The Most Excellent Order of the British Empire is a British award for chivalry.
Me 109	Messerschmitt 109 sometimes described as the *Bf 109* Bayerische Flugzeugwerke the firm which designated the aircraft and was reconstituted as Messerschmitt AG.
MET	Mechanised enemy transport. A loose description for any sort of lorry or truck.
Mph	measure of speed; miles per hour.
NASA	North American Space Agency.

No Ball	a German V1, V2 rocket or V3 cannon research, production and launch facility.
Oberfahnrich	the Luftwaffe rank of flight sergeant.
Obergefreiter	the Luftwaffe rank of corporal.
OC	officer commanding, normally a wing or squadron.
ORB	Operational Record Book an official record of the Squadron's operational activities.
OTU	Operational Training Unit for advanced instruction of flying.
Panzer	German word for a tank.
Pitot tube	a cylindrical tube located on the underside of an aircraft wing to measure airspeed.
P/O	Pilot Officer.
Pranging	RAF slang for causing damage, whether to an aircraft or an enemy target.
PSP	Pierced steel planking used to prevent runways and taxiways becoming quagmires.
Ramrod	a short-range bomber mission to attack ground targets. In the context of this book given fighter protection by Spitfires from 411 Squadron.
RAF (k) 1250	an RAF identification card.
Ranger	freelance mission over enemy territory by units of any size, to occupy and tire enemy fighters.
RCAF	The Royal Canadian Air Force.
RCN	The Royal Canadian Navy.
Rodeo	a fighter sweep over enemy territory.
R/T	Radio transmitter used by the pilots to communicate with each other and their controllers.
R/V	rendezvous or meeting.
Schnellbomber	a high-speed German bomber.
Sommerfeld	tracking a lightweight wire mesh covering used to prevent aerodromes from becoming quagmires.
Sortie	from the French word for exit meaning in military terms a combat mission undertaken by a single aircraft.
S.F.A	Sweet Fanny Adams.
Spinner	A streamlined fairing fitted over an aircraft's propeller hub.

SS	the 'Schutzstaffel.' A paramilitary organisation of the Nazi party and Hitler's elite bodyguard. Alongside the political arm, the SS comprised military units. They were found by the Allies to be fanatical opponents.
T and Ps	temperature and pressure gauges located on the cockpit instrument panel.
Tiffie	nickname for the Typhoon fighter bomber also called a 'bombphoon.'
Tip and run	raiders. Luftwaffe fighters sent singularly or in pairs to coastal towns to drop single bombs or strafe targets of opportunity before returning to their French bases.
Top brass	senior military commanders.
Trim wheel	a wheel that can be turned to make minute adjustments to the ailerons, elevators, and rudder, thereby setting the aircraft in steady flight and taking the pressure off the control column. In a trimmed aircraft, it's possible to take your hands off the stick and the aircraft will continue to fly at the angle of attack and direction you have set it to.
Unteroffizier	Luftwaffe noncommissioned officer.
U/S	unserviceable or faulty equipment.
V1	pilotless flying bomb known as a "doodle bug" or "buzz bomb."
V2	a rocket which flew near the edge of space and carried high explosives.
Wash out	a characteristic of aircraft wing design which deliberately reduces the lift distribution across the span of an aircraft's wing. The wing is designed so that the angle of incidence is greater at the wing roots and decreases across the span, becoming lowest at the wing tip.
Work ups	the process of training a pilot in all aspects of a squadron's operational procedures in readiness for a combat role.
WREN	The Women's Royal Naval Service.
Wings	awarded to a qualified military pilot upon successful completion of their flight training.
WO	Warrant Officer.
Yaw	the action of an aircraft changing direction.

REFERENCES AND NOTES

The reference source for the history and operational records are the 411 Squadron Operational Records and squadron diaries. The Héritage Project, The Canadian Research Knowledge Network.

CHAPTER 1   411 Squadron

Oliver "Ubangi" Pierce origin of the Roaring Squadron. Three sources: McClenaghan, John and Blatchford, Derek *411 City of North York Squadron History,* Canadian Department of National Defence *The RCAF Overseas: The Fifth Year* and Tommy Wheler, discussions with Nick Oram 21 January 2018 and 7 March 2018.

Reorganisation of RAF in 1943. Shores, Christopher and Thomas, Christopher *2nd Tactical Air Force Volume 1 Spartan to Normandy:* Chevron Publishing Limited 2004.

126 Wing tally of destroyed German aircraft and equipment. Nijboer, Donald *No 126 Wing,* Osprey Publishing 2010.

Buck McNair forced to give up as 126 Wing Commander on 12/4/44 due to eyesight. Shores, Christopher and Thomas, Christopher *2nd Tactical Air Force Volume 2 Breakout to Bodenplatte:* Chevron Publishing Limited 2004.

Johnnie Johnson quote on Spitfire weakness to ground fire. Bader, Douglas *Fight for the Sky: The Story of the Spitfire and Hurricane*: WS Cowell Ltd.

Operation Crossbow. BBC TV documentary Operation Crossbow director Tim Dunn. Additional material: Foreman, John *The Fighter Command War Diaries Volumes 3,4, and 5* Air Research Publications 2002 and Wikipedia.

Ringo operation. Sourced from 411 ORBs.

27 January 1944 Casablanca Conference. http://ww2today.com/27th-january-1943-u-s-bombs-from-u-s-airplanes-with-u-s-crews-hit-germany

Operation Crossbow reference to foret d'Eperlecques fortifications. https://en.wikipedia.org/wiki/Blockhaus_d%27%C3%89perlecques

Dive bombing technique op. cit. Nijboer.

"Good night nurse" quotation. Jimmy Corbin DFC recollections of the Battle of Britain. Interview G-Forces Web Management Limited July 2007.

P51 reference op.cit. Foreman.

Details of the Empire Air Training Plan. Milberry Larry and Halliday Hugh *The Royal Canadian Air Force at War 1939-45* CANAV books 1990.

P/O William "Tex" Ash. Obituary The Daily Telegraph 30 April 2014. Wikipedia. Op. cit. Foreman.

Franks, Norman *Buck McNair Spitfire Ace* Grub Street 2001.

27 March 1944 Operation Steinbock, the" Baby Blitz," Wikipedia.

24/7/44. Ammo dump explosion at B4. Berger, Monty, and Street, Brian Jeffrey *Invasions without Tears* Random House of Canada 1994.

No Ball definition. Wikipedia.

Sailor Malan Ten rules air fighting. Wikipedia.

Joskins the dog travelling to Normandy. Told to Roger Strutt, son of 411 Squadron aircraft mechanic Herb Strutt. Discussed with Nick Oram during Roger's visit to Headcorn Aerodrome 18 July 2018.

Johnnie Johnson on poor ill-trained pilots Johnson, Johnnie *Wing Leader* Chattot & Windus Ltd 1956

Herb Strutt's recollections. Meeting with Roger Strutt 18 July 2018 Headcorn aerodrome.

CHAPTER 2   BRUCE WHITEFORD

The pilot logbook of Bruce Whiteford.

Jimmy Corbin hit by flak. Corbin DFC, Jimmy *Last of the Ten Fighter Boys* Sutton Publishing 2007.

Johnnie Johnson stating the Spitfire Vb was outclassed by the FW 190. Op. cit. Johnson.

Gypsy moth CF0CFQ Civil Aircraft Register Canada. http://www.airhistory.org.uk/gy/reg_CF-4.html

BCATP Borden. Bruce Whiteford on 1st course.

http://www.veterans.gc.ca/eng/remembrance/history/second-world-war/british-commonwealth-air-training-plan and http://www.rcaf-arc.forces.gc.ca/en/16-wing/history.page

29 January 1943 mission. http://www.8thafhs.com/get_one_mission. php?mission_id=641

Sqn Leader Turkington. http://www.craigavonhistoricalsociety.org.uk/rev/gilpindserviceandsacrifice.html

Ian Ormston bailing out in the sea. Op. cit. McClenaghan & Blatchford.

Reference the FW 190 as a fighter. Bader, Douglas *Fight for the Sky: The Story of the Spitfire and Hurricane*: WS Cowell Ltd.

Jimmy Corbin DFC recollections of the Battle of Britain. Interview G-Forces Web Management Limited July 2007.

Ramrod 428 6 January 1944. Op. cit. Foreman.

Reference to the muzzle velocity of a Hispano cannon. www.spitfire.com

Yaw reference. Nichol, John *Spitfire A very British Love Story:* Simon & Schuster UK Ltd 2018.

Exercise Tiger. Exercise Tiger Wikipedia & http://www.dorsetlife.co.uk/2009/05/massacre-at-slapton-sands-the-great-portland-cover-up/

11 June 1944. F/S TW Tuttle burial source www.worldnavalships.com

CHAPTER 3 CHARLIE TRAINOR

Charlie Trainor background. Acesofww2.com and Canadian Veterans Hall of Fame.

15 March 1944 action over Cambrai. Op.cit. Foreman.

13 April 1944 Donkin story of bailing out into the sea. Shores, Christopher and Thomas, Christopher *2nd Tactical Air Force Volume 2 Breakout to Bodenplatte*: Chevron Publishing Limited 2005.

1 July 1944 Charlie's probable versus ORB destroyed. Op. cit. Nijboer.

14 July 1944 Rommel. Who shot Rommel JJ Le Roux. Op. cit. Foreman. Rommel suicide reference Wikipedia.

6 July 1944. Flak Vierling 38. Op. cit. Nijboer.

CHAPTER 4 ROSS LINQUIST

The pilot logbook of Ross Linquist.

1 December 1943 Ramrod 343. Reference www.aircrewremembered.com USAAF Combat Operations Chronology.

8 February 1944 Ramrod 529. Marauder speed 280 mph. http://www.aviation-history.com/martin/b26.html

Sandy Halcrow story Joe at www.flyingforyourlife.com

Gyro gun sight – Wikipedia and preferences of Johnnie Johnson and FW 190 as a fighter. Bader, Douglas *Fight for the Sky: The Story of the Spitfire and Hurricane*: WS Cowell Ltd.

10 July 1944 No 17 (F) Sector HQ RCAF Armed recce planes must carry bombs communique. Op. cot. Nijboer.

18 August 1944. The Shambles around Falaise. Op. cit. Nijboer.

Sept 13 44 MJ852 delivery. Op. cit. Nijboer.

TV interviews with Ross Linquist. Memories of a Spitfire pilot. Interview by Ryan Simeone 1994. Maclean Hunter Cable 12 Presentation 1994. Cogeco Community TV 1998 406 Wing RCAF Alliance.

CHAPTER 5   TOMMY WHELER

Tommy Wheler's pilot logbook dated 1941 to 1962.

29 April 1943 Sir Archibald Sinclair escort. Background Wikipedia.

23 April 1944 Bombing Siracort site. Wikipedia and www.battlefieldsww2.com

CHAPTER 6   DAVE EVANS

Mention of Dave Evans return after bailing out. Op. cit. Berger and Street.

CHAPTER 7   GIBBY GIBSON

[ref-t]No 2 SFTS. Vintage Wings Canada and www.rcafuplands.blogspot.com

8 February 1944 Ramrod 526 "blind bombing – https://en.wikipedia.org/wiki/Pathfinder_(RAF) Wikipedia

Reference to NH196. Shores, Christopher and Williams, Clive *Aces High* Grub Street 1994.

CHAPTER 8   LEN HARRISON

24 June 1943 mission. Reference Caldwell, Donald *JG26 Luftwaffe Fighter Wing Diary* Stackpole Books 2012.

30 August 1943 bombing Foret d'Epelocques www.aircrewremembered.com/USAAFCombatOperations/Aug.43.html

"Light the fires quotation: Brown, Captain Eric "Winkle" *Wings On My Sleeve* Phoenix 2006.

CHAPTER 9 BOB HYNDMAN

Extracts from Robert Hyndman's pilot log book.
Reference family material and memoirs Bob's daughters Brydie Hyndman and Margot Mann.
Robert Stewart Hyndman by Hugh A Halliday Curator of War Art Canadian War Museum.
Wilfrid Reid "Wop" May OBE DFC Wikipedia.
Clennell Haggerston "Punch" Dickins OC OBE DFC Wikipedia.
Recollections from the war: Interview with Robert Hyndman. The Ottawa Citizen article by Bruce Ward and Steven Mazey 2 December 2009.
Interview with Robert Hyndman Legionnaire Magazine By Jennifer Morse 1 March 2002.
Interview with Robert Hyndman The Gatineau Valley Historical Society by Catherine Joyce 28 September 2005.

CHAPTER 10 JIMMY JEFFREY

Family memoirs and reference material Lawrie Jeffrey and Denise Laferrière.
Air Commodore Frank McGill Wikipedia.
6 STFs reference. Jimmy Jeffrey pilot log book.
Jimmy shot down by Waldemar Busch. Kracker Archive. Op. cit. Foreman.
Cosme Lockwood Gomm DSO DFC shot down https://internationalbcc.co.uk/losses/gomm-cl/
Bob Davidson: The Hamilton Spectator 6 September 2018 Article by Mark McNeil.
Spitfire MK531 JJ crash. Hit a mound of earth. Info sourced; http://www.airhistory.org.uk/spitfire/
Jimmy Jeffrey return visit to France - The Scope 12 November 2003.
George Martin DFC 609 Squadron. Bell, George *To Live Among Heroes* Grub Street 2001.
Spitfire bail out procedure. Pilot Notes for Spitfire Mark IX, XI & XVI Sapphire Productions. Crown Copyright.

BIBLIOGRAPHY

The History Hangar: https://sites.google.com/thehistoryhangar.ca/thehistoryhangar/welcome

The Nauticapedia: Celebrating the stories of Maritime Heritage of British Columbia (www.nauticapedia.ca)

Bader, Douglas *Fight for the Sky: The Story of the Spitfire and Hurricane*: WS Cowell Ltd

Bashow, David L *All the Fine young Eagles: In the cockpit with Canada's Second World War Fighter Pilots* Douglas and McIntyre (2013) Ltd 2016

Beevor, Antony *D-Day The Battle for Normandy* Penguin Books

Bell, George *To Live Amongst Heroes* Grub Street 2001

Berger, Monty, and Street, Brian Jeffrey *Invasions without Tears* Random House of Canada 1994

Brown Captain Eric "Winkle" *Wings on My Sleeve* Phoenix 2006

Caldwell, Donald *JG26 Luftwaffe Fighter Wing Diary* Stackpole Books 2012

Canadian Department of National Defence *The RCAF Overseas: The Fifth Year*

Carter, Kit C, and Mueller, Bob *US Army Air Forces in World War II: Combat Chronology 1941-45* Center for Air Force History

Joyce, Catherine *Artist Profile: Bob Hyndman Gatineau Historical Society* 28 September 2005

Ministry of Defence *The Drive on Caen Northern France* Crown

Clark, David *Angels Eight Normandy Air Diary* United States of America Bloomington, IN 2003

Clark, David W *Joe's Letters* Authorhouse UK Ltd

Corbin DFC, Jimmy *Last of the Ten Fighter Boys* Sutton Publishing 2007

Crown Copyright *Pilot Notes for Spitfire Mark IX, XI & XVI* Sapphire Productions.

Currie DFC, Squadron Leader Jack *Wings Over Georgia* Goodall Publications 1989

Foreman, John *The Fighter Command War Diaries Volumes 3,4, and 5* Air Research Publications 2002

Franks, Norman *Buck McNair Spitfire Ace* Grub Street 2001

Jackson, Bob *Spitfire The History of Britain's Most Famous World War II Fighter* Parragon 2010

Johnson, Johnnie *Wing Leader* Chatto & Windus Ltd 1956

Nesbit Conyers Roy *An Illustrated History of the RAF* Colour Library Books Ltd 1990

Nijboer, Donald *No 126 Wing,* Osprey Publishing 2010

McClenaghan, John and Blatchford, Derek *411 City of North York Squadron History 411* Tactical Aviation Squadron

Milberry Larry and Halliday Hugh *The Royal Canadian Air Force at War 1939-45* CANAV books 1990.

Morgan Eric B & Shacklady Edward *Spitfire The History* William Clowes Ltd

National Archives and Libraries of Canada *411 Squadron ORB reels C-12278 & C-12279*

Neil Tom *The Silver Spitfire:* Phoenix Publishing 2014

Nichol, John *Spitfire A very British Love Story:* Simon & Schuster UK Ltd 2018

Shores, Christopher, and Thomas, Christopher *2nd Tactical Air Force Volume 1 Spartan to Normandy:* Chevron Publishing Limited 2004

Shores, Christopher, and Thomas, Christopher *2nd Tactical Air Force Volume 2 Breakout to Bodenplatte*: Chevron Publishing Limited 2005

Shores, Christopher and Williams, Clive *Aces High* Grub Street 1994

Wellum, Geoffrey *First Light* Penguin Group 2002

OTHER REFERENCES AND SOURCES

Bravo TV *Bob Hyndman* interview.

Baker, Vic *Private papers, and letters of 126 Wing Commemoration* provided by Julie Baker.

Bob S Hyndman Private papers and recollections. The family of Bob S Hyndman; Brydie Hyndman and Margot Mann (nee Hyndman).

Harris DFC, George HG *101 Squadron Lancaster bomber pilot* private meetings with Nick Oram.

Mason, Patrick *Artist mentored by Bob S Hyndman* private correspondence with Nick Oram.

Strutt, Herb *private correspondence and recollections* Roger Strutt and Nick Oram.

L/Cpl Vidler, Reginald Lionel *B Squadron 1ˢᵗ Special Air Service Regiment (SAS) 1942-45* my grandfather. Numerous informal chats.

Squadron Leader Wellum DFC, Geoffrey HA *92 Squadron* private meetings 16 November 2017 and 12 May 2018 at The Mullion Cove Hotel, Mullion, Cornwall.

PICTURE CREDITS

Integrated

Image 1	411 Squadron Spitfire DB-M at RAF Biggin Hill 1943. © Norm Whiteford.
Image 2	411 Squadron Spitfire at RAF Tangmere with D Day invasion stripes. © Jan Linquist.
Image 3	411 Squadron ground crew with a captured Stuka dive bomber. © Mike Rutledge.
Image 4	411 Squadron Spitfires with Short Stirling bombers. © Mike Rutledge.
Image 5	Bruce Whiteford at RAF Biggin Hill. © Norm Whiteford.
Image 6	Bruce with the Roaring Boys mascot 'Joskins.' © Norm Whiteford.
Image 7	Bruce receiving the Canadian Forces Decoration, Namao, Canada 1963. © Norm Whiteford.
Image 8	Ross with a captured Me 109. © Jan Linquist.
Image 9	Ross with Spitfire 'Letchy Lady.' © Jan Linquist.
Image 10	Tommy with Spitfire 'Little Mil.' © The Wheler family.
Image 11	Tommy's log showing a photo of the Firth of Forth bridge. © The Wheler family.
Image 12	Tommy with DB – D Little Mil II September 1943. © The Wheler family.
Image 13	A crashed FW 190 photographed by 411 Squadron. © Mike Rutledge.
Image 14	411 ground crew with a German 88 mm anti-aircraft gun. © Mike Rutledge.
Image 15	Jimmy in Ontario, 1943. © Lawrie Jeffrey.
Image 16	Doug Wheler pointing at the panel in Spitfire Elizabeth which is signed by Tommy. © Nick Oram.

Plate Section

1, 2, 3, 4, 5, 6, 7, 8, 9, 10, 11, 12, 13 © Norm Whiteford
14 © Imperial War Museum, Duxford
15, 16, 17, 18, 19, 20, 21, © Jan Linquist
22, 23, 24, 25 © The Wheler family
26 © Ady Shaw www.warbirdsphotos.co.uk
27 © Norm Whiteford
28, 30 © Ady Shaw www.warbirdsphotos.co.uk
29 © The Wheler family
31, 33 © Jan Linquist.
32 © Norm Whiteford
34, 35 © Norm Whiteford
36 © Jan Linquist
37 © Norm Whiteford
38, 39, 40, © Margot Mann and Brydie Hyndman
41 © Norm Whiteford
42 © Margot Mann and Brydie Hyndman
43, 44 © Beaverbrook Collection of War Art Canadian War Museum
45 © Jan Linquist
46 © Wayne Marsh
48 © Margot Mann and Brydie Hyndman
47 © Mike Rutledge
49, 50, 51, 52, 53, 54, 55, 56 © Lawrie Jeffrey and Denise Laferrière
57 © Simon Evans
58 © Jan Linquist
59 © Mike Rutledge
60 © Richard Foord
61 © Nick Oram
62 © Richard Foord
63, 64 © Aero Legends Ltd
65 © Richard Foord
66 © Nick Oram
67 © Nick Oram
68 © Richard Foord